The Guest Worker Question in Postwar Germany

This book provides the first English-language history of the post-war labor migration to West Germany. Drawing on government bulletins, statements by political leaders, parliamentary arguments, industry newsletters, social welfare studies, press coverage, and the cultural production of immigrant artists and intellectuals, Rita Chin offers an account of West German public debate about guest workers. She traces the historical and ideological shifts around the meanings of the labor migration, moving from the concept of guest workers as a "temporary labor supplement" in the 1950s and 1960s to early ideas about "multiculturalism" by the end of the 1980s. She argues that the efforts to come to terms with the permanent residence of guest workers, especially Muslim Turks, forced a major rethinking of German identity, culture, and nation. What began as a policy initiative to fuel the economic miracle ultimately became a much broader discussion about the parameters of a specifically German brand of multiculturalism.

Rita Chin is an assistant professor of history at the University of Michigan. She previously taught at Oberlin College. She has received fellowships from the Social Science Research Council and the German Academic Exchange Service and grants from the American Historical Association and the American Philosophical Society. She was recently awarded a fellowship from the Fulbright Program to participate in the German Fulbright Commission's seminar on Muslims in Germany and France.

"This important, thought-provoking book probes the evolution of the postwar 'guest worker' as social and economic phenomenon, political problem, and ideological construct. Spanning the half-century following World War II, Chin explores how the uncontroversial embrace of labor recruitment as economic strategy gradually gave way to skeptical debates regarding the possibility of integrating Muslim Turks into democratic society. Along the way, she convincingly shows that "the guest worker problem" was never a marginal minority issue, but central to our understanding of postwar German history and contemporary Europe. A timely intervention and outstanding achievement."

– Heide Fehrenbach, author of *Race after Hitler* and *Cinema in Democratizing Germany,* Northern Illinois University

"This book could not be more timely. At a moment when Europeans debate whether an expanded European Union should include Turkey and critics of multiculturalism insist on reinforcing the lines that separate people of different ethnicities, Rita Chin offers a superb study of debates over racial and cultural difference in Germany from the 1950s to the present. A model of interdisciplinary scholarship, Chin's book moves from an analysis of guest worker recruitment patterns and migration to insightful readings of literature and film; she follows guest workers into labor markets and the marketplace of ideas and the media. She has much to say about what has facilitated and what has impeded the move toward the acceptance of diversity in Germany."

– Robert Moeller, University of California, Irvine

"A pioneering cultural and intellectual history that shows how a policy initiative designed to provide labor for the West German economic miracle generated far-reaching public debates on the shape of German culture, German citizenship, and the Geman nation. Tracing the key role of Turkish/German writers and artists in initiating or transforming these discussions, the book is a must-read for anyone interested in German multiculturalism, the history of minorities, and the changing spheres of political discourse over the last forty years. A major accomplishment."

– Uta Poiger, University of Washington

"This book by Rita Chin is a highly original combination of political history and literary science. Taking the theory of representation as her point of departure, Rita Chin demonstrates an amazing talent at pointing out interrelations and intersections between texts as different as law codes, political speeches, parliamentary debates, newspaper articles, and novels, without ever succumbing to reductionism. The result is a fascinating ethnography of the *Zeitgeist* and the mood of different periods in the history of the Federal Republic of Germany. The impact of this truly scholarly work goes far beyond migration research. It makes clear how identity, culture, and nation have constantly been re-thought throughout the history of the Federal Republic. With this new and sensational approach to the history of labour migration *and* the history of the Federal Republic, Rita Chin convincingly manages to close the gap between the approaches of political science and cultural studies."

– Werner Schiffauer, Europa Universität Viadrina, Frankfurt/Oder, Germany

The Guest Worker Question
in Postwar Germany

RITA CHIN
University of Michigan

CAMBRIDGE
UNIVERSITY PRESS

CAMBRIDGE UNIVERSITY PRESS
Cambridge, New York, Melbourne, Madrid, Cape Town,
Singapore, São Paulo, Delhi, Tokyo, Mexico City

Cambridge University Press
32 Avenue of the Americas, New York, NY 10013-2473, USA

www.cambridge.org
Information on this title: www.cambridge.org/9780521690225

First published 2007
First paperback edition 2009
Reprinted 2011

A catalog record for this publication is available from the British Library.

Library of Congress Cataloging in Publication Data

Chin, Rita C–K, 1970–
The guest worker question in postwar Germany / Rita C–K Chin.
   p.   cm.
Includes bibliographical references and index.
ISBN-13: 978-0-521-87000-9 (hardback)
ISBN-10: 0-521-87000-3 (hardback)
1. Alien labor – Germany – History.   2. Pluralism (Social sciences) – Germany.
3. Immigrants – Germany – Social conditions.   4. Germany – Social conditions.
5. Ören, Aras, 1939– .   I. Title.
HD8458.A2C45   2007
331.6′2094309045 – dc22   2006018233

ISBN 978-0-521-87000-9 Hardback
ISBN 978-0-521-69022-5 Paperback

For Jay

Contents

Acknowledgments

Over the course of this project, I have often encountered the same question: Why would someone like you write a book about the German guest worker question? The truth is that migration has been a part of my life from the very beginning. Had it not been for my parents' decision to move from Malaysia to the United States when I was an infant, I certainly would not have had the opportunity to become a professional historian. I also like to think that the experience of growing up in a first-generation migrant family has helped me become more sensitive to the complexities of the issues that run through these pages.

My first thanks go to John Toews and Hillel Kieval, who cultivated my deep interest in European history while I was an undergraduate and master's student at the University of Washington. Without their example and encouragement, a Ph.D. in history would have seemed a far less appealing and attainable goal. At the University of California, Berkeley, Martin Jay provided wise and steady counsel during the early stages of this project and has continued to offer unfailing support. I am particularly grateful for his suggestion to explore a somewhat unconventional topic in German cultural history, as well as for his personal generosity and kindness. I would also like to thank Gerald Feldman for his valuable advice and unstinting assistance. His genuine enthusiasm for this topic has been a major asset through the entire process.

Many others were involved during the researching and writing of this book. In Germany, I would like to thank Saliha Scheinhardt, Yüksel Pazarkaya, Zehra Çirak, Sema Poyraz, and the late Kemal Kurt for agreeing to interviews and sharing their experiences with me. My ongoing conversations with Zafer Şenocak have been enormously stimulating and a source of inspiration. Irmgard Ackermann provided invaluable access to her private collection of newspaper clippings and clarified details about the history of the Institut für Deutsch als Fremdsprache. Börte Sagaster was a much-appreciated friend, interlocutor, and playmate in Berlin. Yasemin Yildiz welcomed me into the company of her family in both Söke and Hamburg; she was an important early sounding board for my ideas and has remained a valued discussion partner.

For citations, readings of drafts, conference panels, and general advice, I thank Leslie Adelson, Paul Anderson, Volker Berghahn, Michal Bodemann, Ayşe Çağlar, John Carson, Joshua Cole, Marcia Colish, Matthew Countryman, Dario Gaggio, Deniz Göktürk, Atina Grossmann, Gottfried Hagen, Gabrielle Hecht, Elizabeth Heineman, Dagmar Herzog, Steven Hochstadt, Christhard Hoffmann, Maria Höhn, Nancy Hunt, Kali Israel, Konrad Jarausch, Martha Jones, Anton Kaes, Yasemin Karakaşoğlu, Mary Kelley, the late Eva Kolinsky, Kader Konuk, Wendy Kozol, Harry Liebersohn, David Luft, Ruth Mandel, Andy Markovits, Isaac Miller, Michele Mitchell, Leslie Moch, Gina Morantz-Sanchez, Rainer Ohliger, Damani Partridge, Robin Queen, Sonya Rose, Azade Seyhan, Leonard Smith, Levent Soysal, Scott Spector, Arlene Teraoka, John Toews, Marilya Veteto-Reese, Sabine von Dirke, James West, and Jenny White. Two reading groups at the University of Michigan served as important sites for presenting my work: Alamanya, a fortuitous and unique collective of faculty and graduate students working on Turks in Germany; and the History Department's Junior Faculty Colloquium. I thank the members of these groups for their many forms of helpful commentary. Robert Moeller deserves special mention for reading the manuscript in its entirety and providing incredibly useful criticisms and suggestions. Two other individuals offered friendship and intellectual camaraderie far beyond the usual standards. Heide Fehrenbach gave me feedback on the entire manuscript and has been a valued source of criticism, advice, and moral support. Geoff Eley pushed me to broaden the framework for the project beyond its original form as a synoptic intellectual history; he provided many helpful comments on specific chapters and ultimately read the manuscript from beginning to end.

The book would not have been possible without the financial support of various institutions. A grant from the Social Science Research Council's Berlin Program for German and European Studies facilitated the bulk of my research in Germany. Fellowships from the Department of History at UC Berkeley and Pomona College afforded me the time to write. A Powers Travel Grant from Oberlin College and a Bernadotte Schmidt

Research Grant from the American Historical Association enabled me to return to Germany for follow-up research. The University of Michigan provided generous postdoctoral funding that gave me the opportunity to rethink and rewrite the book in its entirety. For archival help, I thank the staff members of the Institut für vergleichende Sozialforschung and the Freie Universität's Otto-Suhr-Institut für Politikwissenschaft in Berlin, the Institut für Auslandsbeziehungen in Stuttgart, the Institut für Deutsch als Fremdsprache in Munich, and the Deutsche Literaturarchiv in Marbach. I am grateful to Beau Case at the University of Michigan Graduate Library for tracking down some particularly difficult citations. In addition, I wish to thank Lewis Bateman, my editor at Cambridge University Press, for his patience in waiting for the manuscript and his remarkable efficiency once it was done. I am grateful to production editor Janis Bolster and copy editors Jennifer Collier and Marie Deer for shepherding the manuscript through the production process. Thanks also go to Sarah Miller for help with proofreading.

Finally, I want to express heartfelt gratitude to my family. My parents, Lay and Mari Chin, have given me unwavering support and encouragement in everything I set my mind to. Their unconditional love has been a sustaining force in my life. I deeply appreciate Connie and Jim Cook's interest in my work and innumerable kindnesses over the years. Thanks, too, to Amy Cook for providing periodic interludes away from work. Jay Cook has lived with this book from its inception and read each page many times over. His own work and high critical standards have been an inspiration, and our countless conversations about every aspect of this project have made the end product much better. His love, friendship, patience, and steadfast partnership are the foundation upon which this book was written.

Introduction

Conceptualizing the "Guest Worker" Question

The One-Millionth Guest Worker

On 10 September 1964, fewer than twenty years after the end of the Second World War, the one-millionth guest worker arrived in the Federal Republic of Germany. His name was Armando Rodrigues, and he came from the village of Vale de Madeiros in central Portugal. Like the hundreds of thousands of labor migrants who preceded him, Rodrigues moved to West Germany to work in its factories. He was part of a massive foreign labor recruitment program, which began in 1955, to ensure a continuous supply of manpower for the postwar economic miracle. With limited prospects for employment in his homeland, he applied to the Federal Republic as a guest worker and eventually obtained an assignment. His plan was to return from West Germany after a few years with more money than he could save in a lifetime of labor at home. Forsaking family, friends, and familiar surroundings, Rodrigues embarked on a forty-eight-hour train journey into the unknown.

In many ways, Rodrigues fit the typical profile of a guest worker entering the Federal Republic during the mid-1960s. He came alone, leaving his wife and two children in the village. At age thirty-eight, he cut an impressive figure – strong, well-built, in the prime of his life. He possessed precisely the kind of vigorous male body that West German government and industry officials sought to fuel the boom economy. Rodrigues was

NOTE: In the first drafts of this book, I deliberately placed quotation marks around "guest worker" and "foreigner" in order to emphasize the socially constructed and euphemistic nature of these terms. While I have removed the quotation marks from the final version, readers should continue to think of these terms as under interrogation.

I

part of a vast wave of workers from the rural regions of southern Europe, including Italy, Spain, Portugal, Greece, Turkey, and Yugoslavia. But he did not belong to a dominant national group within the broader demographic spectrum of recruitment. During the 1950s, Italians constituted the largest percentage of workers, while from the late 1960s on, Turks outpaced all other nationalities, eventually coming to personify the very image of the guest worker in German public discussions of migration.

Before his arrival, Rodrigues's journey followed the same anonymous trajectory experienced by most guest workers on their way to the Federal Republic. First he traveled within his home country from his village to the urban center where an auxiliary branch of the German Federal Labor Office (Bundesanstalt für Arbeit) had been opened. Next he filed an application for work, underwent physical tests, and endured a long waiting period until he received a job assignment. Finally he embarked for West Germany on a train reserved exclusively for guest workers, with a ticket paid for by his future employer. In Rodrigues's case, however, the endpoint of the migration journey was far from ordinary. Once the train carrying twelve hundred Spanish and Portuguese workers pulled into the station on the outskirts of Cologne, Rodrigues was whisked away from his countrymen by German officials, led across the platform, and positioned in front of flags and laurel trees for a photo opportunity. These "strange men," according to press reports, "presented him with a bouquet of carnations and steered him to the seat of a motorcycle. 'This belongs to you,' they said. 'You are the one-millionth guest worker in the Federal Republic.'"[1] As newspaper photographers' flashbulbs went off, a workers' band from a Cologne cable factory struck up the German and Portuguese national anthems. Journalists on the scene claimed that Rodrigues's fellow passengers let out a cheer: "Viva Alemania!"[2]

This public fanfare signaled a new kind of self-consciousness about the scope and significance of Germany's massive labor recruitment. The event was planned and staged by the Federal Organization of German Employers' Associations, with a host of industry dignitaries and government representatives (including the Minister of Labor) in attendance. Using the celebration to highlight the program's indisputable success, these officials emphasized the crucial role of the guest workers in the triumph of the economic miracle. "Without their collaboration," declared the president of the Employers' Association of the Metal Industry, "this

---

[1] Fritz Mörschbach, "Großer Bahnhof für Armando: Der millionste Gastarbeiter in Köln feierlich empfangen," *Frankfurter Rundschau*, 11 September 1964, 20.
[2] Ibid.

development is unthinkable."[3] The thrust of the message was that West German prosperity directly depended on foreign laborers such as Rodrigues and that recruitment was working out well for all involved.

In 1964, government and business leaders had little sense of the labor migration's long-term social and cultural impacts. Again and again they insisted that guest workers would return home once the economy no longer required supplementary manpower. But, in fact, many foreign laborers chose to remain and eventually sent for their spouses and children. By 1990, well over five million migrants claimed permanent resident status, making West Germany home to the largest foreign population in Europe.[4] This demographic transformation included a second and third generation, which had been born, raised, and educated in Germany with little or no immediate knowledge of their nominal homelands. In practical terms, if not according to official rhetoric, the Federal Republic had become a "country of immigration."

It is important here to consider a second level of historical meaning in the Rodrigues celebration, what might be described as the ideological construction of the guest worker in rhetoric and imagery. Indeed, the very need for a public performance – the fact that German industry and government leaders felt compelled to convince the public of the recruitment's vital importance – suggests that the larger historical significance of the migration cannot be reduced to labor shortages, policymaking, and demographic shifts (even though early government officials certainly tried to do so). It was this media spectacle at the Cologne train station, in fact, that crystallized the initial official position on the guest worker question, conveying very specific messages about the role of foreign laborers in West Germany.

A Deutsche Presse-Agentur photograph (Figure 1), taken at Rodrigues's arrival, documents the event. It shows Rodrigues perched on top of the gleaming new motorcycle, surrounded by a crowd of applauding German dignitaries. Among these officials is the president of the Employers' Association of the Metal Industry, who leans against a podium and prepares to deliver a speech. This carefully scripted scene presents Rodrigues as the guest worker par excellence: he stands for the 999,999 imported

---

[3] Wolfgang Kuballa, "Großer Bahnhof für Armando Sá Rodrigues: Der millionste Gastarbeiter in der Bundesrepublik mit einer Feier in Köln begrüßt," *Süddeutsche Zeitung*, 11 September 1964.
[4] In 1990, the Federal Republic had a foreign population of 5,242,000. France had the next highest number of foreigners at 3,597,000. See Stephen Castles and Mark J. Miller, *The Age of Migration: International Population Movements in the Modern World*, 3rd ed. (New York: Guilford Press, 2003), 81.

FIGURE 1. Armando Rodrigues atop the motorcycle presented to him upon arrival at the Cologne-Dietz train station for being the one-millionth guest worker in the Federal Republic. Courtesy of dpa/Landov.

laborers who have come before him, but he also serves as an ideal type. He is mature, but still young enough to perform the hard work that will be required of him. Neatly yet humbly dressed, he looks like a man of modest means who will apply himself industriously to the job ahead. The fact that the pageant took place at a train station – as opposed to a factory or worker barracks – underscores his status as a transitional, mobile figure who is not permanently rooted in West German society. The motorbike serves as Rodrigues's metaphoric vehicle on the road to prosperity, a promise of the material benefits available to all hardworking recruits. This object simultaneously symbolizes the Federal Republic's phoenix-like recovery from wartime destruction and an emerging era of affluence. Above all, the scene suggests a mantra of mutual benefits: government leaders would maintain national prosperity, business leaders would obtain much-needed manpower, and guest workers would gain access to a higher standard of living.[5]

By its very nature, this public performance served to exclude any of the social and cultural issues that might have undermined the overwhelmingly positive representation. There is no indication here, for example, of the physical dislocation, separation from family, or fear of the unknown that Rodrigues had undoubtedly experienced on the way to Cologne. There is no sign of the strenuous labor, cramped living quarters, meager wages, and social isolation that await him after the ceremony. There is no explanation of Rodrigues's life before his arrival or what he hoped to gain by coming. There is no hint of potential workplace conflict, xenophobia, or public anxiety about the presence of hundreds of thousands of foreigners on West German soil. The media event at the train station, in short, offered a highly circumscribed view of the guest worker question. And the photograph itself reinforced the ideological frame constructed by German officials, quite literally cutting off Rodrigues's past and future. The most famous journalistic image of the guest worker program thus represented the recruitment as a mass-cultural moment of smiles, applause, gift giving, and optimism.

Reports of this remarkable event appeared in virtually every newspaper across West Germany, including regional papers such as *Westdeutsche Allgemeine Zeitung* and nationally distributed papers such as *Frankfurter Rundschau*, *Süddeutsche Zeitung*, and *Der Tagesspiegel*, as well as the

---

[5] Gail Wise has offered an alternative reading of this photo that stresses the anonymity and exchangeability of the foreign worker. See Gail Wise, "Ali in Wunderland: German Representations of Foreign Workers" (Ph.D. diss., University of California, Berkeley, 1995), 12–13.

highly popular national tabloid *Bild-Zeitung*.[6] Rodrigues, in turn, quickly became the labor migration's first national icon. This transformation of labor policy into mass-cultural spectacle cut in two directions. On the one hand, the replication and distribution of the photo all over the country served to disseminate an official narrative of recruitment on a dramatic new scale. For the first time, Germans had a common image – and explanation – of the process that was reshaping the nation. On the other hand, mass circulation carried with it at least the possibility of further ideological complexity.[7] In stark contrast to the hundreds of thousands of nameless, faceless recruits who had come previously, here finally was a guest worker with a public persona – a human being rather than a statistic in a labor report. This process implicitly led to a much more specific set of questions: Who was Rodrigues? What motivated him to leave his homeland for Germany? How was he experiencing his new life as guest worker?

The event, in other words, marked the beginning of a truly public and increasingly multivocal dialogue on the guest worker question in Germany. This is not to suggest that there had been no public comments on the recruitment previously. As soon as the first labor treaty went into effect, the federal government's Press and Information Office issued regular bulletins about foreign workers, replete with statistics and figures that provided economic justification of the program.[8] Popular news magazines such as *Der Spiegel* also started to publish sporadic articles on the labor recruitment and guest workers.[9] Nor do I mean to suggest that ideological struggle and contest began only in the mid-1960s. Italian recruits, for instance, founded the newspaper *Corriere d'Italia* for their own guest worker community a decade earlier. And from the very start,

---

[6] Mörschbach, "Großer Bahnhof für Armando"; Kuballa, "Großer Bahnhof für Armando Sá Rodrigues"; n.a., "'Großer Bahnhof' für den millionsten Gastarbeiter," *Der Tagesspiegel*, 11 September 1964, 5; n.a., "Gastarbeiter Nr. 1000000," *Bild-Zeitung*, 11 September 1964, 1; n.a., "'Großer Bahnhof' erschreckte den Zimmermann aus Portugal," *Westdeutsche Allgemeine Zeitung*, 11 September 1964, 3.

[7] I use the concept of ideology in the sense established by Stuart Hall, which includes the mental frameworks (especially the languages, concepts, categories, images of thought, and systems of representation) that different classes and social groups deploy in order to make sense of and define the way society works. See Stuart Hall, "The Problem of Ideology: Marxism without Guarantees," in David Morely and Kuan-Hsing Chen, eds., *Stuart Hall: Critical Dialogues in Cultural Studies* (London: Routledge, 1996), 25–27.

[8] See, for example, "Ausländische Arbeitnehmer in der Bundesrepublik," *Bulletin des Presse- und Informationsamtes der Bundesrepublik*, 30 March 1965.

[9] See, for example, n.a., "Fremdarbeiter," *Der Spiegel*, 24 August 1955, 17; n.a., "Italien – Saisonarbeiter – Musterung in Mailand," *Der Spiegel*, 4 April 1956, 34–35; n.a., "Arbeitsmarkt – Fremdarbeiter – Export aus Südtirol," *Der Spiegel*, 2 May, 24–25.

workers from multiple backgrounds commented on their day-to-day experiences in letters home, in diaries, and within their ethnic enclaves. A 1998 exhibition on the history of Turkish emigration held at the Ruhrland Museum in Essen included pages from the journal of a Metin Çaglar, documenting his arrival in Germany in December 1963.[10] By the end of the 1960s, small numbers of minority writers who had come to the Federal Republic as migrants began to question the specific terms of public debate, self-consciously re-presenting the guest worker as something more than a beneficiary of the postwar economic boom or a victim of industrial capitalist exploitation. In the photograph of the one-millionth guest worker, then, we can begin to see the intersection of the three major trajectories that comprise the central themes of this book: the labor migration itself, the public discourse and debate surrounding the migration, and the emergence of a primarily Turkish minority intelligentsia dedicated (at least initially) to critiquing what could be said about guest workers.

Guest Workers in West German History

The national debate about the postwar labor migration has often treated the presence of guest workers as tangential (an issue of manpower and labor markets) rather than central to the primary concerns of the Federal Republic. In this respect, the media event around the 1964 arrival of Rodrigues served as part of a larger containment strategy to limit public discussion of guest workers to the issue of mutually beneficial economics. For precisely this reason, it has been difficult to recognize just how crucial the migration has been to the definition and disposition of West German society. Despite such efforts to contain the impacts of guest workers, I argue that the foreign labor recruitment program ultimately produced the opposite effect, a broader and much more consequential debate about the parameters of German identity and the prospect of a new multiethnic nation. Guest workers, in other words, were never marginal to the core concerns of German society. Rather, these migrants occupied a central place in the most important and enduring question of the postwar period: How would West German national identity be reconstituted after the Third Reich?

---

[10] Aytaç Eryilmaz and Mathilde Jamin, eds., *Fremde Heimat-Yaban Silban Olur: Eine Geschichte der Einwanderung aus der Türkei* (Essen: Klartext, 1998). This is the catalogue from the exhibition at the Ruhrland Museum in Essen, which was held from 15 February to 2 August 1998.

In this sense, the postwar labor migration served as the Federal Republic's primary route into the more heterogeneous demographic and cultural landscape we now often describe as the New Europe. In France and Great Britain, such heterogeneity was inextricably linked to the collapse of eighteenth- and nineteenth-century empires, which fed the movement of long-standing colonial subjects into the metropole. West Germany's late twentieth-century diversity, however, did not result from its abbreviated colonial experience. Instead, it grew out of a federal response to economic crisis that targeted foreign populations with which Germans were mostly unfamiliar. The migration of guest workers after 1945 ultimately created the conditions for a major and largely unexpected social-historical transformation – a multinational, multiethnic German society.

It is important to be clear here that the practice of employing foreign labor in Germany was by no means new. Between 1880 and 1914, the eastern agricultural regions and coal mines of the Ruhr valley relied on Poles from Russia and the Austro-Hungarian Empire to supplement the native workforce.[11] And during both world wars, Germany exploited tens of thousands of foreigners as forced labor (*Fremdarbeiter*) to keep industrial production going while its own men fought at the front.[12] Nevertheless, there are crucial distinctions between these earlier uses of foreign labor and the post-1945 guest worker recruitment. Poles entering Germany as seasonal workers during the 1880s, for instance, had specific historical and cultural ties to Prussian Poles, who possessed German citizenship as a result of the Polish partitions at the end of the eighteenth century.[13] By contrast, no group of guest workers in the Federal Republic

---

[11] For more on Polish workers during the Wilhelmine period, see Christoph Kleß-mann, *Polnische Bergarbeiter im Ruhrgebiet, 1870–1945* (Göttingen: Vandenhoeck & Ruprecht, 1978); Richard C. Murphy, *Gastarbeiter im Deutschen Reich. Polen in Bottrop, 1891–1933* (Wuppertal: Peter Hammer Verlag, 1982); Ulrich Herbert, *Geschichte der Ausländerbeschäftigung in Deutschland, 1880 bis 1980* (Bonn: Verlag J. H. W. Dietz, 1986), trans. by William Templer as *A History of Foreign Labor in Germany, 1880–1980: Seasonal Workers/Forced Laborers/Guest Workers* (Ann Arbor: University of Michigan Press, 1990), especially Chapter 1; John J. Kulczycki, *The Foreign Worker and the German Labor Movement: Xenophobia and Solidarity in the Coal Fields of the Ruhr, 1871–1914* (Oxford: Berg, 1994); John J. Kulczycki, *The Polish Coal Miners' Union and the German Labor Movement in the Ruhr, 1902–1934: National and Social Solidarity* (Oxford: Berg, 1997).
[12] Herbert, *Geschichte der Ausländerbeschäftigung*, especially Chapters 2 and 4. See also Ulrich Herbert, *Fremdarbeiter: Politik und Praxis des "Ausländer-Einsatzes" in der Kriegswirtschaft des Dritten Reiches* (Berlin: J. H. W. Dietz, 1999).
[13] Germany, in fact, had a sizable Polish population due to the partitions of the Kingdom of Poland in 1772, 1794, and 1795 by Prussia, Austria, and Russia. The Poles

had long-standing connections to Germany. And at least one major group was perceived as a qualitatively different population: Turks came from a country outside of Europe, practiced a non-Christian religion, and possessed a non-European ethnicity. As far back as the early modern period, in fact, Turks had been understood as the primary social and cultural Other that served to define and consolidate Europe as a historical whole.[14] Furthermore, unlike *Fremdarbeiter*, culled from foreigners already in Germany such as Polish seasonal laborers (in the case of World War I) or enemies and prisoners of war (in the case of World War II) and compelled against their will to work, postwar *Gastarbeiter* (guest

who had been acquired as a result of these annexations were citizens of the German *Reich*, whereas those who came as temporary workers during the 1880s were not. The fact that these two legally distinct groups could not be easily distinguished from one another physically or culturally, however, did create major anxiety about the Polish population as a whole. See William W. Hagen, *Germans, Poles, and Jews: The Nationality Conflict in the Prussian East, 1772–1914* (Chicago: University of Chicago Press, 1980); Richard Blanke, *Prussian Poland in the German Empire, 1871–1900* (Boulder, CO: East European Monographs, 1981); Klaus J. Bade, ed., *Auswanderer, Wanderarbeiter, Gastarbeiter: Bevölkerung, Arbeitsmarkt und Wanderung in Deutschland seit der Mitte des 19. Jahrhunderts* (Ostfildern: Scripta Mercaturae Verlag, 1984). The situation of the seasonal Polish workers, in fact, was quite complicated vis-à-vis their Polish-German brothers. Moreover, during the period of highest demand for foreign labor, Otto von Bismarck was in the process of waging the *Kulturkampf*. One effect of this policy was an attempt to Germanize the *Reich*'s Polish population. For more on the *Kulturkampf* specifically, see Margaret L. Anderson, *Windthorst: A Political Biography* (Oxford: Oxford University Press, 1981), and Helmut Walser Smith, *German Nationalism and Religious Conflict: Culture, Ideology, Politics, 1871–1914* (Princeton: Princeton University Press, 1995).

[14] In the Middle Ages, it is important to note, Islam's otherness was seen primarily in terms of religion, but it also presented a military threat (most of Christendom fell into Muslim hands in the seventh and eighth centuries) and an intellectual challenge (Muslim science and philosophy were heavily influenced by Greek, Persian, and Hindu learning inaccessible to the Latin West until the twelfth century). For a useful discussion of the perceptions of Islam during the medieval period, see John Victor Tolan, ed., *Medieval Christian Perceptions of Islam: A Book of Essays* (New York: Garland, 1996). The classic statement on the perception of Ottomans by Europeans in the early modern period is Robert Schwoebel, *The Shadow of the Crescent: The Renaissance Image of the Turk, 1453–1517* (Nieuwkoop: B. de Graaf, 1967). More recent scholarship in this area includes: David R. Blanks and Michael Frassetto, eds., *Western Views of Islam in Medieval and Early Modern Europe: Perception of Other* (New York: St. Martin's Press, 1999); Aslı Çırakman, *From the "Terror of the World" to the "Sick Man of Europe": European Images of Ottoman Empire and Society from the Sixteenth Century to the Nineteenth* (New York: P. Lang, 2002); Almut Höfert, *Den Feind beschreiben: "Türkengefahr" und europäisches Wissen über das Osmanische Reich, 1450–1600* (Frankfurt: Campus Verlag, 2003). For a specific examination of the Habsburg view of Islam and the Turks, see Charles Ingrao, *The Habsburg Monarchy, 1618–1815* (Cambridge: Cambridge University Press, 1994). For a broader discussion of the place of the Near Eastern Orient in the imagination of the West, see Edward Said, *Orientalism* (New York: Vintage Books, 1978).

workers) came to the Federal Republic voluntarily, with employment and residence permits, under the protection of bilateral recruitment treaties.[15] These crucial differences, along with the fact that the post-1945 importation of guest workers took place in a country where the preceding regime had attempted to eradicate its minorities, produced a unique situation in which the development of a multiethnic society seemed particularly improbable.

This book explores the postwar labor migration and its consequences over a thirty-five-year period, concluding with German reunification in 1990. It is a history that includes a number of crucial milestones. The first and most obvious came in 1955, when the Federal Republic formalized its program of importing foreign workers by signing a labor recruitment treaty with Italy. This agreement set out the legal parameters and procedures for West German employers hiring Italians and became the model for subsequent treaties with other southern European nations. It initially offered work permits for one year, establishing an expectation that foreign laborers would be sojourners. At this point, the central concern of government and business leaders was to keep the economic miracle going, which led them, in turn, to advocate recruitment unequivocally, emphasizing labor statistics and productivity levels in their public presentation of the program.

Another important turning point was the 1973 oil crisis and the economic recession it provoked. In response to rising unemployment, the Federal Republic halted the labor recruitment program and encouraged guest workers to go back to their countries of origin. Efforts to reduce the numbers of foreigners, however, inadvertently produced a net increase in alien residents. Faced with the prospect of restricted access to Germany, many foreign laborers – especially Turks – applied for visas so their families could join them. During the same period, migrant intellectuals, such as the Turkish-German poet Aras Ören, began to enter the national debate about guest workers, publishing texts in German that challenged the predominant stereotypes and assumptions about foreign laborers.

A third pivotal moment occurred in the late 1970s. It was at this time that West Germany first acknowledged the continuing presence of over two million foreigners and initiated a formal policy of "integration." This new era of self-conscious integration witnessed a number of important

---

[15] Historian Ulrich Herbert has written a useful study of Germany's long pattern of employing foreign labor, but a more specific analysis of the similarities and differences across these periods remains to be done. See Herbert, *History of Foreign Labor*.

developments involving demographics and representation. The federal government's policy shift reframed the guest worker question as a vital domestic concern, rather than merely a problem of economics or labor, and spurred a growing public interest in the lives of guest workers. Such an orientation helped create a market for so-called *Ausländerliteratur* (foreigner literature), a genre which German academics originally constructed and promoted as a tool for integration. By the middle of the decade, moreover, Turks had replaced Italians as the largest group of foreign settlers, a trend triggered in part by the establishment of the European Economic Community. The EEC's policy of granting citizens of member states reciprocal labor rights meant that Italians (and eventually Spaniards and Portuguese) could work in the Federal Republic without special permits and thus come and go quite easily. Turks, by contrast, were reluctant to leave, fearing that they might not be able to return. This demographic pattern, coupled with the government's new emphasis on integration, produced a kind of misremembering of the labor migration's early history. The multinational character of the guest worker population increasingly receded as the somewhat more alien cultural and religious practices of Muslim Turks took center stage in policy debates and public discussions.[16] It was around this moment, too, that migrant artists such as the author Saliha Scheinhardt and film maker Tevfik Başer began to focus their texts more squarely on women and gender relations, inadvertently fueling doubts about the capacity of Turks to adapt. In all of these respects, the advent of self-conscious integration policies produced fundamental tensions around the long-term impacts of migrants on a society that continued to describe itself as a "nonimmigration country."

The reunification of East and West Germany marks a final watershed in this book's trajectory. The turbulent aftermath of this long-anticipated event placed migrants in a precarious position. Above all, the social and ideological work of reconstituting a collective German national identity threatened to override the integrationist impulses of the 1970s, as well as the broad public discussions of West German multiculturalism that emerged in the late 1980s. In addition, a growing wave of antiforeigner violence, especially in the former East, led many politicians and government leaders to campaign for and endorse a restriction on the number

---

[16] Italian, Spanish, Portuguese, Yugoslavian, and Greek guest workers, of course, did not disappear from West Germany. My point is simply that public discourse began to emphasize Turks to such an extent that by the mid-1980s, the multinational character of guest worker migration was largely forgotten.

of asylum seekers. This policy served to deflect attention away from the more systemic problem of xenophobia, the virulent resurfacing of which was itself a particularly troubling product of the unification process.

Guest workers and their descendants, then, have been present in German society for virtually the entire postwar period. They began arriving in the aftermath of World War II, before the last traces of the physical destruction had been cleared away. But the seeds of their recruitment were sown in advance of the official treaties by the demographic catastrophe (well over three million German male casualties) wrought by the conflict itself. Multiple generations of migrants lived through every major event in the history of West Germany, from the Grand Coalition and the 1968 student protests to the kidnappings by the Red Army Faction and the fall of the Berlin Wall. Their numbers, moreover, continue to grow (primarily through new births, but also through marriage with foreign nationals) in the unified Federal Republic.

Yet, with a few key exceptions, what is immediately striking about the historiography of the postwar period is the curious absence of guest workers.[17] For the most part, scholarship on the labor migration and

---

[17] Among German academics, Klaus Bade and Ulrich Herbert have considered the postwar labor recruitment from a historical perspective. See Klaus J. Bade, ed., *Auswanderer, Wanderarbeiter, Gastarbeiter*; Klaus J. Bade, *Population, Labour, and Migration in Nineteenth and Twentiety Century Germany* (New York: St. Martin's, 1987); Klaus J. Bade, ed., *Deutsche im Ausland. Fremde in Deutschland. Migration in Geschichte und Gegenwart* (Munich: Beck, 1992); Klaus J. Bade and Myron Weiner, eds., *Migration Past, Migration Future: Germany and the United States* (Providence: Berghahn, 1997); Herbert, *A History of Foreign Labor*. Bade's work looks at the larger phenomenon of migration to and from Germany, while Herbert's scholarship examines foreign workers throughout German history. Neither of them focuses specifically on the postwar labor recruitment. In the last couple of years, however, a younger generation of scholars has begun to address this topic more directly. See Jan Motte, Rainer Ohliger, and Anne von Oswald, eds., *Fünfzig Jahre Bundesrepublik, Fünfzig Jahre Einwanderung: Nachkriegsgeschichte als Migrationsgeschichte* (Frankfurt: Campus, 1999); Ulrich Herbert and Karin Hunn, "Guest Workers and Policy on Guest Workers in the Federal Republic: From the Beginning of Recruitment in 1955 until Its Halt in 1973," in Hanna Schissler, ed., *The Miracle Years: A Cultural History of West Germany, 1949–1968* (Princeton: Princeton University Press, 2001), 187–218; Karen Schönwälder, *Einwanderung und ethnische Pluralität: Politische Entscheidungen und öffentliche Debatten in Großbritannien und der Bundesrepublik von den 1950er bis zu den 1970er Jahren* (Essen: Klartext, 2001); and Anne von Oswald, Karen Schönwälder, and Barbara Sonnenberger, "Einwanderungsland Deutschland: A New Look at Its Postwar History," in Rainer Ohliger, Karen Schönwälder, and Triadafilos Triadafilopoulos, eds., *European Encounters: Migrants, Migration, and European Society since 1945* (Aldershot: Ashgate, 2003), 19–37.

Generally speaking, German historians in Germany have recently begun to examine the post-1945 period, but they remain curiously resistant to addressing the labor recruitment and guest workers. By contrast, the fields of politics, sociology, anthropology, and

its effects has been understood as peripheral to the master narratives of West German history such as Allied occupation, democratization, and the problem of two states and one nation. The labor recruitment has been conceptualized instead as part of a separate field of "migration" or "minority" studies. My goal, by contrast, is to demonstrate some of the ways in which the guest worker question was inextricably bound up with the central issues of German social, political, and cultural history after 1945. How, for instance, might we understand the labor recruitment as a key component of the Federal Republic's early efforts to establish a politically stable state in the aftermath of the Third Reich? Why did normative, German conceptions of gender roles become the primary standard for determining the capacity of migrants to integrate? What role did the enduring desire for a reunified Germany (and the particular notion of Germanness it signified) play in the deep reluctance to expand the boundaries of identity and citizenship to include guest workers and their descendants?

The Guest Worker Question, Racial Formation, and the Public Sphere

Before we can begin to answer these questions, however, it is important to think through the modes of interrogation that help us to connect the migration itself with a broader set of historical issues and problems. The very notion of a guest worker *question* serves as a crucial conceptual tool because it brings together two modes of analysis that have often remained isolated from one another in previous works on the labor migration.[18] Whereas social scientists have tended to focus exclusively on policymaking, economics, and demographic changes, literary critics and

---

literature all have well-developed literatures on the postwar migration. German historians in the United States, too, have been remarkably silent on this topic, although it is worth noting that the sociologist Ray Rist offered a chronology of the labor migration in one of the earliest English-language studies of the phenomenon. See Ray C. Rist, *Guestworkers in Germany: Prospects for Pluralism* (New York: Praeger, 1978).

[18] Stuart Hall has argued that a "politics of representation" and its "discursive machineries" are absolutely crucial to understanding the relationship between identity, ethnicity, and cultural production. See, in particular, Stuart Hall, "New Ethnicities," in Morley and Chen, eds., *Stuart Hall*, 441–49. Key discussions of the importance of discourse in cultural history include: John Toews, "Intellectual History Takes a Linguistic Turn: The Autonomy of Meaning and the Irreducibility of Experience," *American Historical Review* 4 (1987): 879–907; Lynn Hunt, ed., *The New Cultural History* (Berkeley and Los Angeles: University of California Press, 1989); Sarah Maza, "Stories in History: Cultural Narratives in Recent Works in European History," *American Historical Review* 4 (1996): 1493–515.

cultural analysts have generally treated the labor agreements, government policies, and economic rationales as relatively straightforward and static contexts for minority artistic expression and counternarratives.[19] Both policymaking and cultural production, I want to suggest, need to be understood as constituent parts of an ongoing, continually shifting public dialogue on the guest worker question. But discursive analysis is not an end in itself here. Rather, my approach is to follow the public discourse on the guest worker as a narrative thread linking key historical interchanges between labor policy, cultural production, social welfare, and the media. In its most basic form, the larger argument of this book is that debates about the place of the guest worker forced a major rethinking of the definitions of German identity and culture. What began as a policy initiative to fuel the economic miracle ultimately became a much broader discussion about the parameters of a distinctly German brand of multiculturalism.

Between 1955 and 1990, there were several key words consistently utilized in the public debates for designating and explicating difference as embodied in the people who had come to the Federal Republic as part of the labor recruitment. They included "guest worker" (*Gastarbeiter*), "foreigner" (*Ausländer*), and "foreign fellow citizen" (*ausländischer Mitbürger*). Over the course of this period, however, these terms were wielded in constantly shifting ways. At some moments they were used as if their meanings were self-evident, a pattern which both continued and reaffirmed much older conventions of defining German identity through blood and familial lineage. Yet one of the benefits of historicizing the public discourse is that it allows us to see how these assumptions shifted

[19] For examples of social-scientific scholarship on the labor recruitment and migration, see Marios Nikolinakos, *Politische Ökonomie der Gastarbeiterfrage. Migration und Kapitalismus* (Reinbek: Rowohlt, 1973); Rist, *Guestworkers in Germany*; Klaus Unger, *Ausländerpolitik in der Bundesrepublik Deutschland* (Saarbrücken: Breitenbach, 1980); Knuth Dohse, *Ausländische Arbeitnehmer und bürgerlicher Staat* (Königstein: Hain, 1981); Bade, *Auswanderer, Wanderarbeiter, Gastarbeiter*; Herbert, *Geschichte der Ausländerbeschäftigung in Deutschland*; Rainer Münz and Ralf Ulrich, "Changing Patterns of Immigration to Germany, 1945–1995: Ethnic Origins, Demographic Structure, Future Prospects," in Bade and Weiner, eds., *Migration Past, Migration Future*, 65–119. For examples of cultural studies work in the same vein, see Peter Seibert, "Zur 'Rettung der Zungen': Ausländerliteratur in ihren konzeptionellen Ansätzen," *Zeitschrift für Literaturwissenschaft und Linguistik* 56 (1984): 40–61; Monika Frederking, *Schreiben gegen Vorurteile: Literatur türkischer Migranten in der Bundesrepublik Deutschland* (Berlin: Express Edition, 1985); Arlene Teraoka, "Gastarbeiterliteratur: The Other Speaks Back," *Cultural Critique* 7 (1987): 77–101; Heidrun Suhr, "Ausländerliteratur: Minority Literature in the Federal Republic of Germany," *New German Critique* 46 (1989): 71–103; Carmine Chiellino, *Interkulturelle Literatur in Deutschland: Ein Handbuch* (Stuttgart: Metzler, 2001).

and evolved over time. By the 1980s, older assumptions about the constitution of West German identity were increasingly a matter of debate, to be argued or justified among a range of possible models for explaining the boundaries of national belonging. Even during the earliest phases of the labor migration at least a few public commentators drew self-conscious attention to the terms themselves, questioning whether "guest worker," for example, constituted an accurate label for the complex socioeconomic transformations reshaping West German society in the postwar period.

As much as possible, then, I attempt to contextualize these labels and treat them as historical objects, worthy of analysis in and of themselves. The reason is simple: in many cases, the labels represented convenient shorthands for much larger sets of ideological assumptions about West German history, culture, and identity, as well as competing policy approaches to the labor migration. I have also chosen quite deliberately to deploy the labels as they were used in the sources, rather than substitute analytic categories more consistent with contemporary expectations and sensibilities. Throughout this study, for instance, I rarely employ terms such as "race" and "ethnicity" because they seldom, if ever, appeared in West German discussions about the guest worker question.

Here again, the reason grows out of a particular set of historical circumstances. Historian Heide Fehrenbach has demonstrated recently that the word "race" (*Rasse*) carried especially vexing associations in West Germany after the Second World War.[20] For most of the population, this was a term linked to Nazi genocide and therefore one to be avoided, if at all possible. Yet it did not disappear from popular discourse right away. In the immediate postwar period, public debate about racial difference shifted from Jews, the Nazis' ultimate racialized Other, to the offspring of German women and African-American GIs, the so-called *Mischlingskinder*.[21] This displacement of race onto a different set of bodies, according to Fehrenbach, occurred as West Germans quickly absorbed American racial assumptions based on a white/black binary, a model far removed from Germany's own. But because the numbers of *Mischlingskinder* were relatively small (about three thousand in 1950), West German social policymakers declared the problem solved by the early 1960s, as the black occupation children reached young adulthood

---

[20] See Heide Fehrenbach, *Race after Hitler: Black Occupation Children in Postwar Germany and America* (Princeton: Princeton University Press, 2005).

[21] *Mischlinge*, or "mixed bloods," had originally been applied to half-Jews, but it came to connote blacks after 1945. Ibid., 8, 87–88.

and were successfully integrated into the workforce. At that point, the word "race" largely vanished from the public sphere.[22] When Afro-German activists adopted terms that explicitly referenced phenotype – including "black" (*schwarze Deutsche*) and "of color" (*farbige Deutsche*) – as self-conscious appellations during the early 1980s, they did so both to draw attention to their own historical erasure and to forge a common identity among those of African descent in Germany.[23]

The fact that the use of the word "race" waned, however, did not mean that assumptions of racial difference were concomitantly eliminated from public discourse. The very category of guest worker, for instance, presumed clear, immutable distinctions between native and foreigner, permanent resident and transitory laborer. And, as we shall see, one major development in the history of the guest worker question was the emergence of new, more explicitly *racialized* ways of talking about migrant cultures during the 1980s. A good example of this process can be found in texts produced by West German social workers, which sometimes attempted to explain the perceived failure of integration in relation to Muslim religious practices. For these critics, religious differences seemed to indicate an essential incapacity of Turks to integrate into West German society. Thus, if we are to understand German conceptions of difference through apparently neutral terms such as guest worker, foreigner, and migrant, it is important to absorb the crucial lessons that have come out of critical race theory from the United States and Great Britain. This scholarship has powerfully historicized categories of difference that had previously been understood as natural and self-evident. Such work helps us to see that these categories – like their more obvious "racial" counterparts – operate as ideological constructs with very particular implications for how social hierarchy is developed and regulated.[24]

---

[22] Ibid., especially Chapters 3 and 4. Fehrenbach notes (74–75) that even though the numbers of biracial occupation children were small, the figures were grossly exaggerated in contemporary media reports.

[23] May Opitz, Katharina Oguntoye, and Dagmar Schultz, eds., *Farbe bekennen: Afrodeutsche Frauen auf den Spuren ihrer Geschichte* (Berlin: Orlanda Frauenverlag, 1986), trans. by Anne V. Adams as *Showing Our Colors: Afro-German Women Speak Out* (Amherst: University of Massachusetts Press, 1992). For more on Afro-German activism in the 1980s, see Tina M. Campt, "Reading the Black German Experience: An Introduction," *Callaloo* 26.2 (2003): 288–94; and Fatima El-Tayeb, "If You Can't Pronounce My Name, You Can Just Call Me Pride: Afro-German Activism, Gender, and Hip Hop," *Gender and History* 15.3 (2003): 460–86.

[24] My work here thus occupies a somewhat paradoxical position. A vast body of scholarship has demonstrated the social construction of race and ethnicity. See, for example, Stuart Hall, "New Ethnicities"; Paul Gilroy, *There Ain't No Black in the Union Jack: The Cultural Politics of Race and Nation* (Chicago: University of Chicago Press, 1987); Michael

Precisely because the guest worker question highlights ideologies and dominant rhetorics, its history does not simply line up in neat chronological order, with one set of assumptions emerging as another disappears. Rather, it is more accurate to say that one issue became increasingly prevalent during certain moments, overshadowing other issues that faded from view, even as they remained viable positions within the larger debate. Recognizing the discourse around the guest worker as a debate, in other words, allows us to see that there were always multiple issues and categories in play. The chapters in this book are arranged in roughly chronological order around key flashpoints in the ongoing public discussion. Together they offer a historical study of the shifts and emphases within a larger debate, rather than a neat catalogue of successive positions.

This framework also raises some basic issues about scope, participation, and location: if the labor recruitment sparked a national dialogue about the guest worker, who was this "public" that struggled over the meanings of the migration? And through what kinds of institutional, economic, and cultural matrices were such conversations articulated? Or to put it another way: what do we mean by "public" in this particular context? The obvious theoretical touchstone here is Jürgen Habermas's 1962 *Structural Transformation of the Public Sphere*, which sought to explain the social conditions for open debate about matters of public interest by private individuals.[25] For the purposes of this study, three particular

Omi and Howard Winant, *Racial Formation in the United States: From the 1960s to the 1990s* (New York: Routledge, 1994); Noel Ignatiev, *How the Irish Became White* (New York: Routledge, 1995); David Roediger, *The Wages of Whiteness: Race and the Making of the American Working Class* (New York: Verso, 1999); Matthew Jacobson, *Whiteness of a Different Color: European Immigrants and the Alchemy of Race* (Cambridge, MA: Harvard University Press, 1998); and Gail Lewis, *"Race," Gender, and Social Welfare: Encounters in a Postcolonial Society* (Cambridge: Polity Press, 2000). On the other hand, many of these conventional assumptions have been very slow to find their way into the standard practice of modern German history, and for this reason, it seems necessary to rehearse some of the key ideas here. My hope is that this study will contribute to a larger project of approaching questions of nation, culture, and citizenship with the same careful attention to identity formation that has become typical in other contexts.

[25] Jürgen Habermas, *Strukturwandel der Öffentlichkeit: Untersuchungen zu einer Kategorie der bürgerlichen Gesellschaft* (Newied: Luchterhand, 1962), trans. by Thomas Burger as *The Structural Transformation of the Public Sphere: An Inquiry into a Category of Bourgeois Society* (Cambridge, MA: MIT Press, 1989). Habermas's seminal argument about the public sphere has inspired a number of important recent histories. See, for example, Dena Goodman, "Public Sphere and Private Life: Toward a Synthesis of Current Historiographical Approaches to the Old Regime," *History and Theory* 31 (1992): 1–20; Belinda Davis, "Reconsidering Habermas, Gender, and the Public Sphere: The Case of Wilhelmine Germany," in Geoff Eley, ed., *Society, Culture, and the State in Germany, 1870–1930* (Ann Arbor: University of Michigan Press, 1996), 397–426; Steven Pincus, "'Coffee Politicians Does Create': Coffeehouses and Restoration Political Culture,"

issues within the larger scholarly literature on Habermas seem especially relevant.

The first involves the historical trajectory of the public sphere. In Habermas's telling, the bourgeois public sphere emerged as a counterweight to both the absolutist state and the private interests of civil society. This historical ideal relied upon private citizens bracketing their individual concerns in order to engage in rational discussion of matters of common interest. The outcome of such discourse was public opinion, defined as a consensus about the common good. Habermas presented his trajectory of the bourgeois public sphere as a story of transformation and decline in which the possibility for democratic public discourse was increasingly compromised over the course of the nineteenth century. This ideal began to erode once social divisions within civil society and private (especially capitalist market) interests seeped into the public discussion. More recent scholars have rejected this view, emphasizing instead that the public sphere was a site of social and discursive conflict from its very inception, as women and workers devised new political strategies for making their voices heard.[26] The development of the guest worker question

Journal of Modern History 67 (1995): 807–34; John Brewer, "This, That, and the Other: Public, Social, and Private in the Seventeenth and Eighteenth Centuries," in Dario Castiglione and Leslie Sharpe, eds., *Shifting the Boundaries* (Exeter: University of Exeter Press, 1995); Margaret C. Jacob, "The Mental Landscape of the Public Sphere: A European Perspective," *Eighteenth-Century Studies* 28 (1994): 95–113. Theoretical critiques, especially from a feminist perspective, include: Seyla Benhabib and Drucilla Cornell, eds., *Feminism as Critique: On the Politics of Gender* (Minneapolis: University of Minnesota Press, 1986); Nancy Fraser, "Rethinking the Public Sphere: A Contribution to the Critique of Actually Existing Democracy," *Social Text* 25/26 (1990): 56–80. Perhaps the most wide-ranging collection of engagements with Habermas's idea of the public sphere is Craig Calhoun, ed., *Habermas and the Public Sphere* (Cambridge, MA: MIT Press, 1992). For a useful discussion of the current state of scholarship inspired by Habermas's public sphere, see Geoff Eley, "Politics, Culture, and the Public Sphere," *positions* 10 (2002): 219–36.

26 Many scholars have pointed to the exclusions and elisions built into Habermas's idealized public sphere. Feminist historians, in particular, have emphasized the ways that Habermas's conception of the public sphere excludes women. See Joan Landes, *Women and the Public Sphere in the Age of the French Revolution* (Ithaca, NY: Cornell University Press, 1988). Other historians have argued that alternative publics and counterpublics emerged even during the height of the bourgeois public sphere. See Mary P. Ryan, *Women in Public: Between Banners and Ballots, 1825–1880* (Baltimore, MD: Johns Hopkins University Press, 1990); Geoff Eley, "Nations, Publics, and Political Cultures: Placing Habermas in the Nineteenth Century," in Craig Calhoun, ed., *Habermas and the Public Sphere* (Cambridge, MA: MIT Press, 1992), 289–339. These critics also reject Habermas's narrative of an idealized historical moment of the bourgeois public sphere, which declined in the late nineteenth and early twentieth centuries and lost legitimacy under the weight of capitalist society's growing contradictions.

affirms this long history of discursive struggle, but it also complicates the leading critiques of Habermas. The revisionist scholarship has tended to focus on the conventional modes of nineteenth-century protest: strikes, demonstrations in the streets, and grassroots labor activism initiated by those cut off from the electoral process and established channels of economic power. The late-twentieth-century struggles over the guest worker question, by contrast, cut across a somewhat broader terrain. Indeed, as the Rodrigues photograph suggests, these debates played out simultaneously at the levels of labor policy, mass media, and cultural representation. In this sense, the history of the guest worker question helps us to see that ideology and discourse are never confined to the neat disciplinary categories favored by scholars. What the Rodrigues photo demonstrates above all is the interconnectedness of politics, economics, and culture in postwar discussions about the labor migration.[27]

This leads to a second major set of questions: What kinds of voices weighed in on the guest worker question? What sorts of publics did they seek to reach? And what modes of address did they employ? Here the recent work of literary scholar Michael Warner, *Publics and Counterpublics*, is especially helpful.[28] In the broadest sense, the range of voices commenting on the labor recruitment was almost infinite: from German chancellors to immigrant children, virtually every member of West German society during this period no doubt thought about and weighed in on the labor migration in some mode or context. Yet not all of these modes had the same kind of efficacy, and some contexts for public discourse were more engaged with questions of national identity and culture than others. Thus, it is important to be clear about what this

---

[27] Geoff Eley points in this direction when he defines the public sphere "as the structured setting where cultural and ideological contest or negotiation among a variety of publics takes place." Eley, "Nations, Publics, and Political Cultures," 303–304, 306. Over the past decade, scholars have increasingly rejected false separations between political economy and cultural production. See, for example, Miriam Hansen, "Unstable Mixtures, Dilated Spheres: Negt's and Kluge's *The Public Sphere and Experience* Twenty Years Later," *Public Culture* 5 (1993): 179–212; Lawrence Grossberg, "Cultural Studies vs. Political Economy," in John Storey, ed., *Cultural Theory and Popular Culture: A Reader* (Athens: University of Georgia Press, 1998); and Geoff Eley, "On Your Marx: From Cultural History to the History of Society," in George Steinmetz, ed., *The Politics of Method in the Human Sciences: Positivism and Its Epistemological Others* (Durham, NC: Duke University Press, 2005). My work here represents an attempt to trace an ideological history across interpretive categories and subfields.

[28] Michael Warner, *Publics and Counterpublics* (New York: Zone Books, 2002). I thank Jay Cook for making me aware of this important work and pointing out its larger implications for my project.

book does and does not attempt to explicate. Many of the workers themselves, for example, discussed the terms of the recruitment program and the everyday experience of living in Germany, but they did so informally, mostly in conversation and letters circulated within immigrant enclaves.[29] My central concern, by contrast, is with the specific forms and evolution of a self-consciously public debate on diversity that understood itself as national in scope. I am thus interested in those who oriented themselves to a broader public. Although some of these minority voices did not always achieve a national or mass public (especially early on), they were explicitly expansionist in intent, aiming for as wide an audience as possible.

This approach requires us to be particularly sensitive to what Warner describes as the "notional" and "material" qualities of public-making.[30] Many of the documents produced by government officials on the labor recruitment, for instance, cannot simply be taken as transparent, internal records of day-to-day bureaucratic decisions. Rather, they must be understood as self-consciously public statements designed to persuade particular constituencies (e.g., other government officials or the nation as a whole) that importing foreign laborers was necessary for economic productivity or that integration was the only viable option for dealing with permanent guest worker residence. At the same time, greater attention to modes of discourse or address requires us to be precise about the kinds of voices that had access to a broader public. As Warner notes: "To address a public or to think of oneself as belonging to a public is to be a certain kind of person, to inhabit a certain kind of social world, to have at one's disposal certain media and genres, to be motivated by a certain normative horizon, and to speak within a certain language ideology."[31] Migrants striving to reach a national audience needed to employ a specific set of tools: they had to adopt German, frame their statements in terms of personal experience, and use textual genres that could be reproduced and circulated through mainstream channels such as publishing houses, newspapers, and movie theaters. By its very nature, then, this book's emphasis on competing efforts to address a broad German public on the guest worker question means that I focus on individuals (artists, intellectuals, journalists, etc.) who primarily expressed themselves in German and generally used broadly distributed forms of communication.

[29] Ibid., 56–57.
[30] Ibid., 67–74.
[31] Ibid., 10.

But these patterns of uneven access and visibility should not lead us to assume that people such as factory workers who did not adopt modes of public address were voice*less*; rather, they registered their feelings and concerns about the labor migration in other, more localized ways. At various points in the pages that follow, I try to note where labor actions on the shop floor and community activism in neighborhoods intersected with the shifting contours of national debates about the guest worker question. My point is not to privilege one sort of questioning over another, but rather to be clear about the specific ways in which I have tried to understand the larger significance of the labor recruitment for postwar West German history. A study of the labor migration from the perspective of workers' experiences would provide an important counterpart to the national debates that I follow here.

The preconditions for addressing a national audience lead to a third basic question: is it even possible for public debates conducted through mass-circulated media to register oppositional perspectives in any kind of meaningful or efficacious way? To be sure, access and differential power relations are invariably asymmetrical. But my story – which focuses on literature and film, but does not cover television or popular music – also suggests that oppositional voices do operate within market mechanisms and mass-mediated forms of discussion. In this sense, I am trying to build on the insight of Oskar Negt and Alexander Kluge in *Public Sphere and Experience* that it is precisely through market-driven modes of discussion that alternative perspectives and subordinate social groups – previously elided in the classical liberal-bourgeois public sphere – often become visible and audible.[32]

The notion of ideological struggle through market mechanisms runs counter to one of our conventional assumptions about the public sphere. In Habermas's framework, the public sphere ideal relies on setting aside social and economic status to create a forum for open and free discussion. The historical expansion of market capitalism and its encroachment on the liberal public sphere thus spelled decline and impeded truly egalitarian communication. By contrast, Negt and Kluge insist that the commercial

---

[32] Oskar Negt and Alexander Kluge, *Öffentlichkeit und Erfahrung: Zur Organisationsanalyse von bürgerlicher und proletarischer Öffentlichkeit* (Frankfurt: Suhrkamp, 1972), trans. by Peter Labanyi, Jamie Daniel, and Assenka Oksiloff as *The Public Sphere and Experience* (Minneapolis: University of Minnesota Press, 1993), 12–18. This work represents one of the earliest critiques of Habermas's theory of the public sphere. It has recently been the object of renewed academic interest. See Miriam Hansen, "Foreword," in Negt and Kluge, *Public Sphere and Experience*, ix–xli.

aspects of mass-mediated forms of publicity can no longer be separated from the public spheres that they enable. What makes this insight politically significant, according to literary scholar Miriam Hansen, is that "industrial-commercial public spheres depend, for economic reasons, upon a maximum of inclusion": in the effort to extract the greatest possible profit, markets constantly seek new audiences by incorporating social groups and experience previously excluded from representation. Market-driven modes of publicity unwittingly bring into view new "horizons of experience."[33] In the late-twentieth-century history of the guest worker question, the market provided opportunities for minorities to be seen and heard well before they had access to citizenship or voting rights.[34] The question of guest workers entered the public sphere through the mass media – for example, in the media spectacle surrounding the one-millionth guest worker – and in the years that followed, minority intellectuals turned to the cultural marketplace as one of the primary ways to contest and re-present the images produced by government officials, business leaders, and journalists.

This route into the public sphere, it is worth stressing, was particularly important for labor migrants in West Germany precisely because they had no claim to citizenship.[35] Indeed, the guest worker program presumed a basic rejection of permanent immigration, making access to German citizenship an irrelevant issue. Yet the actual practice of foreign labor recruitment created a paradoxical situation: taxpaying migrants permanently settled in the Federal Republic, but were excluded from political

---

[33] Hansen, "Foreword," xxx. "Horizons of experience" here suggests the potential to enlarge one's view and go beyond what one already knows. The phrase actually comes from Reinhart Koselleck, *Vergangene Zukunft: zur Semantik geschichtlicher Zeit* (Frankfurt: Suhrkamp, 1979), trans. by Keith Tribe as *Futures Past: On the Semantics of Historical Time* (Cambridge, MA: MIT Press, 1985). For an interesting recent exploration of Koselleck's "horizon of experience" concept and its theoretical implications, see Michael Pickering, "Experience as Horizon: Koselleck, Expectation and Historical Time," *Cultural Studies* 18.2–3 (2004): 271–89.

[34] An interesting parallel here would be the case of elite African-American artists and intellectuals during the early twentieth century, a period in which legal segregation and ground-level disenfranchisement coexisted with the rise of a "New Negro Renaissance." David Levering Lewis has famously described this mode of cultural politics as "civil rights by copyright." See David Levering Lewis, *When Harlem Was in Vogue* (New York: Knopf, 1981).

[35] Most of the non-European laborers employed in France and Britain, by contrast, were former colonials who enjoyed citizenship or the right to permanent residence based on this status.

representation. During the period examined in this book, German citizenship continued to be defined by blood, and even children of guest workers born and raised in West Germany did not have the right to be naturalized. It was not until the year 2000 that the Federal Republic revised its citizenship law to incorporate labor migrants and their descendants. Thus, the ideological work of writing and representing alternative conceptions of the nation through market channels was absolutely crucial for initiating critical dialogue on the place of labor migrants in postwar German society.[36]

At the same time, it is important to acknowledge that the mass marketplace was always structured by an unequal set of power relations. The market, by definition, only supported those voices and products that it could sell. Consequently, commercial matrices tended to favor cultural images that recapitulated stereotypes and legitimized political and economic subjugation. On the other hand, the mass marketplace often facilitated a much broader circulation of migrant issues than did the voices in the factory barracks and urban tenements. And it also served as the site of the creation of new cultural categories (e.g., the genre of foreigner literature) that enabled ruptures and discontinuities in conventional public discourse.[37] A key aspect of my analysis of minority interventions in German public debate, then, involves tracing this dialectic over time in order to illuminate some of the fraught choices migrant artists and intellectuals encountered as they struggled to reframe the guest worker question in more complex, humane terms.

[36] This is not to suggest that cultural production is more important than suffrage or that culture and politics are not always interconnected. It was precisely the reformulation of German national boundaries that was at stake in these debates. Thus, all of the cultural work led to the more sweeping ideological shifts that were necessary to produce a reformulation of the polity. Still, I would suggest that there is a kind of urgency attached to these cultural struggles, which in many ways resembles the situation of African-Americans in the early twentieth century more than that confronting postcolonial migrants in France and Britain. In the German case, as in the American case, the cultural debates took place in a context where the most basic access to suffrage was still uncertain.

[37] My understanding of the market as a multivalent tool for ideological struggle builds upon the recent work of Paul Gilroy and Stuart Hall, both of whom have emphasized the possibilities for black agency in the culture industries and electronic media of late twentieth-century Britain. See especially Gilroy, *There Ain't No Black in the Union Jack*, Chapter 5; and Stuart Hall's discussion of the politics of representation in "New Ethnicities." For both authors, the story is never simply a straightforward replacement of hegemonic images with minority counterimages. Rather they emphasize the dialectical, ongoing process of intervention and reappropriation that the market fosters.

Migration to Western Europe in the Postwar Period

At this point, it is helpful to situate Rodrigues's story within the larger context of postwar migration to Western Europe. A thorough consideration of the many varieties and histories of migrant experience in the New Europe would require much lengthier analysis. Still, it is possible to point to a number of basic patterns that help us to frame and differentiate the German case. Generally speaking, there were three types of population movements to Western Europe between 1945 and 1990: guest worker migration, postcolonial migration, and the migration of asylum seekers and refugees. These are, of course, ideal types, and the boundaries between them were not always firm. But virtually every nation in the northwestern part of Europe experienced at least one of these influxes. Along with the creation of the European Union and a common currency, migration has had perhaps the most dramatic transformative effect on Western Europe in the second half of the twentieth century. It is a defining feature of the New Europe, the driving force behind the development of more ethnically diverse cultures and societies.

The Federal Republic was not the only Western European nation to implement a guest worker program during the postwar boom years. Foreign, supplemental manpower was also imported by Switzerland and Austria and, to a lesser extent, by every other highly industrialized nation in Europe. Switzerland, in fact, was the first country to adopt this practice, beginning immediately after the war. But its program differed from that of the Federal Republic in two key respects. First, while Germany designed a recruitment apparatus administered through the Ministry of Labor, Switzerland relied on employing firms to find workers on their own and regulated the flow of incoming foreigners on an ad hoc basis. The Swiss government introduced employer-specific quotas for guest workers in 1963 and a countrywide quota on the total number of foreign laborers seven years later. Second, unlike Germany, which eventually drew the bulk of its recruits from Turkey, Switzerland relied primarily on its immediate neighbors, especially Italy, for supplemental manpower. In 1960, Italians made up 60 percent of the foreigners in the country, and until the late 1980s, three out of five Swiss immigrants came from adjacent nations (Italy, France, Germany, and Austria).[38] Austria, by contrast, followed the

---

[38] For more on the Swiss guest worker system and its social impacts, see Rudolf Braun, *Sozio-kulturelle Probleme der Eingliederung italienischer Arbeitskräfte in der Schweiz* (Zurich: Eugen Rentsch, 1970); Hans-Joachim Hoffmann-Nowotny, *Soziologie des Fremdarbeiterproblems: eine theoretische und empirische Analyse am Beispiel der*

West German model more closely. It signed treaties with Turkey (1964) and Yugoslavia (1966) and quickly set up government recruitment offices in those countries to screen potential laborers. Just a decade later, however, Austria officially ended its guest worker program and enacted a law that severely restricted the access of foreigners to employment.

Each of these histories followed a paradoxical pattern that has come to define postwar guest worker migration. On the one hand, Switzerland, Austria, and the Federal Republic all imported laborers as a temporary economic measure and vehemently rejected the idea of permanent immigration. On the other hand, they increasingly found themselves unable to prevent workers from extending their stays or bringing their families, and thus were forced to confront the unintended and unwelcome consequences of shortsighted labor policies – the long-term settlement of migrant groups, which visibly transformed the demographic makeup of largely homogeneous populations. Among these three nations most commonly associated with guest worker recruitment, West Germany developed the system to its fullest extent. In terms of sheer numbers, the Federal Republic enlisted more foreign laborers than any other country in Europe. At the same time, it was perhaps the most resistant to legal changes that would make long-time foreign residents a formal part of the polity.

Other countries that imported foreign labor during the same period included Belgium, France, Great Britain, the Netherlands, Sweden, Denmark, and Norway. But for various reasons, these nations do not quite fit the classic guest worker recruitment model. The Scandinavian countries, for instance, were generally quicker to acknowledge the demographic and social changes produced by labor migration. Sweden and Denmark formulated an official immigrant policy at the tail end of recruitment, giving foreign workers and their families the right to vote and stand for election at the local and regional levels as early as 1975.[39] Sweden, moreover, acknowledged imported laborers as potential immigrants and encouraged them to naturalize.[40] Belgium recruited guest workers from Italy,

---

Schweiz (Stuttgart: Enke, 1973); Hans-Joachim Hoffmann-Nowotny, ed., *Ausländer in der Bundesrepublik Deutschland und in der Schweiz: Segregation und Integration: eine vergleichende Untersuchung* (Frankfurt: Campus, 1982), 32–113.

[39] For an English-language discussion of Denmark's postwar immigrants, see Jonathan M. Schwartz, *Reluctant Hosts: Denmark's Reception of Guest Workers* (Copenhagen: Akademisk Forlag, 1985).

[40] For more on the Swedish guest worker program and its consequences, see Tomas Hammar, "Sweden" in Tomas Hammar, ed., *European Immigration Policy: A Comparative Study* (Cambridge: Cambridge University Press, 1985); Charles Westin, *Settlement and*

Morocco, and other southern European countries for its coal, iron, and steel industries, but it also experienced an influx of postcolonial migrants in the form of political exiles from among the elite classes fleeing the newly independent Democratic Republic of Congo. Other nations with colonial legacies only used guest workers for a short period after the war, relying on postcolonial migrants to meet the bulk of their labor need. Britain, for example, recruited refugees and Italians through the European Voluntary Worker system, which bound laborers to specific jobs and prevented them from bringing their families.[41] But the program was largely abandoned by 1951, when former colonials began to arrive in increasingly large numbers.

Britain, France, the Netherlands, and Belgium have been more closely linked to postcolonial migration. In contrast to the German model of government-sponsored recruitment of guest workers, this second type of migration was in large part spontaneous, fueled by former colonials who enjoyed the right of entry (and thus did not require visas) in the metropole. Britain received immigrants from the so-called New Commonwealth, especially the Caribbean, the Indian subcontinent, Africa, and Asia. These migrants began to arrive soon after the war, expanding in number (541,000 in 1961) until the 1962 Commonwealth Immigrants Act, which made it particularly difficult for unskilled postcolonials to enter the country. In France, North and West Africans came for work even before independence and entered as French nationals. After decolonization the stream of immigrants persisted, but Algerians received special status that gave them an ongoing claim to nationality because Algeria had previously been considered an extension of the metropole. The number of former colonials in France reached nearly 800,000 by 1970. The Netherlands experienced two major influxes of migrants. Between 1945 and 1960, it took in 300,000 repatriates from the former Dutch East Indies (now Indonesia). Most of these migrants had been born overseas, and many were of mixed Dutch and Indonesian parentage, but they all possessed Dutch citizenship. After 1965, workers from the former colony of

---

Integration Policies towards Immigrants and their Descendants in Sweden (Geneva: ILO, 2000).

[41] For more on the European Voluntary Worker system in Britain, see Robert Miles and Diana Kay, "The TUC, Foreign Labour and the Labour Government, 1945–1951," *Immigrants and Minorities* 9.1 (1990): 85–108; and Kathleen Paul, *Whitewashing Britain: Race and Citizenship in Postwar Britain* (Ithaca, NY: Cornell University Press, 1997), 85–88. The numbers of people recruited through the EVW scheme diverge significantly, anywhere from 90,000 (Paul) to 180,000 up to 350,000 (Miles and Kay).

Surinam in South America constituted the primary group of migrants to the Netherlands.

The colonial relationship was a crucial factor in setting the terms for this type of migration. Besides free entry and claim to nationality, most postcolonial migrants possessed at least a rudimentary knowledge of the metropolitan language, customs, and values. Some even followed lines of communication and settlement developed during the colonial period. This stands in stark contrast to the German guest worker model, in which migrants had little or no familiarity with Germany. At the same time, the colonial relationship meant that postcolonial migrants were often subjected to older, entrenched social, economic, and racial hierarchies. Their minority status within Europe was defined not so much by being foreign as by widespread discrimination, both institutional and informal.

Asylum seekers comprised the third major migrant group in Europe during the postwar period. Their numbers remained relatively modest until the mid-1980s, when people from Latin America, Africa, Asia, and the Middle East began to arrive in larger waves, fleeing civil wars, ethnic conflicts, and political persecution in their countries of origin. The figure spiked again after 1989 with the collapse of the Eastern Bloc and the war in Yugoslavia. Between 1985 and 2000, hundreds of thousands of asylum seekers came to Western Europe in search of protection, but their migration situation was quite unlike that experienced by postcolonials or even guest workers. Most nations required them to live in barracks or hostels and barred them from working until their refugee status was formally approved, a process which typically had only a 10 percent success rate and often took many years.

At the same time, asylum became a major political issue throughout Western Europe. In France, Britain, and Germany, in particular, ordinary citizens expressed fear that refugees represented a drain on social resources. Nowhere was this phenomenon as acute as in the Federal Republic. Between 1979 and 1981 alone, over 200,000 people sought refugee status in West Germany. Perhaps the most significant reason for this disproportionate number was Germany's generous asylum provision. As part of the effort to atone for its National Socialist past, the Federal Republic introduced the most liberal asylum law on the continent, which guaranteed refuge for anyone claiming political persecution in his or her country of origin. The 1980s influx of asylum seekers, coupled with already high levels of anxiety about the continuing presence of guest workers, led many Germans to complain that their country was being "overrun" by foreigners. Some critics made little effort to distinguish between those who had recently arrived and those who had resided in the Federal Republic for several decades. Asylum seekers and recruited labor migrants occupied the same fundamental category: they were foreigners who did not belong in German society.

Within this broad spectrum of postwar migration, the Federal Republic established the largest temporary labor recruitment program, importing more guest workers than any other Western European nation. It also outpaced every other country on the continent in terms of its sheer numbers of foreign residents, a fact which immediately disrupts our conventional portrait of Germany as one of the least diverse nations within the New Europe. Yet a large part of the reason that it had such a high number of residents categorized as foreign was its stringent citizenship law, which discouraged many long-term migrants from naturalizing. France and Britain, by contrast, extended comparatively expansive citizenship rights to former colonial migrants and, even after these countries ended automatic citizenship, they urged migrants to naturalize. This is not to suggest that citizenship can be equated with social equality or inclusion and, in fact, a growing scholarship suggests just how contested the process of redefining Frenchness or Britishness has been in the face of nonwhite migration.[42] Nevertheless, the differences among legal frameworks in Germany, France, and Britain do suggest the need for a deeper sense of how the diversification of postwar Europe proceeded in multiple contexts, a story that has been far less rigorously explored in German historiography. The contradictory combination of large numbers of migrants and highly restrictive rules about foreigners becoming part of the polity made Germany distinctive among Western European nations. It was precisely this paradox, moreover, that constituted the key point of contention in public debates about the labor migration.

What the German case demonstrates is just how tricky it is to generalize about the position of minority groups in different national contexts.

---

[42] Gilroy, *There Ain't No Black in the Union Jack*; Stuart Hall, "Race, Articulation, and Societies Structured in Dominance," in *Sociological Theories: Race and Colonialism* (Paris: Unesco, 1980), 305–45; Paul, *Whitewashing Britain*; Maxim Silverman, *Deconstructing the Nation: Immigration, Racism, and Citizenship in Modern France* (London: Routledge, 1992); Patrick Weil, *La France et ses étrangers: l'aventure d'une politique de l'immigration, 1938–1991* (Paris: Calman-Lévy, 1991); Patrick Weil, *La république et sa diversité: Immigration, intégration, discrimination* (Paris: Seuil, 2005); Gérard Noiriel, *Le creuset français: Histoire de l'immigration aux xix–xx siècles* (Paris: Seuil, 1988), trans. by Geoffroy de Laforcade as *The French Melting Pot: Immigration, Citizenship, and National Identity* (Minneapolis: University of Minnesota Press, 1996).

Country of origin, reasons for leaving, and specific legal parameters of residence all shaped the experience of those who settled in postwar Western Europe in vastly different ways. Still, it is important not to lose sight of the fact that these distinctive migration histories overlapped in significant respects as well. In Britain, West Germany, and the Netherlands during the 1980s, for instance, Muslim migrants of different backgrounds experienced what Martin Barker has called the "new racism," a pattern of racialized bigotry in which religion and culture often served as the basis for essentialized claims of incommensurable difference. And the specific patterns of xenophobia and backlash frequently had ripple effects across national boundaries. As we shall see, the so-called Rushdie Affair became a major topic of public discussion in the Federal Republic as German commentators struggled to define the specific terms upon which an increasingly multiethnic society might be understood.

The events of 9/11, of course, emphasized this continuity even more, focusing intense public scrutiny on the Muslim identities of migrants across Europe. Since then, Western European nations have become preoccupied with questions of Islam, fundamentalism, and a perceived clash of civilizations.[43] In Germany, the Turkish community has been increasingly discussed in terms of a "Muslim problem," an ideological development that has spurred renewed public debate about the thresholds of assimilation, integration, and belonging. For precisely this reason, it is crucial to push beyond the visceral reactions of recent years and develop a more nuanced, comparative understanding of migrant experiences of Muslim groups throughout the New Europe. One danger of 9/11 has been our tendency to characterize the challenges of cross-cultural coexistence as singular, or as part of an entirely new political imperative.

For almost half a century, the Federal Republic has struggled to come to terms with the growing diversity fueled by its postwar labor recruitment. Ultimately, then, this is not simply a study of demographic change and its social, political, and cultural impacts. It is also a history of that most elusive of things – a specifically German multiculturalism.

---

[43] See, for instance, Daniel Levy, Max Pensky, and John Torpey, eds., *Old Europe, New Europe, Core Europe: Transatlantic Relations after the Iraq War* (London: Verso, 2005). This collection of essays by prominent Western European intellectuals includes several pieces that define a Judeo-Christian European identity in opposition to Islam and Muslims.

I

Aras Ören and the Guest Worker Question

Because it stands at the intersection of politics, labor, and culture, the guest worker question has always included and supported multiple histories. One obvious place to mark its beginnings, for example, might be the first postwar labor recruitment treaty, which the Federal Republic of Germany signed with Italy in 1955. This document both inaugurated the recruitment program and served to represent it in particular ways. On the one hand, the treaty mapped out the legal and operational aspects of the work trajectory – the application process and placement procedures. On the other hand, it articulated the meaning of "guest," defining labor migrants to West Germany in stark contrast to the category of immigrants who relocate to a new country with the intention of long-term settlement. Another important starting point might be the 1964 public-relations event that celebrated Armando Rodrigues's arrival as the one-millionth guest worker. Like the original labor treaty, this event sought to define what a guest worker was, but it also marked a shift toward more self-conscious modes of promotion. This was perhaps German industry's most important effort to sell the program to the nation. Yet both of these watersheds in the history of the guest worker question run the risk of recapitulating the ideological assumptions and uneven power relations that were built into the labor recruitment. How can we speak of a guest worker question whose beginnings predate the emergence of guest worker voices in the public sphere?

For precisely this reason, the issue of voice has had a special significance in the early scholarship on the labor recruitment. Much of the work of explaining this history has focused on recovering or adding guest worker voices to the official policy statements. At this point, however, it seems worth asking not only what we mean by voice, but also how we might explain the historical origins of a more inclusive public discourse surrounding the *Gastarbeiter*. Most literary studies have pointed to the early 1970s as the breakthrough period when migrant artists and intellectuals began to publish works in German. What makes this moment particularly crucial is that it coincided with the official end of recruitment, a major change in the government's labor policy that had important consequences for the demographic makeup of foreign workers in the Federal Republic. We have never really considered the historical proximity of these two watersheds. Nor have we fully explored their reciprocal relation – the ways in which minority literature both grew out of and simultaneously altered public discussions about the labor migration. The early 1970s, then, offer a crucial but underexplored starting point in the history of the guest worker question – the critical juncture when policymaking and minority critiques converged, as literary texts by migrant intellectuals came into explicit dialogue with government policies and rhetoric.

To make sense of this dialogue, we need to rethink its constituent parts. Early policy statements on the labor recruitment, for example, require examination not only in terms of what they said, but also how they were articulated. In what ways did government officials, industry leaders, and journalists talk about and promote the program to the West German public? What image of the guest worker emerged in the official pronouncements, and what did these images omit? On the other hand, if the first literary works produced by minority writers "added a new voice" to public discussions about guest workers, how exactly did these figures attempt to complicate and contest the earlier policy statements? And in what ways did their interventions differ from other critiques of the labor importation issued by both guest workers themselves and West German intellectuals such as Günter Herburger, Günter Wallraff, Rainer Werner Fassbinder, and Max Frisch?

These questions all point to the prominent Turkish-German intellectual Aras Ören, often described as the father of so-called *Ausländerliteratur* (foreigner literature).[1] Ören's first public statement on the labor migration

---

[1] Arlene Teraoka and Heidrun Suhr have both pointed to Ören as one of the central contributors to minority literature in the Federal Republic of Germany. See Arlene Teraoka, "Gastarbeiterliteratur: The Other Speaks Back," *Cultural Critique* 7 (1987): 77–101; and Heidrun Suhr, "Ausländerliteratur: Minority Literature in the Federal Republic of Germany," *New German Critique* 46 (1989): 71–103. Marilya Veteto-Conrad has dealt extensively with Ören and argued that he represents one of the major voices for Turks in Germany. See Marilya Veteto-Conrad, *Finding a Voice: Identity and the Works of*

came in the *Berlin Trilogie* (1973–1980), a collection of three poetic cycles
that loosely narrated the everyday lives and concerns of both Turkish
and German workers in Berlin's Kreuzberg district. As a Turk, Ören
belonged to what by the early 1970s had become the largest group of
new immigrants in the Federal Republic. Although he wrote these poems
in Turkish, he collaborated in their immediate translation into German
and published the texts with a highly respected, alternative German
press, Rotbuch Verlag. Ören, in other words, did not just add a Turkish voice to the public debates about the labor recruitment. Rather, he
initiated a very particular form of discursive engagement, a voice that
sought out – and existed in – a mass market, a voice that garnered the
widespread attention of West German reviewers, and a voice that problematized the most basic assumptions of the official understanding of the
Gastarbeiter.

Ören's mode of critique in the *Berlin Trilogie* did not remain static.
Between 1973 and 1980, one finds a dramatic shift in the poems' central
concerns – from an impassioned plea for cross-ethnic worker solidarity to
perhaps the first explicitly multicultural characters and themes produced
by a West German writer.[2] Thus, if the initial translation of Ören's work
marked a new kind of literary cultural politics in the West German public
sphere, the development of his work over the next decade demonstrated a
fundamental rethinking of what constituted West German identity itself.

German-Language Turkish Writers in the Federal Republic of Germany to 1990 (New
York: Peter Lang, 1996). Other English-language analyses of Ören's work include: Gil
Gott, "Migration, Ethnicization and Germany's New Ethnic Minority Literature" (Ph.D.
diss., University of California, Berkeley, 1994); and Leslie A. Adelson, *The Turkish Turn in
Contemporary German Literature: Toward a New Critical Grammar of Migration* (New
York: Palgrave Macmillan, 2005), Chapter 3. In German, see especially Irmgard Ack-
ermann, "'Gastarbeiter'literatur als Herausforderung," *Frankfurter Hefte* 1 (1983): 56–
64; Irmgard Ackermann, "Integrationsvorstellungen und Integrationsdarstellungen in der
Ausländerliteratur," *Zeitschrift für Literaturwissenschaft und Linguistik* 56 (1984): 23–
39; Harald Weinrich, "Deutschland – ein türkisches Märchen: Zu Hause in der Fremde –
Gastarbeiterliteratur," in Volker Hage and Adolph Fink, eds., *Deutsche Literatur 1983:
Ein Jahresüberblick* (Stuttgart: Reclam, 1984), 230–37; Monika Frederking, *Schreiben
gegen Vorurteile: Literatur türkischer Migranten in der Bundesrepublik Deutschland*
(Berlin: Express Edition, 1985), 57–81; Heidi Rösch, *Migrationsliteratur im interkul-
turellen Kontext. Eine didaktische Studie zur Literatur von Aras Ören, Aysel Özakin,
Franco Biondi und Rafik Schami* (Frankfurt: Verlag für Interkulturelle Kommunikation, 1992); Sargut Sölcün, "Literatur der türkischen Minderheit," in Carmine Chiellino,
ed., *Interkulturelle Literatur in Deutschland: Ein Handbuch* (Stuttgart: Metzler, 2000),
135–52.
[2] Suhr briefly acknowledged the multicultural implications of Ören's trilogy in 1989. Suhr,
"Ausländerliteratur," 79.

Recruitment Begins

At the most basic level, the Federal Republic's policy of importing foreign labor after the Second World War emerged as a solution to two urgent and mutually reinforcing developments: the unexpected industrial boom of the so-called *Wirtschaftswunder* (economic miracle) and the growing shortage of able-bodied German male workers. Yet these concerns were virtually unimaginable when German army leaders declared unconditional surrender in the spring of 1945. In the immediate aftermath of the war, the devastation of Germany's physical landscape – the ruin of entire cities and their public buildings, factories, offices, and living quarters, as well as railroads, bridges, and other transportation and communication infrastructure – appeared so complete that most expert observers, both German and non-German alike, were deeply pessimistic about the country's economic future. For some, this outward material destruction indicated a more fundamental damage. As one British contemporary put it, the economy seemed to be "cast back to the beginnings of industrialization."[3]

Despite these dismal predictions, the economy of what was to become the Federal Republic experienced a remarkable recovery. Recent scholarship has explained the speed of revival by pointing to the preexisting capacity for industry, which did not sustain as much vital damage as eyewitnesses initially believed.[4] But another important factor was occupied Germany's status as a key site for the emerging Cold War. With tensions mounting between the two superpowers by 1947, the United States and Great Britain increasingly linked economic conditions in Germany with political stability: material prosperity, they believed, would dampen the appeal of political extremism and strengthen loyalty to capitalist democracy. By 1948, the United States and Britain began to initiate economic rebuilding in their zones, which included extending Marshall Plan aid and initiating currency reform. The Western occupation forces as well as the

---

[3] Quoted in Alan Kramer, *The West German Economy: 1945–1955* (New York: Berg, 1991), 1. For a detailed description of the kinds of physical damage sustained by Germany, see page 11.

[4] There has been much debate among economic historians about the causes of West Germany's *Wirtschaftswunder*. Kramer's useful synthesis of the most important literature in this debate attempts to revise what he views as the simplistic assumption that this miraculous recovery can be primarily attributed to "the innate industriousness of the German people, good fortune, hard work and American Marshall aid." He suggests instead that rapid recovery was made possible by the preexisting capacity for industry, low wages, contributions by refugees, and the government's policy of encouraging investment by giving tax breaks. See Kramer, *West German Economy*, 1–2.

state's new leaders thus understood economic health to be a critical component for the democratic success of the Federal Republic founded on 23 May 1949.

Between 1948 and 1952, western Germany's economy began to stabilize and embarked on a path of self-sustaining growth, a development helped by the influx of U.S. capital with the Marshall Plan and later by the demand for West German products during the Korean War. Signs of this upswing included the firm establishment of the new deutschmark, the recovery of industrial production and the gross domestic product beyond the 1936 level, and four successive years of increase for the capital stock of industry.[5] During the first five years of the *Wirtschaftswunder*, the annual economic growth rate rose 8.2 percent and, for the period between 1950 and 1970, averaged slightly more than 6 percent.[6]

At the same time, business leaders and government officials in the Federal Republic confronted a grossly undersized workforce. Even during the 1930s, the number of men available as laborers had been relatively small due to the lost generation of World War I. Germany's high rate of casualties in the Second World War and the thousands of soldiers held as prisoners of war further reduced the number of working-age men available to fill jobs after hostilities ended. The low birthrate during the combat years, moreover, meant that there were fewer young people ready to move into the labor market in the decade after the war.

Yet during the first ten years of economic growth the lack of able-bodied and available German men did not seem to pose a dire problem. The shortage of manpower was alleviated somewhat by the stream of *Ostvertriebene* (ethnic Germans expelled from former territories of the Third Reich) and *Flüchtlinge* (those fleeing the Soviet takeover, especially in the German Democratic Republic) that supplemented the Federal Republic's own relatively meager workforce. From the last months of the war through the early 1950s, as many as fifteen million Germans were driven

---

[5] Ibid., 163.
[6] The first figure is cited in Henry A. Turner, Jr., *Germany from Partition to Reunification* (New Haven: Yale University Press, 1992), 110; the second is provided by Ray C. Rist, *Guestworkers in Germany: The Prospects for Pluralism* (New York: Praeger, 1978), 110. Roy Mellor claims that 1948–50 represented the first real period of *Wirtschaftswunder*, when industrial production rose from 60 percent to 130 percent of the 1936 figure. See Roy E. H. Mellor, *The Two Germanies: A Modern Geography* (New York: Harper & Row, 1978), 150. For more extensive accounts of the West German economy and the economic miracle, see H. C. Wallich, *Mainsprings of the German Revival* (New Haven: Yale University Press, 1955); Eric Owen Smith, *The West German Economy* (New York: St. Martin's Press, 1983); Kramer, *West German Economy*.

out of lands that became Poland, Czechoslovakia, Hungary, Romania, and Yugoslavia. Approximately 8 million of them settled in West Germany, constituting roughly 16.1 percent of the new state's total population. An additional 1.72 million arrived from the Soviet occupation zone and East Germany. Although expellees and refugees faced initial hostility from local inhabitants who resented the prospect of sharing scarce resources with strangers, these ethnic German newcomers became a much-needed source of manpower once the economy took off.[7]

Women also served as an important pool of additional labor. With currency reform in 1948 and the subsequent dissolution of the black market, many women sought jobs that paid real wages. Almost two million women, in fact, took up employment outside the home between 1947 and 1955. As historians have recently demonstrated, this move into the workplace occurred despite the fact that Konrad Adenauer's Christian Democratic government undertook a campaign to redomesticate women, encouraging them to focus on the unpaid labor of "reproducing Germany's future."[8]

While refugees, expellees, and women helped to relieve the initial shortage of workers created by the rapid economic upswing, the West German government also began to explore alternative sources for extra manpower. More specifically, Bonn entered into discussions with Rome about the

---

[7] For more on the expulsion of ethnic Germans from eastern lands, the role of the Allies in this process, and the emergence of expellee organizations, see Pertti Ahonen, *After the Expulsion: West Germany and Eastern Europe, 1945–1990* (Oxford: Oxford University Press, 2003), 15–25. Ulrich Herbert discusses the Federal Republic's use of the *Ostvertriebene* as a primary source of labor in the period roughly from 1948 to 1961. See Ulrich Herbert, *A History of Foreign Labor in Germany, 1880–1980: Seasonal Workers/Forced Laborers/Guest Workers*, trans. by William Templer (Ann Arbor: University of Michigan Press, 1990), 195–201. Mellor cites the 1950 census in the Federal Republic, which showed 7.876 million expellees, with a further 148,000 in West Berlin. See Mellor, *Two Germanies*, 153–54. For more on refugees and expellees in West Germany, see F. Edding, H. E. Hornschu, and H. Wander, *Das deutsche Flüchtlingsproblem* (Kiel: Institut für Weltwirtschaft, 1949); Siegfried Bethlehem, *Heimatvertreibung, DDR-Flucht, Gastarbeiterzuwanderung: Wanderungsströme und Wanderungspolitik in der Bundesrepublik Deutschland* (Stuttgart: Klett-Cotta, 1982); Klaus J. Bade, ed., *Neue Heimat im Westen: Vertriebene, Flüchtlinge, Aussiedler* (Münster: Westfälischer Heimatbund, 1990); Albrecht Lehmann, *Im Fremden ungewollt zuhaus: Flüchtlinge und Vertriebene in Westdeutschland, 1945–1990* (Munich: Beck, 1991).

[8] Robert Moeller, *Protecting Motherhood: Women and the Family in the Politics of Postwar West Germany* (Berkeley and Los Angeles: University of California Press, 1993), especially Chapter 5. See also Elizabeth Heineman, *What Difference Does a Husband Make?: Women and Marital Status in Nazi and Postwar Germany* (Berkeley and Los Angeles: University of California Press, 1999).

possibility of a labor recruitment treaty. Italy, in many ways, was a natural
place for the Federal Republic to turn for additional workers. Switzerland
and Britain, which established the precedent of employing guest workers
immediately after the war, relied primarily on Italians in the first years of
recruiting.[9] The Adenauer government was additionally motivated by the
identification of Italy as an important partner for the Federal Republic's
economic and political integration into Western Europe.[10] Opening up
the labor market to Italians, in this respect, constituted a core component
of the country's policy to liberalize the economy. Thus, on 22 December
1955, Minister of Economics Ludwig Erhard concluded a labor recruitment agreement that facilitated the employment of Italian workers in West
German industry.

By the early 1960s, however, the need for new supplies of labor became
much more urgent. On 13 August 1961, the German Democratic Republic
erected the Berlin Wall, which cut off East from West virtually overnight.
This event dramatically lowered the numbers of workers coming
from the East, curtailing the stream of refugees by more than 90 percent.[11] It also ended the period of relatively free movement along the
border areas between East and West Germany as well as within a divided
Berlin, during which time it had been possible for people to reside in
the East and work in the West. At the same time, the total number of
West German workers continued to shrink, even as the generation of
war babies now entered the labor market. This trend was due to a number of factors: better pension plans that led to an earlier average retirement age, the extended length of required education, the prolongation
of compulsory military service from twelve to eighteen months, and the
drop in the average number of working hours from 44.4 in 1960 to 41.4

---

9   For more on the Swiss recruitment of Italians, see Hans-Joachim Hoffmann-Nowotny,
    ed., *Ausländer in der Bundesrepublik Deutschland und in der Schweiz: Segregation und
    Integration: eine vergleichende Untersuchung* (Frankfurt: Campus, 1982), 32–113. For
    more on Great Britain's European Voluntary Workers program, see Kathleen Paul, *White-
    washing Britain: Race and Citizenship in the Postwar Era* (Ithaca, NY: Cornell University
    Press, 1997), 85–88.
10 Karen Schönwälder, *Einwanderung und ethnische Pluralität: Politische Entscheidungen
    und öffentliche Debatten in Großbritannien und der Bundesrepublik von den 1950er bis
    zu den 1970er Jahren* (Essen: Klartext, 2001), 247–48.
11 According to Mellor, the flow of refugees from the German Democratic Republic was
    drastically reduced after the erection of the Berlin Wall. Between 1950 and 1961, the
    number of East German refugees coming to the Federal Republic was between two hun-
    dred and three hundred thousand per year. After 1961, those numbers declined to figures
    between 20 and 40 thousand annually. See Mellor, *Two Germanies*, 188–89.

in 1968.[12] Together, these changes created a crisis in the West German labor market. As early as the summer of 1959, an article in *Der Spiegel* reported, "the struggle to find more workers has become a stressful and constant effort in which the personnel departments of both large industrial enterprises and smaller firms with fewer employees find themselves embroiled."[13]

Between 1960 and 1968, then, the Federal Republic embarked on a seemingly drastic course of action designed to secure a far larger supply of labor. Following the arrangement it had made with Italy in 1955, the German government signed similar labor recruitment treaties with Spain on 29 March 1960, Greece on 30 March 1960, Turkey on 30 October 1961, Portugal on 17 March 1964, and Yugoslavia on 12 October 1968.[14] This push to import guest workers took place under the stewardship of the Christian Democratic Party (Christlich Demoktratische Union, CDU). In fact, CDU-led governments concluded all of the treaties except the one with Yugoslavia, which was signed during the Grand Coalition. The key figure in this Christian Democratic era was Erhard who, as federal economics minister and later chancellor, sought to bolster a social market economy that balanced high economic growth with low inflation.

The opposition Social Democratic Party (Sozialdemokratische Partei Deutschlands, SPD) did express some skepticism about this solution to the labor crisis. As early as 1955, the SPD pointed out that areas along the East German border actually had high rates of long-term unemployment, suggesting that the economy had not yet reached full employment. In response to the first recruitment treaty, moreover, the party called for an increase in government-subsidized apartments in West Germany's industrial centers as a way to ensure that all unemployed Germans had access to jobs.[15] Despite these misgivings, the SPD agreed to support the foreign

[12] Herbert, *History of Foreign Labor*, 209–10. For further details on the decline in work hours during the 1960s, see Rist, *Guestworkers in Germany*, 110, and Owen Smith, *West German Economy*, 158.

[13] "Volksbeschäftigung – Die dritte Garnitur," *Der Spiegel* 13, no. 34 (1959): 26, quoted in Herbert, *History of Foreign Labor*, 210.

[14] Herbert, *History of Foreign Labor*, 205–13. See also Rist *Guestworkers in Germany*, 137–38. Italy, Spain, Greece, Turkey, Portugal, and Yugoslavia were the main sources of foreign labor, but other countries also had labor agreements with the Federal Republic: Japan (1956), but for miners only; Morocco (1963); Tunisia (1965); and Korea (1970) also for miners only. The numbers of workers who came from these other countries remained quite small. See Heather Booth, *The Migration Process in Britain and West Germany* (Aldershot: Ashgate Publishing, 1992), 110.

[15] Hans Bauer, "Arbeitervertrag Rom – Bonn unterzeichnet," *Frankfurter Rundschau*, 21 December 1955, 1.

recruitment initiative rather than risk an economic slowdown or a rise in general prices.[16]

When the idea of guest worker recruitment first emerged in the mid-1950s, the reaction of the German Trade Union Federation (Deutscher Gewerkschaftsbund, DGB) was also guarded. As the principal representative of labor in the Federal Republic with seventeen unions under its umbrella, the DGB feared that foreigners would create competition for jobs and undercut the favorable working conditions (shorter workweek, overtime, vacation days, etc.) enjoyed by Germans. The federation's officer for foreign laborers, Heinz Richter, explained, "In the early phase of discussions, the question was, above all, whether the foreign workers might possibly be used to force wages down."[17] In order to assuage this concern the government agreed to guarantee non-German laborers the same wages as their German counterparts and pledged to give German workers preference in hiring. The compromise secured union support for the guest worker program throughout the expansion period of the 1960s. This support is somewhat surprising given the late nineteenth-century history of German-Polish struggles around labor issues,[18] but it makes sense in the context of the economic boom. With employment expanding and wages rising, the DGB had little to lose from recruitment as long as the interests of native workers remained protected.

The treaties spelled out the basic terms of the guest worker program, establishing a similar model of recruitment for each of the participating

[16] James F. Hollifield, *Immigrants, Markets, and States: The Political Economy of Postwar Europe* (Cambridge, MA: Harvard University Press, 1992), 60. For more on the SPD criticism of guest worker recruitment, see Bertold Huber and Klaus Unger, "Politische und rechtliche Determinanten der Ausländerbeschaftigung in der Bundesrepublik Deutschland," in Hans-Joachim Hoffmann-Nowotny and Karl-Otto Hondrich, eds., *Ausländer in der Bundesrepublik Deutschland und in der Schweiz: Segregation und Integration. Eine vergleichende Untersuchung* (Frankfurt: Campus Verlag, 1982), 125–94.

[17] Heinz Richter, *Probleme der Anwerbung und Betreuung der ausländischen Arbeiter aus der Sicht des Deutschen Gewerkschaftsbundes* (Düsseldorf: Deutscher Gewerkschaftsbund, 1970), 1.

[18] In his study of Polish workers in Germany's western coal mines during the late nineteenth century, John Kulczycki argues that German union movements, both Christian and socialist, undermined worker solidarity across ethnic lines by excluding Poles and ignoring their interests and concerns. Kulczycki's concern here is to challenge the assumption of many German historians that it is ethnic migrants who undercut worker solidarity. See John Kulczycki, *The Foreign Worker and the German Labor Movement: Xenophobia and Solidarity in the Coal Fields of the Ruhr, 1871–1914* (Oxford: Berg, 1994). For another analysis of tensions between German and Polish workers, see Richard C. Murphy, *Gastarbeiter im Deutschen Reich. Polen in Bottrop, 1891–1933* (Wuppertal: Peter Hammer Verlag, 1982).

countries. Potential laborers applied to work in West Germany at service branches of its Federal Office for Labor Recruitment and Unemployment Insurance (Bundesanstalt für Arbeitsvermittlung und Arbeitslosversicherung) set up in their home countries. The process included a thorough medical examination by German doctors in order to assess an applicant's capacity for physical labor. Files were then forwarded to the main office in Nuremberg, which also handled requests from German companies seeking workers. This agency served as the go-between for employers and possible employees, screening and assigning laborers to specific firms. Successful candidates received a signed contract from their future employer that stipulated a minimum salary and provided details about their accommodations in Germany. Generally speaking, the length of the contract was one year, during which time the foreign laborer could not be fired. While this initial contract gave guest workers a measure of job security, it also functioned to limit their options: during this period, labor recruits could not change positions or leave an unpleasant employment situation without the risk of losing their work permit.[19]

In the early years of the program, imported workers consisted almost entirely of men between the ages of twenty and forty who either were single or left their families at home. For the most part, these guest workers were employed as unskilled or semiskilled laborers in industry, especially in sectors where heavy or dirty work, shift work, and repetitive production methods were common.[20] The construction, mining, and metal industries included the highest concentrations of foreign laborers, which allowed West German nationals to move into more desirable sectors of the economy. In mining and heavy industry, for example, the numbers of Germans decreased by over 870,000 between 1961 and 1971, whereas the number of foreigners in those same areas increased by 1.1 million. From 1961 to 1973, about three million German workers switched to white-collar jobs.[21]

[19] For a more detailed explanation of the recruitment and assignment process, see Verena McRae, *Die Gastarbeiter. Daten, Fakten, Probleme* (München: C. H. Beck, 1980), 13–15.
[20] Bundesanstalt für Arbeit, ed., *Anwerbung, Vermittlung, Beschäftigung ausländischer Arbeitnehmer: Erfahrungsbericht 1963* (Nuremberg: Bundesanstalt für Arbeit, 1964), 6. See also Stephen Castles, Heather Booth, and Tina Wallace, *Here for Good: Western Europe's New Ethnic Minorities* (London: Pluto Press, 1987), 132–37.
[21] See Owen Smith, *West German Economy*, 162–63. Herbert also addresses the kinds of work taken up by *Gastarbeiter* and their impacts on the labor market. In 1966, he states, 90 percent of foreign males were employed as blue-collar workers, whereas only 49 percent of the German male workforce held such jobs. See Herbert, *History of Foreign Labor*, 216.

But men were not the only targets of guest worker recruitment. Between 1960 and 1973, the number of foreign female workers in the Federal Republic jumped from approximately 43,000 to over 706,000. Most of them came from Spain, Greece, Turkey, and Yugoslavia. By 1973, women comprised 30 percent of the entire foreign workforce.[22] This trend was intricately connected with the highly gendered politics of labor in West Germany. As the economy approached full employment in the mid-1950s, rising pressures to bring women into low-wage industrial sectors competed with the belief that working outside the home would threaten women's ability to bear and care for children. Historian Christine von Oertzen has recently argued that part-time work emerged as a compromise solution whereby German women could fill jobs and still have enough time and energy to fulfill their obligations at home.[23] But this resolution did not come close to meeting the labor needs of the textile, clothing, food, electronic, and hospitality industries. By 1960, firms in these sectors actively requested foreign female workers who were young and single. In contrast to their German counterparts, such women presumably would be willing to work without time constraints or physical restrictions and would not refuse overtime, shift work, or piecework.[24]

At least initially, imported laborers tended to lead a modest and circumscribed German existence. They typically lived in housing provided by employers, who were required by law to supply it.[25] The pattern was to build barracks or hostels on or near the factory site, often in areas far removed from city centers, interior neighborhoods, or public

---

[22] Monika Mattes, "Zum Verhältnis von Migration und Geschlecht: Anwerbung und Beschäftigung von 'Gastarbeiterinnen' in der Bundesrepublik, 1960 bis 1973," in Jan Motte, Rainer Ohliger, and Anne von Oswald, eds., *Fünfzig Jahre Bundesrepublik, Fünfzig Jahre Einwanderung. Nachkriegsgeschichte als Migrationsgeschichte* (Frankfurt: Campus Verlag, 1999), 285, 293; for percentage see Table 4, 308. Yüksel Pazarkaya noted this wrinkle in recruitment and migration patterns in the mid-1980s, suggesting that the fine motor skills of female guest workers were especially attractive to the food and garment industries. See Pazarkaya, "Stimmen des Zorns und der Einsamkeit in Bitterland. Wie die Bundesrepublik Deutschland zum Thema der neuen türkischen Literatur wurde," *Zeitschrift für Kulturaustausch* 35 (1985): 18.

[23] Christine von Oertzen, *Teilzeitarbeit und die Lust am Zuverdienen: Geschlechterpolitik und gesellschaftlicher Wandel in Westdeutschland, 1848–1969* (Göttingen: Vandenhoeck & Ruprecht), 1999.

[24] Mattes, "Zum Verhältnis von Migration," 288.

[25] Stephen Castles and Godula Kosack, *Immigrant Workers and Class Structure in Western Europe*, 2nd ed. (Oxford: Oxford University Press, 1985), 244. They further note that if the guest worker changed jobs, his or her new employer was not required to provide housing.

transportation.[26] These barracks generally housed six to eight workers in a room and provided each man with his own bunk bed but little or no common space. Female guest workers generally obtained slightly better accommodations in dormitories and, because they were perceived to be at moral risk in the unknown West German environment, received care and attention from church welfare associations.[27] During these years, the lives of foreign workers appeared to be somewhat one-dimensional, revolving around the most basic activities of working, eating, and sleeping. According to the official reports, recruits generally were more "willing than Germans" to accept unpleasant tasks and jobs, put in overtime hours, and tolerate a low standard of living because they intended to return home as soon as they had earned enough money.[28]

The Guest Worker in the German Public Sphere

The fact that guest workers had relatively little contact with ordinary Germans outside the workplace during the first years of migration did not mean that labor recruits were completely absent from the public sphere. Contrary to the assumption of earlier scholars, who claimed that the subject of guest workers was deliberately underplayed in this period, the mainstream press actually registered the presence of foreign laborers as soon as recruitment began.[29] Both national and local newspapers, for instance, reported on the initial labor treaty between Italy and the Federal Republic in December 1955, announcing that as many as eighty to one hundred thousand Italian workers would arrive in the spring to take up jobs in agriculture, as well as the construction and technology

---

[26] In his investigation of the residential patterns of Turks in Cologne, John Clark discusses the isolation and ghettoization experienced by this guest worker population. See his chapter "Residential Patterns and Social Integration of Turks in Cologne" in R. E. Krane, *Manpower Mobility across Cultural Boundaries: Social, Economic and Legal Aspects* (Leiden: E. J. Brill, 1975), 61–75.

[27] Mattes, "Zum Verhältnis von Migration," 290–91.

[28] Herbert, *History of Foreign Labor*, 215.

[29] The most prominent advocate of this position is Knuth Dohse, *Ausländische Arbeiter und bürgerlicher Staat: Genese und Funktion von staatlicher Ausländerpolitik und Ausländerrecht vom Kaiserreich bis zur Bundesrepublik Deutschland* (Königstein: Hain, 1981), 176–80. Dohse uses the term *Entthematisierung* to describe the lack of West German media attention to guest workers. More recently, Karen Schönwälder has argued against the claim that guest workers were absent in the press, citing articles in *Badische Zeitung*, *Der Tagesspiegel*, and *Frankfurter Allgemeine Zeitung* that covered the conclusion of the recruitment treaty between the Federal Republic and Italy. See Schönwälder, *Einwanderung und ethnische Pluralität*, 161–63.

42   *Aras Ören and the Guest Worker Question*

industries.[30] An article in the *Frankfurter Rundschau* explained the basic
terms of the treaty and emphasized in particular the provision to give guest
workers equal pay and benefits so as to prevent undercutting German
laborers.[31] Just a few years later, the emergence of an Italian "colony"
in the Walsum neighborhood of Duisburg became one of the recurring
human-interest stories of 1957. And through the end of the 1950s, numerous articles appeared about Italian migrants struggling to get used to West
German ways of life – especially speaking a new language, learning how
to drive, and adjusting to a different school system.[32]

Not all press reports were positive, however. A recent study has suggested that Italian guest workers arriving in the 1950s initially served
as a negative reminder of their compatriots who had been employed as
laborers during the Third Reich.[33] According to a *Stuttgarter Nachrichten*
article, "The older population has not forgotten that at the end of the war
thousands of suddenly freed forced laborers took revenge on the people
of Wolfsburg for the injustices they had suffered."[34] In the first decade
of recruitment, then, Italians were sometimes associated with the hardships of the war's end, their presence jogging memories of the rampant
rape and plunder experienced by Germans during the waning days of
Nazi rule.

But by and large, early public statements tended to treat foreign laborers as a kind of curiosity whose unfamiliar cultural traits required explica-
tion. Guest workers were often described as *Südländer*, people from southern Europe (and specifically the Mediterranean region) who demonstrated

[30] "Italienische Arbeiter nach Deutschland," *Der Tagesspiegel*, 21 December 1955, 2.
[31] Bauer, "Arbeitervertrag Rom – Bonn unterzeichnet," *Frankfurter Rundschau*, 21 December 1955, 1.
[32] On the neighborhood of Walsum, see "Italienische 'Kolonie' am Niederrhein," *Welt
der Arbeit*, 29 March 1957; and "Chianti am Rhein," *Die Zeit*, 4 April 1957. For
other early articles on Italians in Germany, see n.a., "Die Frauen sprechen noch nicht
Deutsch. Italienische Familien folgten den Vätern ins Ruhrgebiet," *Westdeutsche Allgemeine Zeitung*, 12 November 1958; "Die Fahrt ins Wunderland. Der Irrtum des Herrn
Zampollini und andere süditalienische Erfahrungen in der Bundesrepublik," *Frankfurter
Allgemeine Zeitung*, 26 May 1962; "Die großen Kinder aus dem Süden sind vereinsamt,"
Frankfurter Allgemeine Zeitung, 9 November 1962; and Schönwälder, *Einwanderung
und ethnische Pluralität*, 161–62.
[33] Julia Woesthoff, "Ambiguities of Antiracism: Representations of Foreign Laborers and
the West German Media, 1955–1990" (Ph.D. diss., Michigan State University, 2004),
28–30. See also, for example, n.a, "Italien – Saisonarbeiter – Musterung in Mailand,"
Der Spiegel, 4 April 1956, 34–35.
[34] Josef Schmidt, "Wolfsburgs Italiener bereiten Sorgen," *Stuttgarter Nachrichten*, 24
November 1962, quoted in Woesthoff, "Ambiguities of Antiracism," 30.

a common set of behaviors that set them apart from Germans. For example, Dr. Giacomo Maturi, an expert on Italian guest workers for the Ford Motor Company in Cologne, attempted to elucidate the contrasting styles of Germans and *Südländer* for the readers of *Die Welt*. Whereas Germans tended to maintain "a reserved attitude" and "impersonal way of dealing," he explained, *Südländer* were often "passionate, temperamental, easily filled with enthusiasm but equally easily discouraged and depressed."[35] In April 1966, the "Nix Amore" series of articles published by the national tabloid newspaper *Bild-Zeitung* presented labor recruits as physically attractive and sexually potent.[36] Even the president of Caritas, the Catholic charity organization that provided social services for Italian, Spanish, and Portuguese workers of the same faith, weighed in on the differences between Germans and guest workers. He declared that *Südländer* had a "totally different mode of being," which affected their "temperament, emotional life, ways of reacting." "Order, cleanliness, and punctuality," he elaborated, "seem like the natural qualities of a respectable person to us; in the south, one does not learn or know this, so it is difficult for [a person from the south] to adjust here."[37] Such popular descriptions clearly relied on cultural stereotypes, yet they functioned more to explain why foreign workers had trouble fitting in than to argue for an intractable clash of civilizations.

The political scientist Karen Schönwälder has criticized the press coverage from this period as somewhat narrow and limited. Newspapers reported on the recruitment process, the presence of foreign laborers, and their (often entertaining) efforts to get used to Germany without addressing the specific causes or consequences of the program itself. In particular, she has emphasized the fact that no major events occurred to force a wide range of media outlets to cover the same story on the same day, a situation which might have produced "a concentrated, relatively intensive discussion and commentary on the foreign workers or foreigner policy."[38] Serious public deliberation over the long-term social and cultural impacts of importing large numbers of guest workers, consequently, remained largely nonexistent in the first decade of recruitment.

---

[35] Giacomo Maturi, "Aus einer anderen Welt," *Die Welt*, 8 August 1964, quoted in Woesthoff, "Ambiguities of Antiracism," 42–43.

[36] Schönwälder, *Einwanderung und ethnische Pluralität*, 166.

[37] Albert Stehlin, "Der ausländische Arbeitnehmer in unserer Gesellschaftsordnung," *Vortragsreihe des Deutschen Industrieninstituts* (1966): 3, cited in Schönwälder, *Einwanderung und ethnische Pluralität*, 167.

[38] Schönwälder, *Einwanderung und ethnische Pluralität*, 163.

This pattern was largely true in the more official representations of the program as well. Most spokesmen for the federal government focused on the immediate needs of the economy. With the convergence of a shrinking German workforce and the cutting off of refugees from the East, Labor Minister Theodor Blank maintained that no viable alternative to the massive recruitment of foreign workers existed if the Federal Republic wanted to prolong its economic expansion and continue the economic miracle.[39] The early reports from the Federal Office for Labor Recruitment and Unemployment Insurance cited the numbers of employed, unemployed, jobs remaining, and foreigners working in German industry with little or no commentary.[40] But by 1963 they began to tie foreign laborers more directly to the large number of remaining jobs. In a report dated 6 July 1963, for example, the title read: "Over 800,000 Foreigners Employed, and Still 597,000 Open Positions – the Situation in the Labor Market."[41] Less than two weeks later, a *Frankfurter Allgemeine Zeitung* article, directly referring to this government report, made the connection even more strongly: "According to this study, the number of employed in 1966 will only be slightly larger than in 1962, if the number of foreign workers stays about the same. A compelling rise in the employment potential of the West German economy can only be reached for the future through a further rise in the employment quota of foreign workers."[42] In this formulation, the very health and prosperity of the West German economy rested on a growing pool of foreign workers.

An editorial written for the same newspaper just over a month later offered a positive commentary on the labor migration. Explicitly calling

---

[39] Herbert, *History of Foreign Labor*, 210. According to M. Nikolinakos, the recruitment of foreign workers was absolutely essential to the continued growth of the West German economy. See M. Nikolinakos, "The New Dimensions in the Employment of Foreign Workers" (Berlin: Wissenschaftszentrum, 1975), quoted in Rist, *Guestworkers in Germany*, 110.

[40] "Die Entwicklung des Arbeitsmarkts im Juni," *Bulletin des Presse- und Informationsamtes der Bundesregierung* 138 (1961); "Die Entwicklung des Arbeitsmarkts im September," *Bulletin des Presse- und Informationsamtes der Bundesregierung* 203 (1961).

[41] "Über 800,000 Ausländer beschäftigt," *Bulletin des Presse- und Informationsamtes der Bundesregierung* 117 (1963).

[42] "Die Beschäftigung erreicht einen neuen Höchststand," *Frankfurter Allgemeine Zeitung*, 15 July 1963. "Nach dieser Untersuchung wird damit gerechnet, daß die Zahl der Erwerbsbevölkerung 1966 nur unwesentlich größer sein dürfte wie 1962, wenn die Zahl der ausländischen Arbeitskräfte etwa gleich bleibt. Demnach kann also auch für die Zukunft eine zu Buche schlagende Erhöhung des Beschäftigtenpotentials in der westdeutschen Wirtschaft nur durch eine weitere Erhöhung der Beschäftigungsquote ausländischer Arbeitskräfte erreicht werden."

readers' attention to the economic situation 15 years before, the author pointed to a dramatic shift in the labor pool: in 1948, there were nearly 1.5 million unemployed, but a decade and a half later, 600,000 jobs remained unfilled. He further warned readers that the economy could now decline again because manpower reserves were in short supply for a number of reasons. Eastern refugees could no longer come to the Federal Republic. New educational requirements forced young people to stay in school longer, and women who had been willing to work were returning to household duties. "The foreign workforce," the author concluded, "thus remains as the single reserve."[43]

At the same time, many employers and industry leaders recognized positive gains from the use of foreign laborers, documenting their views in newsletters such as *Der Arbeitgeber*. They claimed, for example, that the initial expenses incurred in hiring guest workers – including recruitment fees, interpreters, housing, and training costs – were far outweighed by long-term savings, since these workers would, in most cases, contribute their labor and not collect the restricted medical benefits for which they were eligible.[44] Foreign workers also paid income and social security tax, thereby effectively subsidizing the social welfare system.[45] One manager explained: "A foreigner in our employ places the best years of his labor power at our disposal. For employing firms, this results in the advantage that only rarely must an older foreign worker, or one no longer fully fit and able to work, be retained on the payroll for reasons of social policy."[46] From the perspective of business and industry, the prospect of using imported labor seemed like an unqualified good because German firms reaped the benefits of a fully flexible and temporary workforce. Here were thousands of strong, able-bodied persons who

---

[43] Ernst Günter Vetter, "Das Übel der Überbeschäftigung," *Frankfurter Allgemeine Zeitung*, 23 August 1963.

[44] It is worth noting that the initial costs of employing guest workers were quite substantial – they included a recruitment fee of 300 DM per worker, the air or train fare from the German border to the new residence, a medical examination, translation services, on-the-job training, and housing. See Gottfried E. Völker, "Labor Migration: Aid to the West German Economy?" in R. E. Krane, *Manpower Mobility across Cultural Boundaries: Social, Economic and Legal Aspects* (Leiden: E. J. Brill, 1975), 3–45.

[45] State Secretary of the Ministry of Labor Ludwig Kattenstroth detailed these benefits at an information day for the Association of the Federal Union of German Employers in 1966. In addition, foreign workers did not qualify for many extra incentives granted to permanent employees, such as salary bonuses and preventive medical treatment. See Herbert, *History of Foreign Labor*, 212–13.

[46] Hans Stirn and Charles Zwingmann, eds., *Ausländische Arbeiter im Betrieb: Ergebnisse der Betriebserfahrung* (Frechen/Cologne: Bartmann Verlag, 1964), 47.

could be discarded as soon as they were no longer physically capable or needed.

Even IG Metall, perhaps the most important union within the West German labor movement, seemed to accept the economic benefits of foreign manpower recruitment.[47] In a publication from the mid-1960s, the metalworkers' union declared its favorable position on the employment of foreign workers "in the interests of full employment and continued economic growth."[48] At least at the level of union leadership, the desire to maintain the current level of prosperity had priority over concerns about the difficulties of enlisting foreigners as union members or tensions between native and imported laborers.

This shared understanding of mutual economic benefits, as we have seen, was powerfully captured and reproduced at the height of labor recruitment in the widely circulated photograph of Armando Rodrigues, the one-millionth guest worker. Twenty years later, many government officials continued to discuss the recruitment of guest workers as an uncontested, unquestioned policy. A 1984 pamphlet put out by the Federal Central Office for Political Education (*Bundeszentrale für politische Bildung*), for example, asserted: "All socially relevant groups in the Federal Republic bore responsibility for the decision to fill job vacancies with foreign employees. There was no noteworthy discussion about alternatives or social implications. Political parties as well as social groups – from the unions and the employers' associations to the charities and churches – saw in the employment of foreign labor a provisional phenomenon necessary for the meantime."[49] The official voices thus pushed toward a remarkably narrow portrayal of the guest worker question. Above all, they depicted a national consensus on the labor migration. And they strongly suggested that this consensus emerged naturally, almost deterministically from socioeconomic conditions that demanded additional bodies to do the work of the economic miracle.

---

[47] For more on IG Metall and its place within the larger West German labor union movement, see Andrei Markovits, *The Politics of the West German Trade Unions* (Cambridge: Cambridge University Press, 1986), Chapter 4.

[48] *Die Ausländerwelle und die Gewerkschaften* (Frankfurt: Industriegewerkschaft Metall, 1966), quoted in Stephen Castles and Godula Kosack, *Immigrant Workers and Class Structure in Western Europe*, 2nd ed. (Oxford: Oxford University Press, 1985), 129.

[49] Bundeszentrale für politische Bildung, *Ausländer. Informationen zur politischen Bildung 201* (Bonn: Bundeszentrale, 1984), 3–4, quoted in Gail Wise, "Ali in Wunderland: German Representations of Foreign Workers" (Ph.D. diss., University of California, Berkeley, 1995), 15–16.

Yet it is precisely this rhetoric of consensus and self-evident necessity that requires examination. The very same people championing the importation of foreign workers in the early 1960s, after all, had also lived through the Nazi era under a regime whose government and media had promoted a national ideology of racial purity. Therefore it seems at least a little strange, a mere two decades later, to find these officials describing the recruitment of non-German laborers as obviously worthwhile and wholly advantageous. Of course, it was precisely because the Nazi policies of the 1930s and 1940s had gone so terribly wrong that this ideological shift became possible and, in fact, necessary. The heavy burden of guilt inherited by the Federal Republic for the genocide of the Holocaust, committed in the name of a pure German *Volk*, made West German leaders anxious to demonstrate a new sense of openness to non-Germans. In 1964, for instance, Labor Minister Blank cast guest worker recruitment as a sign of goodwill toward the international community, stating that the program made "the merging together of Europe and the rapprochement between persons of highly diverse backgrounds and cultures in the spirit of friendship a reality."[50] A year later, Blank argued that the labor migration would help promote "international understanding" and "European integration," two crucial components of the Federal Republic's national recovery.[51] The fact that this form of internationalism also strengthened the West German economy made the importation of foreign labor doubly useful to the project of normalization.

Still, it seems somewhat surprising that a policy with such potentially massive social consequences received virtually no sustained public questioning or debate. How was it that public dialogue about guest workers in this early period neither engaged the broader effects of the labor migration nor depicted foreign workers as a problem? At least part of the answer has to do with the circumscribed language used to discuss guest workers in the public sphere. The label *Gastarbeiter* not only became the accepted term for referring to foreign laborers during the initial phase of migration, it also crystallized key assumptions about the specific role that these workers would play in the Federal Republic. The term quite literally defined labor recruits as "guests" and "workers": it reduced their presence in West German society to economic function, implying that their impact could be limited to the labor market, and it simultaneously insisted that their

[50] Quoted in Herbert, *History of Foreign Labor*, 213.
[51] Theodor Blank, "Ein Schritt zur Völkerverständigung," *Der Arbeitgeber*, 17. Jg. 1965, 280.

stay would be short lived, taking for granted that most if not all foreign workers would eventually return to their home countries. The emphasis on "guest," moreover, served to differentiate between those who belonged to the nation and those who did not. Being a guest seemed to preclude the possibility of acquiring citizenship. In this way, it was possible for foreign laborers to be physically present on German soil and, at the same time, remain entirely separate from the social body. The rhetorical figure of the guest worker thus made the policy of importing strange and unknown foreigners relatively uncontroversial.

This strategy represented an unacknowledged and perhaps even unself-conscious continuation of older racial ideas. The category of guest worker itself presumed a racialist understanding of difference insofar as it fore-grounded the boundaries between native and foreigner, permanent and transitory, and posited them as impermeable. Yet precisely because this figure was so successful at making such distinctions appear natural and absolute (there was no inkling that Turks might one day become Germans), invoking the language of race proved unnecessary during the period of active labor recruitment.

In practical terms, the assumption that guest worker migration was a temporary phenomenon served as one of the major selling points of the program. In an article about Italians in German industry, for example, the *Frankfurter Allgemeine Zeitung* asserted, "in the event of unemployment in Germany, the foreign workers could be sent back home again."[52] Unlike native workers, who expected to keep their jobs or collect unemployment insurance in times of economic recession, guest workers had no claim to these entitlements because they were brought to West Germany to fill a finite labor shortage. If foreign workers were laid off, it was because the economy no longer required additional manpower, and the presumption was that they would leave. Guest workers, in this view, served as a mobile reserve army of labor whose presence could be readily calibrated to the ups and downs of production.

For Turks in particular the principle of rotation was actually stipulated in the recruitment treaty signed between their home government and the Bonn Republic. The original agreement plainly stated that residence

---

[52] During the recruitment program's first few years, the mobility of foreign workers was perceived as yet another advantage of this already advantageous solution to the labor shortage. See "Italiener in der deutschen Industrie – Ergebnis eines Experiments," *Frankfurter Allgemeine Zeitung*, 21 October 1959, quoted in Herbert, *History of Foreign Labor*, 211.

permits lasting longer than two years would not be granted.[53] Turkish workers, accordingly, would have no choice but to return home after a relatively short period. In this respect, the West German government singled out Turks from Italian, Spanish, and Greek laborers, who were not subjected to an explicit rotation clause. The policy effectively discriminated against Turks and suggests that German authorities may, in fact, have perceived the presence of this group as especially problematic. At the same time, it is important to acknowledge that the earlier recruitment treaties also included mechanisms to prevent other groups of foreigners from staying in the Federal Republic. As one scholar has noted, "Setting the time limit of work permits in principle to a maximum of one year for first-time employment gave German authorities room to maneuver."[54] The regulations to enforce the transient aspect of guest worker migration thus recapitulated the pattern of hindering the settlement of large numbers of non-German peoples, one which had been established in the late-nineteenth century with Polish seasonal workers.

Within a year of full-scale Turkish recruitment, however, the detrimental effects of the rotation principle became apparent. Industry leaders quickly discovered that it cost more money to import new workers every two years than to keep the trained ones and absorb the minor fluctuations in production demands.[55] As rotation proved increasingly unprofitable by the mid-1960s, the government never really enforced the rule of quick return – that is, it almost always granted extensions for the residence and work permits, effectively allowing Turkish and other labor migrants to remain in Germany for as long as they liked.[56] In order to gain maximum profits, then, the government increasingly granted guest workers longer stays.

Policymakers and government leaders nonetheless publicly maintained the position that the presence of foreign workers in Germany was a temporary situation. As at least one scholar has noted, all of those

53 Schönwälder, *Einwanderung und ethnische Pluralität*, 253.
54 Ibid.
55 Marilyn Hoskins and Roy C. Fitzgerald, "German Immigration Policy and Politics," in Michael C. LeMay, ed., *The Gatekeepers: Comparative Immigration Policy* (New York: Praeger, 1989), 97–98.
56 There is some debate about *when* the West German government actually stopped enforcing the rotation policy. Hoskins and Fitzgerald believe that it was not enforced from the very beginning, or at least once recruitment began in earnest, whereas Ertekin Özcan claims that the government maintained it until the recession of 1966–1967. See Ertekin Özcan, *Türkische Immigrantenorganizationen in der Bundesrepublik Deutschland* (Berlin: Hitit Verlag, 1989), 44–45.

formally involved with foreign employment "shared the firm conviction that this was a temporally limited phenomenon, a transitional development that would eventually disappear."[57] This stance was codified in the 1965 Ausländergesetz (Foreigner Law), which outlined special regulations governing the rights of work and residency for foreign nationals from countries outside the Common Market (i.e., Turkey, Yugoslavia, Greece, Morocco, Tunisia). With the signing of the Treaty of Rome in 1957, which formally established the European Economic Community, citizens of Common Market countries enjoyed virtually the same labor and residency rights as their German counterparts. The situation for workers imported from non–Common Market countries, by contrast, was much more nebulous. The new foreigner law declared that non-EEC laborers would be granted residence permits only "if the foreigner's presence does not adversely affect the interests of the Federal Republic of Germany."[58] The vague wording of this guideline – and specifically the failure to define the phrases "adversely affect" and "interests of the Federal Republic of Germany" – conferred on German administrators a great deal of discretionary power over decisions such as granting or denying residence permits, restricting freedom of association, and deporting foreigners.[59] The Ausländergesetz opened the door for officials to claim that any long-term presence of guest workers was detrimental to the interests of West Germany as a nation, especially if such laborers were no longer necessary for the well-being of the economy. Indeed, the only official instructions available to administrators of this law – while still confoundingly general – prompted them to focus on the needs of the labor market in making their decisions.[60]

---

[57] Herbert, *History of Foreign Labor*, 213.

[58] The whole of paragraph 2, which deals with residence permits, reads: "Ausländer, die in den Geltungsbereich dieses Gesetzes einreisen und sich darin aufhalten wollen, bedürfen einer Aufenthaltserlaubnis. Die Aufenthaltserlaubnis darf erteilt werden, wenn die Anwesenheit des Ausländers Belange der Bundesrepublik Deutschland nicht beeinträchtigt." The *Ausländergesetz* is reprinted in its entirety in McRae, *Die Gastarbeiter. Daten, Fakten, Probleme*, 180–91.

[59] Rist, *Guestworkers in Germany*, 135–36. See also Helmut Rittstieg, "Grundzüge des Aufenthaltsrechts," in Gerhard Schult and Heidrun Alm-Merk, eds., *Einwanderungsland Bundesrepublik Deutschland?* (Baden Baden: Nomos Verlagsgesellschaft, 1982), 29–38; and Karen Schönwälder, "'Ist nur Liberalisierung Fortschritt?' Zur Entstehung des ersten Ausländergesetzes der Bundesrepublik," in Motte, Ohliger, and Oswald, eds., *Fünfzig Jahre Bundesrepublik, Fünfzig Jahre Einwanderung*, 127–44.

[60] These instructions appear in "General Administrative Regulations Concerning the Foreigner Law," quoted in Rist, *Guestworkers in Germany*, 136.

The effect of the 1965 Ausländergesetz was to concentrate enormous power over the lives of foreigners in the hands of the state. Yet SPD as well as CDU members of the internal Bundestag (German federal parliament) committee for the law's revision presented the document as "liberal, open-minded, and worthy of a western democracy."[61] What made this claim credible was the fact that the 1965 law served to replace the 1938 Foreigner Police Regulation (Ausländerpolizeiverordnung), which had remained on the books even after the collapse of the Third Reich. This replacement function obscured a crucial detail: in its formulation, the earlier decree was actually less restrictive than the proposed revision; it granted the right of residence to foreigners "who under certain conditions were worthy of hospitality based on their personality and the purpose of their stay."[62] This is not to suggest, however, that the draft of the new law received no criticism. The state of Hesse questioned whether the law could really be represented as a progressive regulation of foreigners' rights, especially in view of human rights concerns. Hessian officials were particularly wary of restricting the freedom of action and travel. They further cautioned that the language of the proposed law was overly vague, leaving bureaucrats with too much room for subjective interpretation.[63] These objections notwithstanding, virtually no debate took place when the Bundestag voted on the proposal. The CDU representative from Hamburg, Dietrich Rollman, hailed the approved foreigner law as an "expression of our transformed relations with those around us. It is an expression of the open-minded foreigner politics of the Federal Republic."[64] Under the guise of eradicating one more vestige of the Nazi past, the Bundestag created a legal instrument that gave the state more control and discretionary power over foreign workers and their efforts to settle in West Germany.

Ultimately, the Ausländergesetz transformed the assumption of temporary residence into a legal regulation. It took the provision for short-term residence specified in the treaties even further by tying residence permits (and the possibility of their revocation at any time) to the "interests of the Federal Republic." In this respect, the 1965 law served as the quintessential expression of the government's early position on the status of guest workers in West Germany, not only reiterating a decade of

---

[61] Schönwälder, "'Ist nur Liberalisierung Fortschritt?,'" 141.
[62] Ibid., 138.
[63] Ibid., 140.
[64] Quoted in Schönwälder, "'Ist nur Liberalisierung Fortschritt?,'" 141.

public statements about "pure labor" and "temporary residence," but also inscribing these assumptions into law. The actual practice of recruitment, however, directly conflicted with the new legal apparatus and circumscribed rhetoric around the guest worker, as the Federal Republic pursued what amounted to a contradictory policy. On the one hand, it remained publicly steadfast in its insistence that guest workers would eventually go home. On the other hand, it continued to renew their visas and extend the lengths of their residence.[65]

Early Critics of Recruitment and the End of the Economic Miracle

By the 1960s, a few isolated critics began to question some of the assumptions at the heart of the public rhetoric. As early as June 1961, Ludwig Kroeber-Keneth, an expert on labor management, wrote an article for the *Frankfurter Allgemeine Zeitung* that offered one of the first public reflections on the recently coined term "guest worker":

The concept of guest worker still sounds foreign and is also not without inner contradiction: usually one does not expect the guest to work for the host, earn money for him, and spend part of it again. Also, the "guest" in actual meaning is not thought of as earning the most money in the shortest possible time, so that he becomes, to one's horror, "a hereditary service person." ... Only the future can show whether the expression "guest worker" takes root. It cannot be forced. But in any case, it would be more welcome and succinct than "foreign workforces" (*ausländische Arbeitskräfte*), to say nothing of the defective and misleading term "alien worker" (*Fremdarbeiter*).... At any rate, it is not unimportant with which term, and that is to say, from which perspective we come to an understanding with foreign workers (*ausländische Arbeiter*).[66]

Above all, this was a critique of rhetoric. "Guest worker," in this view, rolled off the tongue more smoothly than "foreign workforces" and avoided the tainted association of "alien worker" which the Nazis had applied to people used as forced labor. Yet Kroeber-Keneth also stressed that the term was positively loaded with "inner contradictions." Guests

---

[65] For each of the years between 1960 and 1965, in fact, the percentage of migrants from Spain, Portugal, Greece, and Turkey leaving Germany amounted to less than 12 percent of the total of each resident population. See Booth, *Migration Process*, 160, Table 4. The one exception to this trend was workers from Italy. Their returning population remained close to 50 percent during each of these years, a divergence that was due to the different status of Italian workers. Because Italy was a member of the European Economic Community its nationals enjoyed free movement to West Germany and did not need to fear restrictions on labor migration.

[66] L. Kroeber-Keneth, "Die ausländischen Arbeitskräfte und wir," *Frankfurter Allgemeine Zeitung*, 3 June 1961, 5.

by definition did not work – and most certainly not for wages. "Heredi-tary service people," moreover, generally were not treated with the warm welcome normally extended to guests. In both cases, Kroeber-Keneth's point was much the same: the rhetoric itself belied lived experience (as well as common sense). It is this disjuncture between literal and figurative meanings – official rhetoric and actual reality – that dominates the article. And as the article clearly implies, this disjuncture was not simply a matter of linguistic precision. Rhetorical elision was shaping ideology.[67]

Dissatisfaction with the Federal Republic's policy of labor importation was undoubtedly also expressed by guest workers themselves. Literary scholar Heidrun Suhr has observed that almost as soon as the recruit-ment began in the mid-1950s, migrants turned to writing as a kind of survival strategy for "coping with a harsh reality," albeit usually without a specific plan or even the intention to publish their texts.[68] Most of their views found expression in personal journals, as well as in letters to fam-ily and friends at home.[69] A few public venues did exist for workers to publish their writing, particularly among the Italians, who were the ear-liest group of imported laborers and the most active in documenting and collecting their experiences during the initial period of recruitment. Fol-lowing a long-standing tradition of literature written by Italian emigrants, many even paid to have short stories, poems, and novels published back home.[70] As early as 1951, *Corriere d'Italia*, a weekly newspaper for Italian

---

[67] Since Kroeber-Keneth's initial criticism of "guest worker," a number of others have commented on the paradoxical nature of the term. See, for example, Marios Nikoli-nakos, *Politische Ökonomie der Gastarbeiterfrage. Migration und Kapitalismus* (Rein-bek: Rowohlt, 1973), 7–8; Franco Biondi and Rafik Schami, "Literatur der Betroffen-heit. Bemerkungen zur Gastarbeiterliteratur," in Christian Schaffernicht, ed., *Zu Hause in der Fremde. Ein bundesdeutsches Ausländer-Lesebuch* (Fischerhude: Verlag Atelier im Bauernhaus, 1981), 134. For a good overview of the commentary about the neologism "guest worker," see Carmine Chiellino, *Am Ufer der Fremde. Literatur und Arbeitsmi-gration, 1870–1991* (Stuttgart: J. B. Metzler, 1995), 285–89.

[68] Suhr claims that this practice of using writing to deal with difficult experiences in a foreign country grows out of the tradition of Italian migration literature, *Letteratura Gast.* See Suhr, "Ausländerliteratur," 76–78. Suhr cites Gino Chiellino's personal account of his rea-sons for beginning to write; see Chiellino's chapter "Die Fremde als Ort der Geschichte," in Irmgard Ackermann and Harald Weinrich, eds., *Eine nicht nur deutsche Literatur. Zur Standortbestimmung der "Ausländerliteratur"* (München: Serie Piper, 1986), 13–15.

[69] Biondi and Schami have suggested that many workers put pen to paper in order to leave a testament to their experiences and difficulties in a foreign country, documenting the human side of the recruitment program. See Biondi and Schami, "Literatur der Betrof-fenheit." 124–25.

[70] Ibid., 132. Several others discuss the literature that developed out of the long tradi-tion of Italian worker migration. For a broad treatment of Italian emigrant literature, see Francesco Loriggio, ed., *Social Pluralism and Literary History: The Literature of the Ital-ian Emigration* (Toronto: Guernica, 1996). For a more specific focus on Italian literature

emigrants in the Federal Republic, provided a local periodical specifically devoted to the literary productions of migrant workers. But like the more private expressions, these published texts were written in Italian, so they remained largely inaccessible to most Germans and outside the framework of national public debate.

Recent scholarship has convincingly argued that the nature of labor recruitment underwent a fundamental change during the mid-1960s. It was at this moment that the number of foreign workers reached the one million mark, the event officially celebrated with the arrival of Armando Rodrigues. The sheer extent of the guest worker presence prompted at least a few contemporary critics to register some broader implications of the shift. Valentin Siebrecht, president of the Landesarbeitsamt Südbayern (Labor Office for Southern Bavaria), declared in a 1964 editorial for *Die Zeit*: "Most Germans have not yet recognized the consequences of this development. We will now have to get used to the idea that everything that is connected with foreign labor – accommodations, family apartments, schools, cultural institutions, and so forth – will remain continuously on the agenda."[71] What Siebrecht appears to have grasped earlier than "most Germans" was that the labor recruitment affected every aspect of society and that the massive number of guest workers now on West German soil made the expectation of a temporary, circumscribed migration impossible.

Hints of this more critical perspective also appeared in the work of several German writers as they began to incorporate guest workers into their literary texts. In 1963, Günter Herburger, a socialist author who later achieved public recognition in the student movement, published a short story entitled "Gastarbeiter" in the *Stuttgarter Zeitung*.[72] It tells the

---

in the Federal Republic, see Peter Siebert, "'Gastarbeiterliteratur' – und was darunter verstanden wird," *Informationen Deutsch als Fremdsprache* 3 (1985), 198–207; Ulrike Reeg, *Schreiben in der Fremde: Literatur nationaler Minderheiten in der Bundesrepublik Deutschland* (Essen: Klartext, 1988); Gino Chiellino, *Literatur und Identität in der Fremde. Zur Literatur italienischer Autoren in der Bundesrepublik* (Kiel: Neuer Malik Verlag, 1989); Carmine Chiellino, *Am Ufer der Fremde*, especially Part I. This pattern of publishing the writings of Italians in migration remained strong in the Federal Republic well into the 1970s. A good example is the literary journal *Il Mulino*, which was started in 1974 by Antonio Pesciaioli, an electrician by profession. Its mission was to collect and publish literary texts by Italians living away from Italy. Between 1974 and 1981, it published the works of nearly one thousand Italian emigrants.

71 Valentin Siebrecht, "Verdienen in Deutschland: Die zweite Phase der Ausländerbeschäftigung," *Die Zeit*, 22 May 1964, 34, quoted in Schönwälder, *Einwanderung und ethnische Pluralität*, 163.

72 According to Carmine Chiellino, Herburger's story appeared as "Gastarbeiter" on 31 December 1963. See Chiellino, *Am Ufer der Fremde*, 203–204. For more on Herburger's

story of a German contractor: on the job, he treats his foreign underlings harshly, but at home, he must deal with the fact that his own daughter has fallen in love with an Italian laborer, whom she prefers to the "pale little office men." Although the guest worker fails to emerge as anything more than a shadowy figure in this tale, Herburger nevertheless initiated an important cycle. For the first time, a German writer was beginning to challenge – and complicate – the dominant rhetoric. The figure of the sexualized male *Gastarbeiter*, moreover, became a popular trope in the mainstream media several years later. According to a recent study of foreign laborers in the West German press, a flurry of coverage appeared in the mid-1960s commenting on intimate relationships between guest workers and German women. Not surprisingly, these articles reflexively criticized the "unbridled Mediterranean lust" of foreign (mostly Italian) men, but they also worried about the "provocative" and flirtatious behavior of German women that seemed to encourage the attention, a not-so-subtle condemnation of society's increasingly relaxed attitudes toward sex.[73] Herburger's fictional characters anticipated the kind of social commentary contained in these news reports, but at the most basic level began to make publicly visible an existence and set of relations in Germany that far exceeded the image of foreign workers isolated in the factory and barracks.

Two years later, Hans Werner Richter referred to guest workers in *Briefe aus einem Jahrhundert ins andere* (Letters from Another Century), a satirical meditation on West Germany's obsession with the economic miracle.[74] As a founding member of Gruppe 47, one of the main associations to support an emerging post-1945 German literature, Richter's tentative attempt to link labor recruitment to postwar materialism drew the attention of authors in this literary scene to the issue of foreign laborers. And in 1966, Franz Josef Degenhardt (an active participant in Gruppe 61

place in the literary history of the postwar period, see Klaus Briegleb and Sigrid Weigel, eds., *Gegenwartsliteratur seit 1968* (Munich: DTV, 1992), 431–34.

[73] Woesthoff, "Ambiguities of Antiracism," 57–58.

[74] In Hans Werner Richter, *Menschen in freundlicher Umgebung* (Berlin: Verlag Klaus Wagenbach, 1966), 25–45. Richter's satire is presented in the form of a series of letters to Publius Quintus, ruler of Neapolis, from his servant who is traveling in countries of the future. Richter founded the literary circle Gruppe 47, which promoted "humanitarian realism" as a writing style particularly appropriate to its goal of cleansing the German language of its corruption by the Nazis. See Briegleb and Weigel, *Gegenwartsliteratur seit 1968*, 30–32; Keith Bullivant and C. Jane Rice, "Reconstruction and Integration: The Culture of West German Stabilization 1945 to 1968," in Rob Burns, ed., *German Cultural Studies: An Introduction* (Oxford: Oxford University Press, 1995), 222.

and Literatur der Arbeitswelt) more explicitly thematized the presence of foreign workers in his song *Tonio Schiavo*. The lyrics told the tragic story of double revenge. In retaliation for being called a "dago pig," Tonio Schiavo, a construction worker from Mezzogiorno, stabs his foreman. He is, in turn, killed by German fellow workers who want vengeance for the foreman's death.[75] Clearly, these representations suggest a growing awareness among German intellectuals that the labor migration had produced social consequences far beyond what the official pronouncements on the guest worker question allowed.

Around this same time, changes in West German politics helped open up new frameworks for more vocal and rigorous critiques of foreign labor recruitment. In 1959, the SPD promulgated the Bad Godesberg program, a platform which marked a radical move away from its traditional Marxist roots.[76] Social Democratic leaders decided to abandon the party's narrow emphasis on the working class and that social group's specific interests in the hopes of generating a more broadly based appeal. This tactical shift was an attempt to increase the SPD's share of the national vote and help the party break into a ruling federal coalition that had been dominated by the CDU since the founding of the West German state. To a large extent, the strategy worked. In the fall of 1966, the Free Democrats (Frei Demokratische Partei, FDP) left their coalition with the Christian Democrats, opening the door for the SPD to join the CDU in a Grand Coalition led by Kurt Kiesinger. Three years later, Social Democrats gained enough votes to become the senior partner in a ruling coalition with the FDP under Willy Brandt. But the ideological reorientation also produced unintended consequences. As historian Geoff Eley has observed, "The SPD staked its claims to govern by rejecting radicalisms further to the left."[77] The Social

---

[75] In Franz Josef Degenhardt, *Laßt nicht die roten Hähne flattern ehe der Habicht schreit* (Munich: C. Bertelsmann Verlag, 1974), 36–39. Gruppe 61, founded in 1961 by a group of writers from the Ruhrgebiet, sought to provide a forum for workers to write for their fellow workers, as well as to push the boundaries of the West German literary establishment. See Bullivant and Rice, "Reconstruction and Integration," 243–46. For more on *Literatur der Arbeitswelt*, see Anna Picardi-Montesardo, *Die Gastarbeiter in der Literatur der Bundesrepublik Deutschland* (Berlin: Express Edition, 1985), 81–101; Briegleb and Weigel, *Gegenwartsliteratur seit 1968*, 280–86.

[76] For more on the SPD and the unfulfilled reform of the West German Left in this period, see Andrei S. Markovits and Philip S. Gorski, *The German Left: Red, Green, and Beyond* (Oxford: Oxford University Press, 1993), 33–45.

[77] Geoff Eley, *Forging Democracy: The History of the Left in Europe, 1850–2000* (Oxford: Oxford University Press, 2002), 417.

Democrats, in other words, became an accommodationist party, capitulating to the prevailing political, economic, and social order. This redefinition meant that the SPD was no longer perceived as the legitimate site for serious leftist critique, a task which quickly devolved to groups outside of the conformist parliamentary system.[78]

The rise of the New Left and the extraparliamentary opposition movement in the Federal Republic is well known. Less commonly recognized is the fact that it was artists and intellectuals influenced by the New Left and grassroots forms of political protest who began to develop the first sustained and increasingly high-profile West German cultural critique of the labor recruitment. In the process of seeking out new channels for opposition and engagement beyond Social Democratic party politics, radical leftists – especially of the younger generation – began to expand the scope of their social criticism to include the guest worker program. In 1967, for instance, the Swiss playwright Max Frisch, known for his incisive commentary on contemporary society, revisited the question of what imported laborers should be called when he asked: "Guest worker or foreign worker? I am for the latter: they are not guests whom one serves, or off of whom one makes money; they work, and in a foreign land, while in their own land they can by no means prosper. One cannot take offense at that."[79] In contrast to Kroeber-Keneth's earlier rejection of *Fremdarbeiter*, Frisch opted for the more literal and less euphemistic choice, even at the cost of returning to the term associated with Nazi slave labor. He also emphasized the central paradox of the recruitment: "we called for workforces, but people came instead."[80] On the one hand, this commentary exposed the instrumentalization implicit in the practice of recruiting foreign workforces whose presence was regulated according to economic cycles of demand. On the other hand, it suggested that these workers were in fact "people" whose very presence would necessarily reshape German society.

Another example of prominent leftist criticism is Rainer Werner Fassbinder's 1969 film *Katzelmacher*, which portrayed a vicious group of

---

[78] For more on the development of the West German New Left, see Markovits and Gorski, *German Left*, especially Chapter 2.

[79] Max Frisch, *Öffentlichkeit als Partner* (Frankfurt: Suhrkamp Verlag, 1967), 100.

[80] Max Frisch, *Die Tagebücher 1949–1966 und 1966–1971* (Frankfurt: Suhrkamp Verlag, 1983), 416. This meditation has become something of a classic in the scholarship on the labor recruitment, yet we have never satisfactorily examined its historical position within a series of ongoing German and Turkish-German critiques of the government's official rationales for the program.

working-class friends and their dealings with an imported laborer from Greece.[81] Only Fassbinder's second feature film, *Katzelmacher* received high praise from critics as well as a number of prizes, which in turn provided him with production capital for years afterward.[82] The same year, journalist and staunch social activist Günter Wallraff published his first book of reportage on guest workers, *Bilder aus Deutschland – "Gastarbeiter" oder der gewöhnliche Kapitalismus* (Images from Germany – "Guest Workers" or Capitalism as Usual), which investigated the specific living conditions of foreign laborers.

Significantly, there were echoes of this leftist mode of critique in more mainstream arenas as well. In 1970, the broadcasting company Westdeutscher Rundfunk (WDR) sponsored a contest inviting its listeners to propose alternatives to the label "guest worker."[83] It received over thirty-two thousand entries, including "loyal helpers" (*treue Helfer*), "Euro-slaves" (*Eurosklaven*), and "Germany fans" (*Germanyfans*). Even in these somewhat sarcastic suggestions, one gets the sense of a public uncertainty about the meaning of the government's recruitment policy. "Germany fans," for example, can be read as either a wishful caricature of uncritical foreign workers, or as a pointed critique of the government ideology, which quite unironically presumed purely beneficial impacts. Such sarcasm surfaced more clearly in entries like "Euro-slaves," which emphasized the obvious inequities of power built into the rotation principle. In this respect, the contest demonstrated a growing awareness (at least on the part of the some of the station's audience) of the basic contradictions at the heart of the recruitment rhetoric. Labor migrants were never simply "guests." Their lives on German soil were never fully contained by "work." Eventually, though, WDR selected the bland-sounding "foreign employees" (*ausländische Arbeitnehmer*) as the winning entry, a

---

[81] Fassbinder's film was based on a play of the same name, which had its premiere in 1969.

[82] Thomas Elsaesser, *Fassbinder's Germany: History, Identity, Subject* (Amsterdam: Amsterdam University Press, 1996), 45–46. Elsaesser notes that *Katzelmacher* made Fassbinder famous (at least among the avant-garde set).

[83] For a lengthier discussion of this episode, including a list of the entries, see Ernst Klee, ed., *Gastarbeiter: Analyse und Berichte* (Frankfurt: Suhrkamp, 1972), 149–57. Shorter mentions of the contest can be found in Sargut Sölcün, "Türkische Gastarbeiter in der deutschen Gegenwartsliteratur," *Kürbiskern* 3 (1979): 74; John Bendix, "On the Rights of Foreign Workers in West Germany" in Ilhan Basgöz and Norman Furniss, eds., *Turkish Workers in Europe: An Interdisciplinary Study* (Bloomington: Indiana University Press, 1985), 30; Ruth Mandel, "'We Called for Manpower, But People Came Instead': The Foreigner Problem and Turkish Guest Workers in West Germany (Ph.D. diss., University of Chicago, 1988), 25; Carmine Chiellino, *Am Ufer der Fremde*, 288–89; Wise, "Ali in Wunderland," 24.

choice which obscured the critical commentary contained in some of the competition's more provocative submissions.

In contrast to the charges leveled by radical leftists and at least some of the WDR contest participants, German workers who no doubt interacted directly with foreign laborers on the factory floor registered more immediate complaints. On 31 March 1966, *Bild-Zeitung* ran a headline that asked: "Are guest workers more industrious than Germans?"[84] In response to this question, thousands of German metal-industry workers in the southwest part of the country went on strike for a day. Press reports suggested that the German laborers were particularly upset by the implication that they were somehow inferior to their foreign colleagues. One representative of the IG Metall union called the headline a "denigration of metalworkers," while another defended the native workforce by asserting that the economic miracle could have been achieved without the contribution of foreign labor.[85] Some angry Germans, according to the *Frankfurter Rundschau*, tried to provoke brawls with foreign workers in Mannheim and had to be restrained in order to prevent violence.[86]

These protests against the *Bild-Zeitung* headline represented the first major demonstration by German laborers against guest worker recruitment. Though short-lived, the strikes pointed to rising tensions between Germans and their foreign colleagues. A survey commissioned by IG Metall at the Ford plant two years earlier, in fact, found that 31 percent of the 331 workers interviewed agreed with the statement that foreign labor put German workers at a disadvantage.[87] The *Bild-Zeitung* incidents thus made public a hostility that had been simmering for at least several years.

Seven months later, the combination of economic slowdown and political upheaval seemed to produce a new and increasingly volatile situation. Clear signs of economic recession were emerging by the summer of 1966: the number of unemployed rose from 105,743 in August to 145,804 in October, reaching a peak of 673,572 by February of the next year.[88]

---

[84] "Sind Gastarbeiter fleißiger als Deutsche?" *Bild-Zeitung*, 31 March 1966, 1, quoted in Schönwälder, *Einwanderung und ethnische Pluralität*, 158.

[85] "Da platzte den Metallarbeitern der Kragen," *Frankfurter Rundschau*, 4 April 1966, cited in Schönwälder, *Einwanderung und ethnische Pluralität*, 170.

[86] "Arbeiter über 'Bild' empört. Protestkundgebungen gegen Schlagzeile des Springer Massenblatts," *Frankfurter Rundschau*, 1 April 1966, cited in Schönwälder, *Einwanderung und ethnische Pluralität*, 171.

[87] Institut für angewandte Sozialwissenschaft, *Arbeiter-Vertrauensleute-Gewerkschaft* (Bad Godesberg: Infas, 1964).

[88] *Statistisches Jahrbuch für die Bundesrepublik Deutschland* (Stuttgart: Kohlhammer, 1967), 149.

The economic downturn only lasted about a year and was relatively mild, but it created great anxiety for many West Germans. As historian Christoph Kleßmann has explained, this was the first hint of economic uncertainty after a two-decade period of continuous boom, productivity, and prosperity.[89] At the end of October 1966, moreover, the FDP abruptly left the ruling coalition with the CDU because of Chancellor Erhard's inability to stave off recession and reign in federal spending. This governmental crisis continued for just over a month, but in the interim, the recently formed far right National Democratic Party (Nationaldemokratische Partei Deutschlands, NPD) won 7.9 percent of the vote in the state elections of Hesse and 7.4 percent in the Bavarian elections two weeks later.[90]

The unexpected success of the NPD was partially a response to the ideological consolidation of the CDU and SPD, insofar as many Germans on the far right and left began to see meaningful opposition being pushed outside the mainstream political parties. But these electoral victories also have to be understood in terms of increasing antagonism to the presence of guest workers, especially in view of rising unemployment. The NPD platform explicitly addressed the issue of labor recruitment, declaring: "The German worker has a first-priority right to a guarantee of his job against foreign labor."[91] In an interview with the popular newsmagazine *Der Spiegel*, Fritz Thielen, the chairman of the NPD, asserted: "Long-term contracts with foreign workers confirm the danger that Germans where possible will become unemployed, while foreigners here still have jobs and bread."[92] Although the party emphasized the rebuilding of the German empire, it also quite deliberately featured anti-*Gastarbeiter* slogans as part

[89] Christoph Kleßmann, *Zwei Staaten, eine Nation: Deutsche Geschichte, 1955–1970* (Bonn: Bundeszentrale für politische Bildung, 1988), 197.

[90] Studies of the German National Democratic Party proliferated in the years immediately following its founding in 1964. These include: Reinhardt Kühnl, *Die NPD: Struktur, Programm und Ideologie einer neofaschistischen Partei* (Frankfurt: Suhrkamp, 1969); Lutz Niethammer, *Angepasster Faschismus: politische Praxis der NPD* (Frankfurt: Fischer Verlag, 1969); Erwin K. Scheuch, Hans D. Klingemann, and Thomas A. Herz, eds., *Die NPD in den Landtagswahlen, 1966–1968* (Cologne: Institut für vergleichende Sozialforschung, 1969); and John David Nagle, *The National Democratic Party: Right Radicalism in the Federal Republic of Germany* (Berkeley and Los Angeles: University of California Press, 1970). Since then, however, scholarship has focused on other organs of the far right, especially the Republikaner. For more on this phenomenon, see Claus Leggewie, *Druck von rechts: Wohin treibt die Bundesrepublik?* (Munich: Beck, 1993).

[91] NPD Parteivorstand, *Manifest der Nationaldemokratischen Partei Deutschlands NPD* (NPD, 1965).

[92] *Der Spiegel* 15 (1966), 42.

of its campaigns. In this respect, the NPD exploited the xenophobia that was beginning to intensify among ordinary Germans during this period.

Indeed, during this same period between 1966 and 1967, media coverage of migrants started to paint a far more negative picture of foreign workers. Newspaper articles emphasized too much foreign influence, the threats posed by continued recruitment for the labor market, as well as the dangers to German women and girls presented by seductive *Südländer*. Above all, the press underscored the growth in criminality among foreigners, suggesting that the rising number of offenses by non-Germans was driving up the general crime rate. Over the course of about an eight-month period, for instance, numerous articles appeared that featured Turks involved in stabbings provoked by jealousy, card games gone wrong, and family conflicts. It is difficult, of course, to draw a direct correlation between these images and public opinion. Nevertheless, it is worth noting that a 1967 survey conducted by *Der Spiegel* found that 67 percent of respondents agreed there were too many guest workers in the Federal Republic.[93]

The mounting critique of the guest worker program from both ends of the political spectrum – and from a variety of social groups – seemed to be pushing toward a more open public debate about the costs and consequences of labor migration. This possibility was cut short, however, as the leaders of the Grand Coalition became preoccupied with a series of social crises around the increasingly radicalized student movement. In June 1967, a policeman fatally shot West Berlin student Benno Ohnesorg during a protest against a visit by the Shah of Iran. The German Socialist Students Federation (Sozialistischer Deutscher Studentenbund, SDS) interpreted this incident as a political murder by an oppressive state. In response, over one hundred thousand students throughout West Germany took to the streets. The next spring, SDS leader Rudi Dutschke was shot by a disgruntled worker on West Berlin's Kurfürstendamm, precipitating a succession of violent confrontations between masses of demonstrators and the police. Under these circumstances, the challenges to German society posed by the labor migration became a back-burner issue and sustained public discussion of the guest worker question was deferred for a half decade.

In the meantime, three major changes occurred in the migration itself that began to fundamentally alter the public's perceptions of guest workers. The first was a demographic shift in the kinds of laborers coming to the

[93] *Der Spiegel* 21 (1967), 92.

Federal Republic. From 1955 to 1960, Italians had made up the lion's share
of recruits, but in the following decade, workers from Greece, Portugal,
Spain, Turkey, and Yugoslavia diversified the labor pool. And more than
any other group of potential laborers, it was Turks who responded overwhelmingly to the employment opportunities offered by West Germany.[94]
This trend, however, was not immediately apparent: only in 1971 did the
number of Turkish workers surpass that of laborers from other countries,
but the jump was quite striking. In 1970, there were 469,200 Turks in
West Germany, compared to 573,600 Italians and 514,500 Yugoslavians.
By 1971, the Turkish population had risen to 652,800, while the number
of Italians and Yugoslavians remained relatively constant. Significantly,
it was at this point that Heinrich Böll produced the first Turkish guest
worker character in German literature – Mehmet, the lover of heroine Leni
Pfeiffer in *Gruppenbild mit Dame* (*Group Portrait with Lady*).[95] Overall,
between 1970 and 1973, the Turkish population in the Federal Republic nearly doubled.[96] By 30 September 1973, nearly 297,000 Turks had
been living in West Germany for at least four years, of which 37,300 had
resided there for more than a decade.[97] In the following years, the figures
for Turks coming to West Germany continued to increase, whereas those
from other countries steadily decreased. Soon Turks became the dominant
minority group within the larger category of guest workers. This demographic pattern was mirrored and magnified in publications and statements by government officials, policymakers, and the media. The cover
story for a 1973 issue of *Der Spiegel*, for instance, announced, "The Turks

---

[94] Turks, like guest workers from other countries, were attracted by the numerous job
opportunities and the chance to make relatively large sums of money quickly. In addition,
unlike the other groups of foreign workers who tended to repatriate after several years,
Turks were deterred from returning to their home country because of the tumultuous
political situation. According to Mandel, Turkey was reduced to a state of near civil war,
which produced economic and political disaster. See Mandel, "We Called for Manpower,"
43–45.

[95] This novel was wildly successful. It was singled out by the Swedish Academy, which
awarded Böll the Nobel Prize for Literature in 1972, and became a bestseller, with more
than a quarter of a million copies sold by 1974.

[96] For the 1970 figures, see *Statistisches Jahrbuch für die Bundesrepublik Deutschland*
(Stuttgart: Kohlhammer, 1971), 42. For the 1971 figures, see *Statistisches Jahrbuch 1973*,
52. For the 1973 figures, see *Statistisches Jahrbuch 1974*, 51.

[97] The number of Turks who remained in the Federal Republic also exceeded the number of
nonreturnees from other countries, but the large wave of new immigrants that arrived at
the beginning of the decade added to an already expanding group of Turkish residents.
See *Statistisches Jahrbuch für die Bundesrepublik Deutschland* (Stuttgart: Kohlhammer,
1974), 51.

are coming – run for your lives."[98] Increasingly, Turks and guest workers were treated as one and the same, and the fact that the labor recruitment program and subsequent migration had encompassed multiple national groups quickly disappeared from public consciousness.[99]

Meanwhile, large numbers of foreign workers from many countries had started to make their voices heard through labor activism. One point of contention was the stratification of skills and wages along ethnic lines. In the metal processing industry, for example, foreigners and women tended to occupy lower-paying jobs than their male, German coworkers. Another major issue was representation in the trade union leadership and factory councils. All foreign laborers had the right to vote in works council elections, but guest workers from non-EEC countries were not allowed to stand as candidates, a situation which meant that they had a limited ability to make their particular concerns heard.[100] In the spring of 1973, metal-industry workers – both German and non-German – staged a series of spontaneous strikes in an effort to obtain bonuses that would offset the income they were losing to inflation. For the most part, IG Metall did not support the actions, although the union later tried to suggest that its mobilization process had laid the foundations for them.[101] The wave of agitation culminated in the widely publicized wildcat strike of August–September 1973, a confrontation sparked when five hundred Turkish employees of the Ford plant in Cologne returned to work late after the summer vacation period only to learn that they had been fired.[102] During the weeklong occupation and forced

---

[98] "Die Türken kommen – rette sich wer kann," *Der Spiegel*, 26 March 1973.

[99] For examples of this pattern see Ernst Klee, "Die Nigger Europas," *Frankfurter Rundschau*, 16 January 1971, which discusses the exploitation and social discrimination experienced by guest workers but features a large picture of Turks carrying luggage; "Ein Arbeitsplatz in der Bundesrepublik," *Vorwärts*, 19 April 1973, 18–19, which explicitly addresses the question of why so many Turks seek work in Germany; and Bundesanstalt für Arbeit, "Beschäftigung von Ausländern: Arbeitsplätze in Deutschland oder in der Heimat?," *Bayernkurier*, 22 December 1973, 12–13, an advertisement placed by the Federal Ministry of Labor that provides a list of many different foreign workers but is overshadowed by a large picture of a Turkish man. On the ways in which the figure of the guest worker has been conflated with Turks, see Mandel, "We Called for Manpower," 120–22; Leslie A. Adelson, "Migrants' Literature or German Literature? TORKAN's *Tufan: Brief an einem islamischen Bruder*," *The German Quarterly* 63 (1990): 383–84; and Sabine von Dirke, "Multikulti: The German Debate on Multiculturalism," *German Studies Review* 17 (1994): 523.

[100] Castles and Kosack, *Immigrant Workers*, 130–31.

[101] Markovits, *West German Trade Unions*, 226–27.

[102] Summer vacation was a particularly contentious issue between foreign workers and their employers and a good example of the failure of German union representatives

shutdown of the plant, several violent clashes occurred between foreign laborers and German nonstrikers, as well as between police and strikers. These militant demonstrations – and their coverage in the mainstream press – presented a newly dangerous and menacing image of the guest worker to the West German public. In contrast to the earlier paeans to foreign recruits for their economic contributions, *Der Spiegel* now cast the *Gastarbeiter* as ungrateful agitators in a "Turkish revolt."[103]

Finally, the recession of 1973 brought the Federal Republic's boom economy to a screeching halt. Now led by an SPD-FDP coalition government, West Germany entered a period of economic crisis, which proved to be much more serious than the slump in 1966–67 because of the worldwide oil crisis. For the first time in twenty years, sustained unemployment set in, and by 1974 more than half a million West Germans had joined the ranks of the jobless. Public attention now fixated on the large number of foreign workers, which reached a peak of 2.595 million in 1973. With more and more Germans out of work, a chorus of political and journalistic commentators called for restrictions on importing laborers, especially Turks. The decisive moment came on 23 November 1973, when the federal government announced a halt to all foreign labor recruitment, the so-called *Anwerbestopp*.[104]

Aras Ören and the Beginnings of *Gastarbeiterliteratur*

It was at this critical juncture – with cultural representations of guest workers, public debates about their presence, and German unemployment all on the rise – that the first installment of Ören's *Berlin Trilogie* appeared. Unlike the representations produced earlier by Italian workers, which addressed a narrow, Italian-language enclave, *Was will Niyazi in der Naunynstraße* (*What's Niyazi Doing on Naunyn Street?*) targeted a different sort of audience. Ören composed the poems in Turkish but

---

to recognize guest workers' unique concerns. While foreign laborers wanted extended summer leave time in order to return to their homelands and visit families, employers insisted on maintaining strict rules about the amount of time allowed for vacation in the summer. For more on the wildcat strikes of 1973, see "Faden gerissen," *Der Spiegel*, 10 September 1973; Mark J. Miller, *Foreign Workers in Western Europe: An Emerging Political Force* (New York: Praeger, 1981), 104–11; Mandel, "We Called for Manpower," 54–59; and Wise, "Ali in Wunderland," 53–54.

[103] *Der Spiegel*, 10 September 1973.

[104] On the numbers of unemployed West Germans, see Turner, *Germany from Partition to Reunification*, 164–65. On the numbers of guest workers and the subsequent public concerns, see Herbert, *History of Foreign Labor*, 230.

quickly had them translated into German. He also wrote from a distinctly Marxist perspective, emphasizing the class position of his characters, and enlisted the left-alternative Berlin press Rotbuch Verlag to publish and distribute the work.[105] These choices suggest a deliberate effort to hail a specific kind of reader, namely progressive Germans engaged in leftist social criticism. Ören's stylistic and publishing decisions, in other words, positioned him to speak to the emerging debate taking place among New Left artists and intellectuals about guest workers.[106] Yet, in contrast to the representations produced by Germans, which generally treated foreign laborers in brief and vague terms, Ören's poems explored the life of a Turkish laborer over sixty-eight pages. This distinction was clear in the work's title, which established a particular subject (Niyazi) within a specific neighborhood (Berlin's Kreuzberg) and then drew public attention to his individual concerns (*wollen*). Thus, from his very first literary gesture in German, Ören offered a challenge to the atemporal, rootless, and largely faceless guest worker images that had dominated public discussions of the recruitment for the previous two decades.

Ören added further complexity to these images by stressing his characters' diverse motivations for choosing to migrate to the Federal Republic. Several characters (e.g., Halime and Ali) sign up to work in Germany because they need to support their families. Others (e.g., Sabri San) do so because they want to amass enough money to return to Turkey and open their own businesses. The title character, Niyazi Gümüskiliç, a poor laborer from Istanbul, embraces the chance to work in Germany (which he calls "little America") because he wants to live like a member of the Western bourgeoisie. Only in America, he assumes, can

> everyone have a car,
> modern apartments with bath,
> ready-made suits,
> nylon shirts
> and a girlfriend who kisses him in public
> just like in the movies.[107]

---

[105] The title can also be translated as "What Is Niyazi's Business on Naunyn Street?" but for the sake of continuity, I have chosen to adopt the English translation first used by Heidrun Suhr. See Suhr, "Ausländerliteratur," *New German Critique* 46 (1989): 86.

[106] In this respect Ören's engagement follows a pattern identified by Michael Warner: "all discourse or performance addressed to a public must characterize the world in which it attempts to circulate and it must attempt to realize that world through address." See Michael Warner, *Publics and Counterpublics* (New York: Zone Books, 2002), 113–14.

[107] Aras Ören, *Was will Niyazi in der Naunynstraße*, trans. by H. Achmed Schmiede and Johannes Schenk (Berlin: Rotbuch Verlag, 1973), 25. Hereafter cited as *WWN*.

Initially, Ören emphasizes the material conditions of guest workers over their ethnic and cultural identifications. He builds this vision into the very foundation of *Was will Niyazi* by structuring it around a particular place – Naunynstraße – rather than specific characters. The street not only acts as a backdrop for the comings and goings of the poems' many characters, but also marks who they are. Naunynstraße is located in the heart of Berlin's Kreuzberg district, a neighborhood historically inhabited by the working class. During the postwar labor recruitment, this district became a prime settlement area for Turks, one of the few places where guest workers found landlords willing to rent to them. Naunynstraße thus signifies the socioeconomic condition that all of its inhabitants share – regardless of where they came from, their family histories, ethnicities, or cultural traditions.

Ören underscores this common socioeconomic position in a series of metaphoric and historical parallels between Niyazi and his German neighbors, the Kutzers. As Niyazi trudges through the icy cold from Naunynstraße to his night shift job, dreaming of "blue fish time" on the Bosphorus, Frau Kutzer lies in bed in her Naunynstraße apartment, unable to sleep because her feet are frozen blue. As Niyazi passes the hours in an aluminum factory, Frau Kutzer's mind drifts back to her husband's years in the Borsig industrial yards, where he tightened axle screws on locomotives and used his extra money for tea at the fancy Café Bauer. Again and again, Ören weaves a common thread of proletarian experience. Niyazi and the Kutzers live in the same sort of apartments, suffer the same sort of hardships, and engage in the same sort of daydreaming. And it is Naunynstraße that ultimately connects those experiences and dreams. Both figuratively and historically, it binds these diverse members of the German working class together.[108]

As the poetic cycle unfolds, the similarities between Niyazi and the Kutzers extend even further. Frau Kutzer's family, the Brummels, came to Berlin from East Prussia in the 1880s during the major economic shift from handwork and guilds to heavy industry and corporate capital. In the midst of the socioeconomic upheaval, Frau Kutzer's father – who was just a handworker – set up and maintained his own smith shop, employed journeymen, and enjoyed civil rights (*Bürgerrechte*). With their day-to-day existence assured, the Brummels entertained aspirations for a grander life

---

[108] Monika Frederking discusses the role of Naunynstraße from a literary perspective. See Frederking, *Schreiben gegen Vorurteile*, 58–62.

without recognizing the basic divisions of class and status that kept them in their place. As Ören explains:

> Once in a while they played the gramophone.
> But the overtures of Léhar operettas already
> were for them imposed doors
> to a world which remained strange and
> full of secrets.[109]

The futility of the Brummels' aspirations becomes clear in the economic collapse following World War I, when the smith shop no longer provides enough income. Their social standing falls even further after Elisabeth Brummel marries Gustav Kutzer, a working-class mechanic and a member of the communist party.

At this point, Frau Kutzer becomes fully aware of her class position. As the daughter of an independent small-business owner, she had previously spent her days at leisure, listening to music, knitting, or embroidering. But as the wife of a mechanic who sells his labor for wages, she is now forced to work as a cleaning lady for a rich woman in the adjacent neighborhood of Neukölln and grumbles about her hardship. By contrast, her husband, outraged at the injustices heaped upon the workers, criticizes the Social Democrats of the Weimar Republic, calling them "bastards of the rich" who make "golden promises in the name of the workers." Herr Kutzer champions radical communists such as Rosa Luxemburg and admonishes his wife:

> To be a proletarian
> is nothing to be ashamed of.
> Tomorrow the proletariat will
> take power,
> and if the proletariat has no fear before its masters,
> the masters will fear the proletariat.[110]

In the end, however, Herr Kutzer stifles his communist sympathies in the face of Nazi persecution – a silence that, Ören suggests, amounts to nothing less than psychological suicide.

Like Frau Kutzer's family, Niyazi also comes to Berlin in search of a better life. In Istanbul, Niyazi led an impoverished existence as a longshoreman, a position set in stark relief by the proximity of his lodgings to the

[109] Ören, *WWN*, 14.
[110] Ibid., 18.

upper-class neighborhood of Bebek along the Bosphorus. He welcomes the opportunity to work in Germany, expecting rapid upward mobility. But just as with the Brummel family's aspirations, Niyazi's hopes for living like the rich do not materialize. He observes,

> These seven years have changed a lot with me,
> I have understood, where my place
> in society is.
> I have a closet full of suits;
> and I have a car, but
> it is not enough,
> to wish away the boundaries between those,
> who eat sweets and meat pies
> and those who eat unripe melons.[111]

The sheer volume of his material possessions, in other words, has increased in the Federal Republic. Yet he continues to occupy the same lowly socioeconomic position because he remains a powerless worker with only his labor at his disposal. This realization prompts Niyazi to enter into radical politics: he asserts that even the lowest worker deserves an equal share of profit for his labor, a position that echoes the sentiments of the young Herr Kutzer. Indeed, the ideals that Kutzer lacked the courage to act upon in the face of National Socialist opposition are now revived through Niyazi's founding (with his German neighbor Horst) of a multiethnic socialist club that organizes demonstrations and letter-writing campaigns.

In later sections, Ören delineates the ways in which Turkish and German laborers are similarly seduced by industrial capitalism's fantasy of self-determination. In an effort to raise the consciousness of his Turkish neighbors, Niyazi explains the futility of saving wages to his friend Sabri:

> What we have saved,
> without eating, without drinking, without experiencing anything,
> will flow into the pockets of others.[112]

The single-minded drive to save – often in hopes of returning home and opening a business – represents a form of blindness that prevents Turkish workers from understanding their collective exploitation. A second form of blindness emerges in Ören's discussion of Sabri's German counterpart, Klaus Feck, who defines his social mobility in terms of consumer

---

[111] Ibid., 26.
[112] Ibid., 40.

goods. Although his wages barely provide him with enough money for basic survival, he nonetheless is determined to acquire all the luxuries that he associates with a successful worker. For these – a motorbike, a color television, built-in cabinets for the kitchen, furniture for each room of his apartment – Klaus must work overtime, leaving for the factory every morning at five o'clock and returning home every evening at six o'clock. The result, according to Ören, is a "consumer chaos," which seeps into every aspect of Klaus's existence. He has become a materialistic "plow horse" who plods through his work without reflection. Klaus is a slave to consumer desire and, like Sabri, is so caught up in the pursuit of an unattainable goal that he fails to recognize how he is being manipulated.

Ören, the New Left, and the Lingering Problem of Ethnicity

It is worth pausing here to examine this political program more carefully. Born near Istanbul in 1939, Ören initially came to the Federal Republic during the early 1960s as part of a Turkish theater troupe, which had been invited for an extended series of performances at the Frankfurt New Theater. He went back to Turkey for his mandatory military service, but returned to West Berlin in 1965. Influenced by Bertolt Brecht's consciousness-raising theater and conception of art as a tool for Marxist critique, he and several friends established a collective with the intention of performing plays for guest workers.[113] When the project collapsed, Ören returned once more to Istanbul, where he continued to act and write plays, but his marriage to a German meant that he visited Berlin on a regular basis. In 1969, he settled permanently in the West German city, making ends meet with odd jobs until his success with *Was will Niyazi* enabled him to work full-time as a writer and journalist.[114]

---

[113] Frederking, *Schreiben gegen Vorurteile*, 76–79.

[114] Very little biographical information has been published on Aras Ören. The most detailed account of his life appeared in a series of informational portraits of Berlin authors published by West Berlin's popular biweekly entertainment guide, *Tip*. See "Seemann in der Wasserlache," *Tip*, 8–21 July 1977. More perfunctory descriptions have appeared in the following: Heinz Friedrich, ed., *Chamissos Enkel. Literatur von Ausländern in Deutschland* (Munich: DTV, 1986); Carmine Chiellino, *Die Reise hält an. Ausländische Künstler in der Bundesrepublik* (Munich: Verlag C. H. Beck, 1988); Robert Bosch Stiftung, ed., *Viele Kulturen – eine Sprache: Chamissos Enkel zu Gast in Stuttgart. Veranstaltungsreihe mit den Preisträgern des Adelbert-von-Chamisso-Preises der Robert Bosch Stiftung vom 19. bis 22. Oktober 1998* (Stuttgart: Robert Bosch Stiftung, 1999); and Adelson, *The Turkish Turn*, 140.

The precise details of this early biography remain fuzzy, but it seems clear that Ören shared many of the ideas and artistic programs that we now associate with the New Left and the extraparliamentary opposition movement of the late 1960s and early 1970s. In fact, all of the themes and concerns that we have considered thus far resemble those contained in many of the works that came out of this milieu, such as Fassbinder's *Katzelmacher*, Wallraff's *"Gastarbeiter" oder der gewöhnliche Kapitalismus*, and Böll's *Gruppenbild mit Dame*. In each case, a similar set of socioeconomic targets emerges: the self-congratulatory economic prosperity of the Federal Republic, the social conformity and ideological complacency that accompanied this new affluence, and the recruitment of guest workers as the most extreme example of postwar West Germany's indifference to the human costs of the economic miracle.[115]

Ören's poems, however, added a number of distinctive features to this larger ideological program. For Fassbinder and Böll, guest workers function as abstract figures with no individual identities. In *Katzelmacher*, the foreign laborer Jorgos is virtually silent because of his inability to understand or speak much German, and his background remains obscure except for the fact that he has come from Greece.[116] Similarly, Mehmet, the Turkish lover of the protagonist in *Gruppenbild mit Dame*, appears only a handful of times, primarily as an illustration of her uncharacteristic openness to the "outcasts" of conservative West German bourgeois society. Ören, by contrast, presents Niyazi and Sabri as more fully realized working-class characters with specific histories, dreams, plans, and disappointments. Simply put, this was the first comprehensive history of the labor migration told from the bottom up.

This explicit focus on the lives of recruited laborers added a new representational depth to the New Left's broad critique of capitalism. For Fassbinder and Wallraff, guest workers do not so much represent a German social problem as serve as exotic victims.[117] Significantly, Fassbinder played the role of Jorgos himself, a directorial choice that expressed

---

[115] For more on the emergence of the New Left, see Markovits and Gorski, *German Left*, 4–18.

[116] See Linda Alcoff, "The Problem of Speaking for Others," *Cultural Critique* 20 (1991–92): 5–32.

[117] Miller, in fact, points out that many members of the Federal Republic's extreme left saw guest workers as part of the "oppressed Third World." See Miller, *Foreign Workers*, 106. Wise argues, however, that for all of the solidarity expressed by the West German student movement with the victims of colonization, they "seemed unaware of the abuses directed against foreign workers in Germany." See Wise, "Ali in Wunderland," 40.

a sort of empathy for the difficulties of foreign workers, yet ultimately employed this foreignness as a vehicle for his own feelings of social and political alienation rather than those of the immigrant.[118] As Fassbinder later explained, he did not set out to make a film about guest workers per se; his representation of Jorgos was simply one of many techniques for pointing out the human and ideological costs of embracing unbridled capitalistic growth.[119] This was also true of Wallraff's reportage, which sought to expose the poor living conditions of recruited workers. His more fundamental critique was directed at the very idea of a surplus army of laborers held in reserve to absorb the unpredictable fluctuations of the economy and to facilitate "capitalism as usual." To the extent that members of the New Left acknowledged ethnic conflict or antiracist struggle, they did so by criticizing the social conditions in other countries.[120] The weekly *Welt am Sonntag* recognized this pattern as early as 1966: "Germans who work through their past by being outraged about apartheid in South Africa or race riots in America obviously do not have anything against the apartheid of alien workers [*Fremdarbeiter*] in the Federal Republic, against their social boycott and their displacement into ghettos."[121]

In this respect, the most interesting contrasts with Fassbinder, Wallraff, and Böll begin to surface in the moments when Ören specifically addresses ethnic tensions within West Germany's diverse working class. The scenes with the character Ali, in particular, demonstrate how ethnicity

---

[118] On Fassbinder's decision to play the role of Jorgos, including the question of a German "speaking for" a guest worker, see Wise, "Ali in Wunderland," 32–36; and Katrin Sieg, "Ethnic Drag and National Identity: Multicultural Crises, Crossings, and Interventions," in Sara Friedrichsmeyer, Sara Lennox, and Susanne Zantop, eds., *The Imperialist Imagination: German Colonialism and Its Legacy* (Ann Arbor: University of Michigan Press, 1998), 303-07. Other scholars have explored Fassbinder's use of immigrant characters. See, for example, Kaja Silverman, *Male Subjectivities at the Margins* (London: Routledge, 1992), especially Chapter 3.

[119] Rainer Werner Fassbinder, "Gespräche mit Rainer Werner Fassbinder," *Rainer Werner Fassbinder. Werkschau* (Berlin: Argon, 1992), 36, quoted in Wise, "Ali in Wunderland," 34.

[120] In her discussion of West German feminism's blindness to the question of race, Sara Lennox briefly notes that members of the student movement and New Left supported anti-imperialist and antiracist struggles outside of the Federal Republic during the 1960s and 1970s. She suggests that it was not until the 1980s that West German feminists began to consider racism within the ranks of German feminism itself. See Sara Lennox, "Divided Feminism: Women, Racism and German National Identity," in Susan Castillo, ed., *Engendering Identities* (Porto: Universidade Fernando Pessoa, 1996), 30.

[121] H. von Studnitz, "Sind wir unfair zu den Gastarbeitern?," *Welt am Sonntag*, 20 March 1966, quoted in Woesthoff, "Ambiguities of Antiracism," 61.

complicates and divides class consciousness. As Ali leaves his job at the
refrigerator assembly plant, he encounters two German colleagues who
order him to haul garbage to the back of the factory before going home.
Ali refuses, and the Germans begin to harass him. When Ali returns the
hounding, however, they become angry and blame him for their economic
difficulties:

> "Because of you –"
> "Because of all of you –"
> " – you dirty foreigners...."
> "You do overtime, overtime, there you have it.
> And we celebrate Christmas this time without cash,
> next week the short-term work will be over."[122]

While Ali and his German colleagues perform the same tasks on the
assembly line, the Germans place themselves in a symbolically superior
position by telling Ali to see to the trash, thereby relegating him to the
dirtiest work. These German workers blame Ali for taking away their traditional source of extra holiday income and depriving them of comforts to
which they have grown accustomed. Significantly, as they make him into a
scapegoat, their mode of address changes. Early on, the German workers
employ the familiar singular form of "you" (*deinetwegen*), but quickly
shift to the familiar plural form (*euretwegen*), treating Ali as an ethnic
representative. Finally, they explicitly call him "you dirty foreigners" (*ihr
dreckigen Ausländer*). By depersonalizing Ali and making him the stand
in for all guest workers, his German colleagues establish an ethnically
defined hierarchy. Rather than understanding their exploited situation as
fundamentally linked to Ali's, the German workers assert ethnic essentialism, both in an effort to make sense of their new economic difficulties,
and as a kind of psychic compensation.[123]

---

[122] Ören, *WWN*, 51.
[123] This tendency of indigenous workers to scapegoat newcomers and foreigners as a
response to economic hardship is one of the most basic observations that has been
made in recent historical scholarship, especially in the American case, about the relation
between race and class. See David R. Roediger, *The Wages of Whiteness: Race and the
Making of the American Working Class* (London: Verso, 1991). A number of political
scientists and sociologists observe that "native" workers perceive foreign workers as
taking away their jobs in times of economic decline. In the German case similar out-
cries were made, although studies show that foreign workers – and particularly Turks –
actually performed jobs that were so undesirable that most Germans would not consider taking them even in an economic crisis. See, for example, Hoskins and Fitzgerald,
"German Immigration Policy and Politics," 98; Klaus J. Bade, "Immigration and Social
Peace in United Germany," *Daedalus*, Winter 1994, 85–106.

Ören further explains how managers manipulate ethnic identifications among laborers for the benefit of production:

> Ali often worked overtime,
> because the boss wanted it like that.
> And the others, instead of saying something to him
> about short-term work and other harassment,
> opposed him
> instead of opposing the bosses,
> who take advantage of the situation.[124]

The bosses know that Ali and other Turkish laborers will accept overtime because of their desire to accumulate as much money as quickly as possible and their fear of losing their jobs and residence permits. The managers, Ören suggests, understand this dynamic and exploit it: they deflect attention away from the real problem of unfair labor practices and wages by using the foreigners to undermine unionized German workers, a strategy which provokes a racial backlash. The assumption driving the hostility of Ali's German co-workers is that the willingness to do the boss's bidding indicates a different work ethic and code of conduct, a demarcation of ethnic difference that relies on the belief that Germans would not undercut their fellow native workers.[125] This pattern is a good example of what Paul Gilroy has recently described as a shift in "raciology." The sense of incommensurable cultural difference inscribed into forms of behavior, according to his argument, belongs to a new racism that is uncomfortable with a biologically based conception of race.[126]

---

[124] Ören, *WWN*, 51–52.

[125] Ören actually implies that the Turkish workers do operate according to a different set of assumptions about work, but instead of rooting them in ethnic differences, sees them as the outcome of a particular set of circumstances. According to Ören, many of the Turkish guest workers, particularly the ones who came from rural areas, are accustomed to being dominated and oppressed by landowners and do not realize that they have rights. Without the recognition of rights, he implies, these workers allow themselves to be exploited – in both Turkey and Germany – and turn to violence as a way to exert their subjectivity. See Ören, *WWN*, 66.

[126] Paul Gilroy, *Against Race: Imagining Political Culture Beyond the Color Line* (Cambridge, MA: Harvard University Press, 2000), 32–33. Gilroy here draws on the work of Martin Baker, *The New Racism* (London: Junction Books, 1980); Martin Thom, *Republics, Nations and Tribes* (London: Verso, 1995); Jeremy Black, *Maps and History* (New Haven: Yale University Press, 1997); and Guntram Henrik Herb, *Under the Map of Germany: Nationalism and Propaganda* (London: Routledge, 1997).

These ethnic tensions are not one-sided, however. Ali, too, fails to recognize the plight he shares with his German colleagues and allows his frustration to turn into resentment and anger. On the U-Bahn, after the confrontation at the factory, he daydreams about his village:

> And if one day
> a German should lose his way there,
> Ali decided,
> to beat him up
> until his energy drained out of him –
> for that,
> which he had to put up with in these days.[127]

This daydream of vented frustrations, moreover, foreshadows a very real – and deadly – brawl between Ali and his coworker Klaus.

Following his normal routine of drinking on Fridays after work, Klaus sinks into an alcohol-induced existential crisis. In a remarkable, quasi-hallucinatory scene, Ören recounts Klaus's disillusionment with both the postwar economic miracle and the larger culture it has produced:

> "Protect our basic free and democratic constitutional order" –
> the newspapers were full of such words.
> Along with stories of murder and pictures of naked women.
> "Protect our free and democratic legal system" –
> the television programs were full of such statements.
> Along with advertisements and gangster films.[128]

Here liberal values and democratic rights are counterposed with the ugly consequences of capitalism – exploitation of women, a vacuous mass culture, and violence. The point is to suggest that they are actually two sides of the same ideological coin: freedom and democracy are secured in the name of free trade and the protection of private property, yet that very system is sustained by the exploitation of society's most vulnerable groups. Seduced into spending his meager wages on consumer junk, Klaus recognizes that he has been entrapped by the very values he had cherished. He asks himself:

> What do these have to do with me?
> What do I gain from them?
> What do I understand about them?
> I am suffocating.[129]

---

[127] Ören, *WWN*, 52.
[128] Ibid., 47.
[129] Ibid., 48.

At this moment, he spies his co-worker Ali on the street and beckons his friend to join him for a drink. In the bar, a traditional locale for working-class bonding, Klaus turns violent, landing a punch in the face of the "miserable little boozer," as he now refers to Ali. He shouts:

> "What is standing around here so stupidly?
> Can't you even chit-chat properly,
> dirty foreigner, what do you really want here?"[130]

These questions reveal a number of important features of Klaus's frustration. Instead of using the subjective, personal pronoun "who" (*wer*), Klaus employs the object pronoun "what" (*was*), a rhetorical shift that reduces Ali to an object. When Klaus does identify the person to whom he speaks, moreover, it is no longer Ali – his friend – but a "dirty foreigner." Klaus is particularly enraged because Ali cannot even "chitchat properly," a linguistic inadequacy that serves as the ultimate symbol of the Turk's foreignness.

This rapid disintegration of Ali's subjectivity in Klaus's eyes marks the tragic breakdown of the cross-ethnic working-class solidarity envisioned in the earlier scenes with Niyazi and the Kutzers. Once Klaus fully realizes his own oppression, he seizes on Ali's difference as a kind of ideological compensation. He punches Ali mercilessly, mumbling to himself:

> Don't cower,
> before anyone, not even yourself.[131]

Ören then complicates matters even further. In the stanza immediately following Klaus's descent into drunken incoherence, an eerie specter emerges:

> In their hands no submachine guns.
> On their heads no steel helmets,
> on their feet no boots,
> they wore no brown uniforms
> and no swastikas.
> They were seven or eight men,
> the others in the bar.
> The arms tattooed pale blue,
> patent leather shoes,
> and their thoughts nourished a snake
> that spat unhindered poison.

---

[130] Ibid., 48.
[131] Ibid., 48.

And they all
agreed with Klaus,
they shared a common joy.
They went to work on Monday with ease.[132]

Especially interesting here is Ören's use of analogy by negation. He
invokes images of Nazi terror even as he acknowledges that the men
are *not* Nazis.

These disturbing images can be read in a number of different ways.
On one level, Ören juxtaposes the negative effects of capitalism with
images commonly linked to fascism – a linkage that was entirely typical
of the West German New Left. As Andrei Markovits and Philip Gorski
have argued, the 1968 student protest movements in the Federal Republic
took on a specifically "German" character deeply connected to the "Holocaust effect" because their "critique of the complacency and accommodation of the Bonn republic's institutions and political culture" was formulated "vis-à-vis the Nazi regime."[133] In their criticisms of West Germany's
wholehearted embrace of capitalism, Fassbinder and Wallraff argued that
postwar society's obsession with economic prosperity obscured a failure
to deal with its fascist past. In the opening epigraph of *Katzelmacher*,
for instance, Fassbinder warns his audience that "it is better to make new
mistakes than to reconstitute the old ones ad nauseam." Wallraff's exposé
on the conditions of guest workers similarly culminates with the troubling
revelation that a German company housed its imported laborers in the
barracks of the former concentration camp Dachau. Ören makes this connection by invoking the menacing apparition of tattooed men with patent
leather shoes at precisely those moments when the realization of economic
inequity and exploitation leads to violence against foreigners. He suggests
that such connections are fundamental to the ideological legacy that has
infected the minds of Klaus's and Ali's German co-workers.

But Ören also takes the conventional German New Left linkage
between capitalism and fascism in new directions. First and foremost, he
uses this association to point out the tragic consequences of the German
working class's failure to see its own immiseration as fundamentally

---

[132] Ibid., 48–49. The first three lines of this stanza also appear just before Ali's confrontation
with his German colleagues about taking out the trash at the refrigerator assembly plant.
See page 51.

[133] See Markovits and Gorski, *German Left*, 21. They also point out that the emergence
of fascism as a topic of concern among the New Left students and intellectuals corresponded to the "sudden electoral successes" of the right-wing National Democratic
Party.

similar to that experienced by foreign guest workers. Ören also stresses that this neo-Nazi specter was *not* outfitted in brown shirts, steel helmets, or swastikas; that it was *not* the same as the fascism of the Third Reich. For precisely this reason, the violence is all the more tragic: even though Klaus and Ali live under an ostensibly democratic regime, neither side is able to see beyond ethnic affiliations to recognize their common class position. In spite of similar work experiences, mutual economic complaints, and common public spaces in Kreuzberg, the "poisonous snake" seems to emerge with distressing ease. Thus, Ören both reaffirms and complicates the conventional critiques of the West German New Left. In this case, a fascist *mentalité* functions not merely as an ideological legacy that had been elided and ignored in the name of economic rebuilding. It also marks an ideological problem particular to the postwar period – the ethnic essentialisms of exploited workers unable to recognize their common plight.

"Secret Bestseller"

When it appeared in 1973, *Was will Niyazi* was heralded by West German critics as a major cultural milestone. Much of the praise focused on the relationship between the subject matter of the poetic cycle and Ören's ethnicity, noting that the poems represented the "first literary chronicle of the coexistence of Germans and Turks – not from the outside."[134] Another writer applauded Ören for taking "up the exceptional situation of his countrymen" and representing "the life of Turks in Berlin" for the very first time.[135] Here, the critics emphasized, was an author who had the ability to "translate the observations and experiences from an immediate neighborhood... in a half-documentary but extremely poetic language."[136] One of the earliest reviewers even hailed Ören as the "poet of guest workers," who "presented the first full literary work to have emerged from the ranks of the Turkish guest workers."[137] Critics also praised his identification of new kinds of issues related to the labor

---

[134] Ulf G. Stuberger, "'Wir machen szammen Geld für die Fabrika Dirketor...,'" *Deutsche Volkszeitung*, 17 January 1974.
[135] Ingeborg Drewitz, "Poem von den Kreuzberger Türken," *Der Tagesspiegel*, 16 December 1973.
[136] Harald Budde, "Niyazi in der Naunynstraße, oder: Das Leben in der Trümmerlandschaft," *Die Tat*, January 1974.
[137] Anneliese Gottschalk, "Dichter der Gastarbeiter: Mit Sensibilität spürt Aras Ören den Alltagsproblemen nach," *Berliner Stimme*, 29 January 1972.

migration. Drawing attention to topics previously left unspoken, he dealt with "the mistrust, racism, and enmity which surround the colony of Turks in Kreuzberg."[138]

This was, of course, only partially true. Ören's was not the first minority voice to weigh in on the guest worker question. But his was the first to be targeted and distributed to a more mainstream literary market. Rotbuch Verlag printed 6,000 copies of *Was will Niyazi* in 1973 and another 7,000 in 1980; it officially recorded 12,000 books sold.[139] This sales figure was relatively modest, even for its day, but it meant that the work had a far larger audience than any migrant literary text up until that point. What is perhaps even more significant is the fact that Ören's poems resonated beyond the leftist intellectual public that they explicitly addressed. Articles about the work appeared in the arts section of virtually every Berlin periodical, as well as a handful of other regional and national newspapers. *Was will Niyazi* produced a transformation in the readership for minority literary expression: it broadened the scope of the audience and provoked a mass-mediated dialogue in the German-language press.

Within this context, it becomes easier to make sense of what was perhaps the most interesting of Ören's early reviews. In the *Nürnberger Nachrichten* the young literary critic Ludwig Fels pointed to another sort of accomplishment: "I regard this volume as a secret bestseller: whoever reads it will no longer be able to think in the old way."[140] This statement begs an obvious question – how can a bestseller be secret? As Fels no doubt understood, this was not a bestseller by any commercial criterion. Rather, he seemed to be marking a moment of historical transition. By describing Ören's work as secret, he acknowledged the fact that, even in 1973, most German readers were unaware of the labor migration's impact in producing minority literary voices. In this sense, Fels's use of this term connoted an intervention, a literary breakthrough from the margins. Yet by pairing "secret" with "bestseller" he also implied that the distinction between commercial center and literary margin was beginning to change. With thousands of copies selling and reviews in media outlets across the

---

[138] N.a., "'Nur wenn man wie ein Amerikaner lebt, kann der Mensch sagen, er habe gelebt,'" *Frankfurter Rundschau*, 2 June 1973.

[139] Frederking, *Schreiben gegen Vorurteile*, 31–32.

[140] Ludwig Fels, "Geheimer Bestseller. Aras Örens 'Was will Niyazi in der Naunynstraße' – Ein türkischer Gastarbeiter," *Nürnberger Nachrichten*, 13–14 October 1973. The same review appeared several months later; see Ludwig Fels, "Vom Slum ins Getto: Aras Örens Poem 'Was will Niyazi in der Naunynstraße,'" *Frankfurter Rundschau*, 22 December 1973.

nation, it was now difficult to describe Ören's work as a secret except in a purely figurative sense. For the first time, a migrant voice had crossed the mass-cultural threshold and was speaking to the nation.

Fels further asserted that "whoever reads this book will not be able to think in the old way." This audacious claim suggested that Ören had inaugurated a change in West German perceptions of the guest worker, even new modes of thought. According to Fels, *Was will Niyazi* offered a "socially critical lesson" in its final poem, a quote from a Turkish worker written in the form of a letter to his German colleague that reiterates their shared socioeconomic status. What Fels seemed to recognize here was Ören's unique contribution to the political and ideological program of the New Left. This was the volume's crucial breakthrough – an extension of the neo-Marxist critiques of West German capitalist society to include "all the Niyazis in all the Naunyn streets," which in turn made it increasingly difficult to think about guest workers in the "old way" (either as pure labor forces or as pure victims).

As Ören continued to publish in German, a growing number of critics recognized the significance of what he had accomplished. In *Neues Forum* one reviewer declared that "Ören is the first author to lift the situation of the so-called guest workers out of the realm of dry statistics and onto the level of literary imagination and reflection."[141] Another pointed to his emerging status as a public intellectual: "He is heeded, praised, and even presented now as the 'renowned Turk' who writes poetry whenever it is a matter of expressing the Federal Republic's interest in the culture and literature of the largest minority – the Turks – living among us."[142] Twelve years later, Yüksel Pazarkaya, a fellow Turkish-German intellectual, paid tribute to Ören as the recipient of a new major national literary prize, explaining that with the publication of *Was will Niyazi*, "a wave of enthusiasm swept the German critics. They recognized in the verses of this poem an original, powerful, yet tender, matter-of-fact, but also graphic, descriptive, and at the same time unmediated experiential voice from life."[143]

This "wave of enthusiasm" dramatically transformed Ören's career. On the strength of the book's critical acclaim, the West Berlin radio and

---

[141] Heidi Pataki, Review of *Der kurze Traum aus Kagithane*, *Neues Forum* 22 (1975): 66.

[142] Petra Kappert, "Die Verse der Sprachlosen: Ein Gedichtband des in Berlin lebenden Türken Aras Ören," *Frankfurter Allgemeine Zeitung*, 12 March 1981.

[143] Yüksel Pazarkaya, "Über Aras Ören," in *Chamissos Enkel. Zur Literatur von Ausländern in Deutschland* (Munich: Deutscher Taschenbuch Verlag, 1986), 15.

television station Sender Freies Berlin (SFB) commissioned a film version less than a year after the poem's publication. Renamed "Frau Kutzer and the Other Inhabitants of Naunynstraße," this television film demonstrated the double-edged impact of mainstream success. In adapting the story, the network chose to focus on Frau Kutzer rather than Niyazi, even as it included lengthy recitations of Ören's poetry, archival photos, reportage, and dramatizations of particular scenes from the story.[144] It is worth noting, too, that much of the press reception for the television version of Ören's poetic cycle concentrated almost entirely on the German actress who played Frau Kutzer. A lengthy article in the *Berliner Morgenpost*, for example, devoted a total of three sentences to the fact that this story in verse had been written by a Turkish-German author and featured guest worker characters.[145]

Nevertheless, the collective impact of this media attention facilitated further opportunities for Ören. Soon after the debut of the television film he was hired by SFB as editor-in-chief for a thirty-minute daily radio program on news and cultural events, the first Turkish-language broadcast of any kind in the Federal Republic. This position brought Ören's role as public intellectual full circle. By directing *Was will Niyazi* toward a German-language readership, Ören had expanded the public's consciousness of the migrant community and initiated a collective rethinking of how this community was being represented in the public sphere. This, in turn, led SFB to include Ören's fictional and journalistic work in its programming, giving him access to a far broader sort of public (something closer to what we might describe as a national or mass audience), as well as a more prominent, authoritative voice among Turkish migrants.

In all of these respects, the rapid transformation of *Was will Niyazi* during the early 1970s from Turkish lyric poem to German television film stands out as a critical turning point in the larger history of the guest worker question. On one side of this historical divide, public discussion about labor migrants was primarily characterized by a fractured dialogue in which government leaders spoke in economic statistics, foreign workers spoke through strikes, and German leftists spoke through pure victims such as Fassbinder's Jorgos. On the other side, a more complex sphere of communication began to emerge in which migrant intellectuals like Ören

---

[144] The magazine *Spontan* published a page-long article promoting this television film. See Harald Dieter Budde, "Leben in Klein-Amerika. Ein neuer Fernsehfilm über Gastarbeiter," *Spontan* 11 (1973), 48.

[145] Irene Sieben, "Frau Kutzer und Niyazi aus Istanbul: Filmszene aus Kreuzberg: Wie leben Deutsche und Türken zusammen?," *Berliner Morgenpost*, 25 May 1973.

attempted to fashion new modes of representation specifically targeted for nonlocalized cultural markets. This process, it is important to emphasize, was never simply characterized by straightforward co-optation or autonomous resistance. Rather, it was more akin to what Stuart Hall has described as the "dialectic of cultural struggle," an ideological "battlefield where no once-and-for-all victories are obtained but where there are always strategic positions to be won and lost."[146]

Imagining a German Multiculturalism

At the same time, however, a subtle shift was taking place in the way that Ören approached the subject of guest workers and their families. Even in the closing pages of the first installment of the *Berlin Trilogie*, Ören seems to have found himself at cross-purposes. For nearly fifty pages the poems focus relentlessly on the construction of a multiethnic German working class. And despite the tragic bar fight that results in Klaus's death, Ören's final poem depicts Niyazi and Horst vowing to unite the neighborhood around common labor concerns and to pursue grassroots political activities such as public demonstrations and letter-writing campaigns. Yet the specter of fascism haunts these final lines, serving as a brutal reminder that workers are never exclusively economic beings and that ethnic differences drive worker consciousness just as powerfully as common experiences in a Kreuzberg apartment building, factory, or tavern. Despite the utopian vows of Niyazi and Horst, these ethnic tensions both in the characters' lives and in Ören's larger literary program remained unresolved. The cycle of poems concludes with clear reassertions of multiethnic worker cooperation, but we read these stanzas well aware of the crushing ethnic prejudices that have (thus far) prevented such cooperation from being realized.

A year later, in 1974, Ören's second volume of the trilogy appeared. Entitled *Der kurze Traum aus Kagithane* (The Fleeting Dream from Kagithane), it expanded the boundaries of his migration history, adding important new dimensions to his portrait of the guest worker experience. One of the central narrative threads focuses on Halime, who has come to work in Berlin to support her family because her husband is a political prisoner in Turkey. After five years alone with her children she begins a relationship with a fellow guest worker, but abruptly ends it when she discovers that she is pregnant. Although Ören had mentioned Halime briefly

---

[146] Stuart Hall, "Notes on Deconstructing 'the Popular,'" in John Storey, ed., *Cultural Theory and Popular Culture: A Reader* (Athens: University of Georgia Press), 447.

in *Was will Niyazi*, she became a principal character only in the second installment, a development which represented the first extended portrayal of a Turkish woman in modern German literature. In addition, this volume widened Ören's original ideological program by offering a neo-Marxist interpretation of Turkish history. Niyazi, attempting to come to terms with the past in order to change the future, sees the Ottoman Empire as a rule based on conquered lands, exploitation, and colonization with basic affinities to Western bourgeois capitalist societies. These ties are strengthened as the collapsing empire, led by the "hero" Enver Pasha, forges an alliance with Germany that brings industrial capital to Turkey. Since World War II, Ören suggests here, three powers – the military, bureaucracy, and capital – have ruled the Turkish state, a combination which has exacerbated the divide between rich and poor.

Der kurze Traum also re-presented the historical origins of the Federal Republic's recruitment program, pushing the narrative's starting point back to a much earlier stage in the migration process, well before Turkish workers arrived in Germany. Here, Ören focuses on the Istanbul district of Kagithane, a shantytown that sprang up when hundreds of thousands of rural villagers poured into the city to apply for work in the Federal Republic. This new geographical orientation emphasized the fact that for many Turkish laborers the first phase of migration occurred when they moved from the rural regions of Turkey to Istanbul. Previously, guest workers had been presented (both in official statements and in the cultural production of the New Left) as somewhat passive figures, outside of history and largely devoid of any pre-German past. Ören insisted, by contrast, that their lives in the Federal Republic could not be understood without tracing the full trajectory of their migration.

In 1980, Ören published the trilogy's final installment, *Die Fremde ist auch ein Haus* (*A Foreign Country Is Also a House*). This volume focused on Turkish laborers who had lived in the Federal Republic for many years with no plans to resettle in Turkey, a situation that was occurring more and more frequently in the late 1970s and early 1980s. Contrary to the intentions and expectations of the West German government, the 1973 *Anwerbestopp* prompted an increase in foreigners, particularly Turks. Many workers correctly perceived this law as the first sign of a stricter policy toward guest workers and, consequently, applied for visas to bring their spouses and children to Germany before any other restrictive legislation could be passed. This course of action was made possible by the ruling of the West German courts that forcing guest workers to be separated from their families for unusually long periods of time violated their basic human rights. Many laborers also decided to remain in the Federal Republic permanently at this time for fear that they might not be able to obtain work permits in Germany again if they left. Ören's portrayal of de facto permanent non-German residents explicitly problematized the assumption of a homogeneous West German society underlying the original conception of the guest worker.

One of the central characters in this poetic cycle is Kemal, a Turkish laborer who has lived with his family in Kreuzberg for nearly a decade. As the family prepares to vacation in Turkey, a conflict arises between Kemal and his fifteen-year-old daughter Emine, which illustrates the very different relationship each figure has to Germany. Ören describes Kemal as a *Heimaturlauber* (homeland vacationer), a term which captures the complexity of Kemal's status in both countries. The juxtaposition of *Heimat* (implying the rootedness and stability of one's home) and *Urlauber* (denoting a temporary visit) demonstrates a transmutation of the original expectation that Turkish workers would return to their homeland permanently once the short-term need for their labor in the Federal Republic was met. Turkey may still be Kemal's homeland as a cultural reference point, but it is merely a vacation destination in actual practice.

In contrast to her father, Emine perceives Germany as her "real" home and Turkey as a place for holidays. She does not want to join her family on vacation and runs away in protest. A member of the second generation, Emine was raised and educated in Germany. For Emine and her brothers, even more than their father, the assumption that the Turks would naturally gravitate back to their homeland belies reality. Emine explains her feelings in a letter addressed to the Turkish general consulate and Berlin's interior minister:

> Foreignness already began in the homeland, but my father
> called it "Germany."
> I now call it "Turkey."
> When I came here, I was five years old.
> I have been here for ten years, my brothers
> were born in Berlin.
> Where is my foreign country now, where is my homeland?
> The foreign country of my father has become my homeland.
> My homeland is the foreign country of my father.[147]

---

[147] Ören, *Die Fremde ist auch ein Haus*, trans. by Gisela Kraft (Berlin: Rotbuch Verlag, 1980), 66.

In many ways this was the same sort of critique that had been offered by writers such as Frisch – a resistance to any public rhetoric that obscured the lived experience of migration. In 1980, however, Ören took this critique a step further, not only questioning the core contradiction built into the term guest worker, but also insisting that the basic binary opposition between *Heimat* (homeland) and *Ausland* (foreign country) had ceased to make sense.

Despite the radically different ways that Kemal and Emine conceive of their relationships to Germany and Turkey, they share a passport that gives them the same paradoxical social status – they are German residents with Turkish citizenship. Emine's letter expresses a practical desire for a citizenship status consistent with lived experience, as well as a growing frustration with essentialized notions of national identity. This attempt to become legally German underscores the fact that Emine already thinks of herself as German socially and culturally.

For any contemporary reader of *Die Fremde ist auch ein Haus* the disjunction between Emine's request and the German citizenship laws must have been clear. In 1980, naturalization constituted a privilege, not a right or entitlement. Initiating the process required at least fifteen years of residence in the Federal Republic, full-time employment during that period, and renunciation of Turkish citizenship and any possible inheritance in that country. The procedure itself was so complicated and arduous that few Turks undertook it. In the same year that *Die Fremde ist auch ein Haus* appeared, only 387 Turks were naturalized, 0.1 percent of Turks who had lived in West Germany for more than ten years.[148] Ören's impact on the guest worker question, then, extended well beyond debunking a few specific stereotypes, offering a Turkish point of view, or even documenting key changes in the history of migration. Between 1973 and 1980, Ören helped transform West German public debate about guest workers in three specific areas: his poems insisted on the interconnectedness of workers' economic and ethnic identities; expanded the spatial and temporal parameters of the migration experience; and finally, challenged the fundamental dichotomy of native and foreign that had long served as the ideological bedrock for West German conceptions of citizenship.

Ultimately, Ören's progression from *Was will Niyazi* to *Die Fremde ist auch ein Haus* also involved a shift in cultural criticism from a New Left critique of the Federal Republic given from a migrant perspective to a much broader reconceptualization of West German identity and culture

---

[148] Castles, Booth, and Wallace, *Here for Good*, 84.

itself – one which we might today describe as "multicultural." When the final installment of the *Berlin Trilogie* came out in 1980, the actual term "multiculturalism" still remained uncommon in West Germany.[149] As we shall see, the bulk of public debate centered on the continuing presence of large numbers of guest workers, with some critics urging repatriation and others championing various models of integration. Yet I would argue that in the course of writing his trilogy Ören began to imagine – even theorize – a distinctly German mode of multiculturalism. This was the first attempt in German literature to capture perpetually hyphenated lives, transnational histories, and mixed cultural affiliations born amidst the upheaval of thirty years of the labor migration.

---

[149] The first example that I have found of the use of "multiculturalism" appears in 1981. This term did not gain common currency until 1988, when a widespread public debate emerged about whether the Federal Republic was a multicultural society. I discuss this debate and its implications in Chapter 4.

2

Minor(ity) Literature and the Discourse of Integration

In the last week of February 1985, the Bavarian Academy of Fine Arts presented the first Adelbert-von-Chamisso Prize, an award newly created to recognize the "contributions to German literature by nonnative German-language writers."[1] Representatives of the prize's three institutional sponsors – the Academy, the University of Munich's Institute for German as a Foreign Language, and the Robert Bosch Foundation – as well as numerous cultural dignitaries from around the Federal Republic attended the ceremony, which honored Aras Ören as the inaugural award winner. At the event, tributes praised his seminal role in the development of a new kind of literature, one written by minorities and specifically directed across boundaries of class, ethnicity, and nation. As Ören himself declared in his acceptance speech: "It is my wish that the written word might become a bridge to communication across all boundaries, which binds fantasies with fantasies, thoughts with thoughts, language with language, individuals with individuals."[2]

Reports on the inaugural prize appeared in many major newspapers throughout West Germany, including *Die Welt, Frankfurter Allgemeine Zeitung, Westfälische Rundschau, Nürnberger Nachrichten,* and *Süddeutsche Zeitung.*[3] A year later, the prominent publishing house

---

[1] Harald Weinrich, "Der Adelbert-von-Chamisso-Preis," in Heinz Friedrich, ed., *Chamissos Enkel. Zur Literatur von Ausländern in Deutschland* (Munich: DTV, 1986), 11.

[2] Aras Ören, "Dankrede zur Preisverleihung," in Heinz Friedrich, ed., *Chamissos Enkel,* 29.

[3] N.a. "Erster Chamisso-Preis für türkischen Autor," *Die Welt,* 28 January 1985, 15; *Frankfurter Allgemeine Zeitung,* 28 January 1985, 21; *Westfälische Rundschau,* 23 February 1985; Albert von Schirnding, "Deutsche Literatur von außen: Aras Ören und Rafik Schami

Deutscher Taschenbuch Verlag (DTV) released *Chamissos Enkel* (Chamisso's Grandchildren), an anthology which included an essay about the significance of *Ausländerliteratur* (foreigner literature) in Germany, encomiums to Ören and Rafik Schami (a Syrian writer who won a secondary prize for younger authors), the winners' acceptance speeches, and selections from each author's writings. The volume served as a kind of primer on the new minority literature as well as a polite manifesto announcing its arrival in the cultural mainstream.

This broad-based support and national press coverage suggests a critical breakthrough, but it also begs a key set of questions. How did minority cultural production move from relatively isolated publications such as *Was will Niyazi in der Naunynstraße* to a literary category sponsored by elite institutions, distributed by major publishing houses, and recognized with its own annual prize? How, in other words, did minority writing emerge as a literature? Who defined its parameters and under what ideological circumstances? Minority literature in the Federal Republic, I want to suggest, had a very specific political and institutional history – a history that cannot be fully explained by pointing to a few critically successful texts.

Beyond Ören's *Berlin Trilogie*, it was unclear which authors or what kind of work would become dominant within minority literature, or that such a category would even emerge. During the 1970s and early 1980s, a number of grassroots organizations facilitated migrant cultural expression through foreign-language newspapers, writers' associations, small publishers, and literary journals. Each of these groups mapped out its own conception of literature written by minorities and coined labels reflecting its specific visions and agendas. These included "guest worker literature," "literature of concern," "foreigner literature," and "German literature by nonnative German speakers."[4] As literary scholar Arlene Teraoka has

erhalten den Chamisso-Preis," *Süddeutsche Zeitung*, 25 February 1985; Reinhard Knodt, "Identität und Kommunikation: Ein Gespräch mit dem türkischen Schriftsteller Aras Ören," *Nürnberger Nachrichten*, 9 March 1985.

[4] The variety of labels for this literature – and the corresponding political agendas for it – has also been reflected in the U.S. scholarship. The first study of this phenomenon published in the United States called it "guest worker literature." See Arlene A. Teraoka, "Gastarbeiterliteratur: The Other Speaks Back," *Cultural Critique* 7 (1987): 77–101. By 1989, scholarship in the United States favored the term "foreigner literature." See Heidrun Suhr, "Ausländerliteratur: Minority Literature in the Federal Republic of Germany," *New German Critique* 46 (1989): 71–103. And by 1990, "migrants' literature" was the label of choice. See Leslie A. Adelson, "Migrants' Literature or German Literature? TORKAN's *Tufan: Brief an einen islamischen Bruder*," *The German Quarterly* 63 (1990): 382–89. All

observed, "what is called *Gastarbeiterliteratur . . .* is really contested territory, and all claims made about or on it are profoundly strategic and political."[5] Through the 1970s, the parameters, goals, and audiences of minority literary production remained relatively fluid and open, with no one group dominating the field and no single approach determining how it would be packaged, disseminated, and understood.

The Institute for German as a Foreign Language (Institut für Deutsch als Fremdsprache, DaF) at the University of Munich ultimately took the lead in defining and consolidating the genre of *Ausländerliteratur.*[6] Yet this role was not at all apparent when DaF was founded in 1978. It began as one of the first institutions in the Federal Republic to provide university instruction, research opportunities, and pedagogical training for German as a foreign language.[7] Over the course of the late 1970s and early 1980s, however, DaF gradually became the most prominent champion of literature written in German by nonnative German speakers, arguing that such creative expression would not only teach linguistic skills but also foster the integration of foreigners.

This evolution in the DaF's conception of minority literary production coincided with a changing federal policy toward the labor recruitment. Just a few months after the founding of the Institute, Helmut Schmidt's SPD-FDP government created a federal position, Commissioner for Foreigners' Affairs (*Ausländerbeauftragter*), to advocate on behalf of foreigners. This appointment represented the first official acknowledgment of the long-term presence of migrants and signaled an increasing engagement with their social well-being.

Thus, between Ören's debut in 1973 and his acceptance of the Chamisso Prize in 1985, both the discourse surrounding the guest worker

of these studies point out the contested nature and the political stakes of these terms. More recently, Leslie Adelson has argued for the phrase "literature of migration" to describe this cultural phenomenon, which she claims "allows us to keep transnational migration and its long-range cultural effects keenly in sight as historical formations, without limiting these effects to the initial influx of guest workers." See Leslie A. Adelson, *The Turkish Turn in Contemporary German Literature: Toward a New Critical Grammar of Migration* (New York: Palgrave Macmillan, 2005), 23.

[5] Teraoka, "Gastarbeiterliteratur," 82.

[6] The role of this institute in promoting integration through literature corresponds with the observation made by scholars of multiculturalism recently that "the main site of multicultural claims-making is education and cultural institutions, with educators and symbol specialists as the main protagonists." Christian Joppke and Steven Lukes, "Introduction: Multicultural Questions," in Christian Joppke and Steven Lukes, eds., *Multicultural Questions* (Oxford: Oxford University Press, 1999), 2.

[7] N.a., "Zwanzig Jahre Institut für Deutsch als Fremdsprache an der LMU München," *dies & DaF* 2 (1998): 1.

and the perceived functions of minority cultural expression changed significantly. What need to be examined further are the common ideological threads that bound these historical developments together. How did the consolidation of foreigner literature interact with prevailing assumptions about the politics of integration? And what might these pivotal developments in the Federal Republic tell us about the larger process by which "minor literatures" merge with – and transform – the dominant cultures around them?

The Guest Worker Question after the Economic Miracle

When Willy Brandt's social-liberal government issued the *Anwerbestopp* on 23 November 1973, it effectively drew the curtain on the first chapter of the postwar migration to West Germany.[8] The decision to halt the flow of guest workers from outside the European Economic Community (EEC) indicated that the economy no longer required – and the nation no longer desired – such a large foreign labor force. This change in labor policy thus eliminated one of the key official justifications for the presence of millions of non-Germans. Yet the fact that so many foreigners remained even after the end of the economic miracle gradually forced the Federal Republic and its citizens to face a new social reality: guest workers had become long-term residents.

At the time of its announcement, the *Anwerbestopp* was viewed by the German public as a direct response to the 1973 oil embargo. A number of scholars have argued, however, that West German government and industry leaders had begun to question the cost-effectiveness of foreign

---

[8] I follow Ray Rist in dividing the labor migration into specific phases. His focus, however, is almost entirely on economic policies – uncontrolled expansion (1960–1972), consolidation (1973–end of 1975), and structural ambivalence (1976–1977). See Ray C. Rist, *Guestworkers in Germany: Prospects for Pluralism* (New York: Praeger, 1978), 111–13. There is not much to quibble with in his periodization, but some of his analytical tropes for explaining what each period meant beg important questions. For example, the consolidation phase raises the question of what exactly is being consolidated. In terms of the discourse of the guest worker question, it is important to recognize that Rist's period of consolidation coincides with the counternarratives articulated by minority artists such as Ören. Whereas Rist sees the period of the mid-1970s as a period of economic and social retrenchment, I see this period as a fundamental shift toward a contested public dialogue on the impacts of the labor recruitment. Similarly, whereas Rist quite correctly emphasizes "structural ambivalences" toward the guest workers during the late 1970s, my broader time frame emphasizes the ways in which the late 1970s begin an ongoing process of policies, social welfare programs, and cultural images that all take the continuing presence of guest workers and their families as a given.

labor somewhat earlier.[9] These questions reflected a growing awareness of new migration patterns. By the late 1960s, guest workers tended to remain in the Federal Republic for longer periods, and increasingly they sent for their families. At the end of 1971, there were nearly 1.8 million labor migrants from Italy, Spain, Greece, Turkey, and Yugoslavia, with the highest concentrations in the states of North Rhine–Westphalia, Baden-Württemberg, and Bavaria.[10] According to a survey published in 1974, 28 percent of those interviewed had been in the Federal Republic for at least seven years. The percentages of respondents who lived with a spouse were 59 (male respondents) and 90 (female respondents). Of the 63 percent who had children, 46 percent had brought them to Germany.[11] These developments strained German social infrastructure such as housing and schools and created tensions in neighborhoods favored by foreigners. In late 1971, Rolf Weber, a representative of the Employers' Associations (*Arbeitgeberverbände*), noted these shifts in an article for *Handelsblatt*:

The economic dampening effect we were able to achieve until now by the employ-ment of foreigners is turning into its opposite: the foreigners and their families now settling here have ... heightened consumption needs. ... To this is added the cost of public investment, far greater than when foreign workers live here housed in communal hostels. It is not merely a matter of providing suitable living quar-ters, as well as schoolrooms and teachers for foreign children – but also that the infrastructure of our municipalities must adjust to a larger population virtually overnight.[12]

A 1972–1973 report by the *Bundesanstalt für Arbeit* (Federal Labor Office) highlighted these changes too, but it also revealed the dramatic rise in foreigners who were not employed at all: in 1967 there were 137,200

---

[9] Marios Nikolinakos has claimed that the oil crisis was just a pretext for a ban that would have been imposed anyway. See "The New Dimensions in the Employment of Foreign Workers" (Berlin: Wissenschaftszentrum, 1975). See also Rist, *Guestworkers in Ger-many*, 31–32; Ulrich Herbert, *A History of Foreign Labor in Germany, 1880–1980: Sea-sonal Workers/Forced Laborers/Guest Workers*, trans. by William Templer (Ann Arbor: University of Michigan Press, 1990), 231–35; and Ulrich Herbert and Karin Hunn, "Guest Workers and Policy on Guest Workers in the Federal Republic: From the Beginning of Recruitment in 1955 until Its Halt in 1973," in Hanna Schissler, ed., *The Miracle Years: A Cultural History of West Germany, 1949–1968* (Princeton: Princeton University Press, 2001), 187–218.

[10] *Statistisches Jahrbuch für die Bundesrepublik Deutschland* (Stuttgart: Kohlhammer, 1973), 52.

[11] Ursula Mehrländer, *Soziale Aspekte der Ausländerbeschäftigung* (Bonn: Verlag Neue Gesellschaft, 1974), 27.

[12] Rolf Weber, "Die BRD ist kein Einwanderungsland," *Handelsblatt*, 12 November 1971, quoted in Herbert, *History of Foreign Labor*, 232.

non-Germans outside the work force, whereas in 1973 there were 1.37 million. These totals included guest workers who had been laid off and were unemployed, but also spouses and children of employed aliens. Such demographic transformations raised serious concerns about the impact of the labor recruitment on West German society and gradually led many government and industry officials to conclude that the massive numbers of foreign laborers and their dependents were worth neither their monetary nor their social cost.[13]

Behind the discussions of cost-effectiveness lay the still unspoken realization that the presence of millions of foreigners in the Federal Republic had become an issue with implications stretching far beyond questions of manpower and economics. One year after the 1969 dissolution of the Grand Coalition in favor of an SPD-FDP federal government, the Ministry of Labor (Bundesministerium für Arbeit) created the Coordination Committee for Foreign Workers (Koordinierungskreis "Ausländischer Arbeitnehmer") to address the social consequences of the labor recruitment and act as a vehicle of information exchange. The committee included representatives from all the major political parties, the Protestant and Catholic churches, the Federal Organization of German Employers' Associations (Bundesvereinigung der Deutschen Arbeitgeberverbände), and the German Trade Union Federation (Deutscher Gewerkschaftsbund, DGB), but its mandate came from the Labor Ministry and its work remained confined to an advisory role. The committee published its recommendations two years later in the report "Principles for the Incorporation of Foreign Workers," which outlined key issues – such as residence, family reunion, leisure, religion, and education – that required the attention of policymakers.[14] Yet it had no authority to develop programs or policy in these targeted areas. Throughout most of the 1970s, in fact, the labor office continued to make most of the official pronouncements and decisions about foreigners, relying on a framework developed in the 1950s that placed West German economic interests above all other concerns.

---

[13] Bundesanstalt für Arbeit, ed., *Ausländische Arbeitnehmer, 1972–1973. Erfahrungsbericht* (Nuremberg: Bundesanstalt für Arbeit, 1974). See also Herbert, *History of Foreign Labor*, 231; Karen Schönwälder, "Migration, Refugees and Ethnic Plurality as Issues of Public and Political Debates in (West) Germany," in David Cesarani and Mary Fulbrook, eds., *Citizenship, Nationality and Migration in Europe* (London: Routledge, 1996), 164–66.

[14] Bundesministerium für Arbeit und Sozialordnung, ed., *Grundsätze zur Eingliederung ausländischer Arbeitnehmer* (Bonn: Bundesministerium für Arbeit und Sozialordnung, 1972). See also Peter O'Brien, "The Paradoxical Paradigm: Turkish Migrants and German Policies" (Ph.D. diss., University of Wisconsin, Madison, 1988), 90, 104.

Meanwhile, the CDU opposition viewed this changing social situation with marked pessimism. According to CDU Bundestag member Jürgen Todenhöfer, "If the federal government does not find a means to check the swelling guest worker stream, difficult social conflicts will develop in our country which will threaten the inner peace of the Federal Republic."[15] Underlying this statement was an anxiety about the possibility of racial upheaval like that experienced by Great Britain in 1958 and by the United States during the civil rights movement in the 1960s. For the CDU, at least, the complications emerging from the settlement of migrant women and children called for drastic policies to stop the inflow of foreigners.

The recession brought about by the oil crisis served as a useful opportunity to curb the increasingly apparent social consequences of labor recruitment. The SPD-FDP government's first act was to issue the *Anwerbestopp* in order to stabilize the unemployment rate by halting the flow of workers. Caught between a declining economic situation, conservative predictions of crisis, and Social Democratic pressure not to cut back on social welfare programs, the ruling coalition hoped this measure would shrink substantially the number of aliens working and residing in the Federal Republic. Between 1973 and 1975, Labor Minister Walter Arendt announced a series of additional decrees. He ordered the federal labor office to cease granting work permits to foreigners already living in West Germany if they were not citizens of EEC countries, a restriction which particularly affected spouses of guest workers. He suspended automatic renewal of work permits and ordered the labor office to determine whether specific jobs could be performed by Germans. Arendt also stepped up efforts to seek out and deport illegal workers and authorized the deportation of laborers who possessed work and residence permits but were collecting unemployment or social welfare benefits. The new regulations represented deliberate strategies to reduce permanently the numbers of foreigners on West German soil.[16]

At the same time, the Ministry of Labor imposed restrictions aimed at countering the trends of long-term residence and family migration.[17] It declared 13 November 1974 the *Stichtag* (deadline) after which no foreign children from countries outside the EEC would be granted work

[15] Bundesvereinigung der Deutschen Arbeitgeberverbände, "Entwicklungspolitisches Gastarbeiterprogramm," *Informationen zur Ausländerbeschäftigung* 1 (1974): 23.

[16] Knuth Dohse, *Ausländische Arbeiter und bürgerlicher Staat. Genese und Funktion von staatlicher Ausländerpolitik und Ausländerrecht vom Kaiserreich bis zur Bundesrepublik Deutschland* (Konigstein: Verlag Anton Hain, 1981), 317–21, 336–41.

[17] Ulrich Spies, *Ausländerpolitik und Integration* (Frankfurt: Peter Lang, 1982), 67.

permits. Children who had come to Germany before this date and who had been born in Germany, according to the new rule, would be eligible for a work permit upon reaching the appropriate age; children who had come after this date would be ineligible for a work permit. The Labor Ministry also announced that beginning on 1 January 1975 the Federal Republic would decrease its childcare compensation for children of foreigners living outside West Germany. Additionally, it designated certain neighborhoods in cities with a high percentage of foreigners "off-limits" to any future non-German inhabitants.[18] These policies sought to discourage further migration to and settlement in the Federal Republic, but like the measures targeting work permits, were carried out under the banner of labor policy. Indeed, West Germany did not have an immigration policy because it thought of itself as a "nonimmigration country."[19]

These strategies for dealing with the social costs of guest workers were entirely typical of the Ministry of Labor's approach to manpower recruitment: it had long praised the "flexibility" of alien workers – and, more specifically, the use of work and residence permits to calibrate the level of imported manpower with the needs of production – as an important advantage of its labor recruitment policy. Yet, one could argue, it was precisely because the Federal Republic refused to treat the question of guest workers as a domestic social issue that these consolidation measures backfired. In actual practice, the ministry's attempts to shrink the foreigner population produced the opposite effect. Stricter rules for obtaining work permits initially reduced the number of aliens, but the *Anwerbestopp* itself made guest workers fear further restrictions and acted as a catalyst for a dramatic increase in family reunions.[20] Likewise, the reduction in childcare assistance actually created an incentive for foreign laborers to bring over their dependents before the lower rates went into effect, while the *Stichtag* generated an even higher incidence of migration among many workers' children. The numbers suggest that these strategies produced somewhat mixed results, but certainly not their desired effect. The number

---

[18] For more on the ways in which the Federal Republic restricted the access of foreigners to certain neighborhoods and cities in the mid-1970s, see Rist, *Guestworkers in Germany,* 79–81.

[19] The lack of any German immigration policy continued throughout the period covered by this book. Change was only made possible with the 1999 revision of the nationality law that gave foreigners the right to apply for German citizenship.

[20] Marilyn Hoskins and Roy C. Fitzgerald, "German Immigration Policy and Politics," in Michael C. LeMay, ed., *The Gatekeepers: Comparative Immigration Policy* (New York: Praeger, 1989), 98.

of foreigners totaled 3,966,200 in 1973 and 4,143,800 by 1979. This constituted an increase, but not a dramatic one. The population of Turks, the group of guest workers considered the most foreign, was 893,600 in 1973 and 1,268,300 by 1979. These figures indicate that while certain groups of labor recruits left as expected, Turks increased their rate of arrival in the Federal Republic. In any case, no significant decrease in the overall numbers of foreigners took place. Thus, the restrictive course of action produced a foreign population that not only was larger, but also (even worse from the perspective of policymakers) took advantage of the benefits of West German society without contributing to it.[21]

The earliest scholarship on these policies – written as they were still taking shape – characterized the Federal Republic's approach to the continuing presence of foreigners as a form of "structural ambivalence."[22] Policymakers failed, that is, to take active steps either to integrate foreign workers into West German society or to facilitate their eventual return to their homelands. More recent scholarship, by contrast, has argued for the emergence of integration as a new emphasis in policymaking.[23] I would argue that both of these positions are accurate. Initially, the government did not simply abandon its efforts to reduce the number of guest workers in favor of integrating them, but went through a period of pursuing ambivalent approaches that produced unintended consequences. By the late 1970s, however, integration was becoming the central strategy. In retrospect, the contradictory policymaking of the 1970s appears to have reflected the enormous stakes involved in putting the issue of recruited laborers on the domestic agenda. After all, articulating a social policy for foreigners was the first step toward accepting millions of guest workers as an integral part of West German society.

A cartoon published in 1973 by the critic Eckhard Tramsen illustrates just how unlikely and laughable the concept of integration appeared to

---

[21] O'Brien, "Paradoxical Paradigm," 86–87. O'Brien characterizes the Federal Republic's attempts to encourage foreigners to leave as an "embarrassing record of blunders." For the 1973 figures, see *Statistisches Jahrbuch* (1974), 51; for the 1979 figures, see *Statistisches Jahrbuch* (1980), 66.

[22] Rist, *Guestworkers in Germany*, 113–14. Part of Rist's shortsightedness, it should be noted, has to do with his temporal proximity to the events in question. His study appeared in 1978, only five years after the *Anwerbestopp* and other restrictive policies were announced.

[23] Klaus Unger, *Ausländerpolitik in der Bundesrepublik Deutschland* (Saarbrücken: Verlag Breitenbach, 1980); Spies, *Ausländerpolitik*; O'Brien, "Paradoxical Paradigm"; Aytaç Eryılmaz and Mathilde Jamin, eds., *Fremde Heimat-Yaban Sılan Olur: Eine Geschichte der Einwanderung aus der Türkei* (Essen: Klartext, 1998).

many Germans on the eve of those changes.[24] It depicts two German men – one with clipboard and the other with cigar in hand – standing in a guest worker barrack. The sparsely furnished room contains a bunk bed, a stool with three mugs on top of it, an oversized bowl, a pail, and a single light bulb hanging from a string. The caption states, "Here we can integrate either three Italians, six Greeks or twelve Turks." The different numbers of workers clearly represents a hierarchy of foreigners based on stereotypical assumptions about living standards. In a room hardly able to hold three, the cartoon suggests that Italians would be willing to put up with the accommodations as offered, whereas Greeks and Turks might tolerate two or four times as many in the room. On one level, the caricature can be read as a relatively straightforward critique of the guest worker program as pure exploitation. On another level, though, the joke revolves around a contradiction between the term "integrate" and the standard of living pictured. The very idea that this barrack – closely associated with the initial stages of worker recruitment – would be described as a site of integration fuels the joke. No one who lives here, it implies, could possibly be integrated into German society. The cartoon is funny precisely because it relies on a shared cynicism about bridging the social gulf between the German officials and the non-German workers they are supposed to integrate.

There is also a more pointed critique lurking beneath the cynicism here: in 1973, those involved with the labor recruitment had little idea of what a successful integration policy might entail. For government officials accustomed to approaching guest workers within the framework of labor policy, the gradual shift to integration required an entirely new ideological orientation. In the years immediately following the *Anwerbestopp*, little detailed information existed about aspects of foreigners' lives that were not directly related to work. This lack of basic knowledge motivated local, state, and federal authorities – including the Labor Ministry, the Friedrich-Ebert-Stiftung of the SPD, and the Konrad-Adenauer-Stiftung of the CDU – to solicit and fund social scientific research on foreigners by the mid-1970s.[25] For the first time, policymakers began to compile

[24] This cartoon is part of a clipping file on guest workers held at the Freie Universität's Otto-Suhr-Institut für Politikwissenschaft. Beyond the artist and year in which the cartoon originally appeared, there are no references attached to the clipping.
[25] Peter O'Brien's dissertation offers an informative examination of social scientific research on foreigners commissioned by West German governmental agencies from the mid-1970s to the mid-1980s. See O'Brien, "Paradoxical Paradigm," especially 100–220.

sociological data on the living conditions, income, saving patterns, family status and structure, education, religion, and long-term plans of recruited laborers. According to the records of the Information Center for Social Scientific Research, the field of *Gastarbeiterforschung* (guest worker research) experienced a veritable explosion during these years. In 1969, it listed 3 projects about guest workers; by 1975, it reported 60; and between 1982 and 1984, the number grew to 428.[26]

Sociologists played a vital role in formulating the parameters of this scholarship and provoked a whole new research agenda during the 1970s. Those who subscribed to systems theory, in particular, exhibited a great interest in the postwar labor migration because the massive movement of populations presented a setting in which the "modern system" encountered the "traditional system." Focusing on Turkey as the most traditional nation of all the labor-sending countries, they pronounced it an incomplete but modernizing society, in contrast to a more advanced West Germany. As these systems came into contact, sociologists argued, two results would ensue. Migration would push West German modernization even further by rationalizing the economy, fine-tuning the division of labor, and allowing Germans to move up the economic ladder. But it would also produce new instability as continued discrimination and marginalization thwarted the expectations of foreigners.[27]

Sociologists who used systems theory overwhelmingly advocated integration as a crucial antidote for the instability created by the clash of the so-called modern and traditional systems.[28] Their projects tended to concentrate on second-generation migrants, diagnosing the children and youth as caught between their parents' desire to preserve cultural traditions and the influence of modern German society.[29] Because of their

---

[26] Ibid., 108.

[27] Ibid., 115–25.

[28] The most important systems-theory-oriented studies of integration are: Hans-Joachim Hoffmann-Nowotny, *Soziologie des Fremdarbeiterproblems* (Stuttgart: Enke, 1973); Hartmut Esser, Eduard Gaugler, and Karl Heinz Neumann, eds., *Arbeitsmigration und Integration. Sozialwissenschaftliche Grundlagen* (Konigstein: Hanstein, 1979); and Hartmut Esser, *Aspekte der Wanderungssoziologie. Assimilation und Integration von Wanderern, ethnischen Gruppen und Minderheiten* (Darmstadt: Luchterhand, 1980).

[29] Some of the earliest and most significant empirical studies of guest workers and their families include: Bundesanstalt für Arbeit, ed., *Repräsentativuntersuchung 1972 über die Beschäftigung ausländischer Arbeitnehmer im Bundesgebiet und ihre Familien- und Wohnverhältnisse* (Nuremberg: Bundesanstalt für Arbeit, 1973); Ursula Mehrländer, *Soziale Aspekte der Ausländerbeschäftigung* (Bonn: Verlag Neue Gesellschaft, 1974); and Ursula Boos-Nünning, Manfred Hohmann, and R. Reich, eds., *Schulbildung ausländischer Kinder* (Bonn: Eichholz Verlag, 1976).

liminal status, these researchers surmised, foreign children possessed a greater propensity for social conflict, which could manifest itself in unemployment, delinquency, crime, and even violence. Schools functioned as particularly important sites of integration because they offered the primary point of contact between migrant children and West German society. Thus, schools were quickly identified as a valuable tool for preventing widespread social dysfunction. Experts urged integration through intercultural education (*interkulturelle Erziehung*), a pedagogical approach which "awake[n]s understanding for foreign cultures and traditions, dismantles prejudices and nationalisms, facilitates tolerance for the strange and different."[30] Intercultural pedagogical strategies rejected separate classrooms for foreign and German children and insisted on ethnically diverse learning environments, which could foster interaction and communication between different cultural groups. Gradually, the terms of debate and recommendations generated by this body of research began to appear in policy proposals and political statements.[31]

By the mid-1970s, every major West German political party had adopted integrationist rhetoric in formulating their positions on the guest worker question. At the same time, each inflected integration with very different meanings and proposed distinct approaches to coping with the long-term presence of resident aliens. The CDU, which had dominated federal politics as the majority party in the ruling coalitions from 1949 to 1966, played a crucial role in drawing up and implementing West Germany's recruitment program. But it was not until 1977, two years later than the Social Democrats and Free Democrats, that the CDU began to address the need for a framework other than labor interests and to articulate its first foreigner policy (*Ausländerpolitik*).

Above all, the CDU advocated the peaceful coexistence of Germans and foreigners. It specifically invoked social integration as a key to this goal, a choice of terms which suggested that the party now acknowledged the impact of guest workers well beyond the economic sector. Yet

---

[30] Helmut Essinger and Achim Hellmich, "Unterrichtsmaterialien und -medien für eine interkulturelle Erziehung," in Helmut Essinger and Achim Hellmich, *Ausländer im Konflikt* (Konigstein: Athenaeum, 1981), 100, quoted in O'Brien, "Paradoxical Paradigm," 151. O'Brien claims here that underlying the development of intercultural education was the belief that foreign families were incapable of socializing their children properly because they remained stuck in their traditional worldview.

[31] O'Brien, in particular, brings together social scientific research, the paradigm of integration, and politics. I am indebted to his synthetic work, but want to fine-tune its scope and the argument it makes about causality and agency.

Christian Democrats failed to offer a straightforward explanation of what they envisioned. "Social integration," the party statement awkwardly proclaimed, "does not mean an assimilation which works toward making foreign workers and their families into Germans. To the concept of social integration also belongs the preservation and support of the foreign workers and their families' ability to reintegrate."[32] The CDU here repudiated any efforts to transform guest workers into Germans and encouraged foreigners to preserve their national and cultural identifications so that they might eventually return to their homelands.

In the same document the CDU presented more concrete policy proposals that were designed to facilitate peaceful coexistence – or at least to prevent open hostility between natives and foreigners. As an attempt to provide an "equal" footing for guest workers in West German social life, the CDU endorsed easier procedures for family reunions, a repeal of the *Stichtag* for foreign youth, more intensive language instruction for non-German children, better housing arrangements, and leisure activities open to both Germans and foreigners. These propositions reversed many of the consolidation measures from the first half of the 1970s and sought to alleviate the most glaring social disadvantages faced by guest workers. The Christian Democratic party, in other words, emphasized a program of provisional integration that sought to ensure a conflict-free society but clung to the possibility that foreigners would ultimately leave.

The FDP, which shared power with the CDU until 1966 and with the SPD from 1969 until 1982, considered the guest worker question from a classical liberal perspective, advocating an approach to foreigners based on a model of fundamental rights and equal protections. In its first statement of *Ausländerpolitik*, the party singled out the issue of unlimited residence permits. It argued that guest workers should have the right of unlimited residence after only three years of employment as long as they demonstrated recognizable integration into German society.[33] In contrast to the CDU's idea of integration, which involved the conflict-free coexistence of radically different, discrete cultures, the FDP's conception emphasized an acceptance of and respect for liberal, democratic principles. While integration did not demand a wholesale renunciation of foreigners' own cultural identities, it did require abandoning any traditional custom that conflicted with basic human rights or values. By following

---

[32] CDU, *Konzept der CDU Ausländerpolitik* (Bonn, 1977), 3, quoted in Unger, *Ausländerpolitik*, 21.

[33] Unger, *Ausländerpolitik*, 25–29.

these tenets, guest workers earned the privilege to enjoy the freedoms and opportunities of West German society.

From 1969 to 1982, the SPD was the dominant party in coalition with the FDP and exercised the greatest influence on guest worker policy at the federal level. In its 1975 platform the party posited integration as a dual process: on the one hand, foreigners needed to become familiar with and accept the customs of Germans; on the other hand, Germans had to adjust to the permanent presence of foreigners and find out more about them.[34] Social Democrats, that is, envisioned a coexistence of multiple cultures grounded in empathy and tolerance and viewed the interaction and exchange between these cultures as a prerequisite for successful integration. While the FDP defined integration in terms of adjustments made by foreigners to German liberal democracy, the SPD understood it as a give-and-take process that involved change not only on the part of guest workers but also on the part of Germans.

By 1978, the Social Democratic Chancellor Helmut Schmidt made this version of integration a centerpiece of his domestic agenda. Under his stewardship that year the Bundestag passed the Verfestigungsregel (Stabilization Statute), which secured the possibility for foreigners to obtain unrestricted residence permits and laid out clear requirements and procedures for such applications. Schmidt also created a new government position, the *Ausländerbeauftragter* (Commissioner for Foreigners' Affairs), to fight for the interests of foreigners at the federal level and organize and promote national integration efforts. Although this post did not have the authority to transform its recommendations into policy, the commissioner became a major player in directing and shaping the federal government's stance on the guest worker question.

Integration as Discourse and Policy

The incorporation of integration into public discourse signaled a fundamental change in the guest worker question from thinking of foreigners as labor to understanding them as residents and families. Social scientific research and governmental policymaking, however, were not the only sites where this reconfiguration took place. One good example is Aras Ören's *Berlin Trilogie*, in which the second and third installments increasingly focus on the broader, family-based challenges of permanent residence (as opposed to male-dominated labor struggles). Indeed, the fact that Ören's

[34] Ibid., 37.

literary celebrity during the late 1970s went hand-in-hand with his new emphasis on spouses, children, and citizenship suggests that the larger discourse of integration was never simply a political issue sparked by social scientific recommendations. While government-sponsored studies reformulated the *Gastarbeiter* question as one of integration rather than labor, the Federal Republic's leading minority intellectual brought the complexities of integration to the German reading public.[35]

Other pockets of West German society also helped push this ideological turn, especially those sectors that dealt with foreigners at the grassroots level. As principal providers of social services in the Federal Republic, charity organizations (*Wohlfahrtsverbände*) were among the first to recognize and address the practical difficulties encountered by guest workers.[36] The charitable arm of the Roman Catholic Church, Caritas, began to minister to Italian workers as soon as the 1955 recruitment treaty went into effect. It initially opened five advice centers throughout the Federal Republic and rapidly expanded both its base of operations and the people whom it served. By the fall of 1975, Caritas supported 293 counseling centers with 340 social workers and extended its aid to Spanish, Portuguese, and other Catholic foreigners. In addition to establishing these offices, Caritas also supplied social welfare workers to supervise dormitories for female guest workers.[37]

Diakonisches Werk, the Protestant charity organization, offered help to foreigners on a case-by-case basis starting in 1957. Specifically targeting Greek laborers, it formalized its services in the early 1960s as that national population grew. Arbeiterwohlfahrt, the SPD's charitable association, commenced its activities on behalf of guest workers in 1962 when it established advice centers for Turks. It broadened its efforts to include aid for other Muslim foreigners throughout the decade, especially Yugoslavians,

---

[35] One pitfall of O'Brien's emphasis on the role of social scientists in directing political policy is an obfuscation of the agency of Turks and other minorities. He ultimately argues that Turks had very little voice in policies that affected them – and to the extent that they were able to articulate their concerns, were forced to use the language of integration set out by the social scientists. Once we see the discourse of integration emerging from a wider array of areas in West German society, the question of Turks' position within the discourse is not so easily confined to contesting a policy agenda that has been imposed upon them. See O'Brien, "Paradoxical Paradigm," 221–25, 267–81.

[36] Unger, *Ausländerpolitik*, 57–76, 82–95. For a specific discussion of churches in the field of German social welfare work, see Franziska Dunkel and Gabriella Stramaglia-Faggion, *Zur Geschichte der Gastarbeiter in München: "Für 50 Mark einen Italiener"* (Munich: Buchendorfer Verlag, 2000), 185–206.

[37] For more on the role of Caritas in offering social welfare to Italian guest workers, see Yvonne Rieker, *Ein Stück Heimat findet man ja immer: Die italienische Einwanderung in die Bundesrepublik* (Essen: Klartext, 2003), 71–81.

Tunisians, and Moroccans. By the end of 1976, the Arbeiterwohlfahrt ran 146 counseling centers, 78 of which exclusively served Turks.

The activities of the *Wohlfahrtsverbände*, political scientist Dietrich Thränhardt has argued, initially relieved state and local authorities of the obligation to care for the social needs of recruited laborers.[38] At first, these charity organizations emphasized assistance to foreign workers that facilitated their dealings with German bureaucracy and helped them adapt to life in the Federal Republic in the most basic sense. Services included translation, German language classes, counseling on legal rights, apartment rental, unemployment benefits, and job hunting. Working directly with foreigners and often employing foreign social workers, charitable organizations were more informed about the specific challenges facing guest workers outside the workplace than most government agencies during the period of recruitment. Because of this intimate engagement they also registered the impacts of the demographic changes that coincided with economic downturn much earlier than policymakers. The three major charities thus stood better equipped to deal with long-term aspects of foreigner settlement (housing, education, second generation) and increasingly stressed programs to foster the broader social integration of foreign families and youth.

In addition to charitable associations, the German Trade Union Federation also extended aid to foreign workers. As the central organization representing labor interests in the Federal Republic, the DGB took an active interest in guest workers from the very beginning of recruitment.[39] Indeed, once it accepted the principle of employing foreign laborers, the DGB turned its attention to the needs and problems of guest workers.

[38] Dietrich Thränhardt, "Patterns of Organization among Different Ethnic Minorities," *New German Critique* 46 (1989): 15–16. For a broader discussion of the place of charity organizations in West German society, see Dietrich Thränhardt, Wolfgang Gernert, Rolf G. Heinze, Franz Koch, and Thomas Olk, eds., *Wohlfahrtsverbände zwischen Selbsthilfe und Sozialstaat* (Freiburg: Lambertus Verlag, 1986); and Dietrich Thränhardt, "Established Charity Organizations, Self-Help Groups and New Social Movements in Germany," Working Paper 3, Institut für Politikwissenschaft der westfälischen Wilhelms-Universität Münster, 1987.

[39] The DGB's position was often torn between an ideological commitment to all workers and efforts to protect the interests of the native workforce. It supported the importation of manpower on the grounds that an expanding economy would benefit German laborers, for example, but fought for a policy of equal pay for equal work as well as all basic benefits so that individual employers would not use cheap foreign labor to undercut German workers. For more on the DGB's stance toward guest workers, see Cynthia W. Rolling, "But People Came: Responses to the Guestworkers in the Federal Republic of Germany, 1961–1976" (Ph.D. diss., University of Wisconsin, Madison, 1982), 145–57. See also Stephen Castles and Godula Kosack, *Immigrant Workers and Class Structure in Western Europe*, 2nd ed. (Oxford: Oxford University Press, 1985), 129–31.

Foremost among union concerns was the effort to ease the transition into a new work culture – especially acquainting foreigners with different production methods, standards, and labor practices. But the major trade unions also sought to alleviate difficulties faced by workers outside the factories, establishing special offices to dispense advice on legal, social, and personal problems. By the mid-1970s, the DGB's advisory committee on foreign workers, which included experts from individual unions as well as representatives from regional districts, began to weigh in on the question of integration. Committee leader Heinz Richter enthusiastically supported the integration of foreign workers into the German work world, but at the same time cautioned against assimilation: "We wish to make no Italian, no Turk, no Yugoslav into a German."[40]

More informal efforts to address the concerns of foreigners supplemented the social work of the charities and unions. Between 1969 and 1975, West German society witnessed a proliferation of citizens' initiatives (*Bürgerinitiativen*), spontaneous and loosely organized groups of individuals that operated outside traditional institutions and representative democracy in order to protest, make demands, and coordinate self-help around specific problems or issues in local communities.[41] These initiatives were part of the groundswell of new social movements that included the Greens as well as antinuclear and anti–Vietnam War associations. Unlike student protestors or terrorists who also formed extraparliamentary organizations in this period, members of *Bürgerinitiativen* tended to be motivated not so much by concrete political ideals or goals but by the experience of being personally affected and concerned (*betroffen*).[42] They saw political meaning in personal causes, a point of view which often led

[40] Heinz Richter, "Der DGB und das Gastarbeiterproblem," in Walter Althammer, ed., *Das Gastarbeiterproblem: Rotation? Integration? Arbeitsplatzverlagerung?* (Munich: Eigenverlag der Südosteuropa-Gesellschaft, 1975), 47.

[41] For more on citizens' initiatives, see Bernd Guggenberger, *Bürgerinitiativen in der Parteiendemokratie* (Stuttgart: Kohlhammer, 1980); Jutta A. Helm, "Citizen Lobbies in West Germany," in Peter Merkl, ed., *Western European Party Systems* (New York: Macmillan, 1980), 576–96; Fred Karl, *Die Bürgerinitiativen. Soziale und politische Aspekte einer neuen sozialen Bewegung* (Frankfurt: IMSF, 1981); and Ruud Koopmans, *Democracy from Below: New Social Movements and the Political System in West Germany* (Boulder: Westview Press, 1995).

[42] Saral Sarkar, *Green-Alternative Politics in West Germany*, vol. 1., *The New Social Movements* (Tokyo: United Nations University Press, 1993), 24, 30. For more on the relationship between citizens' initiatives, the New Left, and the emergence of the Greens, see Saral Sarkar, *Green-Alternative Politics in West Germany*, 2 vols. (Tokyo: United Nations University Press, 1993); and Andrei S. Markovits and Philip S. Gorski, *The German Left: Red, Green and Beyond* (Oxford: Oxford University Press, 1993), 99–106.

them to champion traditionally marginalized groups close to home such as the disabled, mentally ill, homeless, drug addicts, children, homosexuals, and foreigners.

Bürgerinitiativen for guest workers stressed "help for self-help" in the form of German language courses, a variety of adult-education classes, translation services, childcare, support groups for youth and women, homework assistance, and legal aid. They often lobbied for and marshaled community resources to create neighborhood centers to house these services. To the extent that citizens' initiatives promoted and facilitated self-help they obtained financial support from all the major political parties, which recognized that such community work eased the burden on governmental authorities.[43] Thus, at roughly the same time that government agencies commissioned studies by social scientists to guide a new politics of integration, charity groups and citizens' initiatives offered crucial sources of support for foreigners' practical needs and problems. They represented the first tangible efforts to integrate guest workers into the fabric of German society.

A significant consequence of all these integration efforts was the proliferation of *Sozialarbeit* (social work) and *Ausländerpädagogik* (foreigner pedagogy) programs at *Fachhochschulen* (technical colleges) throughout the Federal Republic, which served as the main sources of instruction and preparation for anyone interested in working with foreigners.[44] These fields of study emphasized the need to understand the specific backgrounds and customs of guest workers in order to communicate across cultures. They operated on the basic premise that only by establishing intercultural communication could their students design effective ways to help foreigners adapt to German society. According to a survey conducted in 1982, forty-seven out of fifty West German *Fachhochschulen* offered at least a handful of courses relating to foreigners, and almost three-quarters of them had fully developed study tracks in *Ausländerpädagogik* that required language courses and internships.[45] During the 1970s, social pedagogy became the key field of study both for teachers who wanted to

---

[43] For more on the response of political parties to the emergence of citizens' initiatives, see Sarkar, *Green-Alternative Politics*, vol. 1, 32–35.

[44] In the early 1980s, a number of studies were undertaken to assess the kinds of training offered for social work and social pedagogy at *Fachhochschulen*. See Samir Akel, Maria Arnsberg, Gerda Leitmann, Hans Pfaffenberger, and Friedemann Tiedt, eds., *Sozialarbeit mit Deutschen und Ausländern – eine Aufgabe für Aus- und Fortbildung* (Stuttgart: Robert Bosch Stiftung, 1982).

[45] Akel et al., *Sozialarbeit mit Deutschen und Ausländern*, 53–58.

develop culturally diverse perspectives in their curricula and for social
workers who were employed by charity organizations, ran citizens' initiative projects, and staffed the federal as well as local and state offices of
the *Ausländerbeauftragten*.

Perhaps the best evidence of the shift in the public discourse toward
integration is the way that politics, social welfare, and culture were intricately interwoven during this period. In 1979, the newly installed federal
Ausländerbeauftragter Heinz Kühn released a memorandum that condemned government policy for failing to admit or take responsibility for
the social consequences of the labor recruitment. Kühn openly criticized
its approach for being "obviously too much shaped by the priority of political, labor-market points of view," which he claimed resulted in measures
that alternated between "consolidation" and "temporary" integration.[46]
Kühn proclaimed: "here a development has occurred that is *no longer
reversible*, and the majority of those affected are no longer 'guest workers'
but rather immigrants."[47] This statement marked a major watershed in
the official thinking on the guest worker question. It recognized the inadequacy of treating foreign recruits solely as an expedient labor market
corrective and, for the first time, publicly acknowledged their long-term,
permanent presence in West German society.

Recognition of de facto immigration, Kühn argued, required a complete reorientation of foreigner policy toward making guest workers and
their families into full members of West German society. He proposed
an intensification of integrative measures through the schools, the elim-
ination of all segregation, the optional right for foreign youth to be
naturalized, and the support of foreigners' political rights through local
voting.[48] His recommendations for an "unconditional and enduring integration" targeted specifically second- and third-generation migrants. He
thus stressed the urgent need for programs at the preschool, school, and
vocational training levels that would enable young foreigners to overcome
language difficulties, obtain the best possible education, and give them
equal opportunities for success in West Germany.[49] Drawing on social
scientists' arguments in favor of *interkulturelle Erziehung*, Kühn called

---

[46] Heinz Kühn, *Stand und Weiterentwicklung der Integration der ausländischen Arbeitnehmer und ihrer Familien in der Bundesrepublik Deutschland. Memorandum des Beauf-
tragten der Bundesregierung* (Bonn, 1979), 2, 11. Kühn had been president of North
Rhine-Westphalia until 1978.
[47] Ibid., 15. My emphasis.
[48] Ibid., 3–4.
[49] More than half of the section outlining Kühn's policy recommendations was devoted to
educational issues. Ibid., 18–36.

for the creation of five thousand teaching positions devoted to multinational education.

Kühn's agenda, which was eventually adopted as part of the SPD's political platform, placed cultural understanding at the very center of its push for integration. It proposed teaching German and foreign pupils together in ethnically mixed classrooms and advocated a curriculum that would incorporate the range of customs and traditions practiced by the Federal Republic's migrant groups. His educational program sought to convey the idea that cultures differ but are not superior or inferior to one another. Kühn suggested that integration would only occur through more openness and knowledge about how other cultures worked – understanding cultures, in other words, drove integration.

The appearance of the Kühn memorandum coincided with ecumenical efforts to promote a similar vision of West German society. In 1978, the Protestant Church organized a nationwide event, the first annual *Tag des ausländischen Mitbürgers* (Day of the Foreign Fellow Citizen), which sought to educate Germans about their foreign fellow citizens. On the appointed day, branches of the Protestant Church throughout the country sponsored informational sessions and performances that celebrated foreigners' cultural traditions as a way to enhance mutual understanding. Integration, these activities suggested, could not be achieved through a one-sided adaptation on the part of non-Germans to German society, but rather required an active exchange between both foreigners and natives. The event's title promoted an alternative to the term *Gastarbeiter*, which had dominated public discourse for the previous twenty years. *Ausländischer Mitbürger* (foreign fellow citizen) marked a clear departure from the initial conception of foreigners as pure labor and temporary guests: the guest worker question had now been redefined as a domestic, social question. But this new term was no less fraught than the old label. *Mitbürger* could also be translated as "co-citizen," which is not quite the same as a straightforward "citizen" (*Bürger*). Thus, the expression tacitly acknowledged migrants as permanent residents by calling them "citizens," and at the same time doubly distinguished them from "true" German citizens by invoking their foreignness and qualifying their citizenship status.

Modes of Minority Literature

This same period witnessed a proliferation of groups promoting minority cultural expression, and some of these groups served as institutional vehicles for the integrationist ideology and policy goals articulated by politicians such as Kühn. But what becomes clear as soon as we look at the broader spectrum of minority cultural production is that there was no consensus about either the desirability or the specific terms of integration. While some groups responded to Kühn's mandate by promoting German literature by non-Germans as an instrument to create *ausländische Mitbürger*, others advocated high literature and classical philosophy as vehicles for cultural synthesis, and still others dismissed integration as altogether outside their range of interests.

The University of Munich's Institut für Deutsch als Fremdsprache (DaF) was one important group that encouraged minority cultural expression in the late 1970s. DaF at Munich was established in 1978 with funds from the German Academic Exchange Service and the Goethe Institute by a group of literature professors interested in *interkulturelle Germanistik* (intercultural German literature). This subject had become a formal area of study around 1970, when the Federal Republic's Wissenschaftsrat (Scientific Advisory Council) enjoined German literary scholars to differentiate between German for native speakers and German as a foreign language. Professor Alois Wierlacher, then at the University of Heidelberg, led the effort to theorize the subfield of *interkulturelle Germanistik*, elevating German as a foreign language from didactic language instruction to a kind of cultural anthropology that would offer multiple perspectives on German literature. The emphasis on German as a foreign language seems to have grown out of a new awareness that the study of German was now an academic field around the world.[50] Yet the primary concern remained engagement with German as a national literature, rather than the more international approach associated with comparative literature. In this sense, the development of *interkulturelle Germanistik* was at once outward looking and inward focused.

In dialogue with Wierlacher, the professors at the Munich Institute stressed cultural diversity as an important aspect of studying German and championed the interpretive method of hermeneutics as a key tool for understanding different cultural forms and modes of expression.[51] The Munich group, however, was more self-conscious and explicit about

---

[50] Alois Wierlacher, "Zur Entwicklungsgeschichte und Systematik interkultureller Germanistik (1984–1994)," *Jahrbuch Deutsch als Fremdsprache* 20 (1994): 37–56.
[51] Hermeneutics as an interpretive method often frames the relationship between an interpreter and the text to be interpreted as a kind of dialogue, the point of which is to bridge the divide inherent between them. For more on the ways that scholars in the U.S. have thought about hermeneutics in relation to literary studies, ethnic studies, and minorities in Germany, see Adelson, *The Turkish Turn*, 23–26.

this intellectual program's connection to issues facing contemporary West German society: "We know that two million guest workers in the Federal Republic are learning – mostly in rudimentary form – to speak German as a foreign language one way or another."[52] In many respects, the creation of DaF put the intercultural and contemporary concerns of these professors to practical use. One of the first university-level institutions to study the teaching and acquisition of German as a foreign language, the Munich Institute regularly confronted issues of cultural difference and communication across multiple languages and traditions – after all, its work included training language instructors and teaching foreign students.

The inaugural director of DaF in Munich was Harald Weinrich, a professor of Romance languages and literatures who had previously written on Cervantes and Racine. Under his leadership, the Institute emphasized a wider scope for linguistic understanding, focusing on applied forms of language use rather than on the rules of grammar. The key to this approach was the insistence that linguistic and literary studies must be brought together: literature, in the DaF model, would serve as a crucial vehicle for making language – and language acquisition – more meaningful. The Munich Institute's first academic director, Irmgard Ackermann, a scholar of German literature whose early work focused on drama, combined these traditionally distinct fields by organizing writing contests that invited nonnative German speakers to submit literary works in German. DaF announced the first competition in 1979, calling for submissions on the subject of "Germany – A Foreign Country," and held a second contest in 1980 on the topic "As a Foreigner in Germany."[53] Together the contests elicited about 220 entries from a wide range of people, including an American exchange student, an Italian guest worker, a Chinese teacher of German, a Cameroonian doctoral candidate, a professor of German from New Zealand, and a child of Turkish labor recruits. These entries offered specific examples of the process of learning a foreign language through producing literature, and thus provided DaF scholars with

---

[52] Harald Weinrich, "Deutsch als Fremdsprache: Konturen eines neues Faches," *Jahrbuch Deutsch als Fremdsprache* 5 (1979): 8–9.
[53] The Institute publicized these writing competitions through posters as well as scattered newspaper and radio advertisements. See Harald Weinrich, "Foreword," in Irmgard Ackermann, ed., *Als Fremder in Deutschland: Berichte, Erzählungen, Gedichte von Ausländern* (Munich: DTV, 1982), 10; and Irmgard Ackermann, "In zwei Sprachen leben: Ein literarisches Preisausschreiben für Ausländer," *Stimmen der Zeit* 108.7 (1983): 443–46.

a body of sources from which to theorize connections between literature and language acquisition.

Almost immediately, however, Ackermann and Weinrich began to expand their interest in literature written by foreigners beyond the initial pedagogical program. The competitions, in a sense, provided raw material from which to construct their own literature-based theory of integration. This process took place in two stages: first they theorized the function of writing, and then they enlisted a major German publishing house to make these texts commercially available – which, in turn, fostered new modes of intercultural reading. Weinrich interpreted the contest submissions as contributions to an alternative German literature: "there is... a strong literary desire to express oneself in the German language even on the part of many members of other nations, who have learned German as a foreign language and want to make use of our language, not only when they need to ask directions to the train station on the street. We can call this literature... a German guest literature."[54] In this view, "guest" literature was not defined in terms of specific content, but by the fact that its authors came from "other nations" and learned German. Weinrich also suggested that these texts shared a similar approach to writing and language. They moved beyond the use of German for mundane or utilitarian purposes ("asking directions to the train station") and demonstrated a desire to become immersed in another culture ("expressing oneself in German"). The act of literary creation enabled the foreign writer to enter the German cultural fabric, contribute to it, partake of it, and be a part of it, even if only in a temporary and incomplete way. The Munich Institute's pedagogical program, in other words, did not simply teach German for practical ends à la Berlitz or Goethe Institute language courses, but for the sake of something more substantial and significant – for literature.

In a 1983 essay Ackermann began to describe the products of this process as guest worker literature. Her choice of terms was not particularly surprising since many of the contest entries came from people affiliated with the labor recruitment. By connecting foreigner writing to the labor migration she also began to articulate how literature might function as part of the SPD's mandates of the late 1970s. What made these writings especially powerful, according to Ackermann, was the personal involvement (*Betroffenheit*) of their authors, which imbued this literature with

---

[54] Weinrich, "Foreword," 9.

"its authenticity and immediacy, its true-to-life nature and its breath."[55] Because this literature emerged in a political situation in which foreigners lacked rights, long-term residence visas, and equal opportunities, it transcended purely personal experiences of being foreign and served as a vehicle for consciousness-raising and change. Living between German culture and their native culture enabled writers to translate one for the other, and consequently, this new literature contained the potential to facilitate integration. In directing their work toward German readers, "foreign writers of the German language could contribute much...to raise consciousness about foreigner integration as a reciprocal process which includes all areas of life."[56] Writing and integration, in this view, were part of the same larger ideological process. Migrant authors helped Germans see their culture from the other side, an essential perspective if intercultural communication was to proceed in earnest.[57]

Until Ackermann's 1983 essay, the Munich Institute's theory of writing remained largely inchoate and tended to be framed in terms of pedagogy. One crucial question, then, is how DaF went from a teaching and learning center to a packager and promoter of a much more carefully defined category of *Ausländerliteratur*. In addressing this question it is important to acknowledge that there were quite a few other sites and associations that facilitated writing by foreigners. Ackermann herself identified a handful of specific authors, nine anthologies, and ten literary journals that fit under the rubric of guest worker literature but did not have formal ties to DaF initiatives.[58] Thus, to fully understand the Munich Institute's emerging

---

[55] Irmgard Ackermann, "'Gastarbeiter'literatur als Herausforderung," *Frankfurter Hefte* 1 (1983): 58.

[56] Ibid., 64.

[57] My point in this chapter is to show how political debate around guest workers intersected with theories about the function of cultural texts produced by migrants, a project that illuminates the broader ideological stakes of integration and integrationist politics. Other scholars have focused more squarely on cultural and philosophical stakes of minority writing in the Federal Republic. See, in particular, Ülker Gökberk, "Understanding Alterity: *Ausländerliteratur* between Relativism and Universalism," in David Perkins, ed., *Theoretical Issues in Literary History* (Cambridge, MA: Harvard University Press, 1991), 143–72; Ülker Gökberk, "Encounters with the Other in German Cultural Discourse: Interkulturelle Germanistik and Aysel Özakin's Journeys of Exile," in Karen Jankowsky and Carla Love, eds., *Other Germanies: Questioning Identity in Women's Literature and Art* (Albany, NY: SUNY Press, 1997), 19–55; Azade Seyhan, *Writing Outside the Nation* (Princeton: Princeton University Press, 2001); and Adelson, *The Turkish Turn*.

[58] Ackermann's examples encompassed everything from Turkish authors working in Turkey to Turkish-German writers living in Germany, unknown guest workers as well as leading intellectuals. In addition to Turks, she included Syrians, Italians, and Czechs. Specifically,

conception of writing – and its relation to the politics of integration – it is useful to consider a range of contemporaneous frameworks and their ideological implications.

What Ackermann's discussion of guest worker literature implied but did not make explicit is that many different modes of minority literature existed during this period and each envisioned its own form and function for literary production. Among the earliest figures to articulate a crucial role for a literature written by Turks in the Federal Republic was Yüksel Pazarkaya, a Turk who came to West Germany as an exchange student. Supported by a Turkish state fellowship, he studied chemistry at the Technische Hochschule in Stuttgart during the early 1960s and later pursued advanced degrees in philosophy and *Germanistik*. Pazarkaya initially dismissed the plight of guest workers as a situation unique to Italians, but once large numbers of Turkish laborers arrived he began to thematize recruitment and migration in his texts. He wrote poetry about his laboring countrymen in both Turkish and German, and by the late 1970s devoted much of his time to a collaboration with Ararat Verlag, a publishing house founded in 1977 by Ahmet Doğan. Known for printing bilingual editions the press sought to bring Turkish language and literature to both German and second-generation Turkish readers. It presented Turkish and German pages side by side in an attempt to encourage German readers' basic familiarity with Turkish as well as Turkish readers' knowledge of German. Pazarkaya served as the primary translator for many of his own works, for those of other Turkish writers living in Germany, and even for well-known texts by major Turkish authors such as Nazim Hikmet and Orhan Veli Kanik.

Ararat Verlag's emphasis on classical Turkish literature and folklore fit well with Pazarkaya's ideas about the function of cross-cultural literary production. Like the scholars at the Munich Institute, Pazarkaya

she listed Aras Ören, Fakir Baykurt, Adalet Agaoğlu, Antonio Skarmeta, Güney Dal, Yusuf Toprakoğlu, Franco Biondi, Jusuf Naoum, Yüksel Pazarkaya, and Vera Kamenko; and various anthologies: Franco Biondi, ed., *Im neuen Land* (Bremen: CON Medien- und Vertriebsgesellschaft, 1980); Förderzentrum Jugend Schreibt, ed., *Täglich eine Reise von der Türkei nach Deutschland* (Fischerhude: Verlag Atelier im Bauernhaus, 1980); Carmine Abate, ed., *Zwischen Fabrik und Bahnhof* (Bremen: CON Medien- und Vertriebsgesellschaft, 1981); Jusuf Naom and Rosi Wolf-Almanasreh, eds., *Sehnsucht im Koffer* (Frankfurt: Fischer, 1981); Christian Schaffernicht, ed., *Zu Hause in der Fremde* (Fischerhude: Verlag Atelier im Bauernhaus, 1981); Carmine Abate and Giuseppe Giambusso, eds., *Wurzeln, hier. Gedichte italienischer Emigranten* (Bremen: CON, 1982); Ackermann, ed., *Als Fremder in Deutschland*. See Ackermann, "'Gastarbeiter' literatur," 56–57.

advocated literature as a site of cultural synthesis, suggesting that these texts might allow Germans and Turks to absorb the best of each civilization and create something totally new:

A genuine synthesis is called for, whereby not only a profound acquaintance with both cultures is necessary, but also a kind of living incarnation into German culture, history, and contemporary life. Actually no one is capable of such a synthesis unless he has made Germany into his second homeland, and the German culture into his second culture. This is certainly a daring thesis which may well seem impossible to readers from both cultures. . . . But whoever thinks in global terms, and believes in human history (*Menschheitsgeschichte*) and human culture (*Menschheitskultur*) as a unity out of variety and difference can expect great new syntheses to come from the pens of the "immigrant" Turkish authors in Germany, whether in Turkish or in German.[59]

As one recent scholar has noted, Pazarkaya's invocation of *Menschheitsgeschichte* and *Menschheitskultur* relied on a universalistic humanism to achieve his "vision of mutual recognition."[60] By underscoring the commonality of artistic creation he insisted that different cultures are never fundamentally incompatible. Pazarkaya's emphasis on "second homelands" and "global terms," moreover, pointed to the creation of cosmopolitan readers. In this view, it was the duty of readers to immerse themselves fully in other national traditions, thereby moving from mere "acquaintance" with the foreign to a more vital absorption and "incarnation" of cultural traditions beyond one's own.

Finally, Pazarkaya believed that this kind of literature might provide a medium for the crucial task of intercultural communication. By being introduced to masterpieces of Turkish literature, German readers would begin to see guest workers in a new light – as the bearers of an important and noteworthy cultural tradition – and perhaps even treat them with more respect. He asserted: "If the German population were . . . sufficiently informed about cultural and intellectual history, about Turkish society, the hatred of Turks would have a less fertile breeding ground."[61] Mutual recognition of intellectual achievement, in other words, would simultaneously facilitate cultural synthesis and preclude ethnic prejudice.

---

[59] Yüksel Pazarkaya, "Ohne die Deutschen wäre Deutschland nicht übel. Der 'Gastarbeiter' und seine Erfahrungen als strittiges Thema der zeitgenössischen türkischen Literatur," *Zeitschrift für Kulturaustausch* 31 (1981): 317, quoted in Teraoka, "Gastarbeiterliteratur," 86.

[60] Teraoka, "Gastarbeiterliteratur," 86.

[61] Yüksel Pazarkaya, *Rosen im Frost. Einblicke in die türkische Kultur* (Zurich: Unionsverlag, 1989), 12.

For both functions, it is important to note, Pazarkaya advanced an explicitly "high" conception of culture. The German culture that he admired and championed was personified by Lessing, Leibniz, Heine, Schiller, Feuerbach, Hegel, Marx, and Brecht – the canonical bearers of Enlightenment values.[62] Similarly, the specific cultural forms that he wanted Germans to apprehend were exemplified by the most revered members of the Turkish literary canon. Pazarkaya's efforts to bring classical Turkish literature to the German reading public represented a radical attempt to push Germans to accept Turks on equal grounds – or at least as heirs to an equally important civilization. Yet by focusing on elite culture, he implied that only the most well educated could accomplish the cultural synthesis and mutual recognition that he envisioned.

Part of this emphasis on high culture seems to have come from Pazarkaya's own privileged position as a government-sponsored university student sent to study in the Federal Republic. As he explained: "for me . . . it was highly upsetting to encounter such countrymen in Germany, who had not come as diplomats, tourists or students, but rather as factory workers. . . . I met them speechless, timid and irritated; they often resembled stranded fish. Hardly any of them knew about industrial work, especially in a highly developed industry like that of the Federal Republic."[63] Pazarkaya's shock here highlights the social and class differences that separated many minority authors writing about guest workers from the subjects of their texts. In this respect, Pazarkaya's propensity for canonical texts starkly demonstrates the deep irony, if not illogic, of classifying his work (and that of most other minority authors) as guest worker literature: he himself was not a guest worker and did not address his writings to them.[64] Although Pazarkaya treated the labor migration as a central

---

[62] Pazarkaya's poem, "deutsche sprache," celebrates Germany as his second homeland and German culture as his second culture, explicitly listing all these figures. Yüksel Pazarkaya, "deutsche sprache," in Schaffernicht, ed., *Zu Hause in der Fremde*, 123.

[63] Yüksel Pazarkaya, "Türkiye, Mutterland – Almanya, Bitterland. Das Phänomen der türkischen Migration als Thema der Literatur," *Zeitschrift für Literaturwissenschaft und Linguistik* 56 (1984): 105.

[64] The fact that Pazarkaya and most other minority writers during this period were not guest workers and directed their works toward a German audience caused many scholars to be dissatisfied with the practice of calling this new literary category "guest worker literature." This misnomer provoked numerous academic debates over exactly what this kind of literature should be called. The suggested possibilities included: *Ausländerliteratur*, *Migrantenliteratur*, and *deutschsprachige Literatur von Autoren nichtdeutscher Muttersprache*. See Helmut Kreuzer, "Gastarbeiter-Literatur, Ausländer-Literatur, Migranten-Literatur? Zur Einführung," *Zeitschrift für Literaturwissenschaft und Linguistik* 56 (1984): 7–11; Teraoka, "Gastarbeiterliteratur"; Suhr, "Ausländerliteratur"; and Adelson, "Migrants' Literature."

topic in his texts and openly pushed for integration in his nonfiction, the thrust of his literary program was a synthesis of elite cultural forms, an impulse which severely limited his readership and the ability of Ararat to sell books. Despite a move from Stuttgart to Berlin to find a more viable market among West Germany's largest Turkish population, by the mid-1980s Ararat Verlag had ceased operations.

The Italian-German writer Franco Biondi championed a radically different conception of minority literature during these very same years. From a family of showmen who performed at farmers' markets and fairs around the Italian countryside, Biondi trained as a metalworker and welder. He left Italy for the Federal Republic in 1965 and was employed as a guest worker near Mainz, first in a chemical factory and subsequently at the car manufacturer Opel. In 1971, he began to take evening classes, earning a high school diploma and then studying psychology in order to become a social worker. Biondi initially wrote about his life in Germany as a kind of hobby in his spare time, but increasingly sought out other Italian migrants interested in articulating their experiences through literature. He published his first stories in 1975 with the help of the newly founded Associazione Letteraria Facoltá Artistiche (ALFA), a group that collected the writings of Italian workers and printed them in its own Italian-language newspaper, *Il Mulino*, and in a series of anthologies, *Panorama della Poesia all'Estero*.[65]

The creation of ALFA sparked a major controversy in the pages of *Corriere d'Italia*, the well-established West German Italian-language newspaper. From 1975 to 1983, a debate raged about the form and function of Italian migrant literature.[66] Some writers wanted to continue ALFA's rather narrow agenda for migrant literature, which promoted literary expression by Italians for Italians. These authors viewed writing as a therapeutic activity; their work tended to emphasize themes such as homesickness, hopelessness, the pain of being separated from their families, and the goal of quick return. From the perspective of these writers, Germany remained an uncertain and threatening place, while their Italian homeland appeared as a glorified *dolce terra*. Another group within

---

[65] In their workbook for the Goethe Institute on Franco Biondi, Rüdiger Krechel and Ulrike Reeg provide a useful overview of Biondi's career and the development of the grass-roots literary associations in which he participated. See Krechel and Reeg, *Franco Biondi* (Munich: Iudicium Verlag, 1989), 8–19.

[66] Franco Biondi offers a detailed summary of "Il Dibattito" that gives a blow-by-blow account of each position. See Biondi, "Von den Tränen zu den Bürgerrechten. Ein Einblick in die italienische Emigrantenliteratur," *Zeitschrift für Literaturwissenschaft und Linguistik* 56 (1984): 81–87.

ALFA argued, by contrast, that minority literature should engage with larger political issues and conceived of writing as an important conduit for discussing and criticizing the social conditions faced by labor migrants in the Federal Republic. For these authors, lyrical retreats to an idealized and irrecoverable past represented a kind of ghettoization rather than an active effort to make their present situation better. In order to establish a dialogue with those outside its immediate circle, this group rejected Italian as its primary literary language and urged its authors to write in German, the language common to guest workers of all nationalities.

These divergent agendas eventually precipitated a rupture within the community of Italian emigrant authors. Biondi spearheaded the push for a multinational conception of literature and, together with a group of compatriots that included Gino Chiellino, Vito d'Adamo, Giuseppe Giambusso, and Carmine Abate, split from those who wanted to write within and for the Italian enclave. In 1980, at Frankfurt's Club Voltaire, Biondi and his followers met with other minority authors and established a registered association called Polynationaler Literatur- und Kunstverein (Polynational Literature and Art Association) – better known as PoLiKunst. This new organization, led by Biondi, the Syrians Rafik Schami and Suleman Taufiq, and the Lebanese Jusuf Naoum, encouraged all forms of cultural production by migrants. The association arranged readings and exhibitions of works by minority artists, organized literature conferences around the country, and published three yearbooks between 1983 and 1985 that brought together literary texts, essays, and art created by its diverse membership. Biondi and company also served as the editorial collective for an anthology series called *Südwind Gastarbeiterdeutsch* (Southwind Guest Worker German), started by the small Bremen publishing house Edition CON around the same time as PoLiKunst.

In many ways, PoLiKunst built on the concerns that Ören had articulated about a decade earlier. Attempting to make the issues of workers visible, the PoLiKunst leaders championed a literature of guest workers that, they claimed, offered an authentic, firsthand critique of the Federal Republic's labor policy and the social consequences it had produced. In a manifesto-like essay, Biondi and Schami explained that the group had deliberately adopted the term "guest worker literature" as a political challenge and reclamation: "We consciously use the term 'guest worker' that has been applied to us in order to expose the irony this term conceals."[67] Like Ören, PoLiKunst also stressed the importance of

---

[67] Franco Biondi and Rafik Schami, "Literatur der Betroffenheit. Bemerkungen zur Gastarbeiterliteratur," in Schaffernicht, ed., *Zu Hause in der Fremde*, 134 n. 1.

a multiethnic working class, inflecting the well-established notion of a common proletarian experience and consciousness with an emphasis on the ethnic diversity of late twentieth-century workers. Global capitalism's demand for manpower, the leaders of PoLiKunst argued, had created a new kind of proletariat, a transnational class of multiethnic laborers. Workers' literature now needed to speak across this diversity, forging communication that would allow both German and recruited laborers to recognize the ways in which an international capitalist system simi-larly affected (*betrifft, betroffen*) them all.[68] "Guest worker literature," asserted Biondi and Schami, offered "the possibility to view our problem not as an individual problem of a Mustafa from Istanbul or a Jannis from Kilkis who had the bad luck of coming at the wrong time, working in the wrong factory, or living in the wrong place, but rather as a collective problem of over four million, of even sixty million citizens of the Federal Republic."[69] This literature not only allowed "individual problems" to be recognized as "collective," but also enabled migrant problems to be under-stood as specifically German problems. The key to bridging these gaps of isolation and nationality was to use German – the common language of this multiethnic proletariat – as the medium of literary expression.

But the PoLiKunst program did not just replicate Ören's project. Whereas Ören came out of the Turkish intelligentsia and added an alter-native voice to New Left critiques of postwar capitalism and material-ism, this was a movement conceived by former workers who had moved through the ranks of the industrial proletariat and wanted to use writing as a mechanism for articulating and solidifying working-class concerns. Whereas Ören made class divisions and ethnicity objects of literary repre-sentation for an educated, primarily German reading public, PoLiKunst aimed to use literature to build a grassroots movement of laborers brought together by the shared sociohistorical experiences embedded in the very language (*gastarbeiterdeutsch*) that guest workers used. At the same time, the leaders of PoLiKunst claimed that *Gastarbeiterliteratur* facilitated "cultural exchange between 'natives' and guest workers" and "direct[ed] itself above all against the one-dimensional, folkloristic figure through which the culture of the guest worker is preferably seen." In addition,

---

[68] Biondi and Schami, in fact, claim that they are only now able to break the long-standing pattern of emigrants writing for their own countrymen in their own language because it is now possible to see immigration as a fundamental consequence of ruling economic relationships. While national literatures might have been understandable in the nineteenth and early twentieth centuries, they are ineffective in finding solutions for the international problem of emigrants. See Biondi and Schami, "Literatur der Betroffenheit," 129.

[69] Ibid., 133.

they suggested, this cultural form was especially necessary because of "the increasing decline of the worker and student movement."[70] A central function of guest worker literature, in this view, was to combat popular perceptions of migrant laborers as "folkloristic figures" and the lack of concern for workers and the working class that set in once the grassroots protest and student movements splintered in the 1970s. For PoLiKunst, self-determination and self-representation were intimately connected: it was impossible to create meaningful social or political change until the laborers themselves gained control of guest worker representations. At the level of policymaking, then, integration remained impracticable until Germans abandoned their one-dimensional image of guest workers and began to think about this process from the perspective of migrants.

The PoLiKunst leadership, however, encountered a number of unforeseen complications as they put their project into practice. The anthologies that they published under the Südwind imprint – *Im neuen Land* (1980), *Zwischen Bahnhof und Fabrik* (1981), *Annäherungen* (1982), and *Zwischen zwei Giganten* (1983) – included texts by authors from many countries, some written in German and some translated (but not acknowledged as such). Although the editors initially insisted that German serve as the lingua franca for a multinational proletarian literature, they quickly realized that most guest workers did not possess the language skills to read or write in German. Thus, in an effort to achieve their political goal of making this literature accessible to "affected" foreign laborers, Südwind also put out two bilingual volumes of poetry in Italian and German.[71] Then, in 1983, the four leaders went even further and changed the name of their series from *Südwind Gastarbeiterdeutsch* to *Südwind Literatur*, a decision that marked a retreat from a literature grounded in, and addressed to, a particular guest worker voice that grew out of the experiences of labor migration. What they seem to have discovered, in other words, was a fundamental disjuncture between shared affliction and shared language: although German factories had served to bring this multinational workforce together in terms of industrial capitalism, the goal of a common voice (and even more, a common literature) to articulate this socioeconomic relationship remained elusive. In 1987, both PoLiKunst and Südwind dissolved.

---

[70] Ibid.
[71] Carmine Abate and Giuseppe Giambusso, *Wurzeln hier*; and Gino Chiellino, ed., *Nach dem Gestern/Dopo ieri. Aus dem Alltag italienischer Emigranten* (Bremen: Con-Verlag, 1983).

The Saarbrücken-based journal *Die Brücke* presented yet another model for promoting minority cultural expression. Founded in 1982 and established as a registered association in 1984, *Die Brücke*'s editor-in-chief was the Turkish-German intellectual Necati Mert. The masthead of the journal featured "*Die Brücke*" in large red type, accompanied by translations of the title into all of the major languages of guest workers (including Turkish, Greek, Spanish, Portuguese, Italian, and Serbian) above, and a statement of its governing principles – "equal rights" and "mutual understanding" – below. The masthead itself provided a window into *Die Brücke*'s conception of integration. At the heart of its program was a vision of a multiethnic coalition bound together by a shared dissatisfaction with contemporary policymaking as well as a desire to promote new forms of interethnic communication.

Like PoLiKunst, *Die Brücke* targeted a culturally diverse readership, but one constituted not so much by workers as by like-minded critics of West German integration policies. Whereas the leaders of PoLiKunst saw their initiatives as emerging organically out of an immigrant worker milieu, created by and for those most directly "affected," the journal did not target any single enclave but instead covered and commented on a wide array of issues – including xenophobia, intercultural education, the treatment of women, generational tensions – that went well beyond labor concerns. What brought this range of topics together was an editorial policy of critique vis-à-vis the patterns of interethnic coexistence that were developing in the early 1980s. In its first few years, the journal condemned the *Ausländerpolitik* advanced by Helmut Kohl's newly elected Christian Democratic government, claiming that it demanded as a condition of integration "the assimilation or absolute cultural submission of those who were affected (*die Betroffenen*), their 'Germanization.'" The editors maintained that public discussions about integration could only be truly meaningful if "foreigners in the Federal Republic were recognized as a minority with their own national cultures and equal rights."[72] A striking cover image for the journal brutally criticized what integrationist policies had produced. In a cartoon-like drawing, it depicted the *Woche der ausländischen Mitbürger* (Week of the Foreign Fellow Citizens) as an event that presented migrants as zoo animals, objects of curiosity which Germans ogled at and photographed from outside the cage (see Figure 2).[73] The cover seemed to suggest that even the more liberal versions of integration (such as that promoted by the Protestant church, which originally

[72] *Die Brücke* 9 (September–October 1982), 2.
[73] *Die Brücke* 38 (August–September 1987).

FIGURE 2. Cover image from the August/September 1987 issue of *Die Brücke*. Courtesy of Die Brücke e.V., www.bruecke-saarbruecken.de, bruecke@handshake.de.

sponsored the event) objectified foreigners and failed to treat them as truly equal dialogue partners. At the same time, Mert in particular chastised Turks for retreating to the "ghetto," lapsing into a nationalism that focused on politics in Turkey rather than working to confront the present challenge of being immigrants in Germany.[74] The journal, in other words, condemned German *Ausländerfeindlichkeit* (xenophobia) and what it termed cultural racism, but simultaneously reproached labor migrants who refused to engage with their immediate political landscape.

The membership and structure of the journal's editorial collective further underscored this ideological program. Unlike PoLiKunst, which was run by migrants and only occasionally included texts by Germans in its publications, *Die Brücke* welcomed the full involvement of anyone – minority or German – sympathetic to its goals and political agenda. At its founding, the journal had six Germans on its board and five others who served as contributing editors. Headquartered in Saarbrücken, its multiethnic staff worked out of Hamburg, Frankfurt, Hannover, Essen, Cologne, Berlin, and a host of smaller cities. *Die Brücke*, in other words, cast a wide net for participation. It privileged collaboration among a diverse group of people who all shared a critical perspective on West Germany's foreigner politics over the particular subject positions of its members – whether worker or intellectual, Turk or German.

In contrast to other models that saw literary and cultural exchange as a precursor to integration in society at large, moreover, *Die Brücke* insisted on equal rights and mutual understanding as the prerequisites for this process. To be sure, the editors regularly supported cultural production through the journal, offering as many migrant authors and artists as possible the opportunity to put their works in a public forum. But they never presented minority literature as the primary vehicle for ideological change. Instead, the editorial collective treated literature and art as alternate modes of critique that coexisted with and reinforced editorials, news reporting, political cartoons, and interviews. In this formulation, minority literature was less a conduit for the cultural synthesis idealized by Pazarkaya or the intercultural communication envisioned by the Munich Institute than a key component of an alternative ideology.

Ultimately, the editors of *Die Brücke* envisioned an ethnic engagement with civil society that did not sacrifice migrants' cultural traditions and social customs. But this dialogue, they contended, could never take place in a public sphere structured by political and legal inequalities and misperceptions of difference on all sides. As they proclaimed, we "want a society on better premises. We want our contribution to it to achieve the shaping of public opinion through practical work. We are not satisfied with demanding something from the ruling state, its social order, and its direct

---

[74] *Die Brücke* 19 (June–July 1984), 5–8.

and indirect institutions. On the contrary: we want to build an alternative, *our* media, OUR INSTITUTIONS."[75] The key to their "alternative"
society was to create organs such as the journal through which more critical information could be exchanged, more accurate images of minority
workers could be conveyed, and thus new modes of social relations could
be fostered.

Beyond these largely grassroots associations, more established and
widely recognized institutions also began to pay attention to the phenomenon of minority literary production in the Federal Republic. One
prominent example was the Institute for Foreign Relations (Institut
für Auslandsbeziehungen, IfA), an organization originally established in
Stuttgart in 1917 (as Deutsche Ausland-Institut) to promote the culture
of Germanness abroad and aid Germany's foreign relations. In 1951, it
abandoned its view of culture as a necessary extension of foreign relations and reconceptualized its work as fostering understanding between
peoples.[76] As part of this new program it built an extensive library collection specializing in foreign cultures; published the journal *Zeitschrift
für Kulturaustausch* (Journal for Cultural Exchange), which reported on
international cultural relations; hosted leading non-German artists and
intellectuals; organized art exhibitions and foreign film series; and played
a central role in the city of Stuttgart's annual Third-World Day. All these
resources and events aimed to bring Germans into contact and familiarize
them with distant cultures. Initially, the institute focused on Germany's
Western neighbors and allies such as the United States, France, and Great
Britain. But after the Second World War, it expanded its scope to include
East Germany and Israel as well as countries in Central and South America, Africa, and Asia.[77]

Between 1974 and 1985, IfA devoted three special issues of its journal
to the question of foreigners in Germany: "Foreign Cultural Politics at
Home: Foreign Workers" (1974), "Turks in Germany – Aspects of the
Migration of a People" (1981), and "But the Foreign Is in Me: Migration
Experience and the Image of Germany in Turkish Contemporary Literature" (1985). These volumes suggested a kind of uncertainty about critical distinctions – Self/Other, native/foreign, German/Turk. Because IfA's
entire mission was devoted to German relations with foreigners outside

---

[75] *Die Brücke* 29 (February–March 1986), 3.
[76] Institut für Auslandsbeziehungen, "75 Jahre Institut für Auslandsbeziehungen Stuttgart,
1917 bis 1992," *Sonderdruck aus der Zeitschrift für Kulturaustausch* 1 (1992): 6.
[77] Ibid., 6–15.

the boundaries of the nation, it was a radical decision to focus even one issue of the *Zeitschrift für Kulturaustausch* on guest workers in the Federal Republic. In so doing, the Stuttgart Institute made an enormous epistemological leap: to acknowledge the foreign within the national body was also to problematize the notion of a rigidly homogeneous West German Self. Explaining the significance of the 1974 volume's title, for example, the editor Ernst Tetsch stated that "'Foreign Cultural Politics at Home' is intended to provoke surprise at first; after all this seems to be a contradiction in itself. The second, amplifying part of the title's formulation, 'Foreign Workers,' nevertheless signals connections and simultaneously cancels the supposed contradiction."[78] Tetsch's comments here reflected a growing self-consciousness about the transnational ties of politics and culture created and transmitted through the influx of foreign workers. They suggested that the traditional distinctions of foreign and domestic were no longer adequate tools for making sense of the labor migration. At the same time, by drawing the reader's attention to the contradiction, Tetsch reinforced the idea that foreign laborers remained distinct from Germans. The implication that the presence of guest workers represented a kind of incursion of foreign policy into the domestic arena probably seemed natural in 1974, as West German society was just beginning to register the long-term residence of millions of foreigners after the *Anwerbestopp*. It appeared somewhat more curious in 1985, however, more than six years after the appointment of the federal Commissioner for Foreigners' Affairs and the inauguration of an official integration policy.

The journal's 1985 special issue solicited essays by many of the key promoters of minority literature, including Weinrich, Ackermann, and Pazarkaya. It also contained literary texts by at least fifty-eight Turkish authors working in the Federal Republic, many of whom had already entered Munich Institute contests and published pieces in the PoLiKunst yearbooks and *Die Brücke*. What is immediately striking about the volume is that it placed this body of work within the framework of "contemporary Turkish literature," a rubric that continued to insist on clear cultural distinctions between German and Turkish rather than formulate a new category created by the migration itself. In fact, Günter Lorenz, who coedited the volume with Pazarkaya, attempted to reassert IfA's emphasis on foreigners abroad by celebrating this literature as a vehicle for improving German-Turkish foreign relations. After describing the

[78] Ernst J. Tetsch, "Editorial," *Zeitschrift für Kulturaustausch* 24.3 (1974): 3.

history of friendly alliance and exchange between the two countries, he acknowledged new tensions arising from the treatment Turkish guest workers received in the Federal Republic. These writings, Lorenz suggested, marked a move away from the traditional enthusiasm toward all things German in Turkish literature. Warning that "even a positive image of Germany that still dominates in Turkey in spite of everything is not necessarily formed for all eternity," Lorenz charged that these texts "should ... awaken shame in the German reader and, more important still, a readiness for rethinking, for a more just encounter with the Turkish people who live among and next to us."[79] In his view, the literary works by Turks provided an outsider's perspective on the handling of foreign labor recruits, giving Germans an incentive to change their behavior toward guest workers in order to shore up their image in the eyes of a longstanding ally.

It might strike us as somewhat odd that Pazarkaya, a figure who championed cultural synthesis, would coedit a special issue that stressed the boundaries between Turkish and German literature. But these distinctions made sense considering his ideas about the function of minority cultural production. Although he promoted synthesis in the long term, his goal of cultural mixing first required identifying an independent Turkish culture worthy of participating in exchange with its German counterpart. In his essay for the volume, Pazarkaya categorized writings by Turks in the Federal Republic as a new Turkish literature, a decision that privileged the country and culture of origin of these authors over the immediate context (and in some cases, language) in which they produced their works. But it is also worth pointing out that his ideas were somewhat malleable. Emphasizing the theme of Turkish migration to describe the very same texts, Pazarkaya had published a virtually identical essay the year before in a special issue of *Zeitschrift für Literaturwissenschaft und Linguistik* (Journal of Literary Scholarship and Linguistics) on *Gastarbeiterliteratur*, a genre that its editor explicitly tied to the specific West German social consequences of the labor recruitment.[80]

---

79 Günter W. Lorenz, "Ein Freund gibt Grund zur Klage: Das Deutschlandbild in der Türkei oder Wie man einen guten Ruf aufs Spiel setzt," *Zeitschrift für Kulturaustausch* 35.1 (1985): 10.

80 Compare Yüksel Pazarkaya, "Stimmen des Zorns und der Einsamkeit in Bitterland. Wie die Bundesrepublik Deutschland zum Thema der neuen türkischen Literatur wurde," *Zeitschrift für Kulturaustausch* 35 (1985): 16–27, to Pazarkaya, "Türkiye, Mutterland – Almanya, Bitterland. Das Phänomen der türkischen Migration als Thema der Literatur," *Zeitschrift für Literaturwissenschaft und Linguistik* 56 (1984): 101–24.

In many respects, this special issue of *Zeitschrift für Kulturaustausch* marked the limits of the Stuttgart Institute's mission. Even as it insisted on characterizing the literary works that it contained as Turkish, its title subtly acknowledged a far more complicated situation – namely, that "The Foreign Is in Me." This rather bold assertion in the 1985 volume remained unclear about exactly whom the foreign had penetrated. The title's indeterminacy hinted at the possibility that the migration experience affected Germans and guest workers alike, forcing both to absorb and register cultural difference. This conception of migration and its cultural consequences, however, undermined IfA's raison d'être: to treat guest worker perspectives as an internalized part of the German Self was to transcend the very notion that these internalized guest worker perspectives had anything to do with "foreign cultures" anymore. Significantly, the Stuttgart Institute ceased to cover issues related to guest workers at this juncture, refocusing its programming on German relations with foreigners abroad.[81] This decision ultimately signaled that the guest worker question was outside its institutional scope, an assumption that in turn relied on the more basic premise that the promotion of cross-cultural understanding could only be facilitated in relation to countries and peoples who were identified as fully external. Somewhat paradoxically, IfA continued to offer services in Stuttgart to promote mutual understanding between Germans and more conventionally defined foreigners.[82] In a sense, the third special issue stretched the binary opposition between "German" and "foreign" about as far as it could go without abandoning the distinction all together.

Before about 1985, then, minority literature served as a cultural form through which different groups articulated very different conceptions of how integration might take place – from Pazarkaya, who championed cosmopolitan connoisseurs, to an organization like ALFA, which rejected

[81] While conducting research at the Institut für Auslandsbeziehungen during the summer of 2000, I had occasion to speak with the director of the library, Gudrun Czekalla. She stated that since the mid-1980s, IfA had ceased collecting materials on guest workers or the labor migration. Those topics, she maintained, no longer lay within the purview of the institute, which only dealt with issues and subjects related to Germany's *foreign* relations. Interview with the author, 19 July 2000.

[82] IfA's ultimate rejection of the foreigner within is an example of one of the classic dilemmas of first-generation multicultural thinking. Mike Davis makes a similar point in the context of Los Angeles, which holds numerous multicultural festivals to celebrate the foreign, but the foreign they celebrate almost always references an external foreign and obfuscates the internal foreign. See Mike Davis, *City of Quartz: Excavating the Future in Los Angeles* (London: Verso, 1990).

the very idea that Italian migrants would want to share their experiences with Germans. These modes, however, were never fully distinct. On a structural level, the literary contests organized by Ackermann through the Munich Institute in the late 1970s and early 1980s served as a kind of clearinghouse, bundling together authors with radically different ideas about minority literature. Based on these competitions, DaF produced three anthologies containing the texts of 125 non-German authors: *Als Fremder in Deutschland* (As a Foreigner in Germany, 1982), *In zwei Sprachen leben* (Living in Two Languages, 1983), and *Türken deutscher Sprache* (German-Speaking Turks, 1984), all edited by Ackermann and published by DTV. The volumes, appearing under the imprint of this widely distributed and powerful press, created a niche for minority literature within the mainstream publishing industry and literary marketplace. At the same time, Ackermann and Weinrich wrote numerous state-of-the-field essays for such well-known journals as *Merkur, Stimmen der Zeit,* and *Zeitschrift für Literaturwissenschaft und Linguistik*, which alerted other academics and educated Germans to the existence of this literary phenomenon.[83]

At the level of ideology, too, there were some continuities. Almost all of these conceptions of minority literature relied on a binary distinction between German Self and migrant Other. They advocated intercultural exchange, cultural synthesis, and cooperation among ethnicities in ways that complicated and stretched, but nonetheless remained within, a binary framework. Insofar as they viewed minority literature as a tool for promoting understanding across cultures, their projects contained an ideological tension between integration and difference: only the presence of differences requiring resolution made integration necessary. One anomaly here was *Die Brücke*, which repudiated any coalition forged in opposition to Germans in favor of a fully inclusive arena of multiethnic collaboration that allowed for unresolved heterogeneity. And at the other end of the spectrum, ALFA stressed the isolation of Italian migrants and formulated its entire project on the basis of continued separation. For the most

---

[83] See, for example, Irmgard Ackermann, "In zwei Sprachen leben: Ein literarisches Preisausschreiben für Ausländer," *Stimmen der Zeit* 108.7 (1983): 443–54; Harald Weinrich, "Um eine deutsche Literatur von außen bittend," *Merkur* 37 (1983): 911–20; Irmgard Ackermann, "Integrationsvorstellungen und Integrationsdarstellungen in der Ausländerliteratur," *Zeitschrift für Literaturwissenschaft und Linguistik* 56 (1984): 23–29; and Harald Weinrich, "Betroffenheit der Zeugen – Zeugen der Betroffenheit. Einige Überlegungen zur Ausländerliteratur in der Bundesrepublik Deutschland," *Zeitschrift für Kulturaustausch* 35 (1985): 14–15.

part, though, the desire to collapse the binary provided an ideological common thread. The distinction between German and foreigner somewhat paradoxically served the useful ideological function of justifying and necessitating integration regardless of an author's particular politics or mode of literary production.

The Chamisso Prize and the Canonization of *Ausländerliteratur*

In the larger historical development of both *Ausländerliteratur* and integrationist politics, the Chamisso Prize stands as a major watershed. Named after the French count Louis Charles Adélaïde Chamissot de Boncourt (1781–1838), who was best known for the *Wundersame Geschichte des Peter Schlemihl* (Strange History of Peter Schlemihl), this award recognized the literary accomplishments of nonnative German-speaking authors writing in German. DaF director Harald Weinrich conceived of the prize and orchestrated its creation, obtaining financial support from the Robert Bosch Foundation and the Bavarian Academy of Fine Arts. The Chamisso Prize's fundamental principle, as one of the official sponsors of the prize explained, was that "where important texts of content and form emerge, new perspectives are opened to German literature, and the foreigner proves himself as an independent cultural partner through texts that are only possible for him to write."[84] A jury made up of members of the Bavarian Academy of Fine Arts, DaF, and the Goethe Institute selected the winners from the entire field of foreign authors, generally honoring one established and one fledgling writer each year. The prize also led to several published volumes that provided basic biographical information about the recipients and presented speeches from the award ceremony.[85]

The inauguration of the Chamisso Prize was significant on a number of levels. It signaled DaF's rise to preeminence among the modes of minority literature that had existed in parallel during the 1970s. One cause of this shift was the ability of Ackermann and Weinrich to expand their earlier work on pedagogy theory into a much broader program of boosterism and public promotion for the writings that arrived in response to their solicitations. They also clearly benefited from the access to important journals and publishing contacts that their academic position provided.

---

[84] Dietrich Krusche, "Die Querung des Flusses," in Dietrich Krusche, ed., *Der gefundene Schatten: Chamisso-Reden 1985–1993* (Munich: A1 Verlag, 1993), 8. Krusche attributes this quote, which he does not document, to the Robert Bosch Stiftung.

[85] See Friedrich, *Chamissos Enkel*; Krusche, *Der gefundene Schatten*.

Perhaps most crucial, though, were the ways in which their theory of foreigner literature resonated with the SPD's integrationist politics. Their widely circulated arguments about the function of *Ausländerliteratur* as a catalyst for intercultural communication seemed to answer Kühn's 1978 call for new initiatives to bring labor migrants into the fabric of German society. By the mid-1980s, such linkages held the status of conventional wisdom (at least on the left), which in turn drew support for the Munich Institute's efforts from prominent institutional bases such as the Goethe Institute and the Bavarian Academy of Fine Arts.

The Chamisso Prize had several other immediate impacts. It generated major national attention for its honorees. Winners typically received detailed coverage in the *Süddeutsche Zeitung*, a function of the fact that Munich-based institutions ran the competitions. This reporting was generally excerpted and reproduced in newspapers around the country. Winning the award often sparked greater interest in the authors and their works. Writers such as Rafik Schami and Franco Biondi, for example, had previously spent years publishing in grassroots, left-leaning periodicals such as the PoLiKunst yearbooks or *Die Brücke*, but journalistic interest in the Chamisso Prize served to create for them a public of national scope and greater ideological breadth. The award also opened up a new understanding of minority literature among German cultural elites previously unaware of these authors' very existence. Alfred von Schirnding, a German writer and member of the Bavarian Academy of Fine Arts, underscored its impact in an article on the first Chamisso Prize. Before the Munich Institute requested support for the award, he explained, neither he nor his fellow members had known about a large number of foreign authors who "live among us, whose books deal with life in Germany and have their reading public in this country."[86] The Chamisso Prize thus expanded the volume and scope of press coverage, as well as the consciousness of Germany's leading cultural critics. In so doing, it helped consolidate the category of *Ausländerliteratur* in the mainstream marketplace.

Finally, the Chamisso Prize served to articulate and define a particular historical narrative of *Ausländerliteratur* that began with Ören. The Munich Institute had long pointed to Ören as a key figure. The year before the inaugural Chamisso Prize, Ackermann singled out the *Berlin Trilogie*, praising it as the "most complex representation of the theme of integration" in contemporary literature.[87] And Weinrich proclaimed

---

[86] Schirnding, "Deutsche Literatur von außen," *Süddeutsche Zeitung*, 25 February 1985.
[87] Ackermann, "Integrationsvorstellungen," 34–38.

that Ören would "earn a primary place in the literary history" of Berlin, although he still balked at including Ören's texts within the rubric of a German guest worker literature since they were composed in Turkish.[88] In the first volume of Chamisso Prize proceedings, however, the fact that Ören wrote in his native language was seen as central to his seminal role in the cultural integration the DaF leadership hoped to foster. They now cast him as the crucial transitional author, a figure who still wrote in Turkish but self-consciously addressed a German-language audience. As Pazarkaya explained on behalf of the jury: "The claim that was registered for the first time through the poem 'Was will Niyazi in der Naunynstraße' had the immanent consequence of declaring: I am also your poet." The Chamisso Prize, he concluded, "now carries out this consequence, confirms the claim, which is no longer a mere claim, but rather a living reality."[89]

But what did it mean for Ören to claim the status of a German poet? And what did it mean for the Chamisso Prize to confirm his claim? To understand what sort of "living reality" the prize envisioned, we need to think more carefully about the process of canonization and its relationship to the work of integration. Initial winners included Ören and Schami (1985), Biondi (1986), Chiellino (1987), and Pazarkaya (1989), all of whom thematized the worker recruitment and were centrally involved in the contested terrain of early minority literature initiatives. But the Chamisso jury also chose other authors who had nothing to do with the labor migration and who did not participate in minority-affiliated journals and associations, such as the Czech political dissident Ota Filip (1986) and the Austrian-Israeli exile Elazar Benyoëtz (1988). Zafer Şenocak (1988) and Zehra Çirak (1989), both members of the labor migration's second generation, counted among the honorees as well. One way to interpret this eclectic set of choices is to emphasize the Chamisso Prize's function as a distiller of difference. The jury, that is, lumped writers of radically dissimilar backgrounds into a single, amorphous conception of foreigner literature.[90] The award winners ran the gamut from self-identified

[88] Harald Weinrich, "Gastarbeiterliteratur in der Bundesrepublik Deutschland," *Zeitschrift für Literaturwissenschaft und Linguistik* 56 (1984): 13. Weinrich notes that this essay was initially given as a lecture in 1983.

[89] Yüksel Pazarkaya, "Über Aras Ören," in Friedrich, ed., *Chamissos Enkel.*

[90] My criticism here of the homogenizing effect of the Chamisso Prize is similar to a critique of the Munich Institute anthologies made by several earlier scholars. See Peter Seibert, "Zur 'Rettung der Zungen': Ausländerliteratur in ihren konzeptionellen Ansätzen," *Zeitschrift für Literaturwissenschaft und Linguistik* 56 (1984): 57–58; Teraoka, "Gastarbeiterliteratur," 95; Suhr, "Ausländerliteratur," 90–91.

intellectuals such as Ören, who came out of the Istanbul theater scene, and Pazarkaya, a university-educated exchange student, to figures such as Biondi, who had toiled in West German factories as a guest worker for close to a decade. They extended from Benyoëtz, the son of an Austrian Jew who fled the Nazis, to Çırak, the daughter of Turkish labor recruits. Even the name of the prize reflected this pattern. By choosing Chamissot, a nobleman who abandoned his native estate during the French Revolution, Weinrich and Ackermann collapsed important and obvious differences among the socioeconomic circumstances, nationalities, and emigration motives of minority authors. The common status of being foreign, in short, seems to have outweighed any other distinctions in the authors' subject positions.

But one can also read this evidence to suggest that the Chamisso Prize offered a remarkably inclusive and pluralistic vision of foreigner literature. The very fact that the Chamisso jury "prized" competing modes of minor-ity writing gave all of them legitimacy and seemingly rewarded contradic-tory conceptions of integration. The award celebrated Pazarkaya's rather elitist cultural synthesis right alongside Biondi and Schami's "Literatur der Betroffenheit." This ideological heterogeneity involved an important alteration and expansion of the functions that many authors initially envi-sioned minority literature to serve. In committing their works to the edited volumes and prize competitions organized by Ackermann and Weinrich, such authors as Biondi and Schami moved far afield of their original goal of a worker collective in which literature would provide a vehicle for consciousness-raising.

These two interpretive impulses lead to a more basic question: did the Chamisso Prize contain a core ideological program at all? Did it pro-mote any particular role for minority literature in the larger process of integration? Essays published in connection with the Munich Institute's earlier writing contests and anthologies provide some useful clues here. In the afterword to *In zwei Sprachen leben*, Ackermann offered one of the clearest explanations of the DaF leadership's thinking. She identified bilingualism as an implicit or explicit theme in all their competitions, claiming that "loss of identity as the price for bilingualism runs like a red thread through the texts, above all for those for whom German was a second mother tongue."[91] The fact that foreign authors "lived in two lan-guages," she asserted, meant that they occupied a liminal position, torn

[91] Irmgard Ackermann, "Nachwort," in Irmgard Ackermann, ed., *In zwei Sprachen leben: Berichte, Erzählungen, Gedichte von Ausländern* (Munich: DTV, 1983), 246.

or caught between native and German cultures.[92] By organizing the volume under thematic headings such as "Where Do I Belong?," "Separated through Language," and "Step-Mother Language," Ackermann further underscored the condition of "in-betweenness." To the extent that their linguistic hybridity and divided identities overwrote or trumped their ideological differences, all of the Chamisso Prize recipients conformed to DaF's conception of minority authorship. This fundamentally liminal status gave the winners a degree of ideological coherence within Ackermann and Weinrich's particular vision of *Ausländerliteratur*. And in this respect, authors of foreigner literature in Germany were distinct from most minority writers in France and Britain, who had generally learned the metropolitan language from an early age through the colonial system of education.

A second unifying theme emerged in the view of these liminal figures as facilitators of integration. DaF professors repeatedly argued that a primary goal of the literary contests was to encourage foreign authors to communicate their experiences to Germans.[93] In writing, Weinrich explained, "immigrants themselves say how they see themselves and how they see us. They say it in German and thus achieve a contribution to German literature worthy of note that at least challenges us Germans in the same way as guest workers themselves, because we are given the chance through this literature to perceive ourselves as foreigners and Germany as a foreign country."[94] By articulating their experiences as literature in German, he concluded, minority authors had the power to evoke empathy from German readers – an emotion that enabled them to inhabit the foreigner's mental world and feel the strangeness of being foreign.

This conception of *Ausländerliteratur* as a catalyst for cross-cultural empathy lay at the heart of the Chamisso Prize's organizational structure and encapsulated its model of integration. As the president of the Bavarian Academy of Fine Arts, Heinz Friedrich, explained, a non-German who writes in German "establishes a dialogue in order to make himself intelligible in his initially foreign environment and to enlist understanding

---

[92] The assumption that migrants exist "between two worlds," as Leslie Adelson rightly points out, has dominated discussions of the culture they produce. She has recently argued that the analytical purchase of this trope is now historically obsolete. See Adelson, *The Turkish Turn*, especially 3–5, 20–23. While I agree with Adelson's critique, my goal here is to trace the historical processes through which the notion of migrants caught "between two worlds" came to dominate West German modes of reading migrant literature in the 1980s.

[93] Ackermann, "Nachwort"; Krusche, "Nachwort," in Ackermann, ed., *Als Fremder in Deutschland*, 189–91.

[94] Weinrich, "Betroffenheit der Zeugen," 14.

for his own foreignness."[95] This ideological framework makes it easier to understand how the Chamisso Prize jury was able to venture so widely across literary style and political orientation in picking winners. It also helps elucidate why the award's organizers assembled an all-German jury to evaluate works produced entirely by non-Germans.[96] Chamisso jury members saw themselves as the first and most immediate German receivers of minority words. One might even say that they positioned themselves as a kind of surrogate for the nation as a whole. *Ausländerliteratur*, according to this logic, was a conduit for migrant voices that needed to be heard by West German society at large. Chamisso Prize winners, by extension, were understood as ideal dialogue partners, uniquely positioned to convey their experiences as outsiders. At least in theory, the German public would be transformed by this process, perhaps even inspired to call for broader social changes beyond the act of reading.

The Subversiveness of *Ausländerliteratur*

Another way to measure the impact of the Chamisso Prize is to consider the relationship between cultural mainstream and margin articulated through the category of *Ausländerliteratur*. In thinking about this relationship, the most crucial theoretical precedent is perhaps Gilles Deleuze and Félix Guattari's well-known argument about "minor literature." They propose that any minority group writing in a major language produces minor literature, which has the capacity to destabilize and undermine the dominant language, culture, and discourse in which its authors operate.[97]

---

[95] Heinz Friedrich, "Vorwort," in Friedrich, ed., *Chamissos Enkel*, 7.

[96] Through the 1980s, the Chamisso Prize jury consisted of Weinrich, Ackermann, Krusche, Schirnding, and a rotating representative of the Goethe Institute in Munich. From 1991 (after reunification), Annarose Buscha of Leipzig was added to the original jury, which remained intact until 1995. Since 1995, the jury has consisted of author and Balkan expert Mira Beham (until 1998), writer and literary critic Karl Corino, novelist Sten Nadolny, Pazarkaya, Stephan Wackwitz of the Goethe Institute in Munich, Weinrich (as a member of the advisory board until 1996), and Ackermann (as a member of the advisory board). Irene Ferchl, ed., *Viele Kulturen – Eine Sprache: Adelbert-von-Chamisso-Preisträgerinnen und -Preisträger, 1985–1998* (Stuttgart: Robert Bosch Stiftung, 1998), 9.

[97] Gilles Deleuze and Félix Guattari, *Kafka: Toward a Minor Literature*, trans. by Dana Polan (Minneapolis: University of Minnesota Press, 1986), 16–27. In recent years, scholars of German literature have increasingly pointed to the theory of minor literature outlined in this book as a crucial framework for understanding the development of minority cultural production in a variety of twentieth-century contexts. See, for example, Teraoka, "Gastarbeiterliteratur," 77–101; Suhr, "Ausländerliteratur," 71–103; and Scott Spector, *Prague Territories: National Conflict and Cultural Innovation in Franz Kafka's Fin de Siècle* (Berkeley and Los Angeles: University of California Press, 2000).

According to Deleuze and Guattari, the ability of such a literature to unsettle the boundaries between social center and margin grows out of three unique functions. First, minor literature deterritorializes language, problematizing the assumption that language, culture, and geography develop organically in relation to one another. Second, this literary mode connects its authors and their works to the politicized subject positions that they as minorities occupy in the major society. Finally, because it is defined by its relation to the major, minor literature makes collective – as opposed to individual – statements.[98]

Certainly, there is a great deal in the development of *Ausländerliteratur* that would seem to support Deleuze and Guattari's theory. The very act of Turks and other migrants speaking and writing in the dominant language represented an important deterritorialization of German. For at least the first twenty years of the labor migration, West Germans tended to perceive guest workers, whose languages were unintelligible to native ears, as a silent, voiceless presence in their society.[99] As Ackermann noted, minority authors' "capacity of articulation" distinguished them "from many of their contemporaries and countrymen, who remain *mute* in their suffering."[100] The sound of their own language emanating from foreign mouths forced Germans to hear migrants' voices for the first time and register the concerns of these arrivals in new ways. But perhaps more importantly, this novel situation – not to mention the prospect of migrants producing German literature – began to challenge basic assumptions about the natural correlation between an author's nationality or territorial status and his or her language and culture.

Even the leaders of the Munich Institute, who claimed to have provided the opportunity for many of "these people to start writing literary texts in German in the first place," appear to have been somewhat unsettled at the prospect of non-Germans creating German literature.[101] Weinrich exhorted his fellow countrymen (as well as himself) to "get used to the thought that there are among these foreigners many who know how to go around not only with the broom or the key, but also with the quill, and this must of course be welcome to us because it brings the world to us in

---

[98] Deleuze and Guattari, *Kafka*, 16–18.

[99] Teraoka, "Gastarbeiterliteratur," 77–79.

[100] Irmgard Ackermann, "In der Fremde hat man eine dünne Haut... Türkische Autoren der 'Zweiten Generation' oder die Überwindung der Sprachlosigkeit," *Zeitschrift für Kulturaustausch* 35 (1985): 28. Emphasis is mine.

[101] Weinrich, "Um eine Literatur," 919.

our country and consequently protects us from cultural provincialism."[102] Weinrich suggests here that language – or more specifically linguistic and literary competence – was essential to the ideological process by which postwar West Germans began to conceive of the millions of migrants in their country as something more than manual laborers. The delinking of territory and language, furthermore, was intricately connected to the process of integration in terms of both cultural transmission and sociability. As Weinrich put it, by introducing the foreign through German language, minority authors "bring the world to us *in our country*" and, therefore, must "be welcome."

Works of *Ausländerliteratur*, in other words, were never simply stories or poems. Rather they were implicated in the relationship between the German and foreign. Ackermann drew this connection explicitly: "the literary texts of foreign authors offer a special chance to learn about the ideas of the afflicted on questions of integration which are very concrete for them."[103] DaF's numerous efforts to explain the significance of these writings repeatedly returned to their ability to illuminate and make intelligible the lives and concerns of a much broader constituency – the millions of labor migrants who had arrived in the Federal Republic since the mid-1950s. West Germany's competing modes of minority literature thus existed in what Deleuze and Guattari describe as the "cramped" ideological space that forces each individual work "to connect immediately to politics."[104] Whether minority authors overtly declared a specific political program, as did Biondi, Schami, and the PoLiKunst collective, or focused primarily on aesthetic issues, as did Pazarkaya, their texts were invariably saddled with political meanings and constrained by the circumstances of their creation – by the fact that they were written by non-Germans in German.

Deleuze and Guattari's view that minority works tend to be perceived as part of a "collective enunciation" rather than as the product of a unique individual is useful here too. The Munich Institute's decision to lump authors of radically different social, economic, and historical circumstances together, both in their anthologies and through the Chamisso Prize, provides a concrete example of this process. As the driving force for making the genre of *Ausländerliteratur* known and available in the commercial marketplace, this institutional framework constituted

---

[102] Weinrich, "Betroffenheit der Zeugen," 14.
[103] Ackermann, "Integrationsvorstellungen," 23.
[104] Deleuze and Guattari, *Kafka*, 17.

a centripetal action that ultimately overrode the individuation of authors, whether based on politics, country of origin, or genius. It is the collectivizing function of minor literature that Deleuze and Guattari celebrate for its resistance to "an individuated enunciation that would belong to this or that 'master,'" a resistance that they suggest opens up a "line of escape" from the major culture (which privileges individual genius) and makes possible an absolute subversion of the dominant discourse.[105]

In other respects, however, this history dramatically complicates Deleuze and Guattari's revolutionary project. Again, in their view, collective enunciation leads to a "line of escape" – that is, minor literature serves as an oppositional voice completely outside of or detached from the cultural and institutional center. But this is an assumption that historian Scott Spector has recently criticized as little more than wishful thinking.[106] The history of *Ausländerliteratur* demonstrates another possibility; namely, that the unsettling of language, identity, and values might actually occur from within relatively mainstream cultural institutions. DaF, it is worth stressing, was very much a part of the intellectual and cultural networks that we would associate with the West German establishment. It was attached to the University of Munich, accepted financial support from the Goethe Institute and the German Academic Exchange Service, and had close working relationships with DTV, the Bavarian Academy of Fine Arts, and the Robert Bosch Foundation. Yet it also became the most important champion of minority literary production, specifically targeting the mainstream marketplace for its promotions of foreign-born authors.

This raises the question of whether the Munich Institute – and its conception of foreigner literature – served as an instrument of cultural hegemony. In her important early work on these literary developments, Arlene Teraoka criticized Ackermann and Weinrich for seeking "to define and control the literary phenomenon they study" and thus creating structural inequalities in the ways that *Ausländerliteratur* was constituted.[107] Certainly, the consolidation of this new genre inscribed unequal relations of power. Ackermann and Weinrich controlled the framework for all of their writing contests, formulated the themes for submissions, and

---

[105] Ibid., 17, 26.
[106] Scott Spector's recent study of Czech Jews writing in German affirms the usefulness of the Deleuze and Guattari model, but it also qualifies and complicates its revolutionary implications. Emphasizing that a minor literature is by definition written *within* a major language, Spector insightfully insists that this form can never be wholly oppositional or step fully outside the major or dominant culture. Spector, *Prague Territories*, 28–30.
[107] Teraoka, "Gastarbeiterliteratur," 92.

insisted on the use of German as a second language. This was also true of the Chamisso Prize, which defined eligibility for the award in terms of an author's linguistic status (only authors of "non-German mother tongues" who wrote in German were considered), thereby ensuring a pool of winners who were by definition "caught between two worlds." In this sense, the Chamisso Prize encouraged a hierarchical relationship between writer and reader, in which minority authors served as designated sufferers, perpetually expressing and explaining their foreignness, while German consumers took on the role of enlightened sympathizers. This framework confined the writer's agency to the act of evoking empathy on the part of readers.

Yet this history was never simply a straightforward co-optation of minority writing by German academics who dictated the genre's parameters. One of the most interesting aspects of the emergence of *Ausländerliteratur* was the dialectical relationship between DaF and its authors. Ackermann and Weinrich argued that their literary model developed organically from the early contest entries. Apart from proposing general themes for the competitions, Ackermann explained, they refrained from posing specific questions. They wanted "to make possible a wide spectrum of statements" that "mirrored subjective experience"; their goal was "to preserve uninfluenced reactions and not restrict creativity."[108] Along these lines, they chose quotations from the submissions themselves to serve as section titles within the published anthologies. But the crux of the matter lay in the framework through which texts were originally solicited. While Ackermann and Weinrich no doubt believed that they were responding to patterns in the contest entries, the thematics of the competitions, which regularly emphasized the experience of being foreign, ultimately generated a steady stream of liminal tropes: "Swing of the Pendulum between Two Worlds," "The Faraway yet Close Homeland," "The Borders Traverse the Middle of My Tongue," and so forth.[109]

---

[108] Ackermann, *Stimmen der Zeit*, 444.

[109] The main headings for each of the anthologies suggest variations on the following basic themes: the strangeness of Germany, lack of belonging, being divided, living between two cultures, crossing borders. The pattern becomes clear if we compare the section headings. *Als Fremder in Deutschland* includes: "*Dein Brot schmeckt dir fremd,*" "*Pendelfahrt zwischen den Welten,*" and "*Typisch deutsch?*" *In zwei Sprachen leben* contains: "*Wohin gehöre ich?,*" "*Deutsche Grammatik,*" "*Durch Sprache getrennt,*" "*Stiefmuttersprache,*" and "*Grenzübergänge.*" *Türken deutscher Sprache* lists: "*Die ferne, nahe Heimat,*" "*Die Grenze verläuft mitten durch meine Zunge*" and "*Ich kann nicht sein wie du.*" See Ackermann, *Als Fremder in Deutschland*; Ackermann, *In zwei Sprachen leben*; Irmgard Ackermann, *Türken deutscher Sprache. Berichte, Erzählungen, Gedichte* (Munich: DTV, 1984).

Even here, though, the question of whose conception of minority literature was being expressed in the contests is complicated. In fact, the DaF leadership chose subjects remarkably similar to the rhetoric and ideology produced by social scientists and SPD politicians from the mid-1970s to the early 1980s. The idea of marginalized immigrants caught in between cultures was central to many sociological studies on guest workers and the labor recruitment. An Institute for Marxist Studies and Research report described foreign workers as "alienated," "isolated," and "ripped out of their usual life relationships," which rendered them liminal beings between host country and homeland.[110] Similarly, in an assessment of a Volkswagen-sponsored, seven-year study of the labor migration, one researcher proclaimed: "All in all, the results of this representative investigation make the ambivalent situation clear, which from time to time is described as 'living between two worlds.'"[111] This sort of evaluation became a common justification for integration measures proposed by politicians. Federal Commissioner for Foreigner Affairs Kühn claimed that foreign youth had been pushed into "an outsider's role" and advocated integrative policies in order to counterbalance "the particular set of problems facing foreign families in view of the unaccustomed living environment, problems of bringing up and educating children and in view of the role of the woman that is shaped very differently through the orientation toward the country of origin compared to local relationships."[112] It was not so much that DaF imposed a conception of minority literature on contestants, then, but that both its leaders and many minority authors seem to have thought about the process of writing in ways that resonated with ideas and themes that had become part of the larger public discourse by the time the contests were initiated. Ackermann and Weinrich, in short, constructed a category of *Ausländerliteratur* that operated squarely within the terms of public debate during the late 1970s.

It would also be wrong to conclude that the Munich Institute's homogenizing conception of minority literature corrupted a wholly separate and uniform voice from the margins. The decision to write in German and direct their work to a German audience precluded any ability for minority authors to exist in strict isolation. These choices, in fact, suggested precisely the opposite – that minority writers wanted to reshape the discourse

[110] Rüdiger Bech and Renate Faust, *Die sogenannten Gastarbeiter: Ausländische Beschäftigte in der Bundesrepublik Deutschland* (Frankfurt: Verlag Marxistische Blätter, 1981), 7.
[111] Hermann Korte and Alfred Schmidt, *Migration and ihre sozialen Folgen: Förderung der Gastarbeiterforschung durch die Stiftung Volkswagenwerk, 1974–1981* (Göttingen: Vandenhoeck & Ruprecht, 1983), 5.
[112] Kühn, *Stand und Weiterentwicklung,* 17–18.

and literature of the major culture as participants in it. Even before
the Chamisso Prize, moreover, the distinctions between minority literary
groups were never fixed. While they may have articulated distinctive –
even contradictory – models of literature and integration in the associations and journals that they founded, minority authors rarely confined
themselves to a single forum for their writings. Seeking as many opportunities as possible to put their work before the public, they routinely submitted texts to a range of periodicals and anthologies. Biondi and Taufiq,
for instance, placed works in *Als Fremder in Deutschland* as well as in
the PoLiKunst yearbooks, the *Südwind Gastarbeiterdeutsch* series, and
Die Brücke. Poems by Çırak and Şenocak appeared in *Türken deutscher
Sprache, Die Brücke*, and *Zeitschrift für Kulturaustausch*. In short, these
authors opted for a multitargeted approach to publishing. They entered
German-run, institutionally sanctioned competitions that required them
to address issues of foreignness in specific ways. But at the same time, they
participated in grassroots, often minority-organized publishing endeav-
ors, which were generally more flexible about the choices of themes and
subjects.

This pattern involved an active maneuvering on the part of migrant
authors among competing notions of minority literature rather than exclusive allegiance to a single model. Pazarkaya, for example, never submitted
his literary texts to the Munich Institute contests – a forum that mixed
the works of professionals and amateurs – but his poems and critical
essays were cited in an early Weinrich summary of guest worker literature.[113] Pazarkaya also made himself into a German-language authority
on Turkish culture and guest workers during the early 1980s, writing
two books on those subjects for the Swiss publisher Unionsverlag.[114] In
this capacity he produced one of the earliest state-of-the-field essays on
contemporary Turkish literature for the 1981 *Zeitschrift für Kulturaustausch*, and contributed – along with Ackermann and Weinrich – to several
other special issues of journals that addressed the phenomenon of a literature written by non-Germans.[115] In addition, he composed the Chamisso

---

[113] Harald Weinrich, "Um eine deutsche Literatur von außen bittend," *Merkur* 37 (1983):
916–17.
[114] Yüksel Pazarkaya, *Rosen im Frost: Einblicke in die türkische Kultur* (Zurich: Unionsverlag, 1980); and Yüksel Pazarkaya, *Spuren des Brots: Zur Lage der Ausländischen
Arbeiter* (Zurich: Unionsverlag, 1983).
[115] See Pazarkaya, "Ohne die Deutschen," 1. In subsequent articles, Pazarkaya proclaimed
himself one of the key pioneers of Turkish literature in the Federal Republic. See
Pazarkaya, "Stimmen des Zorns," 17–18; Pazarkaya, "Türkiye, Mutterland," 104–105.

Prize tribute to Ören and accepted the 1989 prize for his own literary efforts. To a large extent, then, Pazarkaya dictated the terms of his involvement with the Munich Institute, refusing to enter its writing competitions even as he accepted its honors as a founder of the canon of foreigner literature.

Integration and Literary Dialogue

Perhaps the best way to gauge the revolutionary potential of *Ausländerliteratur* is to return to the relationship between minority writing and political ideology. The Chamisso Prize provides a useful historical barometer of these issues because it explicitly connected public discussions of social integration and literary merit. In many ways, the award's emphasis on the alterity of its honorees fit neatly with the idea that foreigner literature would serve as a vehicle for intercultural communication in the SPD's new integration policy. As the President of the Bavarian Academy of Fine Arts explained: "A non-German, who writes German, ... opens a dialogue ... in order to attract *understanding for his particular foreignness*. When non-Germans write in German, they attempt ... to *bridge the distance and transform it into closeness*."[116] What the Chamisso Prize jury sought to reward, then, was the minority author who could speak to the German public from the outside in a way that made his or her foreign experience more intelligible, familiar, and even "close." Jury members essentially envisioned integration as a dialogue across ethnic and national difference, but that boundary itself – the distinction between German and foreign – was always necessary for the dialogue to take place.

This function gave rise to new expectations about the role of minority intellectuals in West Germany. As representatives of difference in all its possible forms, migrant writers – and especially Chamisso Prize recipients – became public spokespersons for foreigners in the Federal Republic. Their status as ideal dialogue partners made their participation absolutely crucial to the success of integration policy, and consequently minority authors increasingly served as experts on panels and television shows and at public meetings and conferences. Because of their publicly and institutionally sanctioned roles as cultural intermediaries, these artists and intellectuals gained greater access to publishing opportunities and attained a level of visibility virtually unimaginable for other members of the labor migration. Yet this circumscribed ideological function placed

[116] Friedrich, *Chamissos Enkel*, 7.

limitations on what subjects and issues were appropriate for them to address. Representing the foreign in the category of foreigner literature created pigeonholes that, as we shall see, quickly provoked new modes of minority resistance, critique, and writing.

But while the Chamisso Prize underscored the foreignness of *Ausländerliteratur*, it simultaneously insisted that this category was part of German literature. For Weinrich, the winning authors not only achieved a noteworthy contribution, but had to be "counted as German literature because the poetic reality that they express is part of the reality of Germany today."[117] He made a similar point in relation to the formulation of *Literatur der Betroffenheit* by Biondi and Schami, claiming that it was "already German in its innermost literary substance."[118] Weinrich explained that *Betroffenheit*, which roughly translates into concern/dismay but has no real equivalent in other languages, evokes bureaucratic (as in *betrifft*) and religious (as in *Betroffenheit des Glaubens*) meanings. With this singular term, he argued, the PoLiKunst leaders imbued their conception of oppositional literature with a uniquely German meaning, championing guest workers who habitually experienced "existential dismay" in the "bureaucratized world" of modern industrial capitalism. Minority writers, that is, used German not simply to communicate in the major language but also to express experiences and concerns that were specific to West German social conditions and modes of understanding.

Chamisso winners were therefore prized both as facilitators of cross-ethnic understanding and as hybrid figures who ultimately collapsed the Self-Other distinction on which the discourse of integration depended. As Ackermann observed: "The phenomenon of foreigner literature as such is ... an exceptional document of integration, not only as the result of the far-reaching integration of single authors, which often finds its expression in the astounding command of language, but also in the sense of the sociological criteria for integration.... true integration can first be spoken of not so much when foreigners participate in the economic process at the lowest level as when they achieve active participation in the different areas of social reality."[119] Ackermann pointed here to the possibility of a breakthrough much larger than demographic shifts or even social

117 Harald Weinrich, "Deutschland, ein türkisches Märchen: Zu Hause in der Fremde – Gastarbeiterliteratur," in Volker Hage, ed., *Deutsche Literatur 1983: Ein Jahresüberblick* (Stuttgart: Reclam, 1984), 230–32.
118 Weinrich, "Gastarbeiterliteratur," 22.
119 Ackermann, "Integrationsvorstellungen," 23–24.

policy. Indeed, by emphasizing the crucial participation of minority texts in the discourse of integration, Ackermann suggested that foreigner literature represented the key mechanism through which minority authors participated in German intellectual life and perhaps even reshaped what constituted German culture. Minority writers were the living, breathing conduits; the Chamisso Prize served to facilitate and champion their "exceptional documents of integration." In this sense, the Chamisso Prize was never just about literary merit or even a particular idea of minority literature. Rather it served as a vehicle to consider perhaps the biggest issue of all – what is German. As the preeminent cultural mechanism for the canonization of *Ausländerliteratur*, the Chamisso Prize contained two very different models of cultural integration: one in which minorities entered into dialogue with the West German nation yet remained distinct from it, and a second that celebrated a fusion of Self and Other. It at least flirted with the possibility that a hybridity embodied in these minority authors might now be *prized*.

Ultimately, the consolidation of *Ausländerliteratur* fostered changes that were both closer to the center of political and ideological life and also less revolutionary than what Deleuze and Guattari originally envisioned. The West German cultural establishment embraced and promoted competing modes of minority literature because of their ability to represent and communicate the foreign, a function that resonated quite well with the dominant policymaking voices of the period. For precisely that reason, institutional support existed for publishing and celebrating minority authors that went well beyond the framework which Deleuze and Guattari thought possible for a minor literature. Indeed, the Chamisso Prize collection, a major cache of works by award winners and about the labor migration, now resides at the National Literary Archive in Marbach. Located in the birthplace of Friedrich Schiller, the archive is spatially and symbolically linked to the heart of the German canon. Here texts by the minority writers honored by the Chamisso jurors sit side by side with the papers of Hölderlin, Nietzsche, and Kracauer.

Yet, for all these remarkable changes, the value system that encouraged the proliferation and sacralization of foreigner literature in the 1980s shared the ideological limitations of integrationist politics more generally. During the first six years of the Chamisso Prize, it is crucial to remember, the Federal Republic continued to follow the 1913 Nationality Law, which determined citizenship on the basis of descent from a German national. Naturalization was considered an exception to be granted only under specific conditions – with no guarantee of final approval.[120] This led to a major ideological gap between the ideal of intercultural communication and the political realities of the labor migration: during the 1980s, none of the dialogue partners celebrated by SPD officials, DaF professors, or the Chamisso Prize jury had the right to become a German citizen. As scholars have recently suggested, one of the primary dangers of such promotions of difference and hybridity is that they tend to privilege aesthetics and cultural choices even as they undermine the ethnic self-identification and distinctiveness that is often necessary to mobilize political action in the pursuit of citizenship and equal rights.[121] In this sense, both the political reforms introduced by the SPD during the late 1970s and the Munich Institute's canonization of *Ausländerliteratur* represented an incomplete revolution: Chamisso Prize winners were part of the canon, but not part of the polity.

[120] Such a privilege required fifteen years of full-time residence in the Federal Republic, oral and written mastery of German, the ability to support oneself and one's dependents, and the renunciation of one's former citizenship and any potential inheritance in that country. Helmut Rittstieg, "Dual Citizenship: Legal and Political Aspects in the German Context," in Rainer Bauböck, ed., *From Aliens to Citizens: Redefining the Status of Immigrants in Europe* (Aldershot: Avebury, 1994), 114–15. In 1991, a new Aliens Act was implemented. While it left most of the conditions for naturalization intact, it significantly revised the basic concept of naturalization in the Federal Republic, making it into an option rather than an earned privilege. The new law also reduced the length of legal residence required for application from fifteen to ten years.

[121] Christian Joppke and Steven Lukes, "Introduction: Multicultural Questions," in Christian Joppke and Steven Lukes, eds., *Multicultural Questions* (Oxford: Oxford University Press, 1999), 10–11.

3

Gender and Incommensurable Cultural Difference

Despite the very real limits of foreigner policy during the 1970s, the basic idea that integration was possible – and even desirable – represented a major reorientation in the West German stance toward foreign laborers and their families. This policy innovation suggested a relinquishing of the notion that guest workers should return home and marked the first serious attempt to encourage the peaceful coexistence of radically different groups of people in the Federal Republic. It also led to wide-ranging programs by educators, state and local governments, church-run charities, and citizens' initiatives to facilitate cross-cultural interaction and understanding.

By the early 1980s, however, a major backlash against guest worker integration was beginning to take shape.[1] Following another economic downturn in 1979 and a noticeable rise in the number of asylum seekers around the same time, antiforeigner sentiments increasingly found voice in the Federal Republic. The rather sudden fall of Helmut Schmidt's SPD-FDP coalition in October 1982 (which ushered Helmut Kohl into the chancellorship) and the CDU's subsequent federal electoral victory in March 1983 also signaled the growing attraction of this renewed conservatism. The two central themes of the CDU campaign, in fact, were

---

[1] Studies that consider this backlash include: Christhard Hoffmann, "Immigration and Nationhood in the Federal Republic of Germany," Working Paper 5.42, Center for German and European Studies, University of California, Berkeley, 1996, 15–19; Peter O'Brien, *Beyond the Swastika* (London: Routledge, 1996), 74–82; Karen Schönwälder, "Migration, Refugees and Ethnic Plurality as Issues of Public and Political Debates in (West) Germany," in David Cesarani and Mary Fulbrook, eds., *Citizenship, Nationality and Migration in Europe* (London: Routledge, 1996), 166–69.

the restoration of German patriotism and the failure of the SPD's integrationist *Ausländerpolitik*.

These changes at the level of federal politics marked a third major shift in the guest worker question. The CDU argued that the Social Democratic approach to integration policy had proven ineffective in a number of respects, asking instead whether full integration could ever be achieved and, more specifically, whether foreigners possessed the capacity to integrate at all. Soon after he became chancellor on 1 October 1982, Kohl proposed a much tougher stance on guest workers and their families. In a dramatic reversal of the SPD mandate, Christian Democrats began to claim that integration had little to do with mutual understanding and intercultural exchange. Guest workers, they insisted, should be required to meet specific standards for membership in West Germany's modern, liberal democracy.

Particularly striking about this new debate over the capacity (or incapacity) of foreigners to integrate was its emphasis on questions of gender relations. I do not mean to suggest that the issue of gender was simply absent in earlier public discussions about guest workers. Indeed, as we have seen, migrant women had already served as the targets of social work within the integration initiatives of the late 1970s.[2] But as conservative critics raised doubts about the viability of integration, public debate about migrant gender relations took on a new centrality and form. By the early 1980s, discussions about the difficulties faced by foreign women were no longer predicated on producing a deeper understanding of female experiences, or helping create healthy home lives. Rather, the

---

[2] A number of studies about guest workers stressed that migration to the Federal Republic was much more difficult for foreign women than for children or men. They diagnosed the wives of alien laborers as living in "extreme isolation," a condition exacerbated by their confinement to the home and lack of German language skills. And they proposed programs to ease female foreigners' adjustment to the new environment, including language and sewing courses, counseling services, and women's centers. In 1979, for example, the Bonn Institute for Social Work and Social Pedagogy published a study on Turkish women, which was sponsored by the Federal Ministry of Education. The *Frankfurter Rundschau* reported its findings. See n.a., "Die Frauen von Gastarbeitern leben in extremer Isolation," *Frankfurter Rundschau*, 16 November 1979. Such integration initiatives continued into the 1980s. See, for example, Horst Westmüller, ed., *Frauen zwischen zwei Kulturen. Frauen aus der Türkei in der Bundesrepublik Deutschland. Dokumentation einer Tagung der Evangelischen Akademie Loccum vom 19. bis 21. November 1982* (Loccum: Evangelische Akademie Loccum, 1985); and Horst Westmüller, ed., *Kultur und Emanzipation. Ausländische und deutsche Frauen in Projekten der Sozialarbeit und Sozialforschung* (Loccum: Evangelische Akademie Loccum, 1985).

"oppression" and "victimization" of migrant women now served as evidence for an unbridgeable chasm separating guest workers and Germans. The treatment of women, in other words, became the primary litmus test to determine whether foreigners – and especially Turks – possessed the capacity to function effectively within a Western liberal-democratic society.

In this larger ideological context, two of the most important and widely discussed cultural documents on the guest worker question emerged: Saliha Scheinhardt's enormously successful 1983 short story, "Frauen, die sterben ohne daß sie gelebt hätten" (Women Who Die Without Having Lived), and Tevfik Başer's 1986 breakthrough feature film, *40 qm Deutschland* (40 m² Germany). Both works were produced by Turkish-Germans and both focused on the hardships experienced by women in the process of migration. These documents marked some of the very first attempts to narrate a history of the migration through women's eyes. They also shifted the representational focus to the domestic sphere, problematizing the guest worker experience in new ways. Domestic violence, loneliness, and the displacement of female social networks now became central issues within the broader discourse on migration.

The representational emphasis on the problems of migrant women catapulted Scheinhardt and Başer to prominence within the cultural marketplace. Both artists became minor celebrities during the mid-1980s and gained wide prominence as Turkish-German authorities on guest worker issues. Their authority, however, was inextricably linked to the larger context of policy debate fostered by the new conservative coalition. Indeed, most reviewers read their works in ways that dovetailed with CDU questioning about the capacity of guest workers to integrate. By focusing on the troubled gender dynamics in each narrative, critics encouraged a growing consensus that the problems of migrant women constituted the central framework for assessing the viability of integration.

Yet this pattern of public reception grossly oversimplified major portions of both cultural documents. In actual fact, Scheinhardt and Başer delineated images of migrant women far more complex than those presented by the CDU or the mainstream West German press. Ultimately, the central dilemma facing both artists was a tension between authorial intent and public reward. While the public's intense interest in the victimization of Turkish women in the Federal Republic made Scheinhardt and Başer overnight celebrities, their celebrity itself was built upon essentialized notions of patriarchal violence and highly circumscribed readings of that violence's social origins.

The Return of the Right and the Political Backlash against Integration

The 1978 creation of the *Ausländerbeauftragter* post, as we have seen, marked a key watershed in West Germany's turn toward integration. By devoting a federal office to foreigner affairs, Schmidt's SPD administration moved the guest worker question into a new kind of political and ideological context. The office shifted the focus of federal engagement with labor migrants from foreign relations to domestic issues, from labor policy to social services. The *Ausländerbeauftragter*, in short, restructured the priorities of federal policymaking to emphasize integration over manpower.[3]

Yet this shift also altered the status of the guest worker debate within the broader political landscape. Once labor migrants were recognized as a major issue on the domestic agenda, political parties outside the ruling coalition felt free to assess the efficiency of integration or ask whether such goals were even feasible. These kinds of questions, in a sense, opened the door for the CDU's 1982–1983 campaign on the "foreigner problem." The Christian Democratic strategy was not simply to criticize the *Ausländerbeauftragter* or the programs it promoted. Rather, in order for the CDU to attack SPD integration policy, there had to be a broader public consensus that foreigners actually constituted a problem. This consensus began to emerge between 1978 and 1982 in a variety of ways.

First, the Federal Republic's economy entered its second major recession in less than a decade. The catalyst was an OPEC oil embargo imposed in the wake of Iran's Islamic fundamentalist revolution in 1978. This oil shock produced high rates of inflation and transformed the West German trade balance from a surplus of DM 18.5 billion in 1978 to a deficit of DM 9.5 billion in 1979 and DM 29 billion in 1980.[4] Over a period of several years, these trends had a disastrous effect on unemployment. The absolute number of out-of-work persons jumped from just under one million in 1979 to over two million by 1983.[5] By the spring of 1982, Josef

---

[3] Karen Schönwälder has argued that a politicization of immigration and the presence of aliens took place around 1980, a marked shift from an earlier period in which there was an absence of public controversy over the labor migration. Here I want to build on her insights about a new kind of public debate spearheaded by political parties, but I also want to insist that the guest worker question was political from its very inception. See Schönwälder, "Migration, Refugees," 159–69.

[4] Dennis L. Bark and David R. Gress, *A History of West Germany*, vol. 2 (Oxford: Basil Blackwell, 1989), 295.

[5] Bundesanstalt für Arbeit, ed., *Amtliche Nachrichten der Bundesanstalt für Arbeit* (ANBA). *Sondernummer: Arbeitsmarkt 1997* (Nürnberg: Bundesanstalt für Arbeit, 1998).

Stingl, the president of the federal labor office, described the country's labor market as "nothing short of catastrophic."[6]

This dire economic situation and especially the growing number of unemployed impacted the guest worker question directly. Even as early as 1976, the *Frankfurter Allgemeine Zeitung* seemed to suggest that the idle status of one million German laborers was intimately connected to the two million guest workers employed in the Federal Republic.[7] Of particular concern to West German commentators was the ratio of employed to unemployed foreigners. According to a 1982 *Die Zeit* article, only 588,012 of the 1,546,311 Turks (or 38 percent) living in the Federal Republic possessed gainful employment.[8] These numbers placed enormous additional pressures on the West German economy and social infrastructure. Even as foreigners accepted unemployment benefits and welfare aid, the argument went, they simultaneously drove up education costs for many *Länder* (states) by flooding schools with their children. For this *Die Zeit* reporter, the primary lesson was that "a threshold of tolerance had been reached." The already dangerous "exploitation mentality" of Germans now threatened to become a full-blown "hatred of foreigners."[9]

To make matters worse from the West German perspective, the number of foreigners continued to increase even as the Federal Republic struggled to deal with long-term high unemployment and a shrinking pool of monetary resources. According to the federal statistical office, for instance, there was a net migration of 105,682 Turks to West Germany in 1979 and 141,671 in 1980.[10] Despite the fact that the recruitment of guest workers had been abandoned seven years before, Turks kept arriving in relatively large numbers on the basis of family reunion.

Tensions were further exacerbated by a sudden spike of asylum seekers between 1979 and 1981. Conceived as a "conscious act of redemption and atonement" for the atrocities of the Nazi period, Article 16 of the

---

[6] Quoted in Klaus J. Bade, *Vom Auswanderungsland zum Einwanderungsland? Deutschland, 1880–1980* (Berlin: Colloquium Verlag, 1983), 104.

[7] Jürgen Eick, "Gastarbeiter – mehr, weniger, gar keine?," *Frankfurter Allgemeine Zeitung*, 23 March 1976, 1.

[8] Hans Schueler, "Die Angst vor den Fremden," *Die Zeit*, 1 January 1982, 3.

[9] Ibid.

[10] For the 1979 figures, see *Statistisches Jahrbuch für die Bundesrepublik Deutschland* (Stuttgart: Kohlhammer, 1981), 66; for the 1980 figures, see *Statistisches Jahrbuch für die Bundesrepublik Deutschland* (Stuttgart: Kohlhammer, 1982), 78. Interestingly, foreigners in the federal statistics office's *Statistisches Jahrbuch* series during the late 1970s and early 1980s are counted in terms of in- and out-migration. There are no figures provided for the total number of resident foreigners or of specific nationalities.

Basic Law stated unconditionally that "persons persecuted for political reasons have the right to asylum" – a policy more generous than that of any nation in postwar Western Europe. In practice, this meant that any individual who claimed to be politically persecuted in their home country enjoyed the right of entry to the Federal Republic and full protection under its law.[11] From 1953 to 1978, only a total of 178,000 people (or roughly 7,100 per year) sought political refuge in West Germany. But these numbers were suddenly eclipsed when over 200,000 applied for asylum in the following three years, including 108,000 in 1980 alone.[12] Part of this massive increase resulted from Turkey's military coup in 1980, the introduction of martial law in Poland during 1980–1981, and a new wave of Vietnamese boat people in the early 1980s.[13] The surge was also related to the Federal Republic's halt of labor recruitment, which left asylum as "the only significant avenue" for legal permanent residence.[14] Indeed, more than half of the one hundred thousand individuals who applied for asylum in 1980 were Turks, by this time the largest single group of migrants in Germany.[15]

The public discourse on asylum after 1980 treated the unexpected explosion of applications with suspicion and skepticism. A wide range of commentators focused their discussion on so-called *Scheinasylanten* (bogus asylum seekers), who, they suggested, accounted for the bulk of the new arrivals. The widely circulated newsmagazine *Der Spiegel*, for instance, claimed that "Turks discovered a new gateway into the economic miracle country" with the liberal asylum law. "Most of the asylum seekers throng to the Federal Republic," the magazine explained, "not

[11] Christian Joppke, "Asylum and State Sovereignty: A Comparison of the United States, Germany, and Britain," in Christian Joppke, ed., *Challenge to the Nation-State: Immigration in Western Europe and the United States* (Oxford: Oxford University Press, 1998), 122–23.

[12] Rainer Münz and Ralf Ulrich, "Changing Patterns of Immigration to Germany, 1945–1995," in Klaus J. Bade and Myron Weiner, eds., *Migration Past, Migration Future: Germany and the United States* (Providence, RI: Berghahn Books, 1997), 84–85.

[13] Vietnamese boat people began to flee after the fall of Saigon in 1975, with most people resettling in neighboring countries such as Thailand, Malaysia, and Indonesia. In 1979, U.S. President Jimmy Carter increased resettlement numbers of Vietnamese to fourteen thousand per day, a decision that produced a spike of boat people between 1980 and 1981. Some of these boat people were rescued from the South China Sea and resettled in West Germany.

[14] Gary Freeman, "Migration Policy and Politics in the Receiving States," *International Migration Review* 26.4 (1992): 1155.

[15] Joppke, "Asylum and State Sovereignty," 125. The actual figure for Turks who applied for asylum in 1980 is 57,913 out of a total of 107,818. See *Statistisches Jahrbuch für die Bundesrepublik Deutschland* (Stuttgart: Metzler-Poeschel Verlag, 1989).

because of political persecution, but rather because they want to earn money."[16] The message was that refugees came under false pretenses to take advantage of Germany's strong economy and extensive social welfare system. This argument, it is worth noting, circulated broadly in the mainstream press well before it became a standard critique of the far right.

The sudden influx of asylum seekers, in short, fueled growing anxiety about too many foreigners. A *Die Zeit* article from January 1982, entitled "Fear of the Foreigners," announced that "a ghost" was haunting the Federal Republic: "the fear of too much influence by foreigners and overcrowding. All of a sudden everyone is talking about the fact that we could be flooded and crushed in our own country by foreign guest workers and their families, by false – and even real – asylum seekers."[17] For some Germans, according to the report, it was difficult and ultimately unnecessary to distinguish among different kinds of migrants. Guest workers, legitimate refugees, and bogus asylum seekers were conflated into the general category of foreigner, as anxieties about being "flooded" and "crushed" by so many non-Germans mounted. In April of that year, *Die Zeit* ran a follow-up article that declared that half of all West German citizens felt *ausländerfeindlich* or hostile toward foreigners.[18]

This antipathy began to manifest itself in vicious acts of violence and even deadly aggression. In 1980 alone, German right-wing extremists perpetrated four different attacks. Ethiopian refugees were forced to relocate to a hotel room after their house near Stuttgart was burned. Vandals destroyed a Turkish store in Hannover. Police in the small town of Lörrach engaged in a street battle to protect a dormitory for asylum seekers after several bomb threats. And two Vietnamese refugees were killed in Hamburg when Molotov cocktails exploded in their hostel.[19]

Hostility to foreigners also produced less violent, if no less xenophobic responses. In November 1981, the right-wing newspaper *Deutsche Wochenzeitung* published a version of the so-called Heidelberg Manifesto, a document that raised a cry of alarm at the "infiltration of the German *Volk* by the immigration of millions of foreigners." The text, according to one report, had not yet been published "officially," but was subsequently leaked to the more mainstream press by leftist student groups who

[16] N.a., "Da sammelt sich ein ungeheurer Sprengstoff," *Der Spiegel*, 2 June 1980, 17.
[17] Schueler, "Die Angst," 3.
[18] Hans Schueler, "Last des Vorurteils," *Die Zeit*, 23 April 1982, 5.
[19] N.a., "Raus mit dem Volk," *Der Spiegel*, 15 September 1980, 19. See also Schueler, "Die Angst," 3.

managed to obtain a copy.[20] Newspapers such as *Die Zeit* and *Frankfurter Rundschau* reprinted this unofficial version in early 1982.[21]

The manifesto was written by Helmut Schröcke, a physicist and mineralogist at the University of Munich also known for his extreme right-wing views. Fourteen other professors signed the statement, including humanists, historians, theologians, and scientists with appointments at Frankfurt, Mainz, Bochum, and Munich.[22] At least two of this group had previously been members of the Nazi Party.[23] Known as the Heidelberg Circle, the professors called for the founding of a *Schutzbund für das deutsche Volk* (Association for the Protection of the German People) that would bring under a single roof "all the associations, organizations, and citizens' initiatives dedicated to the preservation of our people, its language, culture, and customs."[24] These goals echoed policy objectives of the far-right National Democratic Party, which in fact counted some of the Heidelberg Circle among its ranks.

The document urged readers to preserve "the German people (*Volk*) and its cultural identity on the foundation of our Christian and Western heritage," invoking populist rhetoric to argue that peoples with different cultural backgrounds simply could not live together on the same territory.[25] "People (*Völker*) are (biologically and cybernetically) living systems of a high order," declared the Manifesto, "each with its own systemic characteristics which are transmitted genetically and through tradition. For this reason, the integration of large masses of non-German foreigners is impossible for the simultaneous preservation of our people, and leads to the well-known ethnic catastrophes of multicultural societies. Each people, including the German people, has a natural right to preserve its identity and uniqueness in its own environment."[26] Here "*Volk*" was

[20] Hanno Kühnert reported that leftist student groups from Munich found a copy of the Heidelberg Manifesto in a telephone booth in Bonn. See Hanno Kühnert, "Rassistische Klänge," *Die Zeit*, 5 February 1982, 61.

[21] See "Heidelberger Manifest," *Die Zeit*, 5 February 1982, 13; n.a., "Aus dem Wörterbuch des Unmenschen und Bürokratenjargon," *Frankfurter Rundschau*, 4 March 1982, 14.

[22] Kühnert provides short descriptions of the professor signees who agreed to be interviewed. They included Manfred Bambeck, a scholar of Rome at the University of Frankfurt; Kurt Schurmann, a professor and the director of the university's neurosurgery clinic in Mainz; Peter Manns, a Catholic theologian and professor at the University of Mainz; Theodor Schmidt-Kaler, a professor of mathematics and astrophysics at the University of Bochum; and Helmut Schröcke, a professor of physics at the University of Munich. See Kühnert, "Rassistische Klänge," 61.

[23] This includes Werner-Georg Haverbeck and Theodor Oberländer.

[24] *Die Zeit* reprinted the "Heidelberger Manifesto" from the *Deutsche Wochenzeitung* in conjunction with a critical article by Hanno Kühnert. See *Die Zeit*, 5 February 1982, 13.

[25] Ibid.

[26] Ibid.

understood as a genetically similar group of people that maintained its own unique language and customs through propagation. This definition returned to an overtly race-based model of nationhood that had been discredited after the Nazis. At the same time, the author worried that the "genetic transmission" of culture would not be enough to preclude a mixing of "our Volk" if foreigners remained on German soil. While the Heidelberg Manifesto invoked an older rhetoric of essential biological difference, then, it also expressed fear that the 1970s integrationist policies might actually be effective.

Above all, the document suggested, this troubling situation was specifically tied to a "Turkish problem."[27] Turks, the author noted, continued to arrive despite the recruitment halt. Turks were having too many babies. Turks made many Germans feel like foreigners in their own neighborhoods and at their workplace. Turks were unwilling to assimilate and not capable of adapting to German society. Turks with their powerful Muslim faith presented a serious threat to Germany's occidental, Christian heritage. For the first time since early postwar discussions of Afro-German *Mischlingskinder*, the older language of race was invoked to describe a group of people as fundamentally incompatible with Germans.[28]

But it is important to be clear here about the Heidelberg Manifesto's status and impact. Certainly, the statement made unabashed racism more visible in the public sphere and provided a kind of academic legitimacy for such views. Yet the document represented an extremist position: it had only limited influence and attracted little open sympathy outside of the radical right. In fact, the text's inflammatory rhetoric provoked energetic criticism in the mainstream press. *Die Zeit* described the manifesto as full of "prejudices, banalities, barroom wisdom, and bombastic definitions well below the schoolboy level."[29] Journalists further condemned the Heidelberg Circle for inciting "nationalism" and "racism."[30] One critic even blamed the document for underwriting "old Nazis, the NPD,

[27] This term was used in Kühnert, "Rassistische Klänge," 61.

[28] Even though race-based ways of describing difference were discredited by the Nazis, according to Heide Fehrenbach, Germans in the immediate postwar period used this approach to talk about the offspring of African-American GIs and German women. See Heide Fehrenbach, *Race after Hitler: Black Occupation Children in Postwar Germany and America* (Princeton: Princeton University Press, 2005), 87–88.

[29] Kühnert, "Rassistische Klänge, 61.

[30] See, for example, Nina Grunenberg, "Die Politiker müssen Farbe bekennen," *Die Zeit*, 5 February 1982, 5–6; Kühnert, "Rassistische Klänge," 61; Hanno Kühnert, "Von Flöhen und vielen unklugen Menschen," *Frankfurter Rundschau*, 25 February 1982; n.a., "Unser Land hat keinen Nachholbedarf für Nationalismus und Rassismus," *Frankfurter Rundschau*, 4 March 1982.

those who scrawl 'Turks out,' German children who ignore their foreign classmates, and highly educated racists at the more distinguished level of society."[31]

The fact that such an openly racist statement emerged at this particular moment is no accident. As long as guest workers continued to be understood as a temporary presence, separate from West German society, it was possible to suspend the whole question of difference, or more specifically, to explain it away using the language of market expediency and the rationale of mutual benefits. Once the federal government admitted that Turks and other labor migrants were a long-term and perhaps permanent part of society, however, the situation began to change. Now, more explicitly racialized distinctions seemed useful and even necessary as a way to continue marking fundamental differences between Germans and immigrants. What makes this pattern particularly complex is the fact that the Heidelberg authors deliberately invoked older Nazi rhetoric as a tool of provocation within a political landscape hardly comparable with that of the Third Reich. The key lesson here is not that the Heidelberg Manifesto marked a reemergence of Nazi racial politics, but rather that this document signified a new set of racialized concepts specifically designed to inflame a public debate at the very moment when the Federal Republic was beginning to consider the question of multiethnic integration in earnest.

This early 1980s groundswell of concern about the foreigner problem made SPD integrationist policy an easy target for Christian Democrats, who increasingly hammered on *Ausländerpolitik* as a key issue on the domestic front. On 4 February 1982, a heated Bundestag debate on the topic took place in which the CDU laid out its criticisms. Speaking on behalf of his party, Alfred Dregger, a longtime Bundestag representative and the outspoken leader of the Christian Democratic–Christian Socialist (CSU) caucus, accused the ruling coalition of willful neglect in dealing with the foreigner problem during the 1970s.[32] "The government," he charged, "let things drift, repressed the problems, and shifted the burdens to others, especially the states and church organizations."[33] Dregger's strategy was to dismiss SPD integrationist policy as a failure to take meaningful

---

[31] Hans Jakob Ginsburg, "Türken, paßt euch an!," *Die Zeit*, 2 April 1982, 53.

[32] Alfred Dregger served as mayor of Fulda from 1956 to 1970. In 1972 he became a member of the Bundestag and served as leader of the CDU/CSU caucus in the German parliament from 1982 to 1991.

[33] Bundestag, *Verhandlungen des Deutschen Bundestages: Stenographische Berichte*, 9. Wahlperiode, vol. 120 (Bonn: Deutscher Bundestag und Bundesrat, 1982), 4892.

action: the Social Democrats had ignored key warning signs such as the growth of the foreign population and the rise of illegal immigration. He thus rejected the SPD's recent efforts to introduce new restrictions on the numbers of foreigners entering the country as too little, too late.

As an alternative, Dregger outlined a set of policies to fight the foreigner problem head-on. First, he argued for a reconsideration of a "humane" rotation policy.[34] Reintroducing this issue was crucial to the party's attempt to forestall future claims of permanent settlement and family reunion on the part of any foreigner who might come to Germany for work or education. Rotation, Dregger explained, would prevent overcrowding and allow other foreigners to pursue training or vocational opportunities in Germany in the future. Second, the CDU explicitly repudiated the right of foreigners to become German citizens. Dregger justified the position by pointing to a failure of acculturation: "As the example of Turks already shows, there are foreigners even in the second generation who have remained and want to remain foreigners in terms of mentality and language. If that is the case, naturalization is not possible."[35] Christian Democrats claimed to respect the desire of foreigners to preserve their national identities, but at the cost of citizenship. For the CDU, in other words, naturalization required full "Germanization." Finally, the party put forward new parameters for social integration, arguing that "the task of social integration lies squarely with the foreigners who do not want to become German, who come from other cultural circles, and who want to protect their characteristics."[36] Unlike the SPD, which defined social integration as a mutual process that would transform both Germans and foreigners, the CDU transferred the work of integration to migrants alone.

In addition to these specific proposals, Dregger offered a more general opinion on the question of foreigners. "It is always false," he asserted, "to disregard human nature and people's ways of thinking when making political decisions. People, not only Germans, place value on preserving their national identity in principle. This permits the acceptance of only a limited number of foreigners."[37] The presence of too many unassimilated migrants, in this view, would make it impossible to maintain the integrity of German culture. At the same time, Dregger distinguished among four

---

[34] Ibid., 4895.
[35] Ibid., 4895.
[36] Ibid., 4895.
[37] Ibid., 4892.

categories of foreigners, suggesting that some were more compatible with Germans than others. People from the south Tyrol, Austria, and Switzerland, who were foreign citizens but spoke German, presented no integration problem. Other Europeans shared the common Christian roots of European culture, which made integration and eventual assimilation likely. But Turks, along with people from Asian and African countries, brought such unfamiliar cultures, religions, and values that accommodation was virtually impossible.

Focusing on Turks as the key group of unassimilable foreigners, Dregger stressed differences of culture and mentality. "The Turkish people," he argued,

were not shaped by Christianity, rather by Islam – another high culture, and I stress, high culture. The fact that the state founded by Ataturk in 1918 is secular and understands itself as European changes nothing, anymore than the fact that our state is also secular rather than the earlier Holy Roman Empire. Even in its more secular form, the cultural impulses of Christian and Islamic high culture have a lasting effect on our peoples. This contributes, in addition to a pronounced national pride of the Turks, to the fact that they are not assimilable. They want to remain what they are, namely Turks. And we should respect this.[38]

Turkey's embrace of the outward trappings of European secularism, in other words, did not mitigate the fundamental, irreconcilable differences that existed between Turkish and German culture. As evidence of this, Dregger pointed out that largely insular Turkish "ghettos" had developed in all the major West German cities. While he praised the instinct of Turks to keep to themselves and maintain their unique culture, he argued that they should do so in Turkey rather than Germany.

What Dregger offered here was a particular theory of ethnicity and culture. German culture, in this conception, was neither superior nor inferior to Turkish culture; the two were simply different. Dregger did not question the legitimacy or value of multiple cultural traditions. Indeed, he celebrated the fact that significant, historically rich cultures, by definition, operated according to distinct and specific logics. Yet the very strength and persistence of Islamic culture presented a new dilemma for postwar West German society. Turkish "ghettos" created pockets of an enduring minority culture within an equally strong majority culture. Dregger likened this form of mixing to the unstable combination of oil and water, in which both cultures – discrete, impenetrable, and with fundamentally incompatible interests – coexisted uneasily in isolated enclaves. Deeming such

[38] Ibid., 4893.

a scenario unacceptable, Dregger's solution was to relocate Turks within their natural and historical home. Ultimately, his was a theory of culture that posited an unwavering, largely immutable ethnic core or essence. Culture, in other words, became virtually synonymous with ethnicity.

This new approach to *Ausländerpolitik* marked a dramatic shift in the political discourse away from SPD discussions about how best to facilitate integration and toward the question of whether guest workers possessed the *capacity* to integrate. The opinion of the general public also seemed to follow this pattern. Whereas only 39 percent of the native population had believed guest workers should return home in 1979, over 60 percent affirmed this statement in 1982. And the 42 percent of West Germans who had endorsed active integration efforts in 1979 dropped to a mere 11 percent in 1982.[39] That same year, several local citizens' initiatives organized campaigns to limit or reduce the overall number of foreigners on German soil. In Hamburg, for example, the NPD created the *Liste für Ausländerbegrenzung und Beseitigung von Mißständen* (Electoral Slate for the Limitation of Foreigners and Removal of Social Evils) as part of its campaign for mayor.[40] And Bochum's *Bürgerinitiative Ausländerstopp* (Citizens' Initiative for Halting Foreigners) put up posters around the city that featured a young, apparently blonde German woman and three smiling children with the slogan, "Stop foreigners...so that we have a future!"[41]

The growing consensus that the foreigner problem had spiraled out of control made the CDU's more restrictive *Ausländerpolitik* particularly appealing to many West Germans. This ideological shift on the guest worker question was a contributing factor to the larger political crisis facing the Social Democrats, a crisis which generally has been explained in terms of tensions between conservative and progressive factions within both the SPD and FDP.[42] The trouble came to a head when the FDP decided to leave the ruling coalition and partner with the Christian Democrats. Without a clear parliamentary majority for his party, Schmidt called for a vote of confidence. The results on 1 October 1982

---

[39] Schönwälder, "Migration, Refugees," 166.

[40] Charlotte Wiedemann, "Sauber und deutsch," *Die Zeit*, 2 April 1982.

[41] In addition to the citizens' initiative in Bochum, the two other most important local initiatives were the Hamburger *Liste für Ausländerstopp* and the Kieler *Liste wider die Überfremdung*. For a contemporary discussion of the growth of these right extremist movements, see Dietrich Strothmann, "Witterung der Braunen," *Die Zeit*, 23 April 1982, 5.

[42] Bark and Gress, *History of West Germany*, vol. 2, 368–80.

constituted a clear defeat for the SPD and enabled Kohl, as head of the Christian Democratic Party, to assume the chancellorship. General elections held the following spring produced a landslide victory for the CDU/CSU, which marked the culmination of a political sea change and underscored the extent to which SPD integrationist politics had lost their public mandate.[43]

One source of the CDU's success during the early 1980s was the fact that it took seriously the fears and concerns articulated by the far right while simultaneously providing a somewhat softer approach to the foreigner problem. Dregger harshly criticized the SPD for placing the interests of guest workers above those of Germans. He even warned that if West Germany became a country of immigration, it would "pave the way for a new right radicalism."[44] At the same time, Dregger sought to distinguish the Christian Democrats' position from that of the extreme right. In contrast to the Heidelberg professors, who insisted on "genetically transmitted" differences between groups of peoples, Dregger claimed that such distinctions resulted from strong cultural traditions. On one level, this position foregrounded a public expression of respect for others and used the characteristics of cultural strength and durability not so much to demonize foreigners explicitly as to construct a more reasoned argument about the impracticality of expecting migrants to assimilate. Yet Dregger's theory ultimately produced the same kinds of conclusions as the gene-based theories of the far right. Whether defined in physiological or cultural terms, both lines of conservative argument presumed that migrant identities were immutable and therefore incommensurable with an equally immutable German culture. The CDU position also shared the extreme right's predilection for zero-sum logics: in each case, the presence of the foreign was understood as something that supplants rather than enriches or expands.

It is worth noting that similar arguments were circulating in Great Britain around this same time. As Martin Barker first demonstrated in 1981, Margaret Thatcher's rise to power (and the rebirth of conservative ideology that preceded it) was supported by what he termed "new racism," a mode of public discourse based on the assumption that

---

[43] The CDU/CSU won in the spring of 1983 with 48.8 percent of the vote. Only the 1957 election gave the CDU/CSU a higher margin of victory, with 50.2 percent of the vote. See Bark and Gress, *History of West Germany*, 387.

[44] Bundestag, *Verhandlungen des Deutschen Bundestages*, 4894.

immigrants threatened the British "way of life." British conservatives advocating this view emphatically eschewed any connection to racists, who, they claimed, propagated hatred by insisting on the superiority of one group over another. Instead, according to Barker, Tories suggested that "human nature" impelled people "to form a bounded community, a nation, aware of its differences from other nations."[45] The instinctive desire to defend one's "way of life, traditions and customs against outsiders" arose not because immigrants were "inferior" but because they belonged to "different cultures."[46] This new theorization of race by British conservatives, like that of their German counterparts, drew considerable power from its ability both to avoid older, biologically based explanations of race and to reframe racial distinctions in terms of national and cultural difference. In the process, a new commonsense emerged that viewed cultural differences as fundamentally irreconcilable and thus understood immigration as antithetical to the natural desire for a homogeneous national community.[47]

The stance on foreigners espoused by Kohl and the CDU, however, took shape in the context of a uniquely West German set of issues. It emerged alongside a larger *Tendenzwende* or conservative turn in German intellectual life after 1977.[48] One of the most significant aspects of this shift was a renewed public discussion of national identity in which conservatives argued that Germans required a positive image of the national past and strove to create the basis for a new and healthier patriotism. Franz Josef Strauss, the head of the CSU, declared:

It's high time that we emerged from the shadow of the Third Reich . . . and become a normal nation again. . . . To idolize the nation is catastrophic and disastrous; but to deny the nation, to deny one's national identity, to destroy our national identity, to refuse to return to it, to a purified national consciousness, is just as disastrous. . . . German history can't be reduced to the twelve years of Adolf

---

[45] Martin Barker, *The New Racism: Conservatives and the Ideology of the Tribe* (London: Junction Books, 1980), 21.

[46] Ibid., 23–24.

[47] Ibid., 1–53. Paul Gilroy has discussed Barker's work recently within the larger context of a "crisis of raciology." See Paul Gilroy, *Against Race: Imagining Political Culture Beyond the Color Line* (Cambridge, MA: Harvard University Press, 2000), 32–39.

[48] For elaborations of the *Tendenzwende* in the context of the West German *Historikerstreit* (historians' debate), see Richard J. Evans, "The New Nationalism and the Old History: Perspectives on the West German Historikerstreit," *Journal of Modern History* 59 (1987): 761–97; and Geoff Eley, "Nazism, Politics and the Image of the Past: Thoughts on the West German Historikerstreit, 1986–1987," *Past and Present* 121 (1988): 171–208.

Hitler or even to the years 1914–45. German history can't be presented as an endless chain of mistakes and crimes, and our youth thereby robbed of the chance to recover some genuine backbone among our people and toward the outside world.[49]

For Strauss, pride in the nation was a key element to West German "normalization." The atrocities of the Third Reich should now be understood as the exception rather than the rule. National identity and history, in this view, were intimately linked. Upon assuming office, Kohl developed a similar position with two large-scale national historical projects: the construction of the German Historical Museum in West Berlin and the House of History for the Federal Republic in Bonn. The goal in each case was to provide ordinary citizens with historical narratives that would inspire pride – rather than shame or guilt – in the nation.[50]

The ideological stakes of this push to reconstitute national identity became clearer in the spring of 1985, as the Federal Republic began to mark the fortieth anniversaries surrounding the end of the Second World War. For one of these occasions Kohl invited U.S. President Ronald Reagan to lay a wreath at the Bitburg military cemetery to commemorate the fortieth anniversary of Germany's unconditional surrender.[51] Although the request provoked an international uproar once it became known that SS soldiers had been buried there, Reagan nevertheless completed the visit as planned and justified the decision by explaining that the ceremony was intended not to reawaken bad memories but to commemorate the day peace began.[52] In many ways, the Bitburg ceremony was an audacious feat. As historian Geoff Eley has argued, Kohl orchestrated the event as "an act of symbolic resolution . . . the consummation of Germany's long-earned return to normalcy."[53] Central to this process was an interweaving of democratic self-congratulation and the production of new historical narratives. Precisely because the Federal Republic had achieved four decades of democratic stability, it had earned the right to honor its war

[49] Franz Josef Strauss, "Mehr aufrechten Gang," *Frankfurter Rundschau*, 14 January 1987, quoted in Geoff Eley, "Nazism, Politics and the Image of the Past," 182.
[50] For more discussion of the historical context for the German Historical Museum project, see Harold James, *A German Identity: 1770–1990* (New York: Routledge, 1989), 203–205; and Sabine von Dirke, "Multikulti: The German Debate on Multiculturalism," *German Studies Review* 17.3 (1994): 516–17.
[51] For an excellent sourcebook on the Bitburg event, see Geoffrey Hartman, ed., *Bitburg in Moral and Political Perspective* (Bloomington: Indiana University Press, 1986).
[52] Evans, "New Nationalism," 789.
[53] Eley, "Nazism, Politics" 176.

dead (many of whom had no specific ties to the Nazi Party) like other democratic nations.

A similar impulse to relativize and ultimately supersede the Nazi past lay at the heart of the *Historikerstreit* (historians' debate) that erupted the very next year. The public uproar began when the conservative philosopher Ernst Nolte published an article in the *Frankfurter Allgemeine Zeitung* entitled "The Past That Will Not Pass Away." In the essay, he questioned the singularity of the Holocaust and presented the Nazi policy of genocide toward the Jews as a response to an equally heinous threat to themselves from the Soviets. This unpleasant episode, Nolte suggested, was just that – a single twelve-year period in a long and otherwise highly distinguished German historical record.[54]

Our inclination has been to read the *Tendenzwende* and its conservative ideology as a broader retrenchment against a generation of late-1960s leftist critics who participated in the student movement and promoted such forms of extraparliamentary politics as antinuclear protests, the rise of the Greens, and grassroots citizens' initiatives.[55] Less well understood and acknowledged are the ways in which this neoconservative discourse also focused directly on the guest workers. The calls for a new, more energetic nationalism were never simply an issue of moving beyond Nazi guilt or *Wiedergutmachung* (reparations) for the Holocaust. A revived national identity needed historical narratives capable of inspiring pride, but also required a reassertion of borders and clear definitions of cultural membership. For conservatives, raising national consciousness was always interwoven with an insistently homogeneous conception of the nation and a less sanguine view about the possibility of multiethnic cohabitation.[56] The push for patriotism, moreover, seems to have undergirded the zero-sum logic central to the CDU *Ausländerpolitik*. As the party encouraged and championed a restored German self-esteem, it increasingly maintained that strong national cultures could not cross-pollinate and ultimately belonged in their natural homes.

---

[54] For the most important scholarly discussions of this affair, see Evans, "New Nationalism"; Eley "Nazism, Politics"; Charles S. Maier, *The Unmasterable Past: History, Holocaust and German National Identity* (Cambridge, MA: Harvard University Press, 1988); and Hans-Ulrich Wehler, *Entsorgung der deutschen Vergangenheit? Ein polemischer Essay zum "Historikerstreit"* (Munich: C. H. Beck, 1988).

[55] See, for example, Evans, "New Nationalism," 782–84; Eley, "Nazism, Politics," 184–90.

[56] Several scholars have alluded to a connection between the resurgence in nationalism and the efforts to deal with the "foreigner problem." See especially von Dirke, "Multikulti," 515–17; and Schönwälder, "Migration, Refugees," 166–68.

Rethinking Integration on the Left: Gender as Litmus Test

Thus far, we have traced the legacy of SPD integration and, in particular, the backlash that developed as many leading voices on the right side of the political and ideological spectrum came to doubt the policy's efficacy. At this point it also seems worth asking, What about the left? What happened to the nexus of SPD political officials, social workers, church volunteers, academics, and public intellectuals who had been central to the formulation of integration policy as well as its grassroots implementation? Although the CDU coalition came to dominate politics after the early 1980s, it would be a mistake to neglect the ideological trajectories of these diverse groups. Their thinking about integration certainly did not remain static. Indeed, the changes in their approaches tell us a great deal not only about the shifting balance of power in West German politics, but also about a new pessimism toward the possibility of forging a multiethnic nation. Most important, it is only by following the trajectory of leftist thinking about migrants during the ascendancy of the CDU that we can begin to excavate the origins of a crucial development in the history of the guest worker question – the emergence of gender roles as a litmus test for integration.

A good place to begin is the SPD response to the upsurge in antiforeigner sentiment and conservative attacks on integration policy. Forced into a defensive posture, the Schmidt administration largely shelved the recommendations outlined by the Commissioner for Foreigners' Affairs in 1978, Heinz Kühn. Members of the cabinet rejected Kühn's declaration that West Germany had become a country of immigration as too risky and refused to accept the high costs of his integration proposals.[57] Frustrated by the lack of support for his progressive ideas, Kühn resigned the position in October 1980; he was replaced by Liselotte Funcke of the FDP.

Subsequently, the social-liberal coalition began to espouse a more restrictive *Ausländerpolitik*, proposing to limit the numbers of foreigners entering the country under the principle of family reunion.[58] In early 1982, the Schmidt government distanced itself even more from the Kühn position: "There is unity [in the government] that the Federal Republic ... is not a country of immigration and should not become one. The cabinet

---

[57] Dieter Düdig, *Heinz Kühn, 1912–1992: Eine politische Biographie* (Essen: Klartext Verlag, 2002), 316–17.
[58] Barbara Marshall, *The New Germany and Migration in Europe* (Manchester: Manchester University Press, 2000), 13.

agrees that a further influx of foreigners from outside the European Community should be prevented by all possible legal means.... Only by a consistent and effective policy of limitation can the indispensable agreement of the German population for the integration of foreigners be secured. This is essential for the maintenance of social peace."[59] The incidents of violence against foreigners and general rise in xenophobia seem to have forced the Schmidt administration to rethink the basic conditions under which integration would be effective. West Germans, this statement suggested, possessed the capacity to tolerate difference, but only when they did not feel overwhelmed by it. Limiting the number of migrants thus became a necessary prerequisite for a successful integration policy.

Social Democrats strongly affirmed this position during the *Ausländerpolitik* debate in the Bundestag in February 1982. The speaker for the SPD was Representative Hans-Eberhard Urbaniak, an established member of the Bundestag from Dortmund active in trade-union politics. "We are for integration and consolidation," Urbaniak declared, outlining his party's new two-pronged approach to the opposition.[60] Without jettisoning integration altogether, he insisted on "consolidation" – measures to reduce the size of the foreigner population. The Federal Republic, Urbaniak acknowledged, had reached a threshold for absorbing foreigners, especially Turks, and allowing more to enter "would be irresponsible for both population groups in our country and would work against integration."[61] Responding to heightened public anxieties about being overrun by foreigners, the SPD pledged to halt the influx of migrants as well as curtail the increase in illegal workers. At the level of party politics, then, Social Democrats countered CDU criticism of integration by tempering their earlier progressive stance on foreigners with a new sense of limits.

By contrast, the Green Party had a far less clearly articulated position on the guest worker question in the early 1980s. This is not all that surprising since the Greens only emerged as a regional political force in 1978 and did not surpass the 5 percent threshold in national elections (giving the party its first seats in the Bundestag) until 1983. To the extent that the party represented a merging of the alternative subcultures and the citizens' initiatives movement, many Green activists and supporters (especially women) had long been engaged with the practical, grassroots

---

[59] Bundesministerium des Inneren, *Aufzeichnungen zur Ausländerpolitik und zum Ausländerrecht der Bundesrepublik Deutschland* (Bonn: Bundesministerium des Inneren), 3, quoted in Marshall, *New Germany*, 13.
[60] Bundestag, *Verhandlungen des Deutschen Bundestages*, 4888.
[61] Ibid., 4890.

work of integrating migrants. But in terms of formal policy statements, it was really through the issue of asylum that the Greens initially addressed the presence of foreigners in the early 1980s. The occasion for the Green Party's questions about enforcement of the asylum law was the death of Turkish dissident and political refugee Kemal Altun, who committed suicide in 1982 upon learning that he would be sent back to Turkey. Speaking to the Bundestag, Joschka Fischer, the student radical turned parliamentary representative, compared Altun's death to that of Walter Benjamin, who took his own life on the Spanish-French border as he fled the Nazis.[62] For Fischer and the Greens, West Germany's liberal asylum law served as a cornerstone of the nation's efforts to overcome its shameful past. The Altun tragedy was problematic not so much because it was an effect of the far-reaching conservative attempts to curtail the numbers of foreigners, but rather because it indicated a wavering commitment to the project of democratization. The Greens' staunch insistence that atonement and remembrance belonged at the center of West German political culture made the party the most outspoken advocate for upholding the asylum provision to the letter of the law.

The pattern of retrenchment within the sphere of partisan politics and among the more mainstream Left did not mean that integration was abandoned in other areas. For example, the Commissioner for Foreigners' Affairs at both the federal and state levels retained its function as official advocate for foreigner interests and concerns. Religious organizations and grassroots social welfare groups maintained their efforts to help guest workers navigate the German environment with language classes, legal advice, childcare, and counseling. And agencies such as the Federal Ministry for Youth, Family, and Health and the Institute for Research on the Future continued to commission and conduct research on migrants.[63]

Yet one can also detect an epistemological shift taking place in the very discourse of integration, especially among academics, social workers, and feminists. This shift emerges most clearly in the growing number

---

[62] Bundestag, *Verhandlungen des Deutschen Bundestages: Stenographische Berichte*, 10. Wahlperiode, vol. 125 (Bonn: Deutscher Bundestag und Bundesrat, 1983), 1313–17. Reprinted in Joschka Fischer, *Von grüner Kraft und Herrlichkeit* (Hamburg: Rohwohlt Verlag, 1984), 150–59.

[63] See, for example, Franz Brandt, *Situationsanalyse nichterwerbstätiger Ehefrauen ausländischer Arbeitnehmer in der Bundesrepublik Deutschland* (Bonn: Bundesminister für Jugend, Familie und Gesundheit, 1977); and Ute Welzel, ed., *Situation der Ausländerinnen: Fachtagung am 19.–21. September in Berlin* (Berlin: Institut für Zukunftsforschung, 1981).

of German-language publications about migrant women produced during the late 1970s and early 1980s. One major subcurrent within this discourse was the body of research compiled by academic scholars and religious leaders.[64] These studies identified the particular situation faced by foreign women in West Germany as a central problem for the work of integration: migrant women experienced overwhelming isolation and oppression, suffering from such feelings much more acutely than their husbands or children. A 1977 report sponsored by the Federal Ministry for Youth, Family, and Health, for instance, explained that women from Italy, Greece, Yugoslavia, and Turkey all lived with some form of gendered spatial segregation. Most generally interacted with the outside world through their husbands and did not leave the house unaccompanied.[65]

But the larger goal of this research was to understand the cultural context of these practices, which produced uniquely gendered effects in the Federal Republic. Above all, the studies stressed structural causes over essential cultural differences for female migrants' isolation. A 1980 Berlin conference sponsored by the Institut für Zukunftsforschung (Institute for Research on the Future) and the city's Senatorin für Familie, Jugend und Sport (Senator for Family, Youth and Sports), for example, suggested that the strict separation of male and female worlds gave foreign women "security" and a "sense of belonging" in their homelands.[66] In addition to providing them with clear roles and a place in the family hierarchy, gender segregation fostered a strong sense of solidarity among women. Female isolation and oppression, the conference group maintained, was not intrinsic to the cultural practice itself, but developed in the process of migration. In many cases, the move to West Germany cut women off from their familiar village milieu and created new language barriers, which made communication beyond the immediate family circle virtually impossible. Relocation also placed migrant women in an environment

---

[64] Works that fall into this group include: Brandt, *Situationsanalyse*; *Informationsdienst Bildungsarbeit mit ausländischen Arbeitern, Sonderheft/Frauen* (Bonn: Deutscher Volkshochschul-Verband e.V., 1981); Welzel, *Situation der Ausländerinnen*; Christine Huth and Jürgen Micksch, eds., *Ausländische Frauen: Interviews, Analysen und Anregungen für die Praxis* (Frankfurt: Verlag Otto Lembeck, 1982); Peter Schmuck, *Der Islam und seine Bedeutung für türkische Familien in der Bundesrepublik Deutschland* (Munich: DJI Verlag, 1982); Rita Rosen and Gerd Stüwe, *Ausländische Mädchen in der Bundesrepublik* (Opladen: Leske & Budrich, 1985); Westmüller, *Kultur und Emanzipation*; and Rita Rosen, *Muß kommen, aber nix von Herzen: zur Lebenssituationen von Migrantinnen unter besonderer Berücksichtigung der Biographien türkischer Frauen* (Opladen: Leske & Budrich, 1986). For an extensive list of the work on foreign women, see Alice Münscher, *Ausländische Frauen: Annotierte Bibliographie* (Munich: DJI Verlag, 1980).

[65] Brandt, *Situationsanalyse*, 180–206.

[66] Welzel, *Situation der Ausländerinnen*, 17–19.

with radically different social norms, which often provoked fathers or husbands to regulate their movements far more strictly than in the home country.[67]

A striking feature of this literature was its willingness to acknowledge findings that complicated or contradicted researchers' initial assumptions. A good example is a 1982 Protestant Church study coauthored by a scholar and a prominent pastor, which observed that many of the earliest migrant women came as guest workers before their husbands. "This was astounding," the authors declared, "because being employed does not correspond to the traditional Turkish ideas about the role of the woman."[68] While this report expressed great surprise at the inversion of customary gender roles, it simultaneously recognized the flexibility of "traditional Turkish ideas." A similar pattern appeared in a 1982 examination of Islam and its meaning for Turkish women in the Federal Republic. For over fifty pages, the book depicted a social order shaped by seemingly static customs and behavioral norms. "Family life and education," it argued, are in considerable measure "restrictively shaped through Islam: at the very least, half of the population – the women – are robbed by Islam of fundamental human rights."[69] In the next breath, however, the author complicated this argument by acknowledging that economic shifts, generational changes, and the migration experience itself all routinely reshaped Turkish-German family structure. "In the course of emigration," he concluded, traditional structure is "broken, just as it is disrupted within Turkey through economic and political developments."[70]

The emphasis on women in these studies, it is important to note, developed out of a progressive impulse to move beyond the caricature of the male guest worker that dominated German public imagination in the era of labor recruitment. The new focus was part of the growing push to recognize migrants and their families as de facto immigrants and to understand the full complexity of guest worker lives. But what is particularly interesting in the first half of the 1980s is that the attention to migrant women shifted from highly nuanced efforts at cultural understanding to a recurring trope of the imprisoned, imperiled Turkish woman. The trope itself was inextricably connected to the emergence of a new context for the guest worker question – what in Germany is often described as "reportage."

[67] Ibid.
[68] Huth and Micksch, *Ausländische Frauen*, 31.
[69] Schmuck, *Der Islam*, 52.
[70] Ibid., 51.

Trope and context are not easily separated here. It was precisely the movement of guest worker representations into a domain associated with popularly accessible, journalistic treatments of contemporary social problems that fueled the new trope's force.

One of the earliest examples of reportage on migrant women was *Die verkauften Bräute: Türkische Frauen zwischen Kreuzberg und Anatolien* (Sold Brides: Turkish Women between Kreuzberg and Anatolia), published by Rowohlt Verlag. The fact that a widely distributed, sales-driven press like Rowohlt began to exhibit interest in foreign (especially Turkish) women is itself instructive. For the first time, we can begin to see public fascination with the migrant experience moving beyond the context of academic studies and specialty presses into the commercial mainstream.[71] It is also instructive to consider the promotional process. While it is difficult to determine who precisely constituted the audience for this kind of reportage, Rowohlt's marketing choices for *Die verkauften Bräute* offer some useful clues. The book appeared in the "Frauen aktuell" (contemporary women) series, a list which also included: *Die Hausfrauengruppe oder Wie elf Frauen sich selbst helfen* (*The Housewives Group or How Eleven Women Help Themselves*), *Was haben die Parteien für die Frauen getan?* (*What Have the Political Parties Done for Women?*), and *Frauen gegen Apartheid* (*Women against Apartheid*).[72] Advertisements for the series as a whole ran in national feminist magazines such as *Courage*. From the vantage point of the Rowohlt marketing department, at least, the target audience for *Die verkauften Bräute* seemed relatively clear. This was a book specifically addressed to West German women sympathetic to leftist political causes and grassroots activism.

---

[71] Other books on migrant women (and girls) published in this vein include: Erika Fekete, *Eine Chance für Fatma: Jeder von uns könnte mit türkischen Kindern arbeiten* (Hamburg: Rowohlt, 1982); and Gaby Franger, *Wir haben es uns anders vorgestellt: Türkische Frauen in der Bundesrepublik* (Frankfurt: Fischer, 1984).

[72] The series advertisement appeared in *Courage*, November 1979, 46. The full list of advertised books includes: Carola Stern, ed., *Was haben die Parteien für die Frauen getan?* (Hamburg: Rowohlt, 1976); Herta Däubler-Gmelin, *Frauenarbeitslosigkeit oder Reserve zurück an den Herd!* (Hamburg: Rowohlt, 1977); Cheryl Benard and Edit Schlaffer, *Die ganz gewöhnliche Gewalt in der Ehe* (Hamburg: Rowohlt, 1978); Lukrezia Jochimsen, *Sozialismus als Männersache oder Kennen Sie "Bebels Frau"?* (Hamburg: Rowohlt, 1978); Pro Familie Bremen, ed., *Wir wollen nicht mehr nach Holland fahren* (Hamburg: Rowohlt, 1978); Carmen Thomas, ed., *Die Hausfrauengruppe oder Wie elf Frauen sich selbst helfen* (Hamburg: Rowohlt, 1978); Susanne von Paczensky, ed., *Frauen und Terror: Versuche, die Beteiligung von Frauen an Gewalttaten zu erklären* (Hamburg: Rowohlt, 1979); and Ruth Weiss, ed., *Frauen gegen Apartheid: Zur Geschichte des politischen Widerstandes von Frauen* (Hamburg: Rowohlt, 1980).

The book's foreword, written by the well-known and highly respected feminist activist Susanne von Paczensky, demonstrates a similar mode of public address. For Paczensky, the larger purpose of the project was to "make visible the difficulties and discrimination of Turkish women in the Federal Republic of Germany – with the goal of changing them. Whoever wants to help or work with them must first of all understand their situation, and that can only happen when one knows about their origin."[73] Like the Rowohlt advertisements, Paczensky's foreword hails a broad constituency of liberally minded teachers, social workers, counselors, and feminist sympathizers. Yet what are we to make of her simultaneous invocation to ameliorate migrant "difficulties" by going to their "origin"?

To some extent, the project introduced by Paczensky operated within a broader pattern of leftist discourse. Much like the scholarly studies we have already considered, *Die verkauften Bräute* looked to Turkey, and especially to the social customs of the village, to diagnose the problems migrant women faced in Germany.[74] Still, it is possible to detect a difference in tone and emphasis from one genre to the other. In the academic studies, the goal was to account for the impacts of the migration process on women by comparing social practices across cultures. The reportage in *Die verkauften Bräute*, by contrast, presented Islam as the root cause of a fundamental crisis within Turkish gender relations. "In almost all areas of women's lives," the authors Andrea Baumgartner-Karabak and Gisela Landesberger explained,

the influence of Islam is recognizable. Marriage and divorce are often carried out according to Islamic law. The Koran contains exact prescriptions relating to the treatment of women, against whom it discriminates strongly. Orientation to the world, moral ideas, and customary behavior are prescribed by religion, whose content is enforced by relatives and the village community. Firmly fitted within the patriarchal family, the trajectory of women's lives is completely predetermined. Decisions are first made for them by the father; after the wedding, by the husband. They have little influence on the choice of marriage partner. Their role in the household is characterized by unconditional subordination to the husband and the head of the household. Their social place within the family and in the village is defined by their sons.[75]

---

73 Susanne von Paczensky, "Frauen aus Anatolien: Vorwort," in Andrea Baumgartner-Karabak and Gisela Landesberger, *Die verkauften Bräute: Türkische Frauen zwischen Kreuzberg und Anatolien* (Hamburg: Rowohlt, 1978), 8.
74 The book's authors, Andrea Baumgartner-Karabak and Gisela Landesberger, described the experience of Turkish women on the basis of a visit to rural Anatolia, personalizing their discussion with journal entries and pictures from the trip.
75 Baumgartner-Karabak and Landesberger, *Die verkauften Bräute*, 67–68.

Islamic custom, in this view, left virtually no room for female agency. Women's lives were "predetermined"; decisions were "made for them"; their "social place" was fully defined by the men around them.

The larger point of the argument, however, was not so much to critique village customs as to comment upon their transfer to West Germany via the labor migration. In the foreword, Paczensky made this clear by instructing German readers to consider the book's information about village culture in relation to the behavior of the migrant women in their midst. "Turkish women now live in our cities," she declared,

> as unassimilable, strange bodies. It is no wonder that they provoke prejudice.... They walk humbly two steps behind their husbands, and even relinquish the particular domain of women – shopping for food and clothes – to their husbands or children. They contradict every imaginable image of woman: they do not do justice to the traditional role of an efficient mother, who self-confidently manages the household, much less do they meet emancipated demands in their own ways of life.[76]

As the passage unfolds, it becomes clear that the problem facing migrant women is also a threat to the liberal, democratic values upheld by West German feminists. Turkish women, according to Paczensky, fail to live up to Western society's most basic standards, not even fulfilling "traditional" female roles. Her implication is that the Islamic customs described in *Die verkauften Bräute* "contradict" – and ultimately prove incompatible with – the historical emancipation of European women.

It is important to stress that Paczensky's critique was designed, first and foremost, to invite further study by progressive-minded Germans and encourage sympathy with migrant women. Her stated purpose was to foster intercultural understanding, as opposed to overt xenophobia or stricter foreigner policies. Yet Paczensky also makes it clear that the ultimate goal of intercultural understanding was to extricate non-Western women from customs and practices deemed illiberal or even destructive. Certain types of behavior, in short, simply had to be discarded for integration into West German society to succeed. This stance was not unexpected given that most of those working with migrants at the grassroots level were

[76] Paczensky, "Frauen aus Anatolien," 7. Susanne von Paczensky, it is worth noting, is considered a major activist of the post-1945 period. As a young woman she was one of the few Germans allowed to observe the Nuremberg trials. A journalist, author, and sociologist, Paczensky became very politically active and participated in the women's, peace, and environmental movements. I include this quote precisely to demonstrate that West German discomfort with the possibility of reciprocal change in the process of integration has not been restricted to those on the Right.

self-identified feminists who read the situation of Turkish women through the lens of their own struggles. The sight of migrant women wearing head-scarves, walking behind their husbands, and being cooped up in their homes seemed to undermine the basic gender equality for which German feminists had fought so hard. What thus begins as an expression of con-cern and desire to study the problems of Turkish patriarchy eventually becomes an articulation of thresholds between West and East, progres-sive politics and reactionary tradition, feminist practice and unreformed patriarchy.

Other examples of reportage from the same period deploy a subtler version of this same logic. Consider, for example, Sigrid Meske's *Sit-uationsanalyse türkischer Frauen* (*Analysis of the Situation of Turkish Women*), published by the smaller, left-oriented press Berlin Express Edi-tion. On one level, this book offered a fuller picture of Islamic practice by distinguishing between two main groups of Turkish Muslims, the Sunni and the Alevi. "The Alevi," Meske asserted, "reserve a respected place in society and the family for women. No strict separation of the sexes occurs.... In addition, the ritual prescriptions of the Alevi are less strict and orthodox than the Sunni. The Sunni represent the view that Islam refuses women every right, humiliates them, and thereby makes every emancipation impossible."[77] Here Islam appears as a multivalent belief system. It was only the Sunni, in Meske's view, who violated Western values and norms.

Yet her subsequent discussion of women's lives ultimately collapses the categories of Sunni and Turk. The section on women in Turkey concludes with the following statement: "A traditional society in Turkey means a developed patriarchal social form. These structures are shaped by Islam and assign women a subordinate position in comparison to men. Western

---

[77] Sigrid Meske, *Situationsanalyse türkischer Frauen in der BRD: Unter den Aspekt ihrer kulturellen Neuorientierung im Vergleich zu ihren Lebensbedingungen in der Türkei* (Berlin: Express Edition, 1983), 40. Meske was one of the first West German authors to recognize and write about the differences between Sunni and Alevi Turks. As Betigül Ercan Argun has noted, it was only in the mid-1980s that Germans and Europeans more generally began to become aware of the ethnic, religious, and political differences within the migrant community of Turkish guest workers. Betigül Ercan Argun, *Turkey in Germany: The Transnational Sphere of Deutschkei* (New York: Routledge, 2003), 67–70. See also Aytaç Eryilmaz and Mathilde Jamin, eds., *Fremde Heimat-Yaban Sılan Olur: Eine Geschichte der Einwanderung aus der Türkei* (Essen: Klartext, 1998), 24. For a helpful analysis of the Sunni and Alevi with respect to the practice of wearing the headscarf, see Ruth Mandel, "Turkish Headscarves and the 'Foreigner Problem': Constructing Difference through Emblems of Identity," *New German Critique* 46 (1989): 27–46.

influence and political shifts bring about changes in the ways of thinking and living, especially in the big cities."[78] In this formulation, Sunni
practice stands in for Turkish social organization as a whole and serves as
an unqualified evil. The ideological assumptions become even more evi-
dent in Meske's analysis of Turkish housewives' experience in the Federal
Republic: "Because of her socialization, [the housewife] has no possibility to leave the house or interact with neighbors. She also hardly has the
opportunity to come into contact with German society. It is thus difficult
for these women to create new values in the Federal Republic."[79] At the
core of this argument is the belief that "contact" with Germans is the
primary catalyst for Turkish women to break free from constricted lives
and achieve more equitable gender relations.

Such assumptions did not go unchallenged by the small numbers of
migrant women active in West German feminist and social work circles
during the early 1980s. A good example is Neval Gültekin-Neumann, a
Turkish-German social worker who sought to draw attention to some
of the ideological blindspots and prescriptive tendencies embedded
in German feminism.[80] In a 1983 issue of *Informationsdienst zur
Ausländerarbeit*, a newsletter for people working with foreigners,
Gültekin-Neumann reported on a conference about female migrants in
Europe. Her summary of the conference provides a powerful critique
of the mainstream feminist assumptions behind the reportage we have
considered:

If a foreign woman complains about certain troubles or even repression in the
family, the European women in most cases wish that she would make herself
independent. This kind of self-sufficiency, however, often means flight from the
family, loneliness, and a hopeless situation for foreign women and girls.... For
the majority of woman emigrants, the family plays the biggest role in the foreign
society.... If they disown it, they lose every contact to the community.[81]

These comments point to a crucial dilemma: for migrant women, any
admission of problems at home seemed to provide further evidence of
their subjugation in the eyes of Western feminists. By insisting on "independence" as the primary escape from "repression," Western feminists

---

[78] Meske, *Situationsanalyse türkischer Frauen*, 54.
[79] Ibid., 101.
[80] In 1984 Neval Gültekin-Neumann founded, and until 1986 she directed, an intercultural
counseling and education center for women in Frankfurt. In 2002, she received a Ph.D.
in sociology and education (*Pädagogik*) at J. W. Goethe University in Frankfurt.
[81] Neval Gültekin-Neumann, "Emigrantinnen in Europa: Eine Konferenz in Oslo," *Informationsdienst zur Ausländerarbeit* 4 (1983): 12.

not only ignored the resistance strategies formulated by emigrants themselves, they also offered solutions (e.g., "self-sufficiency") that often cut
women off from their families and support networks. Gültekin-Neumann
went on to argue that this tendency to impose Western solutions was
built into the very structure of *Ausländerarbeit* (work about and for
foreigners). In her own experience, she had observed "a stratum of
leftist intellectual experts" that "occupied itself in particular with the
'foreigner problematic,' used female emigrants as the object and material
for its own careerist goals, drove research, and was eager for differences,
foreign customs, deviations, and abnormalities." Without disputing or
questioning Western activists' basic desire to help emigrant women,
Gültekin-Neumann pointed to a troubling pattern. Many of the so-called
experts involved in *Ausländerarbeit* were "part of the European feminist
women's movement," and they used their scholarly activity on foreigners
to "secure their own financial existence and simultaneously confirm their
own lifestyles."[82]

The broad outlines of Gültekin-Neumann's critique were anticipated
by West German feminist Dagmar Schultz, the cofounder of an important women's publishing house, Orlanda Frauenverlag. In 1981, Schultz
wrote an article for *Courage* exhorting West German women to consider
how racism and anti-Semitism operated within mainstream German feminism. But this growing awareness of racism, as historian Sara Lennox
has argued, grew out of an engagement with the U.S. civil rights movement and thus tended to frame the problem of race through the American
black/white model.[83] One consequence was that Afro-German women
(whose numbers were much smaller than the number of migrant and
guest worker women) served as the main dialogue partners in the initial
discussions of German feminist racism. It was only in the late 1980s that
antiracist feminists began to interrogate their attitudes toward migrant
women and criticize the ways that assumptions of essential cultural

---

[82] Gültekin-Neumann, "Emigrantinnen in Europa," 12. She specifically observed that European feminists obtained large sums of grant money and personal validation by trying to
force Western notions of female emancipation on the foreign women they were studying.
Despite the fact that this criticism received virtually no response at the time, it was one
of the most powerful to be articulated by a minority woman during the earliest phases of
multicultural feminist debate. It is comparable to the kinds of comprehensive ideological
critiques issued around the same time by U.S. women of color such as bell hooks or
Angela Davis.

[83] Sara Lennox, "Divided Feminism: Women, Racism, and German National Identity," in
Susan Castillo, ed., *Engendering Identities* (Porto: Universidade Fernando Pessoa, 1996),
30–31.

difference drove a wedge between foreign (especially Turkish) and German women.[84]

The ideological blindspots identified by Gültekin-Neumann in the German feminist movement also emerged in the day-to-day work of putting integration into practice. In 1985, for example, a Social Democratic Berlin city councilman publicly objected when a Turkish woman arrived at a local school for her duties as a teaching intern wearing a headscarf. Here again, intercultural understanding came into conflict with leftist principles. As the SPD councilman explained: "The headscarf is a signal and a form of discrimination . . . [that] has negative pedagogic effects on the children. For me, the claim of equality between men and women is such an important educational goal that I will not make any concessions. A teacher with a headscarf would contradict this educational mission."[85] This SPD politician drew the line at mutual understanding when the issue in question was contact between headscarved Turkish women and German children. Cultural integration, he seemed to suggest, should not come at the expense of German youth, who would absorb "discriminatory" attitudes about gender via the headscarf. Especially significant here is the fact that the rupture in integrationist policy came in the context of maternal nurturing. It was precisely because the SPD official perceived the veiled Turkish woman as an agent of socialization – as a professional empowered to transmit basic values to children – that she became a target of particular concern. While many on the left expressed enthusiasm for integration and championed further study of the problems facing migrant women, they also placed clear limits on how far West German society would go to accommodate cultural differences.

The fact that the perceived problems of Turkish women became a major lightning rod for German feminists and leftists should come as no surprise. Migrant women have been the targets of intense interest and scrutiny in most Western European countries since the 1970s and have often served to measure an immigrant group's level of integration.[86] But in the Federal

---

[84] See especially Annita Kalpaka and Nora Räthzel, *Die Schwierigkeit, nicht rassistisch zu sein* (Berlin: Express Edition, 1986); and Ika Hügel et al., eds., *Entfernte Verbindungen: Rassismus, Antisemitismus, Klassenunterdrückung* (Berlin: Orlanda Verlag, 1993).

[85] Quoted in Vera Gaserow, "Die vielen Seiten eines Kopftuchs," *Die Tageszeitung*, 11 November 1985.

[86] For France, see Odile Reveyrand-Coulon, *Immigration et maternité* (Toulouse: Presses universitaires du Mirail, 1993); Sophie Bouly de Lesdain, *Femmes camerounaises en région parisienne: trajectoires migratoires et réseaux d'approvisionnement* (Paris: L'Harmattan, 1999); and Jane Freedman and Carrie Tarr, eds., *Women, Immigration, and Identities in France* (Oxford: Berg, 2000). For Great Britain, see Amrit Wilson and

Republic, the stakes of this concern were understood as particularly high. Historian Dagmar Herzog has argued recently that the West German New Left framed its efforts to come to terms with the nation's Nazi past through a critique of postwar sexual conservatism. The push for sexual liberation, in other words, was not simply a side effect of alternative lifestyles. Rather, sexual repression offered a key explanation for why Nazism took root in Germany.[87] Precisely because the question of sexual domination was inextricably bound up with the New Left's view of fascism, Turkish gender relations posed a major concern for leftist critics.

At the same time, invoking the language of liberal democracy enabled (even authorized) a more explicit articulation of racial or ethnic difference on the left. Turks, the argument went, threatened to reintroduce reactionary behaviors into a country that had worked tirelessly to transform itself into a modern, firmly democratic society. Such foreigners endangered the nation not so much in the older sense of anxieties about Jews as harbingers of modernity, capitalism, and liberalism.[88] Turks, rather, posed the opposite problem: they potentially undermined West Germany's hard-won emancipation from Nazi ideology, especially in terms of women's rights, marriage, and gender roles. It was therefore by making these kinds of progressive claims that leftists – so wary of association with tainted Nazi racial discourse – were able to begin drawing harder distinctions between Germans and Turks.

During the first half of the 1980s, then, we can begin to see a number of crucial shifts taking place in the public discourse surrounding the guest worker question. For the first time, German conservatives began to formulate a public position that fully recognized the fundamental changes wrought by the labor migration. Integration was no longer just a one-party issue. In the process, Christian Democrats articulated a new sort of cultural relativism, acknowledging the depth and historical importance of migrant cultures in much the same mode as they described their own.

Julia Nash, eds., *Asian Women Speak Out: A Reader* (Cambridge: National Extension College, 1979); Dalston Children's Center, *Breaking the Silence* (London: Centerprise Trust Ltd., 1984); Sallie Westwood and Parminder Bhachu, eds., *Enterprising Women: Ethnicity, Economy, and Gender Relations* (London: Routledge, 1988); Rohit Barot, Harriet Bradley, and Steve Fenton, eds., *Ethnicity, Gender, and Social Change* (New York: St. Martin's Press, 1999); Tracey Reynolds, *Caribbean Mothers: Identity and Experience in the U.K.* (London: Tufnell Press, 2005).

[87] Dagmar Herzog, *Sex after Fascism: Memory and Morality in Twentieth Century Germany* (Princeton: Princeton University Press, 2005), 2.

[88] The classic analysis of this mode of thinking about Jews in Imperial Germany is Fritz Stern, *Politics of Cultural Despair* (Berkeley and Los Angeles: University of California Press, 1961).

Yet, for the CDU, such acknowledgements generally led to sweeping pronouncements of immutable ethnic and cultural incommensurability. This position was a considerably softer form of ethnic distinction than that offered by the NPD or the authors of the Heidelberg Manifesto, but the larger policy conclusions were similar: migrants could not profitably coexist with natives, which meant that migrants would be better off returning home.

Those on the left, by contrast, continued to make the case for intercultural communication and the importance of integration. But in the process, they began to use gender relations as the primary litmus test for debating the most appropriate form of multiethnic coexistence. They also encountered major conflicts between integrationist theory and practice. It was one thing for the Munich Institute to champion minority dialogue partners and quite another to inscribe such reciprocal adaptation into the fabric of daily life. Along the way, they learned about their own thresholds of tolerance for cultural difference – especially when the differences in question involved fundamental social issues such as familial relations or cross-cultural contacts between women and children.

Ultimately, the terms of integration set out in more progressive circles converged with the conservative logic of cultural incommensurability. By the mid-1980s, both ends of the political spectrum framed integration according to a strict set of parameters and defined it as a one-way process. What separated these positions were the models of culture maintained by each group. Whereas most German conservatives understood migrant culture as timeless, essential, and fixed, German liberals tended to insist on the mutability of migrant culture and devoted enormous energy to the grassroots work of cultural reform.

The Woman Question in Minority Cultural Production

It is within this somewhat contentious national discourse that we can begin to understand the positions of Saliha Scheinhardt and Tevfik Başer, the two minority artists best known for representations of migrant women during the mid-1980s. Scheinhardt first came to the Federal Republic in 1967 from the east Anatolian city of Konya as the young bride of a German student.[89] After working a number of odd jobs (seamstress, waitress, and stewardess) while her husband finished school, she pursued her own education, completing a doctoral degree in pedagogy. Scheinhardt's first literary efforts included *Frauen, die sterben ohne daß sie gelebt hätten*

---

[89] Scheinhardt met her husband when he visited her hometown as a tourist. She was working as a tour guide. Interview with author, Offenbach, Germany, 10 March 1996.

and two subsequent books with the small left-wing, Berlin-based press Express Edition. Her breakthrough came in 1985 when she received the Offenbach prize, the Federal Republic's most lucrative literary award at the time.[90] As demand for her writing rose, first Dağyeli Verlag and then the widely distributed Herder Verlag purchased the rights to *Frauen* and issued new editions in 1991 and 1993.

Başer's professional trajectory followed a similarly rapid rise. Trained as a photographer, Başer learned stage and costume design working on a Studio Hamburg project in his hometown of Eskişehir. During the early 1980s he moved to Hamburg, where he supported himself as a cameraman and film assistant, attended the Hamburg Academy of Fine Arts, and wrote the screenplay for *40 qm Deutschland*. Following an initial rejection from *Zweites Deutsches Fernsehen* (ZDF) he submitted the script to the Hamburg Film Foundation, which awarded him a grant of three hundred thousand DM to realize the film. Başer then entered *40 qm Deutschland* at the 1986 Cannes Film Festival and won the UNESCO prize; later that year, he screened the film at Locarno and won the festival's Silver Leopard award. This enthusiastic critical reception quickly led to additional opportunities. In 1986, *40 qm Deutschland* was the only German production purchased by a French distributor. In the Federal Republic the film became an art-house staple under the distribution of Ari Kino.

In many respects, the specific form of cultural celebrity exemplified by these two careers would have been virtually unimaginable a decade earlier, before the emergence of *Ausländerliteratur* as a distinctive genre and market. At the same time, however, it seems equally clear that the professional successes of Scheinhardt and Başer diverged from the institutional practices of DaF in important ways. Indeed, in Scheinhardt's case, it is worth noting that Irmgard Ackermann and Harald Weinrich rejected her work as incompatible with their efforts to build a canon of *Ausländerliteratur*. In their view, Scheinhardt's stories represented journalistic writing or reportage rather than literary fiction with artistic merit.[91] Perhaps more

---

[90] This prize included a two-year stipend with an apartment in the city's famous library tower.

[91] Interview with Irmgard Ackermann conducted by the author, Munich, Germany, 15 March 1996. Within the German publishing industry, reportage tends to focus on contemporary social concerns, attracting ordinary (as opposed to high-brow) readers with sensationalized or even fictionalized accounts of true stories. It is always clearly distinct from *Belletristik* or literature. Ackermann briefly discusses DaF's criteria for the literary contests in *In zwei Sprachen leben: Berichte, Erzählungen, Gedichte von Ausländern* (Munich: DTV, 1983), 242.

importantly, what distinguished the Offenbach prize and the Hamburg Film Foundation grant from the DaF writing contests and the Chamisso Prize was their status as open competitions, which neither restricted the types of artists that might enter nor advanced an explicit agenda for promoting minorities. Scheinhardt's and Başer's ability to compete in more mainstream institutional contexts suggests a growing sentiment that the issues addressed in their work were now of interest to a broader public. In both cases, moreover, the commercial marketplace played an increasingly crucial role in building this public. For Başer, the film festival circuit provided the necessary nexus – and catalyst – for transforming his story of Hamburg guest workers into a widely circulated cultural commodity. During the same period, Scheinhardt's *Frauen* sold thirty thousand copies in the span of four years, a figure far exceeding Ören's "secret bestseller," which sold about twelve thousand between 1973 and 1984.[92]

Yet these stories of minor cultural celebrity raise a more fundamental question: what exactly attracted German audiences of the mid-1980s to their work? Significantly, both artists were best known for their depictions of female imprisonment. Scheinhardt's *Frauen* traces the fate of Suna S., a young Turkish woman jailed in the Federal Republic for murdering her guest worker husband. The novella surveys her prison life, but devotes most of its attention to explaining the events leading up to Suna's incarceration. Başer's *40 qm Deutschland* focuses on Turna, a Turkish woman who leaves her rural village in Turkey to join her new husband Dursun in Hamburg. Each day Dursun locks Turna inside the apartment while he is away at work, and the film follows her mundane daily activities as she passes time almost completely alone.

This similarity notwithstanding, the novella and the film were not strictly of a piece. More accurately, they emphasized different forms of imprisonment and successive moments in the migration process. Başer's Turna arrives in West Germany at the very beginning of the film. She is a captive of her husband, who refuses to let her venture outside the apartment or have face-to-face contact with the world beyond those four walls. By contrast, Scheinhardt's Suna has already lived in the Federal Republic

---

[92] The figure for Scheinhardt's sales is cited in Sven Michaelsen, "Anwältin der Sprachlosen," *Stern*, 2 April 1987. Her sales also exceeded those of one of the most popular nonfiction books about Turkish women, Baumgartner-Karabak and Landesberger, *Die verkauften Bräute*, which sold twenty-seven thousand copies. This figure and Ören's sales numbers appear in Monika Frederking, *Schreiben gegen Vorurteile: Literatur türkischer Migranten in der Bundesrepublik Deutschland* (Berlin: Express Edition, 1985), 31–32.

for a number of years. She is a prisoner of the German state, convicted of killing her spouse in self-defense. But she somewhat paradoxically experiences her six-year custody as a kind of liberation from the same sort of patriarchal confinement that Turna endures.

What makes these cultural documents especially interesting are the parallel ways in which German reviewers read them. In both cases, critics focused on a single aspect of the narrative and also used these representations to mark the limits of the integration process. Reviewers of Scheinhardt's *Frauen* repeatedly pointed to one basic fact: Suna murders her husband.[93] Again and again, they stressed the causal link between Suna's tragedy and a crushing patriarchy assumed to be typical of Muslim households. A *Stern* magazine review, for example, devoted long passages to the humiliation and sexual violence meted out by Suna's husband, informing readers that "this was what made the Turkish woman into a murderer."[94] The fact that the abuse eventually drove her to kill her husband, the piece suggested, only proved the stifling nature of Turkish patriarchy. Another critic explained Suna's act as a justifiable response to a longer pattern of suffering. "The bloody deed," she asserted, "was just the tip of the iceberg of loneliness, threat, and alienation."[95] It is precisely on these kinds of questions that we can see the broader resonance of the West German New Left's concern with sexual repression. On one level, such reviews suggested the possibility of cross-ethnic feminist empathy. But they also used the specter of patriarchal oppression to argue for the incommensurability of ethnic differences.

This pattern emerges even more clearly in the media coverage of Başer's film. Here, critics focused on Dursun's irrational suspicion and fear of the outside world. Summing up the plot for readers, a reviewer for the *Frankfurter Allgemeine Zeitung* wrote: "Turna lives in a square made up of a room, kitchen, and bathroom, the prisoner of her husband Dursun, a Turkish guest worker, who wants to know that she is protected from the treachery of their foreign world."[96] Dursun's distrust of the German environment is so great, the reviewer explained, that he perceives

[93] N.a., "Frauen, die sterben, ohne daß sie gelebt hätten," *Frau und Mutter*, October 1993; Christine Feldner-Repolust, book review of *Frauen, die sterben ohne daß sie gelebt hätten*, *Östereiches Bibliothekswerk*, 30 June 1993, n.p.

[94] Sven Michaelsen, "Anwältin der Sprachlosen."

[95] Feldner-Repolust, 30 June 1993.

[96] Hans-Dieter Seidel, "Sein kostbarer Besitz: Ein bemerkenswertes Filmdebüt: 'Vierzig Quadratmeter Deutschland' von Tevfik Başer," *Frankfurter Allgemeine Zeitung*, 13 August 1986, 21.

mundane occurrences such as a "car speeding by" or a "retiree hobbling down the street" as "treacherous." An article for *Die Zeit* suggested that this paralyzing fear triggers the film's central narrative of imprisonment: "Turna is a prisoner. She was brought to Germany by Darsun [*sic*], a Turkish worker. And because he mistrusts German society, he forbids his wife every encounter with the outside world. He locks the door when he leaves the apartment. Turna remains with only the view of the outside: a shabby back courtyard, a small piece of a sad street."[97] From this perspective, Turna is a passive victim in the whole process – "brought to Germany" rather than coming of her own accord (a claim which, in fact, remains ambiguous in Başer's film), "forbidden" by her husband to engage with the outside world. "Darsun [*sic*]," *Die Zeit*'s film critic concluded, "is a despot, who is not interested in the feelings of his wife."

The crux of the problem for these critics was a system of gender relations unacceptable in an enlightened liberal-democratic society. *Der Tagesspiegel* explained, Dursun "forces [Turna] into isolation; above all, he doesn't treat her like a person – at most, as the mother of his child.... This is the domination of the man over the woman, a practice which continues to be observed in Turkey."[98] Here the reviewer appears especially disturbed by Dursun's failure to respect his wife as a person, a behavioral standard assumed to be typical in a Western democracy. Other critics echoed this sentiment, using the highly charged metaphor of a caged animal to describe Turna's predicament.[99] Such assessments seemed to justify the larger chorus of doubts about integration. How could educated, liberally minded West Germans be expected to accept foreigners into their democratic society when guest workers refused to abide by its most basic values and standards?[100]

An article in the *Rheinischer Merkur* drew clear limits on what kinds of cultural differences ought to be tolerated in the process of integration. Dursun, it asserted, is "wholly bound to the moral conceptions of

---

[97] Anne Frederiksen, "40m² Deutschland von Tevfik Başer," *Die Zeit*, 1 August 1986, 33.

[98] Volker Baer, "Eingeschlossen in der Fremde: Tevfik Başers Debütfilm '40m² Deutschland," *Der Tagesspiegel*, 30 July 1986, 4.

[99] See, for example, Heike Mundzeck, "'40m² Deutschland': Ein türkischer Regisseur dreht in Hamburg einen Kino-Film über eine Gastarbeiter-Ehe," *Frankfurter Rundschau*, 18 January 1986, 13; Hans-Jürgen Fink, "Wie ein Tier im deutschen Käfig: Türkenbesichtigung: Der Film '40m² Deutschland,'" *Rheinischer Merkur*, 4 July 1986, 18; Kathrin Bergmann, "Wie ein Tier im Stall," *Die Welt*, 1 August 1986, 25.

[100] Heike Mundzeck's review of the film also follows this pattern of judging Dursun according to the standards and norms of German society. See Mundzeck, "'40m² Deutschland,'" 13.

the distant homeland," a statement which implied that such practices
and beliefs were simply incompatible with life in the Federal Republic.
The reviewer further described Turna as "torn between the traditional
command of obedience to one's husband and a first silent, then more
open resistance to Dursun."[101] In contrast to the CDU's rhetoric, which
assumed that the two cultures were essentially different and impervious
to transformation, the *Rheinischer Merkur* critic detected the possibility
of choice in Turna's anguish. Yet this choice was inevitably superseded by
the bounds of custom and tradition.

The hypothetical ability of migrant women to choose a different life
was more fully elaborated in the press coverage of Scheinhardt's *Frauen*.
Ironically, many journalists identified a second key message in this novella
about life in a German women's prison – the possibility of *freedom* from
patriarchy. In a story on women in Islam, for instance, *Süddeutscher
Rundfunk*'s radio program *Journal in the Morning* used Scheinhardt's
book as a central example. After noting that Suna's husband had confined
her to the house for nearly a year before the murder, the host continued:
"she spends six years in prison, where she finds more warmth and understanding among the inmates than outside.... Suna, who had hardly seen
more than her own four walls in Germany up to this point, emancipates
herself from the strict rules and prescriptions of her Islamic culture, wears
Western clothing, eats pork, works, comes to life in prison."[102] Integration, in this view, could only be achieved according to a logic of cultural
replacement: it was up to Muslim women to abandon one way of life
for another. Even a German prison offered more freedom than a Turkish
household.

A second kind of doubt about the efficacy of integration emerged in
a *Süddeutsche Zeitung* article on *40 qm Deutschland*. The review began
with the description of a key outburst by Dursun:

Dursun sits on the bed and grumbles. He lives with barbarians. The men do
not wear any head covering, the women lie bare-breasted in the parks, social
welfare agencies care for raped married women and place abused children in
foster homes. Nothing is sacred to the Germans; not beliefs and morality, not
families and tradition. Welfare agents particularly disturb him. They interrogate
the workers at his factory, butt into private affairs, and question the man's role as
absolute lord and guardian of the family. What we would designate as everyday
or progressive, Dursun takes with the self-same understanding as depraved and

[101] Fink, "Wie ein Tier," 18.
[102] Sibylle May Lang, "Frauen in Islam," *Journal am Morgen*, Süddeutscher Rundfunk,
    10 March 1994.

degenerate. His tirade is the central scene in the film because it makes concretely clear . . . its meaning: different countries – different customs.[103]

The point here was not to suggest that Turks (as opposed to the Germans whom Dursun identifies) were the real "barbarians"; in fact, the article goes to great pains to express sympathy for Başer's characters. Instead, the film critic seized upon the scene to demonstrate that Turks were unable to understand and appreciate "social welfare agencies" and services initiated by the SPD coalition during the late 1970s. From this perspective, the real tragedy lay in the fact that Dursun rejects the agencies as "depraved and degenerate." Indeed, the review seems to perceive Dursun's outburst as a clear sign that the institutional apparatus promoted by the SPD had failed. This reading of the film suggests that the failure did not originate with the programs themselves, but occurred because the objects of charity proved incapable of recognizing the ameliorative benefits and instead demonized the state-sponsored mechanisms for integration as a threat to custom.

Somewhat paradoxically, this position, which appeared in one of the Federal Republic's most consistently left-liberal newspapers, dove-tailed with the more conservative CDU approach. While the *Süddeutsche Zeitung* critic recognized that Dursun was not "evil" and avoided char-acterizing Turkish culture as essentially "bad," he also emphasized that German integration efforts were not working. In this view, migrant cul-ture was simply too strong because it resisted efforts to incorporate guest workers into the fold of West German liberalism.

Central to these readings was a perception of ethnographic trans-parency. As a *Rheinischer Merkur* reporter explained, in *40 qm Deutsch-land* Başer "opened a window through which German fellow citizens could see how his Turkish countrymen live when they are not working at the construction site, in the factory, or collecting garbage."[104] In this view, Başer played virtually no constructive role in writing or directing the film; his function was merely to record a typical guest worker mar-riage with his camera. Similarly, an article in *Die Welt* declared: "It only looks as if Turkish women cover themselves up with headscarves when they walk on the street. But they also wear scarves at home, according to the film '40 m² Deutschland' by the Turk Tevfik Başer."[105] Such asser-tions about the private practices of Turkish women indicated a particular

---

[103] Michael Althen, "Zwischen zwei Kulturen: '40m² Deutschland' – der Debütfilm des Türken Tevfik Başer," *Süddeutsche Zeitung*, 31 July 1986, 35.
[104] Fink, "Wie ein Tier," 18.
[105] Bergmann, "Wie ein Tier," 25.

approach to the text: reviewers read the film as an accurate source of basic information about guest workers. Even critics who acknowledged more of an authorial voice in the filmmaking process tended to assume that Başer depicted genuine, representative experiences. "Is what Tevfik Başer presents an exception, or can the story claim overall relevance?" asked the reporter for *Der Tagesspiegel*. "Even if much seems exaggerated, it appears to be neither an extreme example, nor a game that aims at effects or a big dramatic response."[106] Time and time again, German critics concluded that this fictional portrait simply made visible the everyday lives of millions of guest workers.

The press coverage for Scheinhardt's *Frauen* likewise relied on an assumption of ethnographic transparency. A critic for the magazine *Woman and Mother* put it this way: "The Turkish woman author, living in Germany for decades, recounts these authentic fates succinctly and precisely.... This book can teach us to see Turkish women on the street with different eyes."[107] Other reviewers described Scheinhardt as an "advocate of the speechless" who served to make the concerns of migrant women audible to the nation. Her publisher emphasized precisely this function in the promotional literature. On the back cover of Scheinhardt's second book, a volume of short stories, the blurb proclaimed: "They live in our midst, but we do not know them. What does it mean to be a Turkish woman in Germany? Saliha Scheinhardt recounts three authentic fates, which get under one's skin."[108]

---

[106] Baer, "Eingeschlossen," 4.

[107] N.a., Review of *Frauen, die sterben ohne daß sie gelebt hätten*, *Frau und Mutter*, October 1993.

[108] A useful point of comparison here is British Commonwealth literature. For example, the author Buchi Emecheta, a Nigerian woman who came to the United Kingdom at age eighteen with her student husband, began to achieve literary acclaim in Britain around the same time as Scheinhardt. One reviewer summed up an early novel, *Second Class Citizen*, in the following manner: "Moving sociological documentary about a bright young Ibo wife who comes to her Promised Land of London and finds it not at all what it promised to be, what with brutal husband, her own instant fertility, and being stranded between two cultures." (Philip Howard, "Fiction," *The Times*, February 13, 1975, 12.) Here, the familiar themes of patriarchal oppression, the struggle to reconcile two conflicting social systems, and assumptions of native ethnography emerge quite clearly. An important element distinguishing the reception of Commonwealth literature from that of so-called *Ausländerliteratur* is the way concerns about the Nazi past and postwar democratization informed many West German critics. For progressive West German readers, stories of subjugated, sexually repressed women were implicated in the New Left's understanding of fascism. In this respect, the works of Scheinhardt and Başer offered important lessons about the dangers of advocating unqualified cultural tolerance.

These tendencies emerged even more starkly after 1985, when Schein-hardt became the first non-German author to win the title of City Writer of Offenbach.[109] An article for *Die Zeit* about the prize eschewed questions of literary form and style entirely, emphasizing instead that the Offenbach honor stemmed from her "ability to understand the otherness of people who come from strange cultures."[110] As this critic saw it, Scheinhardt grasped such otherness not based on literary skill or a gift of the imagination, but because she herself was a Turkish woman. This subject position, in turn, entitled her to speak for other Muslim women and make their experiences accessible to Germans. Scheinhardt thus functioned as something like anthropologist James Clifford's figure of the "classic ethnographer," an individual uniquely qualified to perform the work of cultural translation by virtue of having been in the field.[111] But in this case, Schein-hardt's ethnographic authority was further bolstered by her status as a migrant woman. She served, in short, as a *native* ethnographer, dutifully recording evidence of unbridgeable difference for a mass reading public.

It is important to note that Scheinhardt herself had a hand in encouraging this mode of reading. While she always insisted on the literary qualities of her work – and routinely described her writing as fiction – she also emphasized that her stories were based on research and interviews with migrant women. Aesthetically, too, Scheinhardt blurred the boundary between her own voice as author and Suna's voice as narrator by adopting a first-person perspective and stream-of-consciousness style. This mode of representation made it easier for readers to assume that the story was at least in part autobiographical.[112]

Following the success of *Frauen*, Scheinhardt quickly became a recognized authority on the problems of migrant women. An article in *Westdeutsche Allgemeine Zeitung*, for example, reported that there was a recognizable core of "like-minded, well-informed people" who routinely

---

[109] City Writer of Offenbach was a major award in Germany at the time, carrying the largest stipend of any literary prize. As City Writer, Scheinhardt became Offenbach's preeminent cultural representative.

[110] Anton J. Weinberger, "Und die Frauen weinten Blut," *Die Zeit*, 24 January 1986.

[111] James Clifford, "Introduction," in James Clifford and George E. Marcus, eds., *Writing Culture: The Poetics and Politics of Ethnography* (Berkeley and Los Angeles: University of California Press, 1986), 1–9. Clifford here contrasts the classic ethnographer (typified by Margaret Mead) who engages in participant-observation in order to understand a foreign culture with a figure that is more self-conscious about his or her ability to perform the work of cultural translation. Clifford is highly critical of the classic ethnographer.

[112] Interview with Saliha Scheinhardt conducted by the author, Offenbach, Germany, 10 March 1996.

attended Scheinhardt's public readings.[113] Scheinhardt herself elaborated
on the specific demographics, noting that it was precisely those invested
in the work of guest worker integration – teachers, counselors, social
workers, and church volunteers – that she encountered again and again
at her increasingly frequent book events.[114] As one commentator noted
in 1987: "Just five years ago, not even thirty people came to her readings; at a church-sponsored event in the past year, four hundred women
attended."[115]

The limited evidence available on reading practices suggests that this
growing public often approached Scheinhardt's works within a very spe-
cific framework – they saw them as pedagogical and social welfare tools.
Her November 1986 reading for a group of high school students in
Marbach is a good case in point. The larger context was the Schiller-
Feier (Schiller celebration), an event designed to mark the birthday of
the nation's literary patriarch. Marianne Wagner, a teacher organizing
the festivities, explained why she had invited Scheinhardt to read: "Many
Turkish students... are affected by the problems depicted in her books.
And especially Turkish girls face an acid test between the two cultures.
Contact and now perhaps even more intensive engagement with the work
of a woman who has suffered, felt, and come to terms with similar things
ought to give them valuable help."[116]

What, then, are we to make of this paradoxical reception, a new form
of commercial success clearly built upon images of female suffering and
ethnographic transparency? On the one hand, these developments seem
to have been inextricably connected with a larger ideological shift during
the mid-1980s. At the very same moment that West German politicians,
journalists, and social workers were increasingly using the problem of
migrant women to question the viability of multiethnic integration, two
young Turkish-German artists achieved unprecedented commercial success by producing images of anguished, even violent domestic relations
in guest worker households. On the other hand, it seems somewhat simplistic to cast these complex cultural texts as one-dimensional catalysts

---

[113] Waltraut Knecht, "Erstmals wurde eine Türkin Offenbachs Stadschreiberin," *Westdeutsche Allgemeine Zeitung*, 14 January 1987. The exact same article was reprinted as
"Brücken schlagen mit Literatur," *Lüdwigsburger Kreiszeitung*, 16 January 1987, 18;
and "Möglichst viele Anstöße," *Rhein-Neckar-Zeitung*, 19 January 1987, 7.
[114] Scheinhardt elaborated on this pattern in an interview conducted by author, Offenbach,
Germany, 17 March 1996.
[115] N.a., "Wir sprachen mit Saliha Scheinhardt," *Schwäbisches Tagblatt*, 20 March 1987.
[116] N.a., "Eine Brücke schlagen," *Marbacher Zeitung*, 11 November 1986, 9.

for political reaction. While the reception patterns clearly suggest that these artworks were understood in large part as evidence of unbridgeable difference, the texts themselves reveal a deeper complexity once we push beyond the portions routinely seized upon by German commentators. Indeed, it is to these largely ignored sections of the texts that we now need to turn if we are to explain the efforts of the period's most prominent minority artists to weigh in on the specific problems of migrant women.

The Missing Chapters

As a first step it is important to sort out the significant gaps in the journalistic coverage, which routinely failed to discuss much of the texts by Scheinhardt and Başer. Reviews of Scheinhardt's *Frauen* focused almost exclusively on the heroine Suna's desperate killing of her husband as the crucial catalyst for her incarceration. This choice is particularly striking when we consider that Scheinhardt devoted a mere 10 out of 121 pages to the murder. Indeed, the structure of the story actually deemphasized what the media reception portrayed as the central event. Employing a first-person, stream-of-consciousness voice, the vast majority of pages recount the protagonist Suna's village life, early years in Germany, and prison existence. The reader, in fact, only learns the specifics of the crime through a legal document inserted into the text, which acts as a jarring stylistic break from the rest of the story and comes about eighty pages into the book. Given what the narrative actually contains, it is somewhat surprising that not a single reviewer mentioned the extended accounts of village life and the migration to the Federal Republic.

More specifically, virtually all of the critics missed the major events in Suna's personal development: her birth in the fields of rural Anatolia, her much envied arranged marriage to a fellow guest worker of her brother, even her highly anticipated arrival in Germany. Also absent from the reviews was Scheinhardt's detailed depiction of the profound effects of West German labor recruitment on the village. Suna, for example, recalls the young men leaving each fall to work in Germany and returning in the summer with gifts. Several reviews did allude to her time behind bars. In particular, they highlighted her petition for exemption from deportation, an action born out of Suna's fears of retribution by her husband's family in Turkey.

The reception of Başer's *40 qm Deutschland* followed a similar pattern, invariably focusing on Dursun's decision to lock his wife in their apartment. Most reviewers described two key scenes: the moment when Turna realizes that she is imprisoned and Dursun's unexpected death (which eventually enables Turna to gain her freedom). Remarkably few articles acknowledged Turna's repeated attempts to challenge Dursun's spatial restrictions. And no reviewer devoted much attention to Turna's experiences within the apartment. These long, slow scenes at the center of the film (which, in fact, constituted the bulk of Başer's visual narrative) critics generally distilled to a single sentence about Turna's loneliness and utter isolation.

How might we begin to explain these omissions? This question forces us to go beyond the issue of critical preferences and take into account what Scheinhardt and Başer were trying to accomplish in the neglected scenes. Above all, we need to consider the surprising absence of attention to Turkish village life, despite the fact that both artists emphasized this setting as a key touchstone for explaining their characters' experiences in West Germany. By weaving their stories back and forth between rural Anatolia and the Federal Republic, Scheinhardt and Başer continued to expand the basic historical narrative of the labor migration, a process which Ören had initiated with the 1974 installment of his *Berlin Trilogie*. Scheinhardt now added a discussion of the recruitment's profound impact on the village itself. And both Scheinhardt and Başer stressed the crucial role of rural socialization in shaping migrants' responses to their new urban industrial lives.

Quite fortuitously, recent anthropological work has provided a much deeper sense of the gender dynamics and cultural practices of women in Anatolian village life. This body of scholarship, in turn, enables us to flesh out a more subtle understanding of the social subtexts that both artists drew upon in developing their narratives. Women in rural Turkey, according to Emelie Olson, tend to be relegated to a more "closed," private sphere, where they are responsible for bearing and taking care of children, managing the household, and working the fields. In contrast, men operate primarily in the public domain. They are generally in charge of the shopping and conduct business in "open" arenas such as the mosque, market, or cafe.[117] Donna Lee Bowen and Evelyn Early have explained this pattern of sexual segregation in terms of the concepts of "honor" and "shame," both of which depend entirely on a woman's sexual behavior and reputation. In order to avoid shame and protect their honor, fathers,

---

[117] Emelie A. Olson, "Duofocal Family Structure and an Alternative Model of Husband-Wife Relationship," in Ciğdem Kagitcibasi, ed., *Sex Roles, Family and Community in Turkey* (Bloomington: Indiana University Press, 1982).

husbands, and brothers must ensure the chastity and fidelity of the women in the household.[118]

Carol Delaney has argued that honor and shame are bound up with ideas about procreation: "a man's power and authority, in short his value as a man, derives from his power to generate life. His honor, however, depends on his ability to guarantee that a child is from his own seed. This in turn depends on his ability to control 'his' woman."[119] For a woman within this social order, venturing into the unprotected world of the street without cover or accompaniment exposes her to the advances of unknown men and calls into question the father of any children she might have.[120] Female sexuality, in this view, is perceived as indiscriminate. According to Delaney's model, the woman provides the "soil" in which the man's "seed" grows; the soil has no capacity for discretion, but nurtures any seed that has been sown. The point of spatial restrictions on women is to eliminate any ambiguity about the origin of the seed.

In practice, however, the control over women's movement is never absolute. As Delaney explains, many women circumvent the letter of the law while respecting its intent. They venture onto the street, but only at specific hours when men are generally absent. Perhaps more importantly, village women compensate for their confinement to the domestic sphere by cultivating close relationships with female neighbors. Outside of the immediate family, these neighbors provide a woman with most of her daily companionship and help in virtually all household matters: "The boundaries between women who are close neighbors are fluid; the gates, doors, thresholds are open.... There is no formality involved in these visits; her house is yours and yours hers. Close neighbors are enclosed in an open world by proximity."[121] Women, in this view, transform the household into their own private sphere of activity and exchange, separate from but equal to the public sphere reserved for men. Ayşe Berkin likewise argues

---

[118] Donna Lee Bowen and Evelyn A. Early, eds., *Everyday Life in the Muslim Middle East* (Bloomington: Indiana University Press, 1993).

[119] Carol Delaney, *The Seed and the Soil: Gender and Cosmology in Turkish Village Society* (Berkeley and Los Angeles: University of California Press, 1991), 39.

[120] Delaney's interpretation of rural Turkish female sexuality stands in marked contrast to that of other scholars of Muslim societies. Fatima Mernissi, for example, argues that Muslim societies see women as possessing insatiable sexual appetites that must be controlled. Mernissi suggests that women are restricted to the home to protect them from themselves, whereas Delaney asserts that constraints are imposed on women to protect them from men. See Fatima Mernissi, *Beyond the Veil: Male-Female Dynamics in Modern Muslim Society*, 2nd ed. (Bloomington: Indiana University Press, 1987), 30–45.

[121] Delaney, *Seed and the Soil*, 188.

that this "sexual division of labor results in a separate women's sphere indirectly controlled by men but where women have a certain freedom of movement and autonomy."[122] The regulation of female movement is thus offset by a women's support network.

My point here is not to insist that this recent ethnographic work provides a transparent window into the gendered practices of Turkish guest workers who migrated to Germany from rural Anatolia. Just as each migration experience followed its own particular trajectory, the gendered divisions of labor and space undoubtedly varied from case to case. Still, these studies of village gender practices do help us to complicate the highly circumscribed readings of Scheinhardt and Başer's narratives produced by West German critics. Both artists referenced these women's networks repeatedly in their texts. Scheinhardt, for example, contrasts the sexual difficulties of an isolated Suna with those of another woman in the village, who consults with the local *hoca* (religious leader) when her husband forces her to have sex in what Suna describes as "inappropriate" ways. For this woman, the intervention of a respected authority brings about a satisfactory resolution to the conflict. The migration process, however, cuts Suna off from the conventional system of adjudication. Suna's efforts to enlist the help of her brother and his wife during periodic visits ultimately fall on deaf ears, forcing her to endure continual threats and ongoing abuse from her husband. Scheinhardt's point here, it seems, is not to cast Turkish patriarchy as essentially violent and oppressive. Rather, what her story highlights are the potential domestic problems faced by migrant women dislocated from their traditional networks of communication, support, and grievance resolution.

Suna's incarceration likewise acquires a more complex set of meanings in relation to the village. Most critics, as we have seen, seized upon the prison as a paradoxical "freedom" from an abusive domestic situation. Yet it is important to remember that the freedom of the prison is also a freedom from isolation. Indeed, it is only through incarceration that Suna receives her first opportunities in Germany to meet and interact with other women – at meals, during recreation time, and through her work in the prison's laundry and printing press. One might argue, in fact, that Suna's "liberation" is always twofold, based as much on her rediscovery of female social networks within the prison as her protection from patriarchal violence outside its walls.

---

[122] Ayşe Berkin, "A Structural Analysis of the Gastarbeiter Phenomenon in the Federal Republic of Germany and Its Implications for Turkey with Special Reference to the Social Position of Women" (Ph.D. diss., Boston University, 1990), 304.

For most critics of Başer's *40 qm Deutschland*, Turna's forced confinement seemed to violate a basic right of Western democracy – freedom of
movement – as well as the basic conventions of modern domestic life. Yet
Dursun's decision to lock Turna inside their Hamburg apartment can also
be read as a specific reaction to a particularly threatening environment,
which in turn prompted him to replicate the gendered spatial order of the
village.[123] Rebuffing Turna's entreaties to go outside, he exclaims: "You
don't know these people. They are like an infectious disease. Marriage
means little to them. They retain nothing of love and values. They walk
around the streets with naked behinds and without covering their heads."
Here Dursun expresses outrage at German forms of social organization
and public behavior, a system of sociability antithetical to the customs of
the village. In dismissing this response as a knee-jerk rejection of modernity and democracy, however, most reviewers failed to grasp the broader
context for Dursun's unease. As one historian has recently emphasized,
West German society underwent a sexual revolution in the late 1960s that
"reconfigured familial, sexual, and gender relations and all codes of social
interaction."[124] This transformation was visible on the streets, especially
in terms of what women wore, how they acted in public, and the way they
related to men. While such behavior did not appear new or unusual to the
majority of Germans by the early 1980s, it must have been a great shock
to many Turkish migrants arriving from rural Anatolia. For Dursun, the
only viable course of action was to enforce more stringently the social and
moral codes with which he was familiar. Delaney has identified a similar
reaction among villagers who migrate within Turkey: "In the town and
city, women and men mix more openly; they can hardly avoid it. This
inability to control the times and places of such mixing is unsettling for
villagers. It is almost certainly the reason that those who move to town
keep their women at home and under much stricter surveillance than in
the village."[125]

---

[123] Elçin Kürsat-Ahlers has recently argued that reproducing cultural practices from home
in the host country serves as one of the primary means of coping with the disorienting
experience of migration. See her chapter, "The Turkish Minority in German Society,"
in David Horrocks and Eva Kolinsky, eds., *Turkish Culture in German Society Today*
(Providence, RI: Berghahn Books, 1996), 113–35.

[124] Herzog, *Sex after Fascism*, 141–48.

[125] Delaney, *Seed and the Soil*, 42. Similarly, a study of Turkish migrants to the Netherlands
has found that husbands often increased their control over their wives by reducing
freedom of movement in the new environment. See Lenie Brouwer and Marijke Priester,
"Living in Between: Turkish Women in the Homeland and in the Netherlands," in Annie
Phizacklea, ed., *One Way Ticket: Migration and Female Labor* (London: Routledge,
1983), 113–28.

But there is another layer of meaning in Başer's narrative. Compared to life in the village, Turna experiences a double marginalization: she is cut off from an outside environment perceived as chaotic and threatening, but also from traditional female social networks, which ordinarily would alleviate the isolation caused by such spatial segregation. The scenes in *40 qm Deutschland* that chronicle Dursun's epilepsy serve to underscore this gap. In a flashback to the village, we observe Turna's female relatives and neighbors rushing in to assist her when Dursun collapses on the couple's wedding night. As Turna cowers in the corner, they hold him down and wedge an apple into his mouth to prevent him from biting his tongue. In the Hamburg apartment, by contrast, Turna struggles alone, unsuccessfully, to replicate the apple trick when Dursun experiences another seizure. This lack of domestic support in Germany ultimately proves fatal. During a second epileptic fit at the end of the film, Dursun stumbles out of the bathroom, falls to the floor, and dies. By juxtaposing these two medical crises, Başer suggests that Turna's confinement is a matter far more complex than spousal jealousy or abuse. Indeed, the larger point of these episodes is to illustrate how the traditional gender segregation of the village has become dysfunctional in the process of migration.

In the film's long middle section, Turna attempts to overcome the constraining aspects of segregation generated by the unfamiliar West German environment. Her struggles lead to a new critical consciousness that is at once feminist and intricately connected with rural village customs. Başer alludes to this evolution by juxtaposing three scenes. In the first, Turna comes across a hidden key while cleaning the apartment. She rushes to try it in the lock, but sinks to the floor in frustration when the door does not budge. The film then flashes back to the village during a formal visit by Dursun to Turna's house. As Turna listens from another room, Dursun informs her father that he has returned to the village to find a bride. Her father explains the family's desperate need for money, and the two men agree on five hundred thousand lira as the price for Turna's hand. The film then abruptly returns to Hamburg and follows Turna wandering aimlessly around the apartment. As she strokes her plaited hair, she catches a glimpse of herself in a mirror, abruptly picks up a pair of scissors, and lops off both braids.

The third scene comes as something of a shock. Başer gives the viewer no warning, no clues of its climactic act. Consequently, Turna's decision to cut her hair seems to come out of nowhere. How, then, are we to interpret her action? Delaney has argued that girls in the village cover their hair after reaching puberty and never cut it: a sign of female eroticism, it is highly valued and must be protected.[126] At least on one level, then, it is possible to read the scene as a symbolic attempt to move beyond customs, now rendered dysfunctional or irrelevant, in search of something new.

Yet it also seems important to consider another key element of this scene: namely, the mirror which functions as the central device for conveying the narrative action. Başer, in fact, does not film Turna directly, choosing instead to show her mirrored reflection as she wanders around the bedroom, fingers a piece of embroidery, and takes off her headscarf. The viewer watches Turna slowly caress her braids until her gaze fixes on the mirror itself. Staring at her likeness, Turna picks up a pair of scissors, at which point the camera moves downward to the cabinet beneath the mirror. First, we hear the shears cutting through the hair; next we see the braids being placed crisscross on the cabinet. The camera then moves back up to Turna's reflection. She holds the stubs of hair with her eyes closed, but slowly opens them to stare at her likeness once again.[127]

What, exactly, is this scene supposed to signify? Here it is useful to consider the insights offered by a standard tool of filmic analysis, Jacques Lacan's theory of the "mirror stage." For Lacan, the moment in front of the mirror serves as one of the most important steps in the formation of identity. In its initial guise, the mirror stage occurs when the infant, held up to the looking glass by the mother, first recognizes itself in its ideal reflection.[128] At the same time, the mother's gaze functions to "join"

[126] Delaney, *Seed and the Soil*, 130. See also Carol Delaney, "Untangling the Meanings of Hair in Turkish Society," *Anthropological Quarterly* 67.4 (1994): 159–72.

[127] It is worth noting that Başer's use of the mirror in the filmmaking process mimics the rupture taking place in Turna's consciousness. Rather than allowing us to see Turna directly in this crucial scene, the camera only shows her reflection. In this respect, Başer echoed the distancing techniques of Fassbinder, who often framed his shots with mirrors, doors, and windows in order to disrupt the viewer's tendency to imagine him or herself as seamlessly embedded in the film. Başer's strategy of pointing the camera at the mirror creates a similar representational self-consciousness. Only when the angle widens so that the mirror comes into the frame do we understand exactly what we have been looking at. By foregrounding the mechanisms through which the viewer apprehends the image on the screen, Başer thus replicates the disjuncture that has just occurred in Turna's psyche. For a sophisticated analysis of Fassbinder's framing devices, see Kaja Silverman, *Male Subjectivity at the Margins* (London: Routledge, 1992), 129.

[128] Jacques Lacan, *Écrits: A Selection*, trans. by Alan Sheridan (New York: W. W. Norton, 1977), 2–6. For a useful and highly lucid discussion of Lacan's mirror stage, see John P. Muller and William J. Richardson, *Lacan and Language: A Reader's Guide to Écrits* (New York: International Universities Press, 1982), 26–34.

the child with its reflected likeness, facilitating what will become the ongoing process of internalizing external images and making that fusion seem natural. Identification with the reflection, however, is predicated on a basic misrecognition: unlike the infant's present incapacity and fragmented experience, the person in the mirror appears whole. At the same time, the child's desire to become the image is ultimately unattainable because the reflection is a distortion, an inversion of reality. According to Lacan, the child must relinquish its instinctual desire to attain its mirrored image as part of developing into a well-adjusted adult.

The largely silent middle section in *40 qm Deutschland* follows a similar trajectory. Turna's discovery of the locked door not only shatters her acceptance of gender segregation; it also shatters her ability (or willingness) to interiorize those socially produced, external images, thereby destabilizing the very foundations of her identity. Once this disturbance has occurred, Turna in a sense reverts back to the infantile mirror stage in order to reestablish her sense of self, marked in the film by her prolonged periods of gazing into the looking glass. Yet the misrecognition that is so critical to the primordial act of identity construction can no longer take place: Turna now rejects the reflection that looks back at her and refuses to internalize distorted images. Dursun's long absences from the apartment mean that he cannot function effectively as the parental figure who, already fully invested in the social order, would normally ensure the joining of self and image. By cutting her hair, Turna indicates a more self-conscious understanding of the vital connection between the constraints under which she lives and her position as a woman. Life in the Hamburg apartment, Başer seems to suggest, produced a major rupture in Turna's psyche, an unhinging of what had been a seamless identification with her gendered identity and its culturally determined limitations.

Turna's transformation points to a second major goal beyond documenting the difficulties of transplanting village custom into an urban industrial environment. This is also a story about an emerging critical understanding, one we might describe as feminist in orientation. At the same time, it is a feminism interwoven with the particular experiences of a migrant woman from rural Anatolia – Turna's awakening does not take place on strictly Western terms. Indeed, Başer presents the final moment of liberation somewhat ambiguously. After Dursun collapses in the shower he can no longer prevent Turna's exit and she is finally free to leave the apartment. Yet her departure – shot from the dark interior of the building's front hall – is depicted as if Turna was a sightless person moving toward the blinding outside light. Scheinhardt, too, seems to have been reaching for a similar narrative balance that is part feminist critique of traditional Turkish gender relations, but one that is always refracted through a complex migration trajectory rarely noticed by the West German press commentaries.

Ultimately, the new mode of commercial celebrity achieved by Scheinhardt and Başer cannot be separated from the growing fascination with migrant women that dominated public discourse in the mid-1980s. But this celebrity had clear benefits and perils. On the one hand, these cultural texts and careers marked a novel entry point into the West German public sphere, one that did not rely on the gatekeeping mechanisms engineered by DaF (such as the early literary contests and Chamisso Prize). What Scheinhardt and Başer achieved was not only increased sales and visibility in mainstream cultural markets, but also a new authority to speak on issues perceived as central to the guest worker question. Their ability to communicate to a broader audience on the problem of migrant women greatly exceeded any of the individual careers or institutional achievements we have considered thus far. Yet it is also clear that the expanding "horizon of experience" now visible in the public sphere was inextricably tied to a logic of ethnic essentialism.[129] Again and again, German commentators ascribed a larger ethnographic transparency to putatively fictional works (a process of which Scheinhardt and Başer were both well aware). By 1985, the imperiled migrant woman had achieved the status of political leitmotif. And in creating fictional stories around this theme, Scheinhardt and Başer capitalized on burgeoning public curiosity with potentially reactionary consequences.

Yet I do not think it is quite accurate to portray these works as a kind of cultural capitulation to the growing doubts about integration that characterized mid-1980s political discourse. Indeed, the obvious gaps and elisions in the reception of Scheinhardt and Başer's works represent the most crucial piece of evidence here because they underscore the limited

---

[129] The phrase "horizon of experience" comes from Reinhart Koselleck, but is used by Miriam Hansen to describe the range of experiences that become visible through the mass-mediated market, as elaborated by Oskar Negt and Alexander Kluge. See Miriam Hansen, "Foreword," in Oskar Negt and Alexander Kluge, *Öffentlichkeit und Erfahrung: Zur Organisationsanalyse von bürgerlicher und proletarischer Öffentlichkeit* (Frankfurt: Suhrkamp, 1972), trans. by Peter Labanyi, Jamie Daniel, and Assenka Oksiloff as *The Public Sphere and Experience* (Minneapolis: University of Minnesota Press, 1993), xxx.

ability of individual texts to reshape popular assumptions. Both artists clearly sought to introduce more nuanced explanations of the effects of the migration process on the lives of Turkish-German women. But in the end, the most striking feature of the press coverage is its similarity to the reportage produced by Rowohlt, or the pronouncements of failed integration issued by Christian Democrats.

4

Toward a German Multiculturalism

In February 1989, an important meeting on diversity issues took place in Berlin's Kreuzberg district. Featured speakers at the meeting included the city commissioner for foreigner affairs, Barbara John (CDU); the SPD representative expert on foreigners, Eckhardt Barthel; the Alternative List staff worker for foreigner issues, Götz Schwarzrock; and the FDP state secretary, Jürgen Dittberner. In the press coverage of the meeting, John's call for a liberalization of the existing citizenship laws received the most attention. Specifically, she argued that a more "modern" policy would "naturalize the bulk of immigrants without problems," perhaps even allowing for "dual citizenship." For John, the key was to discourage "*völkisches* thinking" on the part of the German majority while simultaneously bringing the nation's resident migrants more fully into the democratic process. Only with such a policy, she concluded, could migrants be "politically equal and nevertheless go their own cultural way. National citizenship would finally be detached from cultural identity."[1]

It would be another eleven years (2000) before John's vision of German diversity began to find its way into regular legislative practice; even then, the SPD-Green initiative to reform the nation's naturalization policy stopped short of allowing dual citizenship. Still, this 1989 meeting in Kreuzberg marked a major historical watershed. It announced the arrival of a new conceptual framework for explicating the guest worker question. A reporter for *Die Tageszeitung*, Elisa Klapheck, referred to this framework as "multiculturalism:"

---

[1] Elisa Klapheck, "Multikulturell – was ist das?," *Die Tageszeitung*, 22 February 1989.

Every couple of years foreigner policy brings forth a new concept. Years ago one demanded the adaptation (*Anpassung*) of labor migrants. Later one spoke with a little more moderation of "integration" (*Integration*). The Commissioner for Foreigner Affairs, Barbara John, finally introduced the key word "incorporation" (*Eingliederung*). Recently, "multicultural society" is in every mouth.[2]

Especially striking in this passage is Klapheck's suggestion that policy-making and public discourse are two sides of the same ideological coin. Clearly, something quite dramatic had changed since the early 1980s, when the CDU-FDP coalition regularly questioned the capacity of West Germany's labor migrants to integrate. This ideological shift from unfinished integration to a broad public discourse on a multicultural society was precisely what Klapheck sought to document.

Yet it is equally clear that, even in 1989, the specific parameters of German multiculturalism remained somewhat vague and unfinished. In the very next sentence, Klapheck issued a somewhat sarcastic rejoinder: "'Multicultural' – that sounds good! But what is it?" She also raised a number of difficult questions about how such a society would work in everyday practice: "Is multiculturalism in fact an equal coexistence of different identities? Or does it not, on the contrary, conceal a pacified class difference between foreign workers and German bosses? Is the clinging to one's own identity not a sign of monoculturalism and how does that fit with the 'multicultural society'? Does 'multicultural' really mean different self-determined identities, or does it not implicitly demand that everyone adapt a little?"[3]

That German multiculturalism was simultaneously "in every mouth," overdetermined, and hotly debated at this late date should come as no great surprise. In his most recent book, Paul Gilroy, one of the leading theorists of multiculturalism in Great Britain, has noted the term's "stubborn imprecision."[4] Similarly, in his recent study of late twentieth-century identity politics across a wide range of Western democracies,

[2] Ibid.
[3] Ibid. Klapheck's questions here echoed criticisms of multiculturalism made by antiracists in Britain, who argued that official multiculturalism "isolated racial and ethnic conflicts from other political antagonisms (between the sexes, labour and capital, first and third worlds, overdeveloped and under-resourced societies) while serving to distract public attention from the radical social restructuring involved in the monetarist 'stripping' of the welfare state and the ongoing exploitation of cheap labor markets worldwide." See David Bennett, ed., *Multicultural States: Rethinking Difference and Identity* (London: Routledge, 1998), 5–6.
[4] Paul Gilroy, *Against Race: Imagining Political Culture beyond the Color Line* (Cambridge, MA: Harvard University Press, 2000), 244. This is particularly striking since Gilroy has

David Bennett has argued that "multiculturalism has served variously as code for assimilationism and cultural separatism; campus Marxism and ethnic nationalism; transnational corporate marketing strategies and minority competition for state resources; radical democracy and cosmetic adjustments to the liberal-democratic status quo."[5] For our purposes, though, the key question is not the *true* or *proper* meaning of German multiculturalism, but how it became the primary ideological framework for discussing diversity in the Federal Republic. The 1989 scene recorded by Klapheck raises a series of interconnected historical questions. When did multiculturalism begin to emerge as a topic of public discourse? How did the specific meanings of German multiculturalism change over time? What triggered these changes?

Two other issues deserve further special consideration, namely the "multi" and the "cultural." Given the fact that this 1989 meeting took place in Kreuzberg (the nation's best-known Turkish neighborhood), there were undoubtedly large numbers of migrants in the hall with John, Barthel, Schwarzrock, and Dittberner. Yet Klapheck failed to register their voices throughout the article. Equally surprising is her lack of attention to the central importance of cultural practices in these debates. As we have seen, literature, poetry, and film were at the heart of West German debates about the guest worker question during the 1970s and early 1980s. And by the late 1980s, the Federal Republic's minority intelligentsia included a rapidly expanding second generation, many of whom had a great deal to say about John's central concern – the need to delink national citizenship from cultural identity.

What quickly becomes apparent when we push beyond Klapheck's article, however, is that the particular method or terms of delinking constituted the very essence of the multiculturalism debates in West Germany (and part of what made the debates *political*). No two politicians, journalists, or intellectuals envisioned this process in precisely the same way. Indeed, the dominant ideological chord on the eve of reunification was an increasing uncertainty about the parameters of Germanness itself. While a growing number of commentators agreed with John about the need to let go of *völkisches* thinking, the question of what might replace it remained a point of debate and controversy across the Federal Republic.

been tracking the political and ideological struggles over a multiethnic British society since the early 1980s.

[5] Bennett, *Multicultural States*, 1–2.

A Country of Immigration?

The decade of the 1980s witnessed continued growth in the number of foreigners in the Federal Republic, a result of family reunions and the high birth rate among migrants. In 1980, 4,566,200 foreigners resided in West Germany, and by the end of the decade that number had climbed to 5,007,200.[6] The Turkish population increased as well, jumping from 1,268,300 in 1979 to 1,523,700 in 1988. By 31 December 1988, Turks made up 33.9 percent of the entire foreigner population. The next largest group was Yugoslavians, who at 579,100 represented 12.9 percent of the total.[7] Coupled with the ongoing problem of massive unemployment and a federal budget deficit, the guest worker question – and its domestic policy corollary, *Ausländerpolitik* – remained an urgent political issue for Helmut Kohl and his ruling coalition.

Based on the volume of press attention, the most significant development in the area of foreigner politics during the mid-1980s was the effort of Interior Minister Friedrich Zimmermann (CSU) to revise the 1965 *Ausländergesetz*. The ultraconservative Zimmermann formally presented his draft of an updated foreigner law to the Bundestag in August 1984. In particular, he recommended two new major restrictions. The first imposed a much lower cutoff age (six rather than sixteen) for children of foreigners still living in the country of origin to join their parents in the Federal Republic. The second stipulated that only those migrants who had lived in the Federal Republic for eight years and been married for at least twelve months would be allowed to bring their non-German spouses into the country. These proposals sought to address the putative failure of integration, evidenced most vividly and alarmingly for conservatives by the growth of foreigner ghettos in West German cities.

In an early statement as interior minister, Zimmermann explained his position on the more controversial of the two policy initiatives, the restriction on migrant children:

I also believe that we must avoid a situation in which the present condition of our public budget is made even worse by the irrational behavior of foreign parents. We have had in the past an extended practice of allowing children to be fetched who are almost of age and who have finished their education outside the country. They enter under the guise of family reunion. This happens at a point in time

---

[6] *Statistisches Jahrbuch für die Bundesrepublik Detuschland* (Stuttgart: Metzler-Poeschel Verlag, 1990).

[7] All the figures for 1988 can be found in *Statistisches Jahrbuch für die Bundesrepublik Deutschland* (Stuttgart: Metzler-Poeschel Verlag, 1990).

when they hardly still need care from their parents. It is obvious here that the parent-child relation is not the decisive motive, but rather the idea of providing entry into the German labor market at the last minute. Since youth who enter have no chance for integration among us because it is too late, I maintain that it is right to establish the age of reunion before schooling begins, that is, at six years old.[8]

At first glance, Zimmermann's plan looks like a culmination of the conservative retrenchment that we considered in the previous chapter. The problem with this interpretation, however, is that Zimmermann's initiative met swift and decisive resistance across a large part of the political spectrum, including from the FDP and CDU.

It is no real surprise that those on the left vehemently opposed a more restrictive *Ausländergesetz*. On 9 March 1984, Berlin's *Die Tageszeitung* reported that over one hundred German and foreigner groups, union organizations, and Catholic and Protestant church associations in more than sixty cities around the country were about to begin a week of activities devoted to foreigners (*Ausländerwoche*) in order to protest against xenophobia and the anticipated tightening of the foreigner law. Plans for the event, the article further explained, had taken shape the previous June, when over a thousand people gathered for a congress in Frankfurt to articulate an alternative vision of foreigner policy. In a collective resolution entitled the "Frankfurter Appell" congress participants – among them such well-known figures as the Green politician Daniel Cohn-Bendit – called for the full legal and social equality of Germans and foreigners (including local voting rights for foreigners) and the unlimited right to bring family members to the Federal Republic.[9]

More unexpectedly, those within the ruling CDU-FDP coalition also voiced major concerns. The FDP, for example, challenged Zimmermann's core assumption that foreigners would continue to flood West Germany. As long as this population held steady, the liberals claimed, the "chance would be greater that Germans would get used to the new cultural and social diversity that their Oriental fellow citizens have brought to this country."[10] Rather than imposing additional restrictions, which might actually stimulate a new wave of migrants, the FDP wanted to redouble efforts to integrate foreigners. An article for *Die Zeit* suggested that the

---

[8] Der Bundesminister des Innern, *Pressemitteilung*, 13 December 1982, quoted in Karl-Heinz Meier-Braun, *Integration und Rückkehr? Zur Ausländerpolitik des Bundes und der Länder, insbesondere Baden-Württembergs* (Mainz: Grünewald, 1988), 29.

[9] N.a., "Erste bundesweite Ausländerwoche," *Die Tageszeitung*, 9 March 1984, 3.

[10] Gerhard Spörl, "Harte Lösung? Kontroverse um das neue Ausländergesetz," *Die Zeit*, 7 September 1984, 1.

interior minister's extreme position amounted to his usual trick of "playing Beelzebub" with Helmut Kohl and the other members of the cabinet. But in this case Zimmermann provoked a standoff with the FDP that even the chancellor had clearly hoped to avoid.[11]

The clash came to a head during a meeting in September 1984 between Kohl, Zimmermann, Foreign Minister and leader of the Liberal Party Hans-Dietrich Genscher (FDP), and Labor Minister Norbert Blüm (CDU). Genscher argued for the liberal position but – as foreign minister – also reminded the cabinet that the proposed restrictions jeopardized the European Union's agreement to make Turkey a full partner (giving all Turks freedom of work and movement within the borders of the Union) by 1987. "When Zimmermann remained adamant," a report in *Der Spiegel* explained, "Genscher used his final weapon: 'this government has accepted responsibilities toward Turkey.' Then he unambiguously added: 'I will no longer be at your disposal as foreign minister if these obligations are not observed.'"[12] With this resignation threat, Genscher gained the support of Kohl and Blüm and worked out a compromise. First, Zimmermann agreed to take the two contentious recommendations off the table, a move that the press registered as a major defeat.[13] Second, the ruling conservative-liberal coalition decided to shelve its efforts to revise the foreigner law for another four years. In hindsight, a commentator for the *Süddeutsche Zeitung* characterized the battle as "a grave conflict that poisoned the climate between the CDU, CSU, and FDP."[14]

Recent scholarship has suggested that these debates reflected a bipartisan "policy of limits" during the mid-1980s.[15] The historian Klaus Bade, for example, has argued that the establishment of limits constituted the central ethos of Helmut Kohl's *Ausländerpolitik*: on the one hand, his administration called for further efforts at integration; on the other, it reaffirmed the *Anwerbestopp* and strongly encouraged guest workers to return to their countries of origin. Journalist and migration expert Karl-Heinz Meier-Braun has similarly pointed to Kohl's early policy

---

[11] Ibid.

[12] N.a., "Aus der Asche," *Der Spiegel*, 8 October 1984, 49–52.

[13] See Udo Bergdoll, "Der Patient – von Zuversicht infiziert," *Süddeutsche Zeitung*, 12 September 1984, 3; and Vera Gaserow, "Rechtsunsicherheit für Ausländer bleibt," *Die Tageszeitung*, 5 October 1984.

[14] Udo Bergdoll, "Beim Ausländerrecht haben die Fronten verschoben," *Süddeutsche Zeitung*, 7 April 1988.

[15] Klaus J. Bade, *Ausländer, Aussiedler, Asyl: Eine Bestandsaufnahme* (Munich: Beck, 1994), 57–66; and Meier-Braun, *Integration und Rückkehr?*, 18–19.

statement that "integration is only possible if the number of foreigners living in our country does not increase."[16] This perceived symbiosis between
a bounded migrant population and successful integration, Meier-Braun
claims, drove the conservative-liberal coalition's first concrete act of foreigner policy – a November 1983 voluntary repatriation program that
offered 10,500 DM to each eligible returnee.[17]

In all of these ways, Bade and Meier-Braun are quite right to suggest an
emerging preoccupation with measured approaches and clear thresholds.
But we also need to be aware of the *limits* that the CDU-FDP coalition set
for its own efforts at political retrenchment. Consider, for example, the
1983 bill that provided money to guest workers willing to repatriate (the
Act to Promote the Preparedness of Foreign Workers to Return). This
measure has not been understood as a major development in foreigner
policy, in large part because its impacts remained fairly circumscribed.
Foreigners had a mere six months to register for financial assistance once
the law went into effect, and only about 250 thousand (out of over 4.5
million) accepted the offer.[18] Yet its very existence helps illuminate the
ideological thresholds of conservative policy during the mid-1980s. The

---

[16] Meier-Braun, *Integration und Rückkehr?*, 28.

[17] *Jahresbericht der Bundesregierung 1983* (Bonn: Presse- und Informationsamt der Bundesregierung, 1983), 94. This financial offer, considered a reimbursement of employee
contributions to retirement insurance, also included a 1,500 DM payment for each child.
It was open to any foreign worker from Yugoslavia, Morocco, Portugal, Spain, Tunisia, or
Turkey unemployed after 30 October 1983. The bill stipulated that workers must apply
for return assistance by 30 June 1984. See Meier-Braun, *Integration und Rückkehr?*,
35–37, 48–54.

   For Bade in particular the concept of limits in this period also applied more broadly
to the pattern of policymaking across the 1982 regime change. The Kohl brand of
Ausländerpolitik, he has observed, hardly differed from the policies pursued at the end
of the Schmidt administration. As accusations of failure mounted against the social-
liberal integrationist policies, the SPD party leadership increasingly began to discuss more
restrictive measures for dealing with foreigners, including new limits on family reunion
and monetary inducements for them to leave the Federal Republic (Bade, *Ausländer,
Aussiedler, Asyl*, 58–59). The CDU-FDP coalition, that is, did not really initiate new
restrictions, but only attempted to carry out policies that the SPD-FDP had already
introduced into the public discussion.

   The idea of limits is a useful conceptual tool for understanding the political discourse
on the guest worker question in the 1980s. Foreigner policy clearly revolved around limits
in the most basic sense – the number of migrants residing in West Germany, the amount
of money allotted for repatriation, or the extent to which the CDU actually deviated
from the SPD policies in any respect other than rhetoric.

[18] This number includes dependents who left the Federal Republic with their parents. See
Jahresbericht der Bundesregierung 1984 (Bonn: Presse- und Informationsamt der Bundesregierung, 1984), 95.

ruling coalition was quite happy to encourage foreigners to leave – and to give them cash to do so. But by making the decision to return home a choice, the bill also suggested that systematic repatriation would have to come through the individual will and agency of migrants themselves. The CDU, in other words, made a clear distinction between monetary incentives and large-scale expulsion. Collective removal was the policy threshold that even conservatives would not cross.

The Zimmermann affair can be analyzed in similar terms. The fact that the interior minister's new version of the *Ausländergesetz* provoked such vehement protests from Genscher and the FDP suggests that these restrictions had exceeded a perceived threshold for policymaking. Critics argued that Zimmermann's plan would "result in a constitutionally damaging two-class law" because it further constrained the ability of foreigners to reunite with their children and spouses and thereby violated the fundamental constitutional protection of marriage and family.[19] While many liberals and moderate conservatives were willing to take action to lower the numbers of migrants – and had no problem with offering financial incentives for guest workers to go home – they refused to follow Zimmermann toward a policy that would effectively break up families. In this respect, Bade's notion of limits is precisely right: what troubled those in the CDU and FDP mainstream, above all, was their sense that Zimmermann was pushing too quickly and moving too far from conventional approaches to solving the foreigner problem.

These examples point to an important new development in the mid-1980s – the implicit acceptance of Germany's de facto status as an immigration country. As we have seen, Heinz Kühn had already asserted this position in 1978, but Helmut Schmidt and the rest of his administration quickly distanced themselves from it as the foreigner problem became an increasingly important issue in partisan politics. In the fight over the *Ausländergesetz*, however, a handful of commentators began to articulate a subtle shift in the larger meanings of the labor migration. An article in *Die Tageszeitung* explicitly tied the new law to the "decisive question": "Has the Federal Republic of Germany become an immigration country or not?"[20] *Die Zeit* reporter Gerhard Spörl, moreover, observed that every major party agreed on the urgent need to revise the nearly twenty-year-old foreigner law, disputes over the specific revisions notwithstanding. The original law, he explained, "was written with different relationships in mind – at that time, guest workers came alone and

[19] Spörl, "Harte Lösung?," 1.
[20] Jürgen Gottschlich, "Deutschland den Deutschen," *Die Tageszeitung*, 9 March 1984, 3.

went back to their homelands after a few years. The Federal Republic of Germany did not want to become a country of immigration. This idea is still valid in principle today, but reality does not allow it to hold."[21] Particularly striking here is the open assertion of an immigrant "reality," despite the "principle" that continued to belie it. Whether or not Germany "wanted" to be a country of immigration, Spörl concluded, developments at the ground level rendered such wishes irrelevant. In an article several weeks later he elaborated on what had occurred: "An ethnic minority has built itself in the Federal Republic that claims its place in local society: as wage and salary recipients, as taxpayers, as an economic factor, as neighbors. This development was originally undesired." West Germany, in short, had become a "nonimmigration country" with lots of immigrants.[22]

This somewhat tortured formulation suggests an ideological struggle in progress. Clearly, the concept of *Einwanderungsland* (country of immigration) still felt like a radical proposition in the mid-1980s. Neither Spörl nor the country's leading politicians could manage an unequivocal affirmation at this point. Indeed, CDU-FDP policymaking sometimes pushed in precisely the opposite direction. Yet Spörl also refused to leave unacknowledged Germany's substantial immigrant presence, an ethnic minority that had staked "its place in local society."[23] And in general, the conservative-liberal coalition's *Ausländerpolitik* recognized this major structural transformation at the ground level. The highly publicized rebuke of Zimmermann in 1984 demonstrated a growing uneasiness with any effort to force foreigners out of the country. Coerced expulsion was now understood within the conservative mainstream as a form of extremism.

When the question of a new *Ausländergesetz* resurfaced four years later in 1988, the ruling coalition's sense of limits had become much clearer. To be sure, Zimmermann remained undeterred by his 1984 defeat and renewed his efforts to push conservative revisions into the law. His second plan, in fact, proved more extreme than his first. In addition to family reunion restrictions, he now proposed reinstating a rotation system with a maximum stay in the Federal Republic of eight years. According to the *Süddeutsche Zeitung*, Zimmermann prefaced these recommendations with a much broader ideological declaration:

The self-understanding of the Federal Republic of Germany as a German state is at stake. A continuing... migration of foreigners would deeply change the Federal

---

[21] Ibid.
[22] Gerhard Spörl, "Die Angst vor den Fremden," *Die Zeit*, 21 September 1984, 9–10.
[23] Ibid.

Republic of Germany. It would mean abandoning the homogeneity of society, which is defined by membership in the nation ... The Federal Republic of Germany would ... develop into a multinational and multicultural society, which would be permanently plagued by minority problems. ... The national interest commands a stop to such a development at its very beginning.[24]

This statement revisited the key question of the *Einwanderungsland* debate: how should West Germany's national and cultural boundaries be defined? Zimmermann clearly perceived labor migrants as a fundamental threat to the "homogeneous" integrity of West German society, an integrity that he defined in strictly ethnic terms. His revisions thus sought to foreclose a "multinational and multicultural society" by reasserting a critical fusion of cultural identification with the boundaries of the national state.

What Zimmermann failed to grasp was the extent to which the ideological center – even within his own party – had shifted on the issue of foreigner policy. In anticipation of a second battle over the foreigner law, *Süddeutsche Zeitung* published an article in the spring of 1988 stating that the interior minister would not be able to muster a majority in the CDU, let alone in the Bundestag, for his bid to reduce the age of foreign children to reunite with their parents. His opposition included not only liberals, Social Democrats, and Greens, but also mainstream Christian Democrats. "The criticism of the church had an effect," the report explained. "Demanding that foreigner policy must be aligned with the 'Union's Christian view of humanity' as well as the 'interest of the German people,' Johannes Gerster attempts – as domestic politics speaker for the CDU/CSU faction – to bring a transformation of consciousness to the C-parties."[25] Most conservatives, in other words, now rejected Zimmermann's proposals as patently inhumane and un-Christian.

At the same time, somewhat more liberal views were beginning to emerge within the CDU. According to the same article, Alfons Müller, the spokesman for eleven Christian Democratic Bundestag representatives who comprised the party's committee on social issues, declared that "the foreigner law should not be conceived any longer as 'resistance to danger,' but rather must place partnership and integration in the foreground."[26]

---

[24] Christian Schneider, "Aus Fremden werden Mitbürger und Landsleute," *Süddeutsche Zeitung*, 10–11 September 1988, 9, quoted in Christian Joppke, "Multiculturalism and Immigration: A Comparison of the United States, Germany, and Great Britain," *Theory and Society* 25 (1996): 471.

[25] Bergdoll, "Beim Ausländerrecht."

[26] Ibid.

The committee suggested giving foreigners a claim to naturalization after five years of legal residence, allowing spouses to come to Germany without a waiting period, and eliminating the age limit for children to join their parents.[27] In an interview with *Der Spiegel* around the same time, the CDU mayor of Stuttgart, Manfred Rommel, went so far as to assert that foreigners should have the right to dual citizenship.[28] The majority of conservatives certainly considered these more progressive positions extreme in the other direction. Gerster, who harshly criticized the Interior Ministry plan for its un-Christian treatment of migrants, dismissed the proposals of Müller's group as "careless" and "unrealistic."[29] Yet it was clear by 1988 that Zimmermann occupied an increasingly marginal position, not just within the ruling coalition but within his own faction. With opposition to the interior minister mounting both inside and outside the CDU, Kohl responded by replacing Zimmermann with the more moderate Wolfgang Schäuble (CDU).

The two political firestorms surrounding Zimmermann's proposed reforms provide an illuminating contrast. During the mid-1980s, both the FDP and the less conservative wing of the CDU exhibited a palpable discomfort with Zimmermann's harsh public rhetoric, although they did not express fundamental opposition to his larger policy goal. They did not object, in other words, to the basic assumption that a reduction in the number of migrants was in itself desirable. By 1988, however, the very idea of active restriction or reduction was perceived as incompatible with mainstream Christian Democratic thinking. The fact that Zimmermann was forced to resign suggests that his particular brand of foreigner politics had become untenable within Kohl's CDU.

Framing a German Multiculturalism

This assessment raises a crucial question: Why exactly did conservatives come to perceive Zimmermann as a political liability? An answer begins to emerge when we examine the broader patterns of public discourse that took place between the 1983 CDU/CSU victory in the federal elections and Zimmermann's 1988 ouster. At the end of the decade, the debate about *whether* Germany had become a country of immigration was increasingly giving way to an explicit discussion about what a multicultural

[27] Meier-Braun, *Integration und Rückkehr?*, 63.
[28] N.a., "Was die wählen, ist mir Wursch," *Der Spiegel*, 30 May 1988, 48.
[29] Meier-Braun, *Integration und Rückkehr?*, 63–64.

society would look like in practice.³⁰ This recalibration of the public discourse signaled a deep shift in values and assumptions. Above all, the
growing willingness to debate the terms and meanings of a specifically
German multiculturalism presupposed that a major demographic and
cultural transformation had already taken place. At the same time, it
is important to be clear that discussing multiculturalism did not signal
collective affirmation. Nor did this discussion simply supersede or cancel
out older debates about the Federal Republic as a country of immigration.
Even today, it remains axiomatic among many conservatives to deny the
notion of an *Einwanderungsland* as a political or civic principle. But in
the late 1980s, one pattern of discourse began to overshadow the other.
Not just the Greens and the SPD but also the CDU began to ponder how
multiculturalism might work in a West German context.

One of the first recorded deployments of the term "multiculturalism"
in West German public discourse was a statement promoting the 1980
Tag des ausländischen Mitbürgers (Day of the Foreign Fellow Citizen), an
event sponsored by the Catholic and Protestant churches. Jürgen Micksch,
a leading Protestant pastor who helped organize the activities, explained
that the planners consciously used the expression "multicultural society"
to broaden the public's understanding of and appreciation for long-term
foreign residents. This term, he noted, encouraged native Germans to see
their "foreign fellow citizens" as bearers of rich customs and traditions
that might enhance German culture in the process of integration. The
main objective was to combat the dominant perception of foreigners as
a burden, or as conduits for new social problems such as ghettos, unemployment, higher crime rates, and religious conflict.³¹

In retrospect, it is somewhat surprising that the organizers of the
Tag des ausländischen Mitbürgers chose the expression "multicultural
society" in 1980. As Ella Shohat and Robert Stam have pointed out,

---

³⁰ Sabine von Dirke has offered one of the earliest considerations of multicultural discourse
   in 1980s West Germany. She has usefully identified the key lines of argument for and
   against multiculturalism. Her goal is more a wide-ranging survey of the German discourse than a systematic analysis of how the discourse changes over time. See Sabine von
   Dirke, "Multikulti: The German Debate on Multiculturalism," *German Studies Review*
   17 (1994): 513–36. For more on multiculturalism in the German political context, see
   Brett Klopp, *German Multiculturalism: Immigrant Integration and the Transformation
   of Citizenship* (Westport: Praeger, 2002); Christian Joppke and Steven Lukes, "Introduction: Multicultural Questions," in Joppke and Lukes, eds., *Multicultural Questions*
   (Oxford: Oxford University Press, 1999), 1–24.
³¹ Jürgen Micksch, *Deutschland – Einheit in kultureller Vielfalt* (Frankfurt am Main: Otto
   Lembeck Verlag, 1991), 5–16, cited in von Dirke, "Multikulti," 516.

"multiculturalism is often seen as the name of a specifically American debate."[32] Thus, the German church activists seem to have imported a foreign term, even if it is not clear that they fully understood how the concept was being used in the U.S. context.[33] They were largely oblivious, for example, to the fact that some groups in the United States use multiculturalism to argue for the preservation of cultural particularity (as opposed to a dynamic mixing of cultures). Nevertheless, this instinct of West German religious leaders to associate their celebration of "foreign fellow citizens" with an American phenomenon is interesting. In so doing, they began to make culture into a primary category of identification, a conceptual move that opened the possibility that West German society might be understood as a diversity of cultures rather than an ethnically defined nation. This early introduction of multiculturalism began the process of revaluing migrants' cultural differences from a source of pathology to a catalyst for enrichment.

It is worth noting that this early German articulation of multiculturalism differed greatly from the theory of cultural integration promoted by the Institute for German as a Foreign Language (DaF) during the same period. In DaF's conception, cultures exist as discrete and somewhat static units that remain largely unintelligible to each other. Migrant authors writing in German become important intermediaries because they enable their readers to slowly expose themselves to foreign ideas. The *Tag des ausländischen Mitbürgers*, by contrast, presupposed a conception of culture that was far more dynamic, fluid, and syncretic. Multicultural, in this formula, not only assumed that it was possible for multiple cultures to coexist in a single society, it also suggested that German culture

[32] Ella Shohat and Robert Stam, *Unthinking Eurocentrism: Multiculturalism and the Media* (London: Routledge, 1994), 46.

[33] David Hollinger provides a useful primer on the multiculturalism debate in the U.S. context. This debate, he argues, has generally divided into "separatists" and "defenders" of Eurocentric domination. But Hollinger also points to the ways in which the term itself is slippery. Both sides, he notes, have at times claimed to be proponents of multiculturalism: "many who do hold up European traditions insist that what makes these traditions worth defending is their multitudinous, decidedly multicultural character. Hence the 'opponents' of multiculturalism sometimes end up claiming its banner as their own, while a more-multiculturalist-than-thou faction simultaneously complains that a merely cosmetic acceptance of multiculturalism masks a conservative victory in the culture wars and a rejection of 'true' multiculturalism." David Hollinger, *Postethnic America: Beyond Multiculturalism* (New York: Basic Books, 1995), 81. See also Chapter 4. For a useful discussion of the issues that gave rise to the multiculturalist debate in the United States, see Gary B. Nash, "The Great Multicultural Debate," *Contention* 1 (1992): 11–26.

would be continuously enriched and expanded by the contributions of its "foreign fellow citizens." Whereas DaF advocated greater communication and mutual understanding, the *Tag des ausländischen Mitbürgers* celebrated the idea of substantive transformation.

Precisely because this latter model moved well beyond the dominant rhetorics and values of guest worker integration, some German critics responded with concern. A good example can be found in feuilleton editor Konrad Adam's 1982 *Frankfurter Allgemeine Zeitung* essay, "The Price of Multiculture," which sharply criticized a conference sponsored by the Protestant Academy of Arnoldshain. Formed in the immediate aftermath of the Second World War, this Protestant association described itself as a progressive forum for the discussion of religious, cultural, and sociopolitical issues. What bothered Adam was the group's declaration of German multiculturalism as a "foregone conclusion." "Utopian calls" by the Academy to "broaden one's horizons" or to embrace "the possibilities of other cultures," he asserted, were not enough. Rather, social progressives needed to answer a set of basic questions: how is "mutual integration" to be "concretely represented, what is given and what is taken; under which conditions and at what price must Germans adapt to 'the new relationships of a multicultural coexistence' and where does this task conversely fall on foreigners."[34] More pointedly, Adam asked, would "renunciation of women's equality, revival of corporal punishment in the schools, or the violent mischief of the Gray Wolves" be "drawn into the cultural exchange"?[35] Which values, in short, would structure this new "multicultural coexistence"?

These arguments did not simply recapitulate the standard conservative critique from the early 1980s – namely that migrants lacked the capacity to integrate. Adam's questions, rather, identified the Protestant Academy's more fluid and decentered notion of cultural formation as the key problem. In his view, such dynamism and relativism brought with them the possibility that retrograde ideologies might filter into West Germany under the guise of cross-cultural enrichment. Adam also expressed concern that a multicultural German society might atomize into a collection of ethnic particularities (*Sonderkulturen*) with no collective ideological framework for valuing one set of principles over another. Undemocratic customs and absolutisms would thus be celebrated along with all the rest.

---

[34] Konrad Adam, "Der Preis der Multikultur. Ausländer und Deutsche – eine kritische Masse?," *Frankfurter Allgemeine Zeitung*, 23 November 1982.
[35] Ibid.

It is not entirely clear which specific examples Adam had in mind as he was issuing these concerns, but recent scholarship has noted that new ethnic particularities were indeed beginning to emerge in a number of different sectors of West German society at roughly the same moment. Betigül Argun has argued, for instance, that the growing prevalence of multiculturalism in West German public discourse resulted in the articulation of more differentiated ethnic and religious identifications among migrants.[36] Before the 1980s, Germans generally thought of guest workers from Turkey as a homogeneous group – as Turks. But in fact, large numbers of Kurds, an ethnic minority within Turkey engaged in a long-term struggle for self-governance, migrated to the Federal Republic in the 1960s and 1970s. Initially, very few of these labor migrants emphasized a distinct Kurdish identity, or even described themselves as Kurds.[37] Similarly, almost 30 percent of all Turks in Germany were Alevi, members of the Turkish Islamic sect that worships Ali rather than Mohammed and has a strong tradition of fighting for social justice and equality. Yet until the early 1980s, most Alevi Turks in West Germany remained silent about their religious beliefs and their historical persecution by the majority Sunni.[38] Events like the *Tag des ausländischen Mitbürgers* and the conference sponsored by the Protestant Academy encouraged migrants to claim more specific identities. And during the 1980s, both Kurds and Alevis established cultural centers around the country, often obtaining financial support from city governments (especially Berlin), which sought to promote the cultural diversity of foreigners.

Thus one early effect of the multicultural discourse on the migrant community was the emergence of what we might call identity politics. In

[36] Betigül Ercan Argun, *Turkey in Germany: The Transnational Sphere of Deutschkei* (New York: Routledge, 2003), 67–69. Argun's book primarily focuses on the impact of the Turkish community in Germany on domestic politics in Turkey. Here she argues that the splintering of identities among Turkish migrants in the Federal Republic, which was prompted by the discourse of multiculturalism, forced Turks in Turkey to begin to acknowledge ethnic and religious diversity within Turkish society.

[37] For a useful discussion of Kurds in this history, see Aytaç Eryilmaz and Mathilde Jamin, eds., *Fremde Heimat-Yaban Sılan Olur: Eine Geschichte der Einwanderung aus der Türkei* (Essen: Klartext, 1998), 24. The discourse of multiculturalism, of course, was not the only factor that produced a new awareness of Kurdish identity. The 1980 military coup in Turkey led to a greater influx of politicized Kurdish asylum seekers in West Germany. And the Kurdish Workers' Party (PKK), which emerged in Ankara in the late 1970s, started a full-blown guerrilla war against the Turkish state in 1984 that spilled over into violent attacks on West German and European soil.

[38] Ertekin Özcan, *Türkische Immigrantenorganisationen in der Bundesrepublik Deutschland* (Berlin: Hitit Verlag, 1989), 59.

the early 1980s, for example, the Kurdish Culture and Information Center in Berlin demanded that in public schools German-language courses designated for foreign children be taught in Kurdish as well as Turkish.[39] Ironically, this emphasis on tolerance and inclusion also created a space for more extreme ultranationalists and religious fundamentalists.[40] Organizations such as the right-of-center, nationalist Federation of European Democratic Idealist Turkish Associations (Avrupa Demokratik Ülkücü Türk Dernekleri Federasyonu, ADÜTDF) and fundamentalist Islamic Community–National Outlook (Islamische Gemeinschaft Milli Görüş, IGMG) established mosques, groups for women and children, sports clubs, and religious schools. Both groups aimed to protect and strengthen the particularistic identities – whether national Turkish or Islamic – of Turks in Germany. The leader of the ultranationalist European Turkish-Islamic Union (ATIB), a splinter group of the Turkish Federation, also used the arguments of multicultural inclusion as a strategy to preserve cultural differences. "We want Islam to be recognized as an official religion in Germany," declared Musa Serdar Çelebi. "We want voting rights and the right to open our own schools to raise and educate our children within our own system."[41] My point here is not that the valorization of multicultural principles simply produced fragmentation; clearly, these tensions had much longer histories and causal motors of their own. Rather, the new emphasis on multicultural tolerance seems to have brought latent tensions more squarely into public visibility and discourse.

A somewhat different model of identity politics emerged around Afro-Germans at about this same time. Spurred by the 1984 visit of African-American poet and activist Audre Lorde to Berlin's Free University, a small group of black German women began to recognize Afro-German as a shared identity. Lorde encouraged these women to think of themselves as "part of a worldwide black diaspora" and thereby "validated their experiences in a way previously unknown" to them.[42] In response, key figures in this group such as May Opitz (later Ayim) and Katharina Oguntoye

---

[39] Argun, *Turkey in Germany*, 67. She does not give specific dates for this development.

[40] The ultranationalist Turkish National Action Party (MHP) was closely connected to the Gray Wolves, a group of paramilitary commandoes that operated in Europe and especially Germany during the 1970s and 1980s. Right-wing extremists, the ultranationalists (later a part of the Turkish Federation) have sought the "unification of the Turkish race." See Argun, *Turkey in Germany*, 139–52.

[41] Ibid., 145.

[42] Fatima El-Tayeb, "If You Can't Pronounce My Name, You Can Just Call Me Pride: Afro-German Activism, Gender, and Hip Hop," *Gender and History* 15.3 (2003): 470.

began to research the buried histories of people of African and African-American descent in Germany, which they collected in the pathbreaking 1986 book *Farbe bekennen* (translated as *Showing Our Colors*). This publication spurred a new self-consciousness among Germans of African descent and prompted the establishment of the Initiative of Black Germans (Initiative Schwarzer Deutsche, ISD) and the Afro-German Women's Association (Schwarze deutsche Frauen und Schwarze Frauen in Deutschland, ADEFRA).[43]

Tina Campt has recently argued that these events represented "the product and process of importing individual, social, and cultural meanings to blackness as a strategic form of self-definition and identification."[44] In other words, precisely because the history of black Germans could not be distilled to a collective migration or displacement – because it included African migrants and refugees, as well as the offspring of African-American GIs and Germans – the very notion of a collective Afro-German identity was a self-conscious choice, a "strategic essentialism" constituted for specific political purposes.[45] The all but complete erasure of black

---

[43] May Opitz, Katharina Oguntoye, and Dagmar Schultz, eds., *Farbe bekennen: Afrodeutsche Frauen auf den Spuren ihrer Geschichte* (Berlin: Orlanda Frauenverlag, 1986), trans. by Anne V. Adams as *Showing Our Colors: Afro-German Women Speak Out* (Amherst: University of Massachusetts Press, 1992).

[44] Tina M. Campt, "Reading the Black German Experience: An Introduction," *Callaloo* 26.2 (2003): 289.

[45] The history of Afro-Germans is just starting to be written. It includes work on German colonies in Africa, the occupation of the Rhineland by French African soldiers, and the interaction of African-American GIs and German women. See, in particular, Reiner Pommerin, *Sterilisierung der Rheinlandbastarde: Das Schicksal einer farbigen deutschen Minderheit, 1918–1937* (Düsseldorf: Droste Verlag, 1977); May Opitz et al., eds., *Farbe bekennen*; Reinhold Grimm and Jost Hermand, eds., *Blacks and German Culture* (Madison: The University of Wisconsin Press, 1986); Katharina Oguntoye, *Eine afro-deutsche Geschichte: Zur Lebenssituation von Afrikanern und Afro-Deutschen in Deutschland von 1884 bis 1950* (Berlin: Hoho Verlag, 1997); Tina Campt, Pascal Grosse, and Yara-Collette Lemke-Muniz de Faria, "Blacks, Germans, and the Politics of Imperial Imagination, 1920–60," in Sara Friedrichsmeyer, Sara Lennox, and Susanne Zantop, eds., *The Imperialist Imagination: German Colonialism and Its Legacy* (Ann Arbor: University of Michigan Press, 1998), 205–29; Leroy T. Hopkins, ed., *Who Is a German? Historical and Modern Perspectives on Africans in Germany* (Washington, DC: The American Institute for Contemporary German Studies, 1999); Fatima El-Tayeb, *Schwarze Deutsche: Der Diskurs um "Rasse" und nationale Identität, 1890–1933* (Frankfurt: Campus Verlag, 2001); Damani J. Partridge, "Becoming Non-Citizens: Technologies for Exclusion and Exclusionary Incorporation after the Berlin Wall" (Ph.D. diss., University of California, Berkeley, 2003); Tina M. Campt, *Other Germans: Black Germans and the Politics of Race, Gender and Memory in the Third Reich* (Ann Arbor: University of Michigan Press, 2004); and Heide Fehrenbach, *Race after Hitler: Black Occupation Children in Postwar Germany and America* (Princeton: Princeton University Press, 2005).

Germans from German history and public discourse impelled a group identity that would force Germans to acknowledge the deep workings of race and racism in their society.

The contrasts here between black Germans and Turkish-Germans are instructive. Whereas Afro-Germans explicitly invoked blackness, migrants of Turkish descent generally did not organize under an "of color" rubric.[46] This tactical choice reflected more than the obvious difference between race and ethnicity. As labor migrants from a non-European Union country, Turks existed as foreigners outside the West German polity for most of the post-1945 period. Their primary struggle was to obtain the basic rights of residence and citizenship. In this context, a strategic essentialism or identity politics based on color would have only served to reinforce conservative claims of incommensurable differences. Most Afro-Germans, by contrast, were citizens of the Federal Republic because of their partial German parentage. Thus, they sought to contest the paradox of their liminality – at once within the German polity, but largely invisible in German culture and history. The very term Afro-German challenged the ongoing erasure of black German citizens in public discourse as well as the conventional insistence that West Germany did not have a race problem.

At this point, an event occurred outside the Federal Republic that considerably raised the ideological and political stakes of the multiculturalism debate, namely the publication of Salman Rushdie's controversial novel *The Satanic Verses* (1988).[47] Most readers will be familiar with the

---

[46] According to Kader Konuk, migrant women from Turkey and other countries did attempt to claim a shared identity as "women of color" within the feminist movement during the late 1980s. The effort to apply the American usage to the German context broke down at a 1991 conference for women of color in Hamburg, when feminists from a variety of minority groups could not agree on which women should count as being "of color." The most extreme contrast was between Turkish women with light skin but no German passport and black German women who regularly experienced discrimination because of dark skin but held German citizenship. One effect of the inability to agree on the "of color" distinction was a more explicit labeling of minority women's subject positions in Germany. See Cathy S. Gelbin, Kader Konuk, and Peggy Piesche, eds., *AufBrüche: Kulturelle Produktionen von Migrantinnen, Schwarzen und jüdischen Frauen in Deutschland* (Königstein: Ulrike Helmer Verlag, 1999).

[47] Numerous scholars have discussed the manifold implications of the Rushdie Affair. They include Peter Jones, "Respecting Beliefs and Rebuking Rushdie," *British Journal of Political Science* 20.4 (1990): 415–37; Aamir Mufti, "Reading the Rushdie Affair: An Essay on Islam and Politics," *Social Text* 29 (1991): 95–116; Afsaneh Najmabadi, "Interview with Gayatri Spivak," *Social Text* 28 (1991): 122–34; Timothy Brennan, "Rushdie, Islam, and Postcolonial Criticism," *Social Text* 31/32 (1992): 271–76; and Talal Asad, *Genealogies of Religion: Discipline and Reasons of Power in Christianity and Islam* (Baltimore, MD: Johns Hopkins University Press, 1993), Chapter 7.

outlines of the ensuing furor. By 1988, Rushdie was one of Britain's most prominent minority intellectuals. Yet many Muslim Britons aggressively protested the novel's perceived insults against Islam, demanding that the book be withdrawn from circulation or even banned.[48] And in the months that followed, Iran's Ayatollah Khomeini issued a *fatwa* against Rushdie. This threat of violence, together with a highly publicized burning of the book in Bradford, prompted the British government to chide its South Asian citizens for their extremism. For our purposes, though, the so-called Rushdie Affair leads to another sort of question. Why did this religious controversy surrounding a British-Asian intellectual resonate so strongly in the Federal Republic?

For many West Germans, this was a moment of reckoning, a historical watershed in which earlier flirtations with American conceptions of multiculturalism gave way to a greater awareness that the issue had specifically European connotations and meanings. The uproar, after all, involved an attack by Muslim "fundamentalists" on a figure widely acknowledged as an exemplar of multiculturalism in the New Europe. In particular, these events seemed to impress upon German commentators that multiculturalism was a matter of immediate and nontheoretical political urgency. Dankwart Guratzsch, a conservative critic writing for *Die Welt*, characterized "Khomeini's command of murder" as a "deathly frost on the blossoming dreams of a 'multicultural society.'" He further observed that even liberal champions such as the Green politician Daniel Cohn-Bendit were forced to qualify their position: they now said "'yes' to a multicultural society, but not at the price of giving up emancipatory ideas that [had] been painstakingly fought for."[49] As Guratzsch was quick to point out, the Muslim fundamentalist response to what it perceived as blasphemy undermined "postmodern" cultural pluralism, which rejected the sacredness of any single idea or tradition and allowed all varieties of difference to coexist without censure. In discrediting multiculturalism, then, Guratzsch highlighted the ironic predicament of leftists such as Cohn-Bendit, who ended up abandoning one key tenet of Western society – freedom of religion – in order to protect another – freedom of expression.

Yet for Guratzsch, the Rushdie Affair illuminated a more fundamental and disturbing problem: "If a single occasion, a misguided (possibly even

---

[48] For a highly useful collection of newspaper articles around the Rushdie Affair as it played out in the West, see Lisa Appignanesi and Sara Maitland, eds., *The Rushdie File* (London: Fourth Estate Ltd., 1989).

[49] Dankwart Guratzsch, "Rushdie und die Multikultur," *Die Welt*, 20 March 1989.

mean) novel, a single man is enough to shake deeply the inner peace of Europe, how could a 'multicultural society' then ever recommend itself as a stable order of peace?"[50] The crux of the problem, he argued, lay in the nature of culture. Contrary to the common belief that culture was "something decorative, delightful, superfluous," Guratzsch maintained that it was an elemental part of human existence whose defense was "unavoidably a question of life and death." Decrying multiculturalists' attempts to explain away the *fatwa* as a reversion to the Middle Ages or to claim that Islam "is tolerant at its root," he insisted that the "death sentence against Rushdie" was far from "a mad, singular decree of the old man Ayatollah." After all, the Muslim jurist Malik Ibn Anas, author of what Guratzsch described as the oldest and most respected Islamic legal text, "saw in apostasy a crime worthy of death." This early example of religious intolerance, Guratzsch argued, represented "the seed of discord for that multicultural vision that has now been so far-reachingly shaken in the case of Rushdie. It can be trivialized, challenged, or whitewashed . . . nevertheless this seed of foreignness between the cultures will grow."[51]

The Rushdie Affair also elicited a strong reaction from Claus Leggewie, a well-known progressive commentator and one of the Federal Republic's most prominent political scientists. In contrast to Guratzsch, Leggewie did not dismiss the idea of multiculturalism out of hand. Rather, he saw this event as a kind of test case for how multiculturalism would be adjudicated in the new polyglot society of late twentieth-century Europe. Notwithstanding the efforts of right-wing hardliners, Leggewie noted that the embrace of multiculturalism had moved beyond strictly partisan lines in West Germany. He pointed, for example, to the fact that Stuttgart's Christian Democratic mayor, Manfred Rommel, and the CDU general secretary, Heiner Geißler, now publicly supported foreigners' right to vote in local elections as well as the easing of federal naturalization laws. For Leggewie, however, the controversy surrounding *The Satanic Verses* raised two major concerns. On the one hand, he argued that those who championed the coexistence of many cultural "communities and colonies" as an alternative to "national homogenization" were in fact promoting a "childish" celebration of differences that often fed the desire for exoticism.[52] On the other hand, he worried that such under-theorized multiculturalism

---

[50] Ibid.
[51] Ibid.
[52] Claus Leggewie, "Multikulturelle Gesellschaft oder: die Naivität der Ausländerfreunde," *Deutsche Volkszeitung/Die Tat*, 10 March 1989, 3.

failed to offer disparate ethnic communities any shared institutions that would bind them to a common set of principles.

In Leggewie's view, the death threat issued by Khomeini boiled down to a clash between "the universally declared right to the freedom of speech and artistic freedom" and the particular "worldwide claim of an Islamic sect to protect and spread the true teaching."[53] It also vividly illustrated the "aporias" created when "cultures that have nothing in common merely coexist." A society that viewed everyone's cultural particularities as worthy of protection but shared no basic values or institutions, Leggewie concluded, would invariably succumb to illiberal acts. The crucial issue was how to adjudicate the inevitable conflicts between cultural differences and determine parameters for democratic accommodation. Leggewie insisted that "the mutual recognition of difference" must be "preserved in the constitution of *universal* rights ... and in protecting *procedures* of interaction."[54]

Yet this framework could only be meaningful if migrants had access to German citizenship. Leggewie therefore called for the easing of naturalization procedures and a redefinition of German citizenship that would include guest workers and their families. As German citizens, migrants would possess guaranteed universal rights and simultaneously be bound to "procedures of interaction." The key to discouraging extremism, in this view, was to give migrants a clear stake in civil society. And to this end, he proposed that Germans embrace the French republican concept of *citoyen*, a general membership status based on loyalty to the state.[55] Leggewie envisioned membership in the West German state as wholly separate from cultural identification. His hope was that migrants might claim citizenship rights while also retaining multiple forms of personal affiliation. This conception of multiculturalism allowed and even encouraged migrants to maintain a wide range of customs and traditions while also binding them to the values and obligations of liberal democracy. Here, Leggewie suggested something akin to constitutional patriotism

---

[53] Ibid.

[54] Ibid. Emphasis in the original text.

[55] This is the meaning of *citoyen* in its classic, revolutionary sense – a substitution of a social order based on common law for one based on estates and privileges. The best-known statement on French conceptions of citizen and citizenship is Rogers Brubaker, *Citizenship and Nationhood in France and Germany* (Cambridge, MA: Harvard University Press, 1992). Recent debates about Muslim women wearing headscarves in French public institutions, however, remind us that the concept of *citoyen* ultimately contains a set of particularistic expectations despite its universalistic claims.

(*Verfassungspatriotismus*), a concept first formulated by the West German political scientist Dolf Sternberger in an effort to rescue the notion of patriotism from its Nazi legacy. Since Nazism had rendered any ethnic concept of nationhood untenable in the Federal Republic, according to Sternberger, the values set out in the West German Basic Law provided the only viable basis for national loyalty.[56] In each case, grounding patriotism in allegiance to the state and its democratic principles detached national belonging from the demand for homogeneous ethnic identity or a uniform set of cultural practices.

The unresolved tensions within Leggewie's vision become more apparent, however, when we consider anthropologist Talal Asad's critique of the Rushdie Affair in Britain. In particular, Asad has emphasized the unprecedented response by the government, which issued three separate official statements to the Muslim community about the need for immigrants to behave like proper Britons. These admonitions "on being British" (the title of one of the statements written by Deputy Home Secretary John Patten) asserted that national belonging meant more than simply paying taxes, voting, using welfare services, or abiding by the laws of the country. The British government further insisted that Muslim citizens accept the core principle of freedom, defined here as both tolerance of diversity and the obligation to respect the rights of others.[57] What particularly upset government officials, according to Asad, was the way in which offended British Muslims politicized their alien traditions. More specifically, Muslim protesters used the language of Western liberalism (i.e., equal rights and freedom of religion) to defend their own strongly held religious convictions, which in turn undermined the government's authority to define the "core of common values" for British society.[58]

In many respects, Patten's definition of Britishness was precisely the social blueprint that Leggewie idealized in his notion of a multicultural German citizenship. The Muslim protesters were British citizens as members of the former empire. They also enjoyed full legal and political rights and even subscribed to some of the basic assumptions of liberal democracy. Yet these benefits of British citizenship did not prevent the

---

[56] Dolf Sternberger, *Verfassungspatriotismus* (Hannover: Landeszentrale für Politische Bildung, 1982). Jürgen Habermas adopted the phrase "constitutional patriotism" in the early 1990s as part of his consideration of European integration and European identity. See Jürgen Habermas, "Citizenship and National Identity: Some Reflections on the Future of Europe," *Praxis International* 12.1 (1992): 1–19.

[57] Asad, *Genealogies of Religion*, 243–44.

[58] Ibid., 267.

pursuit of particularistic absolutisms. Nor did a shared stake in the state or its liberal procedures provide a clear framework for judging the priority of conflicting interests beyond a reassertion of core British values.

What emerges here, then, is a vivid illustration of the built-in difficulties of squaring multicultural ideals with liberal democratic principles. For Leggewie, the great lesson of the Rushdie Affair was the need to move beyond vague platitudes and establish legal mechanisms for sorting out the competing claims of different ethnic groups. Yet, as Asad reminds us, such mechanisms were part of the problem in Britain. Faced with religious claims perceived as illiberal, government officials quickly defined some values as more "British" than others. Many Muslim fundamentalists, by contrast, defended the *fatwa* by reasserting their constitutional rights to freedom of speech and religion.

The staunchest West German defender of multiculturalism in this volatile climate was Hilmar Hoffmann, former head of the Goethe Institute and Cultural Minister for the city of Frankfurt. Three months after Leggewie's highly publicized response to the Rushdie Affair, Hoffmann insisted that the time for debate was over. The Federal Republic, he argued, had "long since become a multicultural society." Yet he also believed that "lived multiculturalism" must "ground itself above all in tolerance." For Hoffmann, multiculturalism "makes any all-inclusive ideology, religion or worldview impossible.... Whoever merely speaks of the preservation of a cultural identity, be it of Germans or foreigners, misunderstands the *dynamic character* of the cultural process."[59] In contrast to church leaders who had earlier simply promoted cross-cultural enrichment, Hoffmann was very clear about how this "dynamic" process should operate. Immigrants, he argued, should not seek to isolate themselves or protect their culture from any outside influence. Neither should they be cut off from the roots of their culture under the guise of assimilation or "Germanization." Rather, they must open themselves to a more syncretic process of cultural synthesis that would allow an intermixture of new ideas and environments with inherited traditions.

Hoffmann further insisted that West Germans would have to engage in the very same process. To that end, he chided his fellow countrymen for failing to recognize that Turks – the most foreign of all guest worker nationalities – belonged to a people whose culture had been important

---

[59] Hilmar Hoffmann, "Im Laboratorium fürs Überleben: Die Utopie von der multikulturellen Gesellschaft," *Süddeutsche Zeitung*, 3–4 June 1989, Feuilleton-Beilage, 1. My emphasis.

for one thousand years. Turkey produced Nobel Prize winners, philosophers, novelists, poets, and filmmakers "just as significant as our own." Hoffmann also pointed to "German-Turkish literature" as the unique product of cultural synthesis in the Federal Republic. Instead of the additive model central to earlier ideas of cultural "enrichment," Hoffmann made it clear that reciprocal adaptation and exchange were the very essence of "lived multiculturalism." In this view, no aspect of German culture could remain unchanged.

Hoffmann was quite willing to admit that conflicts would inevitably emerge in such a multicultural society. Right radicalism, he observed, "vented itself on the foreigner question, in which the threat of an inferior social position for the lower strata of the population manifested itself. It found political expression with the appearance of the Republikaner, a small, right-wing extremist party, and the reanimation of the NPD."[60] He also noted that uncertain or difficult economic conditions made it especially easy for struggling Germans to lash out at foreigners. On the other hand, Hoffmann acknowledged that groups that insisted on fundamentalist positions – the *Republikaner* but also the Islamists – threatened to produce intractable cultural clashes that would make peaceful coexistence difficult. This potential for tension and turmoil, however, did not deter him from insisting upon both the merits and the irreversibility of a multicultural society. For West Germany in particular, he argued, such changes provided a crucial ethical bulwark against the barbarism of the nation's traumatic history.

It is worth noting, finally, that these values were part and parcel of the Goethe Institute's global marketing campaigns during the 1980s, part of the way that Hoffmann promoted a new, more dynamic image of German culture to foreign politicians, students, and tourists. The sources make it impossible to draw fine distinctions here between personal beliefs and self-conscious promotional strategies, but in a sense that is precisely what makes Hoffmann's 1989 public comments so interesting. As a figure associated with the nation's most prominent institution for cultural outreach, Hoffmann's staunch defense of German multiculturalism suggests that these values were now becoming the stuff of political expediency – at least beyond the nation's borders.

The question of pragmatic politics brings us full circle, back to our starting point with the 1989 neighborhood meeting in Kreuzberg. It now becomes possible to situate the comments of Berlin Commissioner for

[60] Ibid.

Foreigners' Affairs Barbara John within a more variegated national debate. John, it is important to remember, specifically called for the possibility of dual citizenship and criticized any form of *völkisches* thinking. She was even willing to support the notion that cultural identity and national citizenship must be delinked from one another. In the very next breath, though, she expressed discomfort with using the term "multicultural society" to describe the Federal Republic. Germany did not yet count as a "true" multicultural society, she told her Kreuzberg audience, because of its relatively small (7 percent) minority population.[61]

Yet at almost the same moment Heiner Geißler, the general secretary of the CDU, began to insist that multicultural principles must be incorporated into the party's foreigner policy. Geißler's decision marked a crucial turning point. For the first time, one of the nation's leading Christian Democratic political figures argued that the older models of citizenship, culture, and nation no longer reflected what the Federal Republic had become. Significantly, this line of argument provoked a level of condemnation from within the party similar to the backlash against Zimmermann. Edmund Stoiber, the leader of the CSU, predictably denounced Geißler's position, but so too did Schäuble, who had recently replaced Zimmermann as interior minister. According to one journalist covering the debates, there were even claims that Geißler harbored "undisguised, un-German machinations."[62] By the time of the CDU national congress in September 1989, Kohl announced that he would not renominate Geißler as general secretary "in the hope that he, and with him, the fight over political concepts like 'multicultural society' would go away."[63] Just as Zimmermann's uncompromising reforms to the Foreigner Law represented one extreme within the CDU coalition, Geißler's unequivocal plea to accept West Germany as a multicultural society seems to have marked the other end of the CDU's ideological spectrum.

These examples suggest a more complex and variable set of limits in 1980s *Ausländerpolitik* than we have previously acknowledged. In the space of just nine months the CDU ousted both Zimmermann, whom it perceived as pandering to right extremism, and Geißler, whose conversion to multiculturalism was understood as a threat to lingering ideals of a homogeneous nation. These events also help to explain why John

[61] Klapheck, "Multikulturell."
[62] Günter Hofmann, "Großes Wort, kleiner Geist. Die multikulturelle Gesellschaft und ihre Feinde," *Die Zeit*, 8 September 1989, 85.
[63] Ibid.

(the CDU official most intimately engaged with the day-to-day problems of managing a multiethnic Germany) steadfastly refused to accept the moniker of a multicultural society in public forums. By 1989, the term multiculturalism itself had become a kind of political litmus test. Even those CDU officials most open to citizenship reform recognized its political dangers.

Yet it is also clear that the expediency question now cut in multiple directions. Zimmermann's dogged resistance to anything resembling multicultural thinking made him seem like an old-fashioned crank – out of touch with the massive demographic changes taking place around him. Geißler's unwillingness to equivocate about these changes, by contrast, was perceived as an impolitic act for precisely the opposite reason. As John's statements demonstrate, one's specific choice of label was often more important for political survival than a particular position on the citizenship law. But when the debate moved beyond domestic politics, the meaning of expediency shifted yet again. Having promoted German culture around the globe for much of the past decade, the Goethe Institute's Hoffmann understood the political stakes of multiculturalism in a very different way. What he seems to have grasped better than most was that *cultural* diplomacy in the late-twentieth century was simply incompatible with the notion of a homogeneous German nation. Cosmopolitan audiences required more cosmopolitan images of German culture.

Beyond *Ausländerliteratur* and the Burdens of the "Minority" Artist

There was no German equivalent to the Rushdie Affair, no political firestorm around the work of a prominent minority intellectual. Yet this should not lead us to conclude that minority intellectuals and artists were somehow disengaged from the public debates about multiculturalism or that their views on the subject lacked political implications. A good starting point for sorting out these views is Martin Greve's 1996 article "Irritated by Questions of Origin." This piece was written during the post-reunification period, almost a decade after the events we have been following. Still, it is a useful place to begin because it registers broader ideological patterns and market forces that did not emerge fully formed in 1996. Indeed, my central argument here is that the cultural developments underlying minority artists' "irritation" with identity questions first started to emerge in the mid-1980s as the issue of multiculturalism and who might serve as its representatives came to dominate public debate.

Greve's article appeared in *Zitty*, one of Berlin's most popular and widely read cultural magazines, and was designed to celebrate a distinctly German multiculturalism assumed to be fully established. It featured Aras Ören along with Zehra Çırak and Zafer Şenocak, the second-generation Turkish-German authors discussed in Chapter 2, who found critical acclaim during the late 1980s. Right from the start, Greve assumes his readers' familiarity with these writers. Ören, for example, is described as "an arrived author," while the accompanying photograph presents him as a kind of literary patriarch, with pipe and wine at hand in his book-filled Charlottenburg apartment. The younger writers similarly come across as part of Berlin's new multicultural mainstream. Their work, we learn, has been published by the leading presses; both authors are described as local celebrities who give regular public readings.

Yet the dominant chord of the article is dissonance. Early on, Greve explains that "Ören does not like interviews.... There are questions that he can no longer bear to hear: What is it 'like to be a Turkish author?' or 'Do you dream in Turkish or German?'"[64] In a similar vein, Şenocak expresses frustration at the fact that his work is often read within the narrow terms of *Ausländerliteratur* – as an expression of a collective migrant experience. Çırak, by contrast, is more willing to engage this line of questioning, but she also makes it clear that doing so represents a kind of trade-off. While she welcomes the exposure that such media interest could bring, she wryly jokes that invitations to recite her work in public are inevitably proposed under the mantle: "Turkish authors read." Thus, what seems to have been intended as a piece designed to showcase Berlin's minority intelligentsia paradoxically served to record lingering cross-cultural tensions. As the title of Greve's article bluntly put it, these artists were "irritated with questions of origin."

This irritation in Berlin echoed concerns that African-American intellectuals had begun to articulate much earlier in the century. The literary critic Ross Posnock has summarized the problem succinctly: "To escape the pressure to conform to the familiar and recognizable, to stereotypes" was also to be "free to delete the first word or to accent the second in the phrase *black intellectual* or to vary one's inflections at will or as circumstance dictates."[65] One of the central dilemmas of early U.S.

---

[64] Martin Greve, "Genervt von Herkunftsfragen. Türkisch-deutsche Schriftsteller: Aras Ören, Zehra Çırak, Zafer Şenocak," *Zitty*, 6–19 June 1996, 29.

[65] Ross Posnock, *Color and Culture: Black Writers and the Making of the Modern Intellectual* (Cambridge, MA: Harvard University Press, 1998), 2.

multiculturalism, in other words, was that it often involved dissolving the binary link between Self/Other or culture/nation, even as it created new markets for those perceived as representatives of racial/ethnic difference. A similar point can be made about West Germany's minority intelligentsia during the late 1980s. Somewhat ironically, the same migrant intellectuals most centrally involved in pushing toward a multicultural conception of West German society now began to resist the very category of minority artist.

It is important to stress that this resistance did not follow any single or uniform model. Indeed, the three most prominent second-generation writers to emerge during the late 1980s – Çırak, Şenocak, and Akif Pirinçci – help us to see the multiple and varied ways of navigating a public persona beyond the constraints of migrant dialogue partner. The early trajectory of Çırak's career provides perhaps the clearest example of the difficult choices faced by the second generation. Of all her peers, she wrestled most self-consciously and explicitly with the competing pressures of the marketplace and her own artistic agenda. In an "author portrait" for *Zitty*, Eberhard Seidel-Pielen, a controversial journalist well known for his reporting on West Germany's foreigner question, explained that until 1983 Çırak wrote texts that had nothing to do with *Ausländerliteratur*.[66] Yet when a wave of interest in this "exciting new literary genre rustled through Germany's intellectual living room," she decided to change the focus of her poetry. As Çırak recounted, "Rowohlt came to me and asked whether I didn't have something on the theme. I saw the chance to be published finally. So I sat myself down and wrote about what they wanted, about my life in a foreign country.... If I had resisted the fashion trend and the wishes of the publishers at that time, I would probably have had a hard time breaking into the literary world."[67]

From the outset, however, Çırak was not entirely comfortable with this decision to conform. In an article for *Die Tageszeitung*, she explained: "I often didn't know what I should write because my texts had nothing

---

[66] Eberhard Seidel-Pielen published a number of books in the reportage genre on the problems of urban youth around ethnic and racial differences. His 1995 book about Turks in Germany created a major controversy in Berlin's Turkish community, which objected to his patronizing treatment of immigrants. See Klaus Farin and Eberhard Seidel-Pielen, *Rechtsruck: Rassismus im neuen Deutschland* (Berlin: Rotbuch, 1992); Klaus Farin and Eberhard Seidel-Pielen, *Ohne Gewalt läuft nichts! Jugend und Gewalt in Deutschland* (Cologne: Bund Verlag, 1993); Klaus Farin and Eberhard Seidel-Pielen, *Skinheads* (Munich: C. H. Beck, 1993); Eberhard Seidel-Pielen, *Unsere Türken: Annäherungen an ein gespaltenes Verhältnis* (Berlin: Elefanten, 1995).

[67] Eberhard Seidel-Pielen, "Ihr könnt uns mal . . .," *Zitty*, no. 6, 1989, 17.

to do with the theme of foreigners in Germany."[68] In another interview she simply remarked: "It is not because I am a foreigner that I
write."[69] These comments rejected the unspoken assumption at the heart
of *Ausländerliteratur* during the early 1980s, namely that what motivated
minority writers to express themselves in German was the experience of
being foreign. Çırak's publishing choices thus need to be understood as a
self-conscious balancing act within a particular set of ideological and market pressures. As she explained to the reporter Klaus Farin, "I write about
what they wanted, although I myself have never felt discriminated against
by Germans, and even tried to smuggle in some of my other poems" on
different topics.[70]

A good example of such "smuggling" can be found in Çırak's poem
"Küçük Çekmece," which first appeared in the 1984 DTV anthology
edited by Irmgard Ackermann, *Türken deutscher Sprache*. Çırak's title
refers to a suburb of Istanbul but also means "little box" in Turkish,
thereby offering several interpretive options:

> Little box feels limited in the drawer
> Drawer in the armoire does not want to remain closed
> Armoire in the room wants to stand somewhere else
> Room in the building would like to be outside
> Building in the area wants to be a city
> And every city, a planet for itself
> Every planet, a box factory
> Boxes
> With quick movements they will be produced
> Through hands which then use them
> To fill and again empty
> Put them then in a drawer
> Close the armoire
> Go outside
> And feel in great shape on this planet[71]

On one level, Çırak's reference to a specific Turkish place makes it possible to interpret the poem as a metaphoric commentary on her country
of origin. And judging from the poem's placement in a section of the

---

[68] Nadja Encke, "Von der Romanze durften die Eltern nichts wissen," *Die Tageszeitung*,
12 August 1991, 22.

[69] Karl-Ludwig Baader, "Ich habe saumäßiges Glück gehabt," *Hannoversche Allgemeine
Zeitung*, 4 July 1987.

[70] Klaus Farin, "Utopie einer Mischkultur: Gedichte der Berliner Autorin Zehra Çırak,"
Berliner Zeitung, 10 September 1991.

[71] Zehra Çırak, "Küçük Çekmece," in Irmgard Ackermann, ed., *Türken deutscher Sprache.
Berichte, Erzählungen, Gedichte* (München: Deutscher Taschenbuch Verlag, 1984), 35.

anthology entitled "The Far, Near Homeland," this is precisely how Ackermann understood the text.[72] Yet the box metaphor can also be read as a comment on the ideological constraints of *Ausländerliteratur* itself. Lines such as "little box feels limited by the drawer" or "the drawer in the armoire does not want to remain closed" convey a kind of aesthetic and ideological claustrophobia.The second stanza, by contrast, suggests an acceptance of the boxes – if only because they are "quickly produced" and will eventually be "emptied."

Çırak's decision to work with Ackermann and DaF, it is important to note, represented a significant professional opportunity. But this also meant that the critical response to her poetry followed a number of predictable patterns. Virtually every review, for instance, discussed her familial background as the eldest daughter of Turkish guest workers and characterized her circumstances as typical of "many of her generational contemporaries."[73] Born in 1960 in Istanbul, Çırak moved with her parents to Karlsruhe when she was three years old. Contemporary articles describe her family as strict and suggest that it was only in the outside world – at school and while playing in the street – that she began to experience German relationships, language, and culture. This simplistic narrative lent itself to the familiar DaF theme of living "torn between two cultures." As a reporter for the *Hannoversche Allgemeine Zeitung* explained, "at home she yielded as a 'well-mannered daughter,' but outside she participated – as much as possible – in the life of her peers."[74]

Çırak continued to live in her parents' house while she trained to be a cosmetician and wrote poetry on the side. Soon thereafter, she met and fell in love with the German sculptor Jürgen Walter. She lived a "double life" for four years until she and Walter secretly fled to West Berlin, a move that provoked her father to disown her. In this respect, Çırak's break from her family fit many liberal Germans' conception of how integration should take place. The review by Farin, for example, concluded that Çırak's flight to Berlin marked a "decision between two cultures in favor of the German."[75]

---

[72] Ackermann, in fact, briefly elaborates on this interpretation of the poem in her afterword to the volume. See Irmgard Ackermann, "Nachwort," in *Türken deutscher Sprache*, 249.

[73] See, for example, Baader, "Ich habe saumäßiges"; Seidel-Pielen, "Ihr könnt"; Encke, "Vonder Romanze"; Farin, "Utopie einer Mischkultur"; and Renate Just, "Wie geht's. Ein Anruf bei Zehra Çırak, 31, in Berlin, deren erstes Buch, der Gedichtband *Vogel auf dem Rücken eines Elefanten* gerade erschienen ist," *Süddeutsche Zeitung Magazin*, 1991.

[74] Baader, "Ich habe saumäßiges."

[75] Farin, "Utopie einer Mischkultur."

Interviews make it clear that Çırak was uncomfortable with this kind of representation of her personal life. But it is equally clear that her decision to work within the representational constraints of *Ausländerliteratur* paid professional dividends. In addition to the texts published in Ackermann's anthology, her poems appeared in several volumes organized by writers and activists independent of DaF, including *Sie haben mich zu einem Ausländer gemacht – ich bin einer geworden* (*They Have Made Me into a Foreigner – I Became One*, 1984), *Ich zerbreche den Kreis* (*I Break the Circle*, 1984), and *Zwischen zwei Kulturen* (*Between Two Cultures*, 1985).[76] These publications, in turn, led to a steady stream of invitations. She was asked, for example, to give the very first literary recitation (along with Ören) at Berlin's House of World Cultures in 1985. In 1987, she won a stipend from the city of Berlin's office of cultural affairs, and two years later, she received the Chamisso Patronage Prize for young authors. According to a *Deutsche Welle* radio program on literature, this honor caught the attention of literature professor Walter Höllerer, who subsequently invited Çırak to a meeting of the famous and influential Gruppe 47 in Dobris near Prague: "She was the youngest author there in the middle of mature literary prominence."[77]

By the end of the decade, Çırak's writing had garnered so much praise that the renowned press Kiepenheuer & Witsch offered to publish an entire volume of her poems. Yet even Kiepenheuer & Witsch reproduced many of the older stereotypes in their marketing materials. As a back cover blurb for the 1991 book *Vogel auf dem Rücken eines Elefanten* (*Bird on the Back of an Elephant*) explained: "Zehra Çırak's poems are the surprising product of a contrary identity between two cultures – the German and the Turkish. Full of wittiness and pleasure in contradiction, they move back and forth between the meanings of the words and images, always on guard against the latent fear of an existence 'on hot ground.'"[78]

Once again, Çırak's own poetry provides a useful barometer for gauging her response to market pressures. Consider, for example, the very different ways that Çırak and Ören employed the "bridge" as a literary

---

[76] Karin Hopmann, ed., *Ich zerbreche den Kreis: Frauen finden ihre Sprache: Neue Gedichte und Prosa* (Kronshagen: Morgenroth Verlag, 1984); Norbert Ney, ed., *Sie haben mich zu einem Ausländer gemacht – ich bin einer geworden: Ausländer schreiben vom Leben bei uns* (Reinbeck bei Hamburg: Rowohlt, 1984).

[77] Hans Georg Schwark, "Über die deutsch-türkische Lyrikerin Zehra Cirak und ihren Gedichtband 'Vogel auf dem Rücken eines Elefanten,'" *Deutsche Welle/Literatur*, 20 February 1992.

[78] This blurb appears on the back of the paperback edition of Zehra Çırak, *Vogel auf dem Rücken eines Elefanten* (Cologne: Kiepenheuer & Witsch, 1991).

trope. In his acceptance speech for the inaugural Chamisso Prize in 1985, Ören referred to the bridge metaphorically to denote the work of the minority artist as a catalyst for integration. He expressed a desire for "the written word" – and in particular, his literary words – to serve "as a bridge to communication across all boundaries."[79] Çırak's 1991 poem "Sich warm laufen" ("Warming Up"), by contrast, employed the bridge metaphor quite differently:

> since we know even bridges have an end
> there's no need to hurry going over
> yet bridges are where it gets coldest.[80]

Here the trope assumes a temporal quality, marking a transitional stage between one point and another. Precisely because the liminal state has "an end," Çırak suggests that the crossing need not be rushed. And yet she describes this in-between place as particularly "cold" (and difficult). By 1991, in other words, the recurring trope of cultural mediation signaled a necessary but also temporary individual positioning.[81] As one reporter explained, "She knows that her free space also depends on the ability of Germans to accept difference and multiplicity, perhaps to perceive it as enrichment. But she does not want to occupy herself exclusively with the problems of her national or cultural membership."[82]

Another poem, "Kulturidentität" ("Cultural Identity"), offers some clues about how Çırak ultimately hoped to move beyond the category of minority artist:

Is [cultural identity] something through which I recognize myself, or is it something through which others can categorize me?

I prefer neither my Turkish nor my German culture. I live and long for a mixed culture. I am forced to live like this because I neither live in Alaska in an igloo, nor in Anatolia deep in a hut. There are cultural objects, which despite my – (citation:

79 Aras Ören, "Dankrede zur Preisverleihung," in Heinz Friedrich, ed., *Chamissos Enkel. Zur Literatur von Ausländern in Deutschland* (Munich: Deutscher Taschenbuch Verlag, 1986), 29.
80 Zehra Çırak, "Sich warm laufen," *Vogel auf dem Rücken eines Elefanten* (Cologne: Kiepenheuer & Witsch, 1991), 93, trans. by Elizabeth Ann Oehlkers in *Where Germany Begins: Translations from the German of the Poetry and Prose of Zehra Çırak, Zafer Şenocak, and Yoko Tawada* (MFA thesis, University of Arkansas, 1996), 18.
81 Moray McGowan, "'Bosporus fließt in mir': Europa-Bilder und Brückenmetapher bei Aras Ören und Zehra Çirak," in Hans-Peter Waldhoff, Dursun Tan, and Elçin Kursat-Ahlers, eds., *Brücken zwischen Zivilisationen. Zur Zivilisierung ethnisch-kultureller Differenzen und Machtungleichheiten. Das türkisch-deutsche Beispiel* (Frankfurt: IKO-Verlag, 1997), 21–39.
82 Baader, "Ich habe saumäßiges."

Strauß) "belonging to the European circle of hygiene" – I refuse. For example, television. As a child and teenager, I had no choice but to look far away [watch television]. I became acquainted with the TV series "Dallas" in Turkey some time before it was broadcast in Germany.

I would rather be intoxicated by other cultures, e.g., through the music of Bach and Mahler, through films of Tarkovsky or Buñuel or Akira Kurosawa.

I recognize myself again.

I should like best to wake up in the Japanese manner on a tatami mat in rooms with transparent paper doors. Then I would gladly breakfast in the English manner, and afterward, with foreign indifference, work in the Chinese manner, diligently and zealously. I should like best to eat French food and, bestially satisfied, bathe in the manner of the Romans, gladly I want to hike like a Bavarian and dance like an African. I should like best to possess Russian patience and not have to earn my money in the American manner. Oh, how I would like a Swiss passport in order to avoid suspicion and hold a numbered bank account. I should like best to fall asleep in the Indian manner as a bird on the back of an elephant and dream in the Turkish manner of the Bosphorus.

Do I also want something through which I can recognize myself, or something through which others can categorize me?[83]

Çırak begins here by highlighting two kinds of work performed by the category of cultural identity: it serves as a vehicle for self-understanding and also as a framework for others to make sense of her. At this point, however, she disavows any effort to assert one function over the other and opts for an explanation of how she sees herself: "I prefer neither my Turkish nor my German culture. I live and long for a mixed culture." Çırak thus rejects both the assumption that she is "torn" between a Turkish and a German identity and the pressure to choose one over the other.

As an alternative, Çırak begins a process of ongoing deterritorialization in which culture is emphatically delinked from nation. She mentions learning about the American television series *Dallas* on a trip to Turkey, an example which suggests that place of birth and national belonging have become far less important for determining the range of cultural identities with which one might define oneself. Culture transcends space in a global world, making the link between art and locale less obvious or natural than it once was. Identity, in this view, relies more on Çırak's position in a cosmopolitan metropolis than on the mere fact of her birthplace. She leads the reader through a kind of catalogue of eclectic tastes and urban selves: Japanese beds, English breakfasts, African dancing, Roman bathing, Bavarian hiking, Turkish dreaming, international art house films.

---

[83] Zehra Çırak, "Kulturelle Identität," *Vogel auf dem Rücken eines Elefanten* (Cologne: Kiepenheuer & Witsch, 1991), 94.

Yet this deterritorialization is only possible because Çırak resides neither in an "Alaskan igloo" nor an "Anatolian hut." Instead, the poem celebrates the metropolis as a quintessentially hybrid space where everyone – migrant and nonmigrant alike – continuously puts on and takes off cultural identities as a matter of course. The voice at the poem's center is a protean subject that remains in constant motion and recreates itself daily. Çırak's emphasis on heterogeneous metropolitan spaces, moreover, revalues migrant culture because difference itself serves as the city's primary source of energy. In this sense, Çırak's poem echoes much older notions of the multiethnic city first produced by early twentieth-century American writers such as Randolph Bourne. In both cases the modern metropolis functions as a kind of contact zone in which momentary cultural affiliations and exchanges across racial and ethnic lines become the very essence of modern cosmopolitan experience.

Çırak concludes the poem by rephrasing her original question: "Do I *want* something through which I recognize myself, or something through which others can categorize me?" The reappearance of the question underscores Çırak's recognition that identity never emerges within a vacuum. Even as she stresses the exhilaration of life in late twentieth-century Berlin, she registers the fact that other people's perceptions have substantive effects. And in this sense, the final lines of her poem remain haunted by the specter of the market. Çırak acknowledges that self-perception and the perceptions of others are always reciprocally intertwined. Perhaps more important, she makes it clear that whichever side of the equation she chooses to emphasize inevitably impacts her standing in the cultural marketplace.[84]

Çırak's market-savvy cosmopolitanism represented perhaps the most common strategy for escaping the constraints of "minority artist" in the last years of a divided Germany. But it was not the only option. Indeed, Akif Pirinçci followed a different path altogether. Pirinçci burst onto the West German literary scene when the large Munich-based press Goldmann published his first novel, *Tränen sind immer das Ende (Tears Are Always the End)*, in 1980. The contract with Goldmann was the culmination of several years of hard work and clever self-promotion. Pirinçci submitted the manuscript to over seventy publishers in a three-month

---

[84] Çırak shares and is highly conscious of the dilemma faced by many black intellectuals in the United States, namely the danger of "falling outside categories" and "losing visibility" when "untethered to the race work that typically defines" the minority artist. See Posnock, *Color and Culture*, 26.

period. And when it was universally rejected, he borrowed 3,000 DM
from his mother to fund a private printing. He produced the book at a
university copy center, using a cover image by his sister, and distributed
the advertising fliers himself. Not surprisingly, the book sold slowly at
first.

Yet within a matter of months, Pirinçci came across an installment of
the *Zweites Deutsches Fernsehen* (ZDF) television program *Tour of Literature* that was featuring books about "love in our time." After watching
the show, he called the moderator Reinhard Hoffmeister and posed two
brazen questions: Why did the program only cover "high" literature?
And why was his novel not included? As a follow-up, Pirinçci sent the
manuscript directly to Hoffmeister, and when ZDF broadcast a subsequent episode of *Tour of Literature*, the young author was invited to
give a six-minute plug for his book. The next day, a representative from
Goldmann called with welcome news: "Your book pleases us very much,
we want to buy it."[85] In less than a week, Pirinçci had a contract with
Goldmann guaranteeing a print run of twenty thousand copies and a
royalty of six pfennigs per copy.

Particularly striking in this tale is the pluck and independence of its
protagonist. Pirinçci, who was only twenty years old at the time, followed
a path into the marketplace utterly unique among minority artists during
the early 1980s. *Tränen* appeared the year after DaF's inaugural writing
contest. But he did not submit material to the competition, just as he chose
not to participate in the migrant author associations emerging during the
same period. Instead, Pirinçci decided to enter the German literary world
on his own terms as a kind of free agent. He approached publishing houses
directly, and when that strategy failed to produce the desired result he
enlisted the mass media.

Pirinçci had begun to write creatively in his early teens. But instead of
focusing on conventional literary forms such as poetry, short stories, or
novels, he wrote radio plays and film scripts. *Die Zeit* explained that he
"'wanted to be in the media,' but that did not happen with his scripts about
Hessian soldiers going astray in the American War of Independence ... or
an archeologist seeing a ghost in Pompeii. ... So he wrote a romance,
one which has everything 'that people today want in it – love, youth,
urban atmosphere.'"[86] At first glance, this account suggests a somewhat

---

[85] Klaus Pokatzky, "Ich bin ein Pressetürke: Akif Pirinçci und der deutsche Literaturbe-
    trieb," *Die Zeit*, 28 May 1982, 63.
[86] Ibid., 63.

crass desire to pander to the masses. Yet it also tells us something about the specific mode of writing Pirinçci envisioned – a mode quite unlike any other form of literature produced by a minority author during the 1980s. On the one hand, Pirinçci quite explicitly rejected the ideal of the politically engaged guest worker literature promoted by grassroots cultural associations such as PoLiKunst. On the other, he did not strive toward the idealized notions of literary merit set out by DaF and the Chamisso Prize. Pirinçci simply refused to play the part of dialogue partner prescribed by the gatekeepers of *Ausländerliteratur*.

Pirinçci repudiated the role of cross-cultural mediator, but he did express a desire to connect with a broader West German reading public. His interviews from the period are peppered with paeans to mass culture. "*Star Wars* is my favorite film," he declared to the *Rheinischer Merkur*'s Michael Fuchs. "Lucas succeeds in speaking to the archaic feelings of humans. His films embody myths that every person understands."[87] Like the American director George Lucas, Pirinçci aspired to tell stories that were accessible and appealing to ordinary cultural consumers. In this respect he was highly critical of artists such as Rainer Werner Fassbinder, the avant-garde darling of German critics, who failed to capture the interest and imagination of the mass marketplace.[88] Pirinçci's preferred genre of *Unterhaltungskunst* (light art), by contrast, encouraged "totally relaxed amusement, enjoyment without the ever-present social criticism."[89] In *Tränen*, he explained, the goal was to write what he imagined "people today want" – a romance between young people in a big city. Above all, Pirinçci championed the ideals of accessibility, pure entertainment, and resonance across market segments.

Within this context it becomes somewhat easier to grasp Pirinçci's decision to reject – even mock – the idea of himself as a "Turkish artist." "I am perceived as a Turk for public relations," he told one reporter in *Die Zeit*, "but whether I am now regarded as a Turk or a German is all the same to me, my culture exists out of what I make. And what my environment does doesn't interest me." The oft-asked question "what do you think of that as a Turk?" was enough to make Pirinçci "puke." Attempting to clarify his

---

[87] Michael Fuchs, "Mit Superman gegen den Tiefsinn: Warum der Türke Akif Pirinçci deutsche Bücher schreibt," *Rheinischer Merkur*, 28 June 1986.

[88] Fassbinder was highly praised by German and international critics; his films resuscitated the German film industry in the international marketplace. But his success at home, among the German public, was mixed at best. Very few Germans, in fact, were interested in or even saw his films.

[89] Steve Crawshaw, "Feline Fantasies," *The Independent*, 18 September 1993, 29.

philosophy, Pirinçci asserted: "All cultures resemble each other, culture doesn't interest me; the world is about fucking and money and nothing else."[90] Such statements were clearly calculated to shock and provoke. But they also served as a way to shut down the efforts of German commentators to push Pirinçci into the conventional role of Turkish-German exemplar or representative.

Somewhat ironically, Pirinçci's *Tränen*, which represented his first attempt to put into practice this self-consciously "popular" art, focuses on an eighteen-year-old Turkish-German man with the very same name – Akif. Kicked out of his parents' house, Akif moves to Cologne to become a freelance writer. The story revolves around his relationship with Christa, a German law student, whom he meets in the city. Their romance deteriorates, however, because of Akif's obsessive need for reassurance about the strength of their relationship. When Christa finally breaks up with him, Akif tries to commit suicide. This traumatic incident drives him to reconcile with his parents and he resolves to write a novel about the experience.

In his review for *Die Zeit*, Klaus Pokatzky began with an enthusiastic declaration: "Let's be honest – we journalists have been waiting for something like this for a long time: a twenty-two-year-old Turk, who has been in the Federal Republic for thirteen years, whose father is a truck driver, whose mother is a factory worker, writes a novel, the story of his lost love with a German law student, Christa. The book becomes a bestseller, the filming is imminent. This makes us happy, we are happy to report it."[91] Several paragraphs later, however, Pokatzky noted with some frustration that "whoever hopes to experience... the thoughts and feelings of the second foreigner generation will be disappointed: he writes virtually nothing about Turks and their problems." In fact, this was completely false. The entire novel focuses on a Turkish-German teenager and a whole host of "problems." Akif experiences first-date anxiety, hates his job as a stagehand at the Cologne opera, pines for his girlfriend when she goes home for Christmas, and so on for over 250 pages. The crucial distinction here, in other words, was the specific type of problems that critics had grown to expect from *Ausländerliteratur*. Pirinçci's novel described the sort of love, angst, and frustration that plagued every teenager. More familiar migrant "problems" such as social isolation, gender tensions, and religious customs simply did not factor in this work at all.

[90] Pokatzky, "Ich bin ein Pressetürke," 63.
[91] Ibid.

Other commentators approached the novel with a very different set of expectations. In his *Rheinischer Merkur* feature article, Michael Fuchs admitted that he had been given Pirinçci's book as a gift for his seventeenth birthday: "Kitsch had been my first thought when I saw the title. Then I read it and made it into the Bible of two different relationships. Akif became my idol; as victim of his suffering, as lonely masochist, but also as total teenager, he embodied my second self."[92] Fuchs, in other words, was not really interested in assessing the sociological lessons of Pirinçci's novel. Rather, he wanted to know whether Akif the author corresponded to Akif the character because the novel resonated so strongly with his own teenage experiences. In this respect Fuchs was precisely the kind of reader that Pirinçci hoped to reach: a lonely adolescent whose most important concerns were the trials and tribulations of first love.

Despite these small, critical victories, Pirinçci continued to insist that he never really encountered his "correct public with the novel." *Tränen*, he pointed out, represented something completely new because "up to that time Turks in Germany had only written about their problems. That a Turk would write a *totally normal love story* had never been done."[93] Fuchs seems to have been aware of these concerns, noting with sympathetic sarcasm that "a writing Turk makes a good attraction in the literary circus." But from Pirinçci's perspective, this kind of media frenzy hijacked the novel from its intended audience and roused the interest of people to whom he was absolutely uninterested in speaking – those looking for insight into the experiences of migration.

Like Çırak, Pirinçci was intensely conscious of the way he was perceived in the public sphere. And he understood the price of his desire to write a "totally normal" book for a "totally normal" audience. He made the point clear in his comments on Tevfik Başer, the Turkish-German film director. Baser, Pirinçci noted, received a lot of praise for his movie depicting the conflict of cultures through the isolation of an Anatolian woman in Germany. "If I were to make a film about the experiences of a Turk in Germany," the young author declared, "my future would be secured. The film foundations would immediately support me." Yet the same article concluded: "he will not do it, will not let himself be pressed into these pigeonholes, rather he writes what he wants, what is fun for him, what is important to him."[94]

---

[92] Fuchs, "Mit Superman."
[93] Ibid., my emphasis.
[94] Ibid.

Pirinçci likewise faced sharp criticism about the novel's "popular" approach and appeal. This was a major issue for *Die Zeit*'s Pokatzky, who reported with amazement that *Tränen* had been compared in favorable terms with the works of J. D. Salinger and Charles Bukowski and praised as a contemporary version of Goethe's *Die Leiden des jungen Werther* (*The Sorrows of Young Werther*). Despite the fact that such claims generally came from regional newspapers and magazines sponsored by the major publishing houses, Pokatzky admitted that his curiosity had been piqued. Upon reading the book, however, he was less impressed:

What Goldmann hails as "a piece of literature of contemporary Germany, which surprises and carries away through its originality" is nothing more and nothing less than a nice piece of entertainment, good to read before bed, in the bath, or on the S-Bahn. It is in places expressed with wit and liveliness; it is written with forcefulness, but also with the strong, humorless, flirtatious, and dumb undertone of a young chauvinist. And very often it is simply obvious and embarrassing. One notices all too clearly that the Goldmann editors were less interested in helping a young author develop his literary talents than in marketing him effectively in the media.[95]

This rather elitist response was precisely what Pirinçci had in mind when he complained to Fuchs that "the arrogance toward entertainment art and the continual search for pensiveness in everything" made it impossible to write a love story with popular appeal.[96]

Nine years passed between the publication of *Tränen* and the appearance of Pirinçci's next novel, *Felidae* (1989). One suspects that this long hiatus reflected the young author's desire to strategize a way out of the usual critical traps. The end result was a shift in genre from teenage love story to detective novel as well as a decision to forego human protagonists in favor of cats (in Latin: *felidae*). The novel's hero is Francis, a clever, wisecracking feline who refers to his owner, Gustav, as a *Dosenöffner* (can opener). After their move to a less desirable part of the city, Francis discovers that a serial murderer is on the loose in the neighborhood and that the killer has targeted one particular species of the cat population. Our hero investigates the mystery with the help of two new feline friends, a cripple named Blaubart and the terminally ill Pascal, who possesses useful computer programming skills. Francis soon learns that the neighborhood felines have been drawn into a religious cult that reveres the martyr figure Claudandus, a cat previously mutilated through scientific

[95] Ibid.
[96] Ibid.

experiments. Over time, we discover that Claudandus is really Pascal. We also learn that Pascal's secret plot is to cleanse the feline gene pool in order to establish a master race of cats strong enough to eliminate humans. The cult of Claudandus is actually a scheme to keep the local cat population ignorant of his larger plan. In the novel's final showdown, Francis kills Pascal/Claudandus and returns to ordinary life with Gustav, a human simpleton entirely unaware of the epochal drama taking place under his nose.

Given the rather eccentric storyline, it is not surprising that Pirinçci once again found it difficult to secure a publisher. Thirty different publishing houses rejected *Felidae* before Goldmann finally decided to take a chance on Pirinçci's cat detective. Yet as soon as the novel appeared in bookstores, it became a national hit. *Felidae* sold over 120,000 copies the very first year, a threshold one commentator claimed had been reached in recent years only by "short mysteries for women or cheap tax-tip books."[97] The novel also won the 1990 Mimi award for best mystery of the year, a prize similar to the Edgar award in the United States. At this point, *Felidae* began to evolve into a major pop-cultural phenomenon. *Westdeutscher Rundfunk* (WDR) quickly acquired the radio rights. And in November 1994, *Felidae* became the most expensive animated film in German history, with well-known actors such as Klaus-Maria Brandauer providing voices.[98] By this time, the book had gone through twenty-three printings, sold more than one million copies, and been translated into twelve languages. As one critic noted, *Felidae* seemed to "be exactly what . . . 4.5 million German cat owners had been waiting for."[99]

For our purposes, though, the more interesting point is that *Felidae*'s bestseller status seems to have facilitated a public discourse in which critics no longer deemed Pirinçci's efforts to "entertain" incongruous for a Turkish-German author. An article in the *Frankfurter Allgemeine Zeitung*, for example, discussed *Felidae* in relation to the larger genre of animal fables and the detective fiction of Raymond Chandler. It even commended Pirinçci for his thorough knowledge of cat biology, psychology, and sociology, as well as the author's ability to anthropomorphize the cat characters in compelling ways. Drawing a parallel between Pirinçci's Francis and Chandler's cat Taki (who, the American author once

[97] Reinhard Jahn, "Alles für die Katz!," *Kriminal Journal*, 5/6 (1991), n.p.
[98] The film reportedly cost over ten million DM to make. Brandauer did the voice of Pascal, Ulrich Tukur played Francis, and Mario Adorf played Blaubart. For a longer discussion of the film version of *Felidae*, see Bruni Mahlberg, "Auf samtigen Pfötchen brachte der Horror Erfolg," *Kölnische Rundschau*, 15 August 1993.
[99] Jahn, "Alles."

speculated, possessed superior writing abilities to his own), the commentator concluded that since "we must relinquish the possibility of a major novel by Taki for all time, we will be very content with what Pirinçci and Francis have related."[100] These statements represented a subtle breakthrough in the reception. For perhaps the very first time, a major German critic was spotlighting the work of a minority author without insisting on authorial subject position as the most essential critical fact.

To be sure, not every reviewer had such favorable things to say. The critic for *Kriminal Journal*, a periodical devoted to mystery novels, grumbled: "But not once does the mystery bring tension into play because Akif Pirinçci is nothing more than a literary hack of the genre; he robs it with the acuity of a grave robber. He includes a little detective brilliance à la Conan Doyle, a little world-domination-craziness in the style of James Bond. The whole thing is garnished with Chandler-like sentences and long-winded Agatha Christie puzzles."[101] In this formulation Pirinçci emerges as nothing more than a clever borrower of well-established mystery-novel conventions. Yet the very fact that such criticism was now appearing in a trade journal on detective fiction – rather than a forum on *Ausländerliteratur* – is interesting. The reviewer's critique was based on differences of opinion about what constituted good crime writing, not the sense that Pirinçci was somehow better suited for other genres or loftier social goals.

Most critics, not surprisingly, continued to acknowledge Pirinçci's Turkish-German identity as a point of information.[102] Yet they often scoffed at the idea that such information was relevant for appreciating the adventures of Francis. A review for the British newspaper, *The Independent*, typifies the pattern. It began in the following manner: "Akif

---

[100] Jochen Schmidt, "Von Katzen und Killern," *Frankfurter Allgemeine Zeitung*, 9 September 1989, 26.
[101] Jahn, "Alles."
[102] For articles that continued to insist that the experience of being "torn between two cultures" was a key to Pirinçci's work, see Matthias Gretzschel, "Ein begabter Zyniker," *Hamburger Abendblatt*, 18–19 July 1992, supplement, 2; and Mahlberg, "Auf samtigen Pfötchen." For articles that treated Pirinçci's ethnic identity as background information, see n.a., "'Krimi-Oscar' für Katzen-Thriller," *Die Rheinpfalz*, 20 April 1990; Brigitte Kramer, "Die Vertreibung aus dem Paradies," *Süddeutsche Zeitung*, 22–23 February 1992, Feuilleton Beilage; Meike Winnemuth, "Instant-Bestseller," *Stern*, 5 March 1992; Stefan Jaedich, "Später Rächer an Nazi verbrechern," *Welt am Sonntag*, 17 May 1992, 58; Susanne Broos, "Weg vom Normalhorror," *Frankfurter Rundschau*, 12 July 1993; n.a., "Die Katze als Detektiv," *Augsburger Allgemeine Zeitung*, 26 August 1993; Christoph Engels, "Francis gegen den schwarzen Ritter," *General-Anzeiger*, 17 September 1993, 15; n.a., "Kater Francis löst den nächsten Fall," *Welt am Sonntag*, 19 September 1993.

Pirinçci is a Turkish-born writer who lives in Germany. He writes about hideous killings and his highly successful first [*sic*] novel refers to the lethal nature of supremacist doctrines. It seems that we must be talking Political Statements. Extreme-right violence against Turks has, after all, been one of the most hotly discussed items in Germany this year."[103] In the very next paragraph, though, the journalist used Pirinçci's own words to mock the notion that literary success made him a "role model" for "integration": "'I wondered if they were missing a cup from the cupboard. If I thought anybody might see me as a role model, I would laugh myself *kaputt.*'"[104]

Given these breakthroughs in popular reception, it is somewhat ironic that some recent scholarly work on Pirinçci has refigured *Felidae* and his subsequent novels featuring the cat Francis (*Francis*, 1993, and *Cave Canem*, 1999) as a kind of allegory for Pirinçci's own experience as an outsider and his vision of multicultural German society.[105] This scholarship argues for Pirinçci's close identification with Francis as cat – an independent, intelligent, and self-reliant species – and as freelance detective – a loner who is alienated from, but also more acute than, those around him.[106] It interprets the standoff between Francis and Pascal/Claudandus as a struggle between two conflicting models of multiethnic society. Claudandus seeks to produce a race of cats capable of killing off humans; he wants a society in which power is concentrated in the hands of a dominant majority but seeks to invert the original power relation in favor of his own species. Francis, by contrast, rejects such attempts to replace human tyranny with feline oppression; he sees interbreeding as desirable and champions a future society in which animals and humans live together in mutual tolerance.[107] Here, the minority author's impulse to represent a multicultural vision is to some extent predetermined. Irrespective of Pirinçci's desire to participate in the discourse of foreigner literature, this critical work suggests that his novel inevitably reads as a tale of interethnic conflict and resolution.

Perhaps. It seems to me, however, that one might draw precisely the opposite conclusion. What the reception of Pirinçci demonstrates above

---

[103] Crawshaw, "Feline Fantasies," 29.
[104] Ibid., 29.
[105] See James Jordan, "Of Fables and Multiculturalism: The Felidae Novels of Akif Pirinçci," in *German-Language Literature Today: International and Popular* (Oxford: P. Lang, 2000), 255–68.
[106] Ibid., 258–61.
[107] Ibid., 263–65.

all is the almost reflexive impulse of late twentieth-century critics to interpret minority art as an expression of the author's life and experience.
The scholarship on *Felidae* has been quite explicit about Pirinçci's own
disavowal of just this sort of function. Yet the very same critics have
invoked postmodernism's rejection of authorial intention in order to insist
on an unconscious intent: Pirinçci, in this view, writes allegorically about
migrant issues and concerns whether he realizes it or not. In many ways,
the *Felidae* novels were a brilliant effort to counteract this impulse. Pirinçci
could not put a complete stop to this line of interpretation, but he could
expose the single-minded logic (one might even say folly) of its assumptions. To the extent that critics and journalists have insisted on maintaining the older stereotype of minority artist as dialogue partner, they have
done so at their own peril.[108]

Ultimately, Pirinçci refused not only the discourse of minority literature
but also the very notion that participating meaningfully in German culture
required living up to an idealized notion of Art with a capital *A*. He tried
to carve out a position for himself as artist that was at once nonethnic
and popular through and through. Invited to comment on the works of
several other contemporary authors for an edition of *Literarisches Quar-
tett*, a television talk show about literature broadcast on ZDF, Pirinçci
complained to the show's host, Marcel Reich-Ranicki, that his own writing had never been discussed on the program. Reich-Ranicki responded,
"When you write a good book." As he had on so many other occasions,
Pirinçci acted here as a *provocateur*. He used this mass-media moment
on camera to question some of the most fundamental, often unspoken
assumptions in public discourse. He both engaged in very clever self-
promotion and exercised his iconoclasm as a kind of intervention in the
received wisdom about what constituted German art and literature.

Zafer Şenocak's career suggests a third set of strategies for resisting
and complicating the conventional pieties of *Ausländerliteratur*. Born in
Ankara in 1961, Şenocak grew up in a highly cultured household full of
discussion about books and ideas. His father was a freelance journalist and
publisher, and his mother was a schoolteacher. In 1970, he moved with

---

[108] Leslie Adelson has offered the most trenchant critique of this tendency – the impulse
to read literature by authors of non-German heritage entirely for their sociological
value. See, in particular, Leslie A. Adelson, "Opposing Oppositions: Turkish-German
Questions in Contemporary German Studies," *German Studies Review* 17.2 (1994):
305–330; and Leslie A. Adelson, *The Turkish Turn in Contemporary German Literature:
Toward a New Critical Grammar of Migration* (New York: Palgrave Macmillan, 2005),
especially 1–30.

his parents to Munich, where he attended *Gymnasium* (academic high school) and completed the *Abitur* (equivalent to a high school diploma) before studying German language and literature, politics, and philosophy at Ludwig-Maximilian University. Soon thereafter, Şenocak became an independent author, working first as a poet and then branching into prose fiction. During the mid-1980s, he translated the writings of Turkish folk poets such as Yunus Emre and Pir Sultan Abdal. He also received a literary prize from the city of Munich in 1984 and won the Chamisso Patronage Prize for young authors in 1988. Since 1990, he has written nonfiction essays and articles for a number of prominent periodicals – most notably *Die Zeit* and Berlin's *Die Tageszeitung* – and given countless readings around the world. He now regularly serves as a visiting lecturer, teacher, and writer in residence at leading academic institutions in the United States, Netherlands, France, and Canada.

Şenocak, in short, has become one of contemporary Germany's most important and critically acclaimed young authors. At the same time, his body of work demonstrates one of the core values of late twentieth-century cosmopolitan intellectuals: the notion that "culture has no color" and that no individual, group, or nation possesses "'special proprietary rights' to culture."[109] During the 1980s and early 1990s, he worked as artist, translator, and critic, an intellectual division of labor that enabled him to speak simultaneously to a wide variety of publics. And in this sense Şenocak's cosmopolitanism has extended across cultural strata as well as geographic boundaries. While his aggregate audience is considerably smaller than that of Pirinçci or even Çırak, Şenocak is known today by a wider variety of educated readers than any other author we have considered in this study.

Şenocak first came to the attention of critics with the 1983 publication of "elektrisches Blau" (*Electric Blue*), a poetic cycle often compared to expressionist or action painting. Consider, for example, the following remarks in an early press notice from *Die Zeit*:

After wild painting, now wild poetry? Expressionistic reminiscences are unmistakable in the poems of the twenty-three-year-old Zafer Senocak [*sic*]. But it is not the ending of worlds and twilight of humanity that are the theme of this lyrical graffiti, rather the remains of the world. Poems as last looks, on the run, pushed

---

[109] Posnock, *Color and Culture*, 10. More than any other recent scholar, Posnock provides a twentieth-century genealogy of intellectual cosmopolitanism. The quotation here builds on an idea first developed by the early twentieth-century African-American intellectual Alain Locke.

into the corner, stuck on the wall. A language, which – without papier-mâché – trusts the rhythm wholly, as fleeing trusts instinct.[110]

For our purposes, the most interesting feature of this review is not so much the particular choice of aesthetic analogies (e.g., lyrical graffiti) as the very fact that they are aesthetic. Here, the reviewer seems to suggest, is an artistic object worth taking seriously. We find no hint of a causal relationship between Şenocak's personal biography and the mode of writing, no suggestion that the poems might be understood as ethnographic artifacts or windows onto foreign values and social practices.

In another review, the literary critic Ulrich Hohoff focused on Şenocak's striking poetic images:

This poetry is intended to be visual: it fixes impressions in the most plastic concentrations of images. The natural environment becomes a glaringly distorted image or appears dead. The flowers are endangered: "Buds out of glass." The trees "stand under the torrent/ and shine like colorful bouquets." The birds disappear as: "The migratory birds on the electric poles/ to the hoods of cars/ struck by lightning/ charred/ are dumbstruck/ in the supermarket shopping cart." Above all, the visual appears unbearable in the artistic light: "Blocked eyes stumble on neon fields." This is no black-and-white painting in which an "innocent" nature is played out against the "despicable" big city. More accurately, "nature" is given a new context, and it is not only charming as a supplier of metaphors: "if in the morning again/ the sun a sweet pastry/ is waiting/ behind the tin horizon." The moon appears as: "aged poet/ swims as an oil pool/ on a partially decomposed fish." The sky "goes somewhat drunk under the people/ smog cap on the head." Fascination and revulsion also mix with other basic motifs of the big city poetry in Şenocak's [sic] cycle: in the forms of loneliness and anonymity and in the continual presence of appeals to buy and consume, which leave marks on contact to fellow humans and not least on erotic images.[111]

Especially interesting are the ways in which Şenocak's images assume a constitutive role in shaping this analysis. For Hohoff, *Electric Blue* is an aesthetic world unto itself. The images exist only in relation to one another, or they conjure metaphoric associations with deracialized abstractions such as "the natural environment" and "the big city." It is also worth noting that Hohoff makes no effort to impose a particular reading of the poems. Rather, he assumes that Şenocak's lyricism is by its very nature ambiguous, that its meanings are open, unfinished, and contingent. These assumptions may not strike us as especially odd or counterintuitive, but during the mid-1980s they constituted an important rupture

---

[110] N.a., "Elektrisches Blau 2," *Die Zeit*, 22 June 1984.
[111] Ulrich Hohoff, "Diktatur der Lichter: Zafer Şenocak," *Literatur in Bayern* 8 (1987).

in the public discourse surrounding the work of minority artists. What Şenocak's poems seem to have confounded, in other words, was the older, critical calculus that assumed that subject position dictates signification.

Şenocak was equally well known as a translator. In public discussions about his translation of Yunus Emre's poetry, Şenocak liked to emphasize the particular choices that informed his method:

> With my translations I set certain priorities. At the beginning is understanding. Emre's texts can only be opened up through knowledge of his philosophy. Although Emre spoke Turkish, he employed many Islamic (Arabic) ideas. I placed value on maintaining the freshness and the simplicity of his language even in German. The language should seem neither antiquated nor constructed. Finally, I tried as much as possible to capture Yunus's rhythm in German. I favored an unrhymed translation because the importance of Yunus lies not in the rhyme, but rather in the clarity of his language, his thought, and the originality of his images.[112]

This is a very different conception of "translation" than we have encountered in previous discussions of *Ausländerliteratur*. For DaF's Ackermann and Weinrich, translation involved bringing the "foreign" into a previously static, homogeneous monolith ("German culture"). In their framework, the minority author embodied the "foreign" culture of his or her birth and, at the same time, served as a conduit for difference to enter the mainstream. This idea of translation assumed a kind of passivity on the part of minority writers: their ability to perform intercultural translation existed as a condition of being.

Şenocak, by contrast, was celebrated precisely for his depth of knowledge and active choices in the translation process. His work as translator was understood as a set of skills to be acquired or a particular expertise that reflected literary virtuosity. This new conception of translation, in turn, allowed a rethinking of the larger category of "foreign" (*fremd*). Consider, for example, the following *Süddeutsche Zeitung* review of Şenocak's translation of Emre: "It offers for the first time the possibility to track down and bridge that foreignness which remains between the European and Islamic traditions."[113] Here, *Fremdheit* no longer refers to an essentialized ethnic identity embodied by the artist. Rather it denotes a condition of ignorance or misunderstanding perceived to exist between cultures. The work of translation itself thus begins to change. For this critic, Şenocak's cross-cultural contribution was not to represent the

---

[112] N.a., "Ein Interview mit Zafer Şenocak: Eine Synthese der gedanklichen Sättigung und der farbigen Gemütsausstrahlung," *Dergi* 6 (1987).

[113] Reinhard Knodt, "Dichter-Derwisch," *Süddeutsche Zeitung*, 21–22 March 1987.

foreign or bring it into German literature, but to eradicate misperceptions and ignorance.

As we have seen, a similar set of exchanges was central to Yüksel Pazarkaya's conception of "cultural synthesis." By showing that Turks had a rich cultural history he sought to raise Germans' estimation of Turkish labor migrants. The key for Pazarkaya was to foster a dialogue of sacralization that would place Turkish masterworks on equal footing with the German canon. Great civilizations would come to understand and appreciate each other's greatest cultural achievements. Yet this emphasis on parallel traditions inadvertently meshed with CDU policymaking during the early 1980s. In both arenas, the public rhetoric encouraged mutual respect, even as it assumed a starting point of wholly separate national cultures.

Şenocak's conception of translation, by contrast, specifically sought to problematize the notion of distinct traditions and literary categories. This more expansive approach to translation first crystallized in the mid-1980s. One sees it, for example, in press accounts for a public poetry reading where Şenocak surprised his audience by delivering an essay on the "situation of foreign authors" writing German literature. According to an unsigned review in the *Frankfurter Allgemeine Zeitung*, the young author argued for a "necessary synthesis of Oriental and European literature and, in the widest sense, of culture."[114] This, in turn, provoked a discussion about whether German-language literature written by "foreigners" should be defined as "guest worker literature." As the reviewer pointed out, this debate had been smoldering for quite some time. Established figures such as Ören and Pazarkaya had already complained that the term did not encompass the full spectrum of themes treated by Turkish-German authors. But Şenocak responded to the question with what the article described as "a clear and enlightening argument." He asserted that "only the examination of a text based on its literary value should be decisive. Categories like 'foreigner literature' or 'women's literature' are 'simply ridiculous.'"[115] More than a critique of a particular set of labels, Şenocak's central concern here was to argue for the obsolescence of identity categories in general. The time had come to let go of categorical boxes and one-dimensional modes of reading.

The fall of the Berlin Wall in November 1989 and the rapid reunification of East and West Germany less than a year later served as important

---

[114] N.a., "Erstochen hab ich den Mond," *Frankfurter Allgemeine Zeitung*, 24 April 1986.
[115] Ibid.

catalysts that led Şenocak to introduce these concerns in terms more conventional to broader national public debate. In January 1990, just two months after the breaching of the wall, Şenocak criticized the continuing influence of identity categories in an essay written with Bülent Tulay entitled "Germany – Home for Turks? A Plea for Overcoming the Crisis between Orient and Occident."[116] As thousands of ethnic Germans from the East arrived in the Federal Republic, he condemned the restrictive citizens' rights available to guest workers and their descendants. The genealogical basis for German citizenship, Şenocak pointed out, meant that an ethnic German from Eastern Europe with only distant family ties to Germany and little ability to speak the language was considered a German, while a second or third-generation Turk who knew German better than Turkish remained a foreigner.[117] The population influx engendered by the collapse of communism revealed the difficulty with older identity categories and affiliations; they quickly erased thirty-five years of separation (on the part of East Germans) and peaceful coexistence (on the part of Turks).

Beyond this call to revise the legal framework regulating citizenship, Şenocak advocated a "comprehensive change of consciousness, a reorientation that links Turks with Germany's problems and perspectives, that enriches the Germans with the cultural legacy of the Turks."[118] Multiethnic society, in this view, required a thorough transformation of both Turkish and German mentalities, a transformation that could not be achieved through the mere exchange of literary texts or expansions of the canon. Şenocak observed that conservative Germans asked Turks to integrate when they really meant "nothing short of absolute assimilation, the disappearance of Anatolian faces behind German masks."[119] But he also criticized liberal Germans for too quickly idealizing difference and romanticizing a multiethnic society in which "cultures and perspectives exist[ed] side by side without touching each other."[120] "Demonization and glorification of things foreign," he concluded, are ultimately two sides of the

---

[116] This essay originally appeared in Zafer Şenocak, *Atlas des tropischen Deutschlands: Essays* (Berlin: Babel, 1992). Its English translation has been included in Zafer Şenocak, *Atlas of a Tropical Germany: Essays on Politics and Culture, 1990–1998*, trans. by Leslie A. Adelson (Lincoln: University of Nebraska Press, 2000), 1–12.

[117] Zafer Şenocak and Bülent Tulay, "Germany – Home for Turks? A Plea for Overcoming the Crisis between Orient and Occident," in Şenocak, *Atlas*, 1–2.

[118] Ibid., 5.

[119] Ibid., 2.

[120] Ibid., 2, 3–4.

same ideological process: neither impulse encourages contact with difference or allows a relationship of true "partnership."[121]

Şenocak was equally impatient with the inclination of Turkish-German
youth to emulate their parents' one-sided cultural and political orientation
to Turkey. He urged the second and third generations not to "cling to the
phantasm of the lost homeland" but instead to engage with Germany's
past and future. For Şenocak, simply existing in a place was not enough.
"Doesn't immigrating to Germany," he asked, "also mean immigrating
to, entering into, the arena of Germany's recent past?"[122] In particular,
he encouraged immigrants in the Federal Republic to concern themselves
with the history of German Jews. By pushing Turks to make an empathetic
leap into a German past that preceded their arrival, Şenocak stressed
that the ideological world they inhabited in the present was inevitably
bound up with the legacies of the past. Immigrants, in short, could not
realistically expect to shape German society's future unless they "entered"
into its history.

Ultimately, history itself served as the crucial vehicle for Şenocak's theory of how to develop a more meaningful model of German multiculturalism. This approach seems to have become urgent with the resurgence in
public debate about national identity as a reunited Germany embarked on
its fiftieth anniversary commemorations of the end of World War II. In a
1995 interview with Berlin's *Der Tagesspiegel*, Şenocak elaborated on history's key role and pointed to some of the obstacles preventing Turks from
entering Germany in the fullest sense. One crucial barrier was the ethnically homogeneous notion of belonging implicit in the national project of
Holocaust commemoration. In the Federal Republic, Şenocak explained,
"history is read as a diary of the 'community of fate,' the nation's personal
experience, to which Others have no access. This conception of history
as ethnic, collective memory was tied to the question of guilt after the
crimes of the Holocaust."[123] Within the framework of "collective guilt"
and "community of fate," the past is always already understood as a
perfect alignment between ethnicity and nation: the lack of genealogical
credentials barred migrants from being recognized as an integral element

---

[121] Ibid., 2–3. The danger of multiculturalism, Posnock suggests, is that it often functions as
the "mirror image of what it sets out to repudiate – racialist, nativist thinking" because
"these alleged enemies both fetishize difference." Posnock, *Color and Culture*, 24.

[122] Şenocak and Tulay, "Germany," 6.

[123] Zafer Şenocak, "May One Compare Turks and Jews, Mr. Şenocak?" in Şenocak, *Atlas*,
53. He refers to this shared experience as a "community of fate" whereby Germans are
bound together by their troubled collective history.

of German society. These assumptions about German history meant that one could "immigrate to a country, but not to its past."[124]

The task of *Vergangenheitsbewältigung* (mastering the past), Şenocak further argued, was "intended to package history, as one packs up things or buildings: in commemorative speeches, in commemorative plaques, in rituals."[125] This mode of collective mourning and remembrance neatly divided German history into discrete periods and discontinuous episodes even as it reinforced the ethnic-based view of history. In particular, it treated the Third Reich and its state-sponsored program of race-based genocide as completely divorced from other periods in modern German history, a perspective that made it especially difficult to recognize continuities and patterns in the nation's ongoing struggles with difference.

Şenocak consequently challenged the impulse to put brackets around the past. "It is time," he proclaimed, "to unpack German history . . . to see causes and consequences. Only then will we understand what resistance there is in Germany today toward immigrants."[126] Precisely because Germans continued to parcel out their history and describe it in ethnic terms, asserted Şenocak, they remained unable to deal with their current diversity. Removing these compartments and dissolving the ethnically homogeneous idea of the past would accomplish significant ideological work for the present.

Şenocak's point, however, was not to reject Holocaust commemoration per se. Instead, he wanted to reformulate the nation's approach to its troubled history by disrupting the binary logic of categories such as Self/Other, inside/outside, German/foreigner. Unpacking German history and recognizing continuities between past and present, Şenocak insisted, required bringing immigrants into the historical imaginary, into the shared burdens and responsibilities that were an inevitable part of living in postwar German society. In short, he proposed introducing a third term into the reflexive commemorations of Jewish victims by German perpetrators. In his 1998 novel *Gefährliche Verwandschaft (Perilous Kinship)*, Şenocak fleshed out this triangular relationship. Describing "today's Germany," narrator Sascha Muteschem, son of a German-Jewish mother and Turkish father, observes:

Jews and Germans no longer face one another alone. Instead, a situation has emerged which corresponds to my personal origin and situation. In Germany now,

---

[124] Ibid.
[125] Ibid.
[126] Ibid.

a trialogue is developing among Germans, Jews, and Turks, among Christians, Jews, and Moslems. The undoing of the German-Jewish dichotomy might release both parties from the burden of their traumatic experiences. But for this to succeed they would have to admit Turks into their domain. And for their part, the Turks in Germany would have to discover the Jews, not just as part of the German past in which they cannot share, but as part of the present in which they live. Without the Jews the Turks stand in a dichotomous relation to the Germans. They tread in the footprints of the Jews of the past.[127]

The literary critic Leslie Adelson has usefully cautioned against a straightforward or linear interweaving of Turkish and German national memory cultures, suggesting that Şenocak "write[s] a new subject of remembrance into being" rather than presenting a transparent window into Germany's struggle with diversity on a sociological level.[128] Yet it is precisely the perspective enabled by this three-way relationship (particularly in his non-fiction essays) that allows Şenocak to ask new, uncomfortable questions. In "Thoughts on May 8, 1995," for instance, he recounts how his father listened to the war on the radio in his Turkish village. When the conflict ended, writes Şenocak, his father "experienced neither a liberation nor a collapse. He was neither victim nor perpetrator," adding: "this vantage point allows me to raise a few questions."[129] For Şenocak, this anniversary was an important occasion on which to connect past and present, especially in light of reunified Germany's newly attained sovereignty. "Germany lost World War II in 1945," he states. "The Nazi regime was defeated. On the other hand, the subtle consequences of National Socialism continue to affect Germany even today. Does the Nazis' brutal effort to render Germany ethnically homogeneous have nothing to do with the present resistance to acknowledging, in Germany in 1995, the ethnic diversity that has arisen through migration?"[130] Here, in plain language, was the crux of the matter: fifty years of democracy and Holocaust commemoration had not brought Germans any closer to recognizing an ongoing pattern of social exclusion. But a triangulated debate among Germans, Turks, and Jews, Şenocak suggested, might help Germans begin to grasp ethnic diversity not simply as a temporary problem or a tragic episode from the past, but as a central narrative of the nation's historical development.

[127] Zafer Şenocak, *Gefährliche Verwandschaft* (Munich, 1998), 40.
[128] Leslie A. Adelson, "The Turkish Turn in Contemporary German Literature and Memory Work," *Germanic Review* 77.4 (2002): 333, quoted in Andreas Huyssen, "Diaspora and Nation: Migration into Other Pasts," *New German Critique* 88 (Winter 2003): 158.
[129] Zafer Şenocak, "Thoughts on May 8, 1995" in Şenocak, *Atlas*, 58–59.
[130] Ibid., 59–60.

In many ways, the attempt to "weld" Germans and Turks through the nation's Jewish past was Şenocak's most ambitious translation project of all, for it involved positioning himself as the intellectual link between Germany's ethnic past and ethnic present. It also represents, arguably, the most fundamental challenge to the conceptions of German culture and nation we have considered thus far. Şenocak did not simply resist the critical convention that assumed minority intellectuals could only serve as spokespersons for their particular ethnic group. More ambitiously, he began to articulate a vision of German history and identity that involved a shared interrogation of the past and present, an interrogation facilitated by the tectonic shift of the Cold War Federal Republic giving way to a reunified, Europeanized Germany. This moment of upheaval, when, as the literary scholar Leslie Adelson has aptly put it, "East is no longer East, West is no longer West, and the past is not what it used to be either,"[131] opened the possibility for fresh interpretations and new definitions of German history that recognized the common ground between natives and immigrants. The deep ideological and historical interconnectedness of Germans, Jews, and Turks, in other words, would revalue the traditional frameworks for self-understanding and produce a novel, syncretic idea of what it meant to be German.

German Multiculturalism on the Eve of Reunification

It is perhaps more accurate, then, to speak of German multicultural*isms* emerging during the late 1980s. Somewhat paradoxically, the process of delinking culture and nation also produced multiple – and hotly contested – conceptions of both categories. In the realm of politics, the crucial point of debate focused on how to square the nation's multiethnic diversity (a diversity increasingly acknowledged by all sides as permanent) with the desire to hold on to the larger idea of shared values, principles, and customs that the nation-state has traditionally signified and legislated. By 1989, "multiculturalism" had become the most pervasive rhetorical means of talking about those tensions, although virtually all public figures defined their version of multicultural German society in slightly different terms. At the same time, almost everyone seems to have understood that the debate itself represented a new kind of ideological work: arguing about the specific terms of coexistence within a permanently multiethnic nation

---

[131] Adelson, "The Turkish Turn," 327.

was very different from acknowledging that pockets of foreigners would have to be integrated into a homogeneous society.

What ultimately connects these political discussions with cultural developments during the late 1980s is a growing willingness in both arenas to contemplate German identity as distinct from one's personal lineage or range of affiliations. But intellectuals and artists thought about the delinking process in somewhat different terms. By the mid-1980s, they seem to have grasped that the ideological function of the "minority" artist was central to the politics of multiethnic Germany. The task of ideal dialogue partner required them to represent their own ethnic group and mediate between two permanently separate cultures. For second-generation authors such as Çırak, Şenocak, and even Pirinçci, challenging the seemingly natural fusion of cultural identity and national citizenship focused on the extent to which they were prepared to fill this role.

Each strategy, of course, had different implications. Pirinçci's embrace of mass-cultural forms and market mechanisms fueled the popularity of his work among a broad German audience, enabling him to bypass literary categories based on ethnicity and difference. Above all, his approach inverted the classic theoretical critique of the culture industry. It was precisely the formulaic, standardizing aspects of mass culture famously disparaged by Theodor Adorno and Max Horkheimer that Pirinçci found liberating.[132] In particular, he exploited a paradox central to modern culture industries: as they search for new markets and raw materials to absorb within the mainstream, they sometimes draw upon "areas of human life previously bracketed from representation – if only to appropriate, commodify, and desubstantiate that material."[133] From Pirinçci's perspective, though, this basic tension within the culture industry – the fact that profit motives require the broadest possible market – offered opportunities for professional mobility as well as a way out of the representational burdens of *Ausländerliteratur*.[134] So-called popular genres (teenage romance and detective fiction) that to Adorno and Horkheimer looked like the death of individual subjectivity were in this case a form of creative breathing

[132] Max Horkheimer and Theodor Adorno, *Dialektik der Aufklärung* (Frankfurt: Fischer, 1969), trans. by John Cumming as *Dialectic of Enlightenment* (New York: Continuum, 1994).

[133] Miriam Hansen, "Foreword," in Oskar Negt and Alexander Kluge, *Public Sphere and Experience: Toward an Analysis of the Bourgeois and Proletarian Public Sphere* (Minneapolis: University of Minnesota Press, 1992), xxx.

[134] Ibid.

room. Here was a trade-off never envisioned by the Frankfurt School –
one set of market-driven formulas as escape from another.

By contrast, Çırak continued to operate within the parameters of the
"minority" artist even as she developed a vision of urban cosmopolitanism
that went beyond the cultural enrichment model promoted through earlier church-organized initiatives. She championed an urban protean self
that did not just seek exposure to difference at multicultural festivals
or foreigner awareness days, but regarded ongoing improvisation and
eclecticism as fundamental characteristics of identity. This celebration of
hybrid subjectivity, in turn, gave new value to the diverse migrant cultures
that constituted urban experience. At the same time, Çırak defined cosmopolitanism largely in relation to the market. Rather than rejecting the
popular demand for cultural difference fed by the works of Scheinhardt
and Baser, she revised the terms of the transaction: Çırak (as migrant
woman) was now the consumer, and consumption was the central vehicle
through which self-fashioning took place. Yet her sensitivity to market
imperatives was not limited to consumption; she was also highly conscious of her own position as a producer within the publishing industry.
Indeed, one of the most interesting aspects of her work is that she treated
Ausländerliteratur itself as an object of artistic commentary. Çırak's decision marked the limits of the genre as such. Foreigner literature not only
became a source of constraint and occasional frustration, but also became
its own subject.

Şenocak's project pushed even deeper. More than any other figure
associated with the migration he offered a concrete vision of the ideological labor involved in creating a multicultural society. Right from the
start, Şenocak introduced two novel ideas: first, any true "dialogue" on
the guest worker question would necessarily be reciprocal, transcend-
ing notions of Self and Other predicated on incommensurable difference;
second, the work of "translation" would demand an active interweaving of multiple traditions rather than mere celebration of the Turkish
literary canon for German audiences. Şenocak's own aesthetic practices
provided a model for what this syncretic culture of letters might look
like in the new Germany. Even more important was his insistence that
any meaningful theorization of a multicultural present entailed rethinking the past. This reconceptualization of German history pushed beyond
Çırak's notion of cosmopolitanism through consumption. For Şenocak,
a more rigorous, collective interrogation of the German past could not
help but disrupt the relation of culture and nation: the core assumption behind this fusion – that Germany had a prior moment of ethnic

homogeneity – would be exposed as an ideological fiction and ultimately cease to make sense.

Of course, one might argue that Şenocak's triumph in eliciting reviews based on his aesthetic choices rather than his ethnographic position was far removed indeed from the socioeconomic struggles faced by most labor migrants and their families. It is also true that the multiple lifestyles celebrated by Çırak were the choices of a member of the cultural elite, someone with the resources and mobility to eat English breakfasts and go to art cinemas. The obvious limitations of this ideological work emerge most distinctly in terms of Pirinçci's commercial success: the fact that his novel about a cat detective became a major bestseller in Germany had very little impact on the material lives of manual workers.

Yet the notion that Pirinçci and the other second-generation authors were responsible for their fellow migrants is in many ways another iteration of the particular cultural calculus that assumed that the professional choices of minority artists were dictated by birth. On another level, too, this kind of critique fails to acknowledge the variety of ways in which intellectuals and artists can effect historical change. Pirinçci, Çırak, and Şenocak were among the first to create new templates for multicultural identity in a context where the distinction between German and foreign no longer prescribed the possibilities of Self in such a rigid, automatic way. To be sure, the ideological purchase of this binary did not simply evaporate. But during the late 1980s, each author began to articulate conceptions of Self and cultural production well beyond the tropes – guest worker, dysfunctional migrant, or perpetually marginal dialogue partner – previously represented in the mainstream media.

The political significance of this ideological labor lay not so much in resisting stereotypes or adding minority voices. Part of what made it so crucial was the *public* status of these figures. As bestselling authors, prizewinning artists, and cultural critics of considerable reputation, Pirinçci, Çırak, and Şenocak disrupted the public imaginary. They began to show in their published statements and professional trajectories alternative models for how a member of the migrant community might inhabit a public identity in Germany. Another factor that raised the political stakes of their cultural production was its broad scope – it did not focus exclusively on migrants. When Pirinçci discussed his goals as an author in the mass marketplace he did not claim a public position or level of success open only to minority artists. When Çırak wrote about her existence in the postmodern metropolis she did so as the daughter of guest workers, but the protean life she celebrated was not restricted to migrants or their descendants. When Şenocak called for an engagement with history he envisioned a process that included and affected anyone residing in the Federal Republic. In their attempts to get out of the binary, these authors presented new possibilities for German identity as such.

It is important, then, to understand that the projects and concerns of Pirinçci, Çırak, and Şenocak were not typical of labor migrants. Their exceptional lives, careers, and experiences were played out in some of the most public forums. Precisely because they as figures were so uncommon and their choices were so public, these authors took on a particular ideological and social importance. This dilemma confronts many prominent minority intellectuals: their representativeness has to do less with their typicality as members of the migrant communities from which they emerge than with the range of experiences and ideas they make visible as exceptional individuals. In this way, they carry a special burden as historical figures.

Ultimately, both political and cultural conversations revolved around reformulating the relationship between culture and nation. One focused on citizenship and *Ausländerpolitik* while the other emphasized cultural production and cultural belonging. We might say that the 1980s witnessed a gradual move toward replacing assumptions of German homogeneity with new conceptualizations of what it meant to be German. But the great paradox of the story is that at this very moment the growing push for a separation of cultural identity and national citizenship was eclipsed by a new preoccupation with reuniting the constituent parts of the older Germany. It was not so much that reunification represented a deliberate attempt to revive *völkisch* (ethnic) notions of the nation and its culture – although the process did stir up this kind of rhetoric. More accurately, the upheaval of reunification itself and the massive problems of reconstituting the historical nation seem to have drowned out and postponed the move away from homogeneous models of culture that had gained considerable momentum during the second half of the 1980s. For this reason it is not surprising that it took close to a decade for national reform of the citizenship law to become a political priority.

By the end of the 1980s, it is clear that many second-generation intellectuals had grown exasperated with questions of origin as well as the expectation that they serve as dialogue partners for a German audience. Yet the three authors we have examined here made very different decisions about the extent to which they were willing to inhabit the category of "minority" artist. Pirinçci assumed perhaps the most extreme position, constructing a career that increasingly hampered any attempt to read him within this rubric. Strategies such as the celebration of mass culture, the emphasis on teenage romance and cat detectives, and the use of market mechanisms as opposed to academic institutions or prizes allowed him to circumvent the entire apparatus that had been constructed earlier in the decade for being a minority author in the public sphere.

Neither Çırak nor Şenocak, by contrast, rejected this role out of hand. Çırak understood the public expectations about her artistic career as a kind of balancing act: she took advantage of the visibility afforded by *Ausländerliteratur* promotional mechanisms to secure a readership for her work but refused to adhere strictly to the terms dictated by the industry and discourse. Çırak "smuggled" into her poems criticism of the limitations placed on minority artists. Alternatively, Şenocak's response was to reinhabit the category of minority intellectual on completely new terms, forcing both migrants and Germans into a qualitatively different relationship with each other. He approached this task as an artist by casting his literary texts in a stylized, aesthetic mode, as a translator by bringing novel kinds of cultural materials into dialogue with one another, and above all as a theorist of multiculturalism by reconceptualizing German history and identity.

Conclusion

Situating German Diversity in the New Europe

The Guest Worker Question and Reunification

One of the most crucial developments leading up to the reunification of East and West Germany was a series of Monday demonstrations that took place in Leipzig during the late summer and fall of 1989.[1] This popular mobilization reached a climax on 9 October, two days after celebrations to mark the fortieth anniversary of the German Democratic Republic. More than seventy thousand Leipzigers marched through city streets heavily fortified by paramilitary units from local factories, police, and state security forces. Anticipating a confrontation in response to this unauthorized demonstration the crowd shouted, "We are staying here" and "No violence," but in the end the armed guards did not attack. This peaceful protest steeled the courage of other citizens, swelling the ranks of subsequent Monday demonstrators to over three hundred thousand. It also produced dramatic political results. Within nine days Erich Honecker,

[1] Early academic analyses of the collapse of East Germany and unification include: Arthur M. Hanhardt, Jr., "The Collapse of the German Democratic Republic and Its Unification with the Federal Republic of Germany, 1989–1990," in Michael G. Huelshoff et al., eds., *From Bundesrepublik to Deutschland: German Politics after Unification* (Ann Arbor: University of Michigan Press, 1993), 207–233; Konrad H. Jarausch, *The Rush to German Unity* (Oxford: Oxford University Press, 1993); Manfred Görtemaker, *Unifying Germany, 1989–1990* (London: Macmillan, 1994); and Charles S. Maier, *Dissolution: The Crisis of Communism and the End of East Germany* (Princeton: Princeton University Press, 1997). The most comprehensive German-language treatment of this topic is the four-volume *Geschichte der deutschen Einheit* (Stuttgart: Deutsche Verlags-Anstalt, 1998). For a useful collection of documents on reunification, see Konrad Jarausch and Volker Gransow, eds., *Uniting Germany: Documents and Debates, 1944–1993* (Providence, RI: Berghahn Books, 1994).

general secretary of the Socialist Unity Party (Sozialistische Einheitspartei Deutschlands, SED) and East Germany's head of state, resigned. And within a month the Berlin Wall fell, creating free movement between the two Germanys for the first time in twenty-eight years. As several scholars have observed, the calls for open discussion and changes to the regime during the Leipzig demonstrations largely sealed the fate of the GDR.[2]

A particularly striking feature of the Leipzig protests was the set of slogans that spontaneously emerged from the crowd. The chants served as an important barometer of the popular movement, which quickly shifted from pressing for political reform of the East German regime to advocating reunification. In October demonstrators proclaimed *Wir sind DAS Volk* (we are THE people), but by the end of November, the protestors now declared *Wir sind EIN Volk* (we are ONE people) and demanded *Deutschland, einig Vaterland* (Germany, united fatherland). The push for reunification, in short, quickly became a kind of public referendum on the boundaries of German nationhood and identity.

Most popular press accounts of the events in Leipzig and Berlin marveled at the rapid crumbling of a totalitarian regime that had held the GDR hostage for half a century. To the extent that contemporary commentators focused on the rhetorical and ideological movement toward Germany as *ein Volk*, they tended to raise concerns about German history, nationalism, and the potential disruption of European integration.[3] An op-ed piece in the *New York Times*, for example, offered a few caveats to the popular enthusiasm. The essay quoted several U.S.-based academics, including David Calleo, professor of European Studies at Johns Hopkins University, who asserted:

The problem is how not to re-create all sorts of old problems that have haunted the European scene for a long time: It is true that the division of Germany and the division of Europe into Cold War blocs has, in a fashion, resolved some of the earlier European problems – and in particular what is often called the German problem. [. . . That] was essentially that a united, centralized Germany was so big

---

[2] Hanhardt, "Collapse," 215; and Maier, *Dissolution*, 139.

[3] This was also true of scholars of Germany who, by the early 1990s, began to reflect on the impact of unification on German nationalism and concepts of nation. What is particularly striking about these discussions is their insular quality; they tackle the question of the nation exclusively in terms of the peculiarities of German history. See, in particular, Jürgen Kocka, "Crisis of Unification: How Germany Changes," *Daedalus* 123.1 (1994): 173–92; and Heinrich August Winkler, "Rebuilding of a Nation: The Germans Before and After Unification," *Daedalus* 123.1 (1994): 107–127.

and dynamic that it more or less automatically threatened all of its neighbors, who tended, naturally enough, to ally themselves against it.[4]

A week later the *New York Times* issued its own editorial on the push for German unity:

No one was prepared for the rush of change in East Germany and the abrupt opening of the Berlin wall. So it's not surprising that the good news is being followed by much disquieting conjecture about a feared old topic: German reunification.... Though President Mitterrand says he does not fear German reunification, France doesn't want it. Reunification complicates Paris's priority of moving ahead quickly with Western European economic integration. A new fatherland of 80 million Germans would tip the balance in the European Community further in West Germany's direction. Britain shares French concerns about an enlarged Germany becoming the economic superpower in Europe. Prime Minister Thatcher's warning against talking prematurely about reunification springs from the traditional British desire to maintain a balance of power on the continent by resisting the emergence of any outsized rival.[5]

The prominent West German intellectual Günter Grass, moreover, specifically tied the question of unification to a reinvigorated nationalism: "Once again, it looks as if a reasonable sense of nationhood is being inundated by diffuse nationalist emotion. Our neighbors watch with anxiety, even with alarm, as Germans recklessly talk themselves into the will to unity."[6] When asked in an interview with the Berlin leftist newspaper *Die Tageszeitung* whether he accused "those in Leipzig who now shout 'Germany, unified fatherland' of lacking historical consciousness," Grass explained: "I don't blame anyone living under the economic pressures in the GDR for calling for unity; I blame the politicians, whose responsibility is not to follow the public attitude, which is in itself justified, but to develop a strategy acceptable to us and our neighbors. If they fail to do this and merely follow the trends, we will find ourselves once again on a historical and political slope that does indeed have its precursors, particularly in Germany."[7] Responding to the prospect of German reunification,

---

[4] Eric Pace, "Clamor in the East: Academics Ask, What's Next? Joy for Germans, With a Few Caveats," *New York Times*, 12 November 1989, Sect. 1, 20.

[5] *New York Times* editorial, 19 November 1989, cited in Jarausch and Gransow, *Uniting Germany*, 83–84.

[6] Günter Grass, n.t., *New York Times*, 7 January 1990.

[7] N.a., "Günter Grass Against the Clamor for Unity," *Die Tageszeitung*, 12 February 1990, cited in Jarausch and Gransow, *Uniting Germany*, 108.

Lech Walesa, the founder of the Polish Solidarity movement, stated flatly: "This is a bomb. We paid a heavy price for the existence of Hitler."[8]

Less widely discussed was the impact of the popular demand for *ein Volk* and political reunification on the guest worker question. Indeed, one might argue in retrospect that the oft-cited danger of renewed nationalistic fervor was far less of a problem than the various ways in which the reunification project obscured the broad efforts of the late 1980s to engage seriously with the problem of constructing and legislating a self-consciously "multicultural" Germany. Of course, these discussions about reunification and multiculturalism were ultimately interrelated. At base, both debates wrestled with the same fundamental questions: What does it mean to be German? And which model of society ought to guide Germany's future?

This shift in focus from multiculturalism to reunification, it is important to stress, did not go completely unnoticed at the time. The federal *Ausländerbeauftragte*, Liselotte Funcke, became so frustrated at the Kohl administration's lack of attention to migrant affairs that she resigned in protest in the summer of 1991.[9] But the most incisive and sustained critiques came from members of the migrant community.[10] Zafer Şenocak, for example, wondered in 1992 whether Germany could be a homeland for Turks: "We have been asking ourselves this question for a year and a half. German unification was in process and stopped past us like a train that we ourselves were sitting on. We were inside this country that we grew up in, bound to its streets, plazas, cities, and people, but we

---

[8] Neil A. Lewis, "Clamor in the East: Walesa Warns on Reunification of Germany, Citing Hitler's Rule," *New York Times*, 17 November 1989, Sect. 1, 15. Even those European nations that did not invoke the past worried about the potential effect of a united Germany on the future. France and Britain, for instance, faced the prospect of being nudged off the center stage of European politics. See, for example, Alan Riding, "Upheaval in the East: On Germany, Not All Is Joy: French and British Are Among Doubters," *New York Times*, 5 February 1990, Sect. 1, 1.

[9] Klaus J. Bade, *Ausländer, Aussiedler, Asyl in der Bundesrepublik Deutschland*, 2nd ed. (Bonn: Bundeszentrale für politische Bildung, 1992).

[10] An important exception here is Andreas Huyssen, "The Inevitability of Nation: German Intellectuals after Unification," *October* 61 (1992): 65–73. Huyssen criticizes the insularity of German discussions about the nation after unification and proposes "a broad public debate about an alternative notion of nation, one that emphasizes negotiated heterogeneity rather than homogeneity imposed from above, federalism rather than centralism" (71). In this respect, Huyssen seems to point to a return to the kinds of discussions that emerged around multiculturalism at the end of the 1980s. His larger point, though, is to suggest that the left's refusal to engage in a public debate about German nationhood has opened the door for militant nationalism and xenophobia; he never sees foreigners themselves as part of this discussion, but only as passive victims.

were also outside it because the symbols which were suddenly resuscitated from the dusty files of history said nothing to us."[11] Part of the difficulty, he suggested, was that "rapid reunification...created the illusion that current events and contemporary phenomena [could] be described with nineteenth-century language, with concepts such as *nation* and *Volk*. We have no concepts for the emotions and psychic structures to which recent historical ruptures have given rise, no concepts for the disarray of the new arrangements. The ones that are used are ripped out of context."[12] What the spontaneous demands for a single German people enacted, according to Şenocak, was a historical erasure on multiple levels. These calls elided forty years of division and, more problematically, raised issues of culture, nation, and citizenship within an ideological framework that excluded Turks and other migrants almost entirely.

Similar criticisms arose at the grassroots level. Several Turkish-German students in Berlin who were involved in publishing a politically engaged, intercultural newspaper described the effects of the fall of the Wall on their lives. "In principle," one of the editors explained, "I have felt quite unwell since November 9 – since I saw these masses in the streets. I already had a foreboding of what was in store for us. I grew up here – but I have never felt as foreign as now." Another student writer argued that the concept of *ein Volk* had a particular ideological resonance for East Germans who experienced "on the one hand, being *German* and, on the other hand, occupying an economic and social position worse than that of immigrants in the West. The people in the DDR could not cope with that psychologically. It was certainly forced by the politicians in the West, so that being German was suddenly so revalorized."[13] By reinvigorating the distinction between German and foreigner, this patriotic shift threatened to naturalize immigrants' status as interlopers at a private family reunion. At stake here was more than thirty years of struggle by the migrant community to expand the basic boundaries of German belonging.

Perhaps the most acute migrant statement on the course of reunification can be found in a photograph from a demonstration that took place at Berlin's Kaiser-Wilhelm-Gedächtniskirche to protest the violence against

[11] Zafer Şenocak, "Ein Türke geht nicht in die Oper," *Die Tageszeitung*, 21 January 1992, 11.

[12] Zafer Şenocak, "What Does the Forest Dying Have to Do with Multiculturalism?" in Zafer Şenocak, *Atlas of a Tropical Germany: Essays on Politics and Culture, 1990–1998*, trans. by Leslie A. Adelson (Lincoln: University of Nebraska Press, 2001), 26.

[13] Andrea Böhm, "Wir werden diese Gesellschaft ein bißchen umkrempeln," *Die Tageszeitung*, 13 November 1990, 12.

foreigners that erupted in the wake of German unity (Figure 3).[14] In the midst of the crowd, a middle-aged immigrant man hoists a homemade placard announcing: *Wir sind auch das Volk* (we are also the people). This clever twist on the original Leipzig slogan infused the old ideal of an ethnically homogeneous German community with a radical new meaning. *Das Volk*, the sign suggested, now included not only ethnic Germans from East and West, but foreign-born guest workers and their descendants as well. In a sense, the demonstrator's appropriation of *das Volk* constituted a vernacular expression of Deleuze and Guattari's "indigestible kernel": it was a public act that cut against commonsensical assumptions about the relationship between ethnicity, language, and national identity. The gesture also took up Şenocak's charge for migrants to engage actively in the project of constructing a collective German future. Here was an effort to reshape the outmoded, nineteenth-century idea of nation into a usable concept for a multiethnic German society.

These critiques from the early 1990s raise a key historical question for this study. What exactly were the broader consequences of reunification for the guest worker question? More than a decade and a half after the event, it may still be too early to assess accurately the effects of what was lost, deferred, or eclipsed as one national debate gave way to another. The key lesson may be that these debates were inextricably interwoven, although it has taken some time for the complex ideological linkages to become fully visible. At the very least, it seems important to consider the various ways in which problems of migration were central to the history of the reunification period. As historian Konrad Jarausch has recently noted, the rush to German unity itself was spurred by the migration of thousands of political refugees from the GDR and the prospect of an even greater influx.[15] Even after East Germany established free movement between the two countries in November 1989, the exodus continued at a rate of around two thousand people per day until the end of 1990. Less well understood is the process by which the volatile flux of reunification began to produce new questions of national identity and belonging.

The most obvious – and chilling – place to begin is with the sharp increase in attacks on foreigners between 1991 and 1993. The wave of violence spread across both eastern and western parts of Germany, as young hooligans, skinheads, and right-wing extremists carried out a series of vicious assaults, often to the chorus of "Foreigners out" and "Germany

[14] N.a., "Schluß mit dem Terror," *Die Tageszeitung*, 1 June 1993, 5.
[15] Jarausch, *Rush to Germany Unity*, 20–32.

FIGURE 3. Protester carrying a placard that proclaims, "We are also the people." Courtesy of Andreas Schoelzel, www.schoelzel.net.

for the Germans." In September 1991, the hostility reached a new level in the depressed eastern town of Hoyerswerda.[16] For nearly a week, gangs of young men, cheered on by hundreds of residents, besieged two apartment complexes that housed contract laborers from Mozambique and Vietnam who had been hired by the now defunct GDR. Armed with knives, rocks, bottles, and Molotov cocktails, the youths surrounded and blockaded the buildings. One man told newspaper reporters, "We are going to stay here until the blacks are gone."[17] Despite dozens of arrests, local police could not contain the violence and eventually used the cover of night to evacuate all 230 foreigners to the safety of a nearby army base. Two aspects of the attack seem especially important: First, this escalated aggression broke out in the weeks leading up to the first anniversary of German reunification. Second, the decision to remove the foreigners marked the first time German political leaders heeded the demands of violent extremists. In the aftermath, residents of Hoyerswerda appeared on national television and jubilantly proclaimed their town "foreigner-free."[18]

A similar attack took place on a refugee hostel in the eastern German city of Rostock in August 1992. Again, several hundred right-wing youths threw stones and homemade explosives into the building, which lodged asylum-seeking Gypsies from Romania and contract workers from Vietnam. Again, thousands of bystanders applauded and supported the assault over successive days. And again, local authorities were paralyzed by the intensity of the outbreak, finally slipping the victims to safety in a nearby former military barracks. This spate of violence intensified with a pair of deadly arson attacks in the West. On 23 November 1992, two skinheads set fire to the home of a Turkish family in Mölln, killing two girls and their grandmother. And on 29 May 1993, four German youths firebombed the house of another Turkish family in Solingen, killing five women and girls.[19] What all of these incidents help us to see is that the

---

[16] Already during 1991 there had been sporadic attacks against foreigners, including an incident in Dresden, where a Mozambican contract laborer hired by the GDR was pushed to his death from a moving street car.

[17] Leon Mangasarian, "Police Evacuate Mozambicans after Racist Attacks in Eastern Germany," *United Press International*, 21 September 1991.

[18] Stephen Kinzer, "A Wave of Attacks on Foreigners Stirs Shock in Germany," *New York Times*, 1 October 1991, Sect. 1, 1.

[19] For several useful scholarly discussions of the violence against foreigners in the Federal Republic during the early 1990s, see Gabriele Nandlinger, "Chronik der Gewalt," in Klaus Henning Rosen, ed., *Die zweite Vertreibung: Fremde in Deutschland* (Bonn: J. H. W. Dietz, 1992), 119–58; Claus Leggewie, *Druck von rechts: Wohin treibt die Bundesrepublik?* (Munich: C. H. Beck, 1993); and Armin Pfahl-Traughber, *Rechtsextremismus: Eine kritische Bestandaufnahme nach der Wiedervereinigung* (Bonn: Bouvier, 1993).

guest worker question was never simply "contested" at the level of representation and rhetoric. Rather, struggles over the boundaries of German national identity routinely spilled over into life-and-death questions of citizenship, civil liberties, and basic protections against bodily harm.

These xenophobic attacks functioned as a kind of grassroots refusal to accept the primary lesson of migrant presence: Germany had become a multiethnic society during the postwar period and the ideal of a reconstituted homogeneous German *Volk* was no longer possible. On one level, at least, the violence itself was a brutal, visceral attempt to keep migrants out of the national body (as well as the post-unification debates about national identity). But there were clearly other socioeconomic issues in play here, too. As numerous commentators noted, skyrocketing unemployment plagued much of the East immediately following unification, fueling deep disappointment about the material rewards of a reunited German state. Meanwhile, resentment grew in the West as the federal government allocated large sums of money and resources to aid the new eastern states. Yet neither of these factors fully explains the ideological significance of the cheering onlookers in Hoyerswerda and Rostock. One source of the applause seems to have been a collective desire to remove migrants from the national imaginary – to create a "foreigner-free" Germany. Or perhaps the goal was actually more modest: to insist that the very presence of migrants on German soil represented an affront to the bystanders' dreams of reunification.

Of course, this scenario constituted an extreme position. Most Germans were deeply troubled by such xenophobic violence and, in fact, thousands protested each of these major attacks. The question of who was protesting in this context is important as well. After the riots in Hoyerswerda and Rostock, several thousand demonstrators from western Germany descended on both cities to condemn the brutality, provoking clashes with the police and local residents. According to a *U.S. News & World Report* journalist on the scene, even casual conversations had the potential to "erupt in rage." When Rostock resident Klaus Goetze criticized Georg Classen for coming from the West to demonstrate, for example, a furious Classen "shouted back: 'I'm here because I'm German, and it's the duty of all Germans to stand up at this moment and protest!'"[20] This sentiment was reaffirmed by tens of thousands who took to the streets all over the country to denounce the attacks in Mölln and Solingen.

---

[20] John Marks, "The Fight for a New Germany's Soul," *U.S. News & World Report*, 113, No. 10 (14 September 1992), 22. I include this American news source because it provides a perspective on the riots quite unlike any of those captured in the German media.

Between December 1992 and January 1993, in fact, nearly two million people (or one in every forty) throughout Germany demonstrated their rejection of the violence by participating in candlelight vigils.[21]

But what precisely was at stake here? Certainly part of the outrage articulated by the protestors seems to have derived from the raw brutality of the attacks on foreigners and the conviction that such horrific acts should never again take place on German soil without vociferous public condemnation. As an editorial in Dresden's main newspaper *Sächsische Zeitung* explained, "The great value of the candlelight vigils is moral and psychological. They tell violent rightwing extremists and those who support them that they are on the wrong side, and that society will not silently accept their acts."[22] But these public demonstrations were also very much a protest against the defilement of Germany's image as a civilized and peaceful European society whose liberal-democratic credentials had been meticulously established over the previous half century.

On the whole, German newspaper coverage of the antiforeigner attacks relayed the details of specific episodes rather than offering commentary on the broader meaning of the violence. Occasionally, however, individual articles pointed to the larger political and ideological implications. In the final paragraphs of a lengthy *Süddeutsche Zeitung* article, for instance, a reporter drew the following conclusion about the Hoyerswerda riots: "Even if this operation [to relocate foreigners] had been staged without violence, it would remain a shameful success for the radical right."[23] By characterizing the police operation in response to the extremists' actions as "shameful," the reporter implicitly extended responsibility for the incident beyond its immediate perpetrators to German society as a whole. What seemed to trigger this "shame" was not so much the violence per se, but the assumptions driving the violence. The Africans and Asians under attack, the reporter noted, were actually scheduled to leave Germany a mere two months later, when their labor contracts expired. The pogrom in Hoyerswerda, in other words, was not really about the presence of these particular contract workers. Rather, it was part of a more general desire to rid Germany of foreigners. The reporter emphasized this point by quoting one of the Mozambican victims: "Even if we're going away anyway, they now want all foreigners to disappear."

---

[21] Stephen Kinzer, "Germany Ablaze: It's Candlelight, Not Firebombs," *New York Times*, 13 January 1993, Sect. 1, 4, cited in Jarausch and Gransow, *Uniting Germany*, 268.

[22] Jarausch and Gransow, *Uniting Germany*, 269.

[23] Knut Pries, "Die Krawalle in Hoyerswerda," *Süddeutsche Zeitung*, 24 September 1991, 3.

Some editorial pages drew much more explicit lessons from the violence. Less than a month after Hoyerswerda, for example, *Süddeutsche Zeitung* argued that the recent riots in the east were part of a resurgence of xenophobia that had begun even before reunification. Evidence of this pattern included the desecration of Jewish cemeteries in the former West by skinheads and the brutal attacks on "contract foreigners" that the SED "carefully hushed up." The collapse of East Germany, the newspaper claimed, "blazed a trail of aggression that no one opposed," creating "a training ground for right-wing radicals from the west who could dare to do in the east what they had not previously risked in the Federal Republic." Whereas the state had exerted all of its power against left-wing terrorism in the 1970s and 1980s, current eruptions of *Ausländerfeindlichkeit* produced surprisingly little in the way of concerted government action. "Every threatened hostel," the essay concluded, constituted a fundamental challenge to the rule of law: "We demand protection of the constitution, police, and justice. We demand a politics which opposes extremism.... And the integration of the foreigners residing here must no longer be the sole task of the groups we call the 'foreigner lobby.' The legal state must begin an offensive against the hatred of foreigners."[24]

A year later, the well-known public intellectual Hans-Magnus Enzensberger echoed these sentiments in a special issue on reunified Germany by the British publication *Granta*. The key question for Enzensberger was not so much the problem of foreigners or the asylum law, but rather the state's monopoly of force: "No one can say that [the government] ever hesitated to make use of this monopoly of might if it seemed threatened.... But in the past months not even the most insignificant use has been made of this arsenal of repression. Indeed, the police and the courts have responded to the mass-scale appearance of gangs of thugs with a previously unheard-of restraint."[25] This "laissez-faire approach" threatened to make Germany uninhabitable for all, "whatever their passport or stamp or legitimacy." "I call a place uninhabitable," Enzensberger explained, "where a gang of thugs is allowed to attack a person in the middle of the street or set fire to his house. Is it possible to live with people who set out on organized manhunts?"[26] He predicted that the state's refusal to protect threatened individuals could force those individuals to arm themselves, leading to gang wars with right-wing thugs: "We will all recognize the political

[24] Heribert Prantl, "Eine deutsche Pubertät," *Süddeutsche Zeitung*, 10 October 1991.
[25] Hans-Magnus Enzensberger, "The Great Migration," *Granta* 42 (1992): 48–51.
[26] Ibid., 48.

conditions: they are the same that Germany experienced toward the end of the Weimar Republic."[27]

For some critics, then, the central problem was the government's striking unwillingness to take action in the face of xenophobic violence. But it is probably more accurate to say that government leaders actively responded to the violence by pushing in a very different policy direction. Local officials such as the interior minister of the state of Saxony, Rudolf Krause, explained the Hoyerswerda attacks by pointing to the abuse of Germany's asylum law.[28] His colleague, Saxon Minister President Kurt Biedenkopf, in turn, demanded a drastic reduction in the number of asylum seekers sent to the new (eastern) states.[29] At the federal level, German President Richard von Weizsäcker publicly decried the assaults as "horrifying and shameful," and one Bundestag representative described the violence as a "return to barbarism."[30] But by and large, leading policymakers emphasized the causal relationship between xenophobic attacks and the nation's liberal asylum provision. Federal Interior Minister Wolfgang Schäuble repeatedly blamed the antiforeigner violence on the massive influx of refugees, adding that "large portions of the population" were alarmed at the "increase in asylum seekers."[31] "Germany is friendly to foreigners and will remain so," Schäuble declared, "but this can only happen if the concerns of our citizens are heeded." He thus urged the Kohl administration to take immediate steps to stem the "uncontrollable flow" of foreigners.[32]

The government's response constituted an ideological step backward, a return to assumptions, rhetorics, and modes of analysis from the early 1980s. Instead of perceiving the attacked as *ausländische Mitbürger* (foreign fellow citizens) who were entitled to legal protection, politicians like Schäuble viewed them as mere "foreigners" whose presence understandably provoked neo-Nazi violence. In this respect, policymakers

---

[27] Ibid., 51. The historian Klaus Bade has also argued that the government reacted "much less systematically to the extremism of the Right than it had years ago to the extremism of the Left," although he attributed this difference to the diffusion and disorganization of skinheads and right extremists in the early 1990s. See Klaus J. Bade, "Immigration and Social Peace in United Germany," *Daedalus* 123.1 (1994): 95.

[28] Pries, "Die Krawalle in Hoyerswerda," 3.

[29] Giovanni di Lorenzo, "Der Mob siegt in Hoyerswerda," *Süddeutsche Zeitung*, 25 September 1991.

[30] Stephen Kinzer, "A Wave of Attacks on Foreigners Stirs Shock in Germany," *New York Times*, 1 October 1991, Sect. 1, 1.

[31] David Gow, "Bonn Condemns Neo-Nazi Clashes," *The Guardian*, 24 September 1991.

[32] Kinzer, "Wave of Attacks," 1.

reinvigorated the older, clear-cut distinction between native and foreigner that had begun to be challenged by the debates on German multicultural-ism in the late 1980s. Their approach collapsed foreigners into a monolith, treating recently arrived asylum seekers and long-resident guest workers and their families as essentially the same. Authorities also reverted to the pattern of fixating on numbers, a mindset that implicitly placed very strict limits on the scope of multiethnic diversity. Such an outlook posited a kind of threshold for migrants in German society: once the size of the foreigner population exceeded a certain level, xenophobic violence would become almost inevitable.

This posture on the part of high-level government officials further fueled and legitimized an already growing public perception that Germany was being flooded with foreigners, an image crystallized in several books of sensationalistic reportage that portrayed the increase in asylum seek-ers as a "storm," "threat," and "invasion."[33] In terms of policymak-ing, the strategy of using asylum seekers to address a much broader wave of antiforeigner sentiment dominated the country's domestic agenda for well over a year, as the Kohl administration focused its energies on passing a more restrictive asylum law. Most opponents of the effort – including both Free Democrats (the CDU's junior coalition partner) and Social Democrats – balked at the prospect of amending Article 16 of the Basic Law because of its historic anti-Nazi significance. Oth-ers expressed reservations about the policy's underlying logic. During a Bundestag debate in September 1992, Hans-Ulrich Klose, parliamen-tary leader of the SPD, declared that "it would be disastrous to say that the attacks against foreigners would not have happened if the asylum law had been changed earlier. Whoever maintains this therefore concedes that the attackers from Rostock and elsewhere were right."[34] Klose here rejected the attempt to explain right-wing violence as a direct result of the high numbers of refugees. Nevertheless, he and many in his party were willing to consider a revision of the asylum law as long as it did not deny the basic principle of an individual's right to apply for political protection.

In December 1992, the CDU reached a compromise with its FDP coalition partner and the SPD opposition that provided the necessary

---

[33] See, for example, Manfred Ritter, *Sturm auf Europa: Asylanten und Armutsflüchtlinge. Droht eine neue Völkerwanderung?* (Munich: von Hase & Koehler, 1990); and Jan Werner, *Die Invasion der Armen: Asylanten und illegale Einwanderer* (Munich: von Hase & Koehler, 1992).

[34] N.a., "Bundestag-Asyl," *Süddeutsche Zeitung*, 10 September 1992.

two-thirds majority for a constitutional amendment. The change did not alter the original guarantee (attached to the individual rather than the state) that "persons persecuted on political grounds shall enjoy the right of asylum." Rather, it streamlined the asylum procedure. The new rules stipulated the immediate rejection of any application by refugees who entered Germany through a European Community country or any other so-called "safe country" where no persecution was believed to exist (e.g., Poland and the Czech Republic). The reform additionally established a quicker decision and appeal process in order to minimize the waiting period for a ruling on applications. These modifications sought to reduce the perceived abuse of the asylum guarantee by economic refugees and to alleviate the burden placed on German social services to house and feed asylum seekers while their status was being determined. But in so doing, it also reinforced the general public perception that neo-Nazi violence had at its core a more reasonable (or at least understandable) list of complaints. Driving the asylum debates was a shared sentiment that something needed to be done about the "foreigner problem" in the Federal Republic.

In one sense, then, the widespread public hand-wringing about asylum seekers can be read as a specific set of responses to the immediate problem of post-unification violence against migrants of varying types and backgrounds. What the asylum debates fostered was a kind of ideological quick fix. By stanching the flow of refugees, government officials sought to position themselves as attentive to public discontent about foreigners more generally. Yet these developments during the early 1990s bring us back to perhaps the most important question of the period after reunification: How can the time lag between assertions in the late 1980s that Germany had become an irrevocably multiethnic society and the passing of a new federal citizenship law that would put such ideological assumptions into political and legal practice be explained? In actual fact, it was not until 1998, when the SPD-Green coalition came to power under the leadership of Gerhard Schröder, that the drive to overhaul Germany's citizenship law became a top priority. And even then, a year and a half of fierce parliamentary struggle ensued before the Bundestag formally enacted the new code on 1 January 2000.

The change in the citizenship law augmented the 1913 definition of German nationality, which had determined belonging on the basis of ethnic descent or blood (the principle of *jus sanguinis*). The law now also granted citizenship according to place of birth (the principle of *jus soli*) and, for the first time, automatically bestowed this status on children born in the Federal Republic to non-German parents. In terms of process, the right to automatic citizenship only accrued to children with at least one parent who had resided in the Federal Republic for eight or more years and held either an *Aufenthaltsberechtigung* (residence entitlement) or an *unbefristete Aufenthaltserlaubnis* (unrestricted residence permit) for at least three years. The new law also required any child receiving German citizenship on the basis of *jus soli* formally to choose German citizenship upon reaching the age of majority or lose German nationality by the age of twenty-three.

Perhaps the best-known analysis of the German citizenship reform process comes from sociologist Christian Joppke.[35] He has explained the Federal Republic's stubborn reluctance to revise its citizenship law by pointing to the country's founding national self-definition: because West Germany "defined itself as a vicarious, incomplete nation-state, home for all Germans in the communist diaspora," it "prioritized the immigration of co-ethnics" at the expense of a more expansive policy that would include guest workers and their families.[36] As soon as the Federal Republic had fulfilled its historic obligation by reconstituting the German nation-state, according to Joppke, political leaders abandoned their insistence on an exclusively ethno-cultural model of state member-ship and liberalized the requirements for citizenship status.

The strength of this approach is that it underscores how much the battle over ideology matters. Joppke helps us to see the particular ide-ological framework for German identity, culture, and nation that drove the resistance to citizenship reform prior to 1990. Still, several points in his interpretation suggest the need for further analysis. His argument, for example, hinges on a very specific ideological inheritance that shaped the thinking of government authorities on citizenship. The relative speed of the legal reforms after reunification demonstrates for Joppke that it was simply overcoming the problem of two Germanys that triggered the willingness of legislators to revise the parameters for national belonging. It is no doubt correct to suggest that the long-harbored dream of reunifica-tion carried some weight. Yet this framework is very selective in terms of what kinds of ideological struggle count. If one brings the public debates

---

[35] See especially Christian Joppke, "How Immigration Is Changing Citizenship: A Compar-ative View," *Ethnic and Racial Studies* 22.4 (1999): 629–52; and Christian Joppke, *Immi-gration and the Nation-State: The United States, Germany, and Great Britain* (Oxford: Oxford University Press, 1999). My point here is not to issue critiques specific to Joppke himself, but rather to make a case for the need to historicize the ideological process through which citizenship reforms emerge over time. As a comparative sociological study of citizenship, Joppke's work is an important and helpful intervention. It is at the level of historical causality that I seek to complicate his story.

[36] Joppke, *Immigration and the Nation-State*, 63.

on multiculturalism into the historical narrative of citizenship reform, the impact of reunification seems to push in precisely the opposite direction. West German society was on the verge of a real ideological breakthrough in the late 1980s when the CDU's Heiner Geißler and cultural critics such as Hilmar Hoffmann publicly declared the Federal Republic to be a multicultural society. But both the euphoria and the unexpected difficulties of forging a unified nation constituted a massive disruption that upended and postponed serious engagement with the legal consequences of this heterogeneity for more than a decade.

Another key issue involves the questions of how and where to mark the origins of the citizenship reform process. Joppke's political study focuses on juridical status as the key criterion for measuring meaningful change. In his portrait, the moment of citizenship revision – enacted by politicians and legislators – largely overshadows the broader ideological, social, and cultural struggles over the previous forty years that made the legal reform desirable or even possible. What disappears from this framework is the agency of migrants themselves and their decades-long efforts to claim a space within the national body. Even before migrants enjoyed officially sanctioned channels of political participation they found alternative ways to shape the terms of public debate about a new set of core principles for sociability and belonging. A much more complex picture of the change emerges if we view the 2000 citizenship reform not as the starting point for the reevaluation of German identity, but rather as the culmination of a much longer cultural and ideological process extending back to the mid-1950s.

This argument points to a broader need to reconsider the place of the guest worker question within the master narratives of postwar Germany. In recent decades, scholars have built an image of the period around a familiar set of issues: Allied occupation and the Cold War, the legacy of the Holocaust and process of mastering the past, the development of the welfare state and ideologies of domesticity, the "economic miracle" and the politics of consumption, and democratization and reunification.[37] For the most part, the guest worker question has been understood as

---

[37] For a highly useful overview of historical work on West Germany, see Robert G. Moeller, "Introduction: Writing the History of West Germany," in Robert G. Moeller, ed., *West Germany under Construction: Politics, Society, and Culture in the Adenauer Era* (Ann Arbor: University of Michigan Press, 1997), 1–30. For a more recent and somewhat broader topography of twentieth-century and especially postwar German history and historiography, see Michael Geyer and Konrad H. Jarausch, *Shattered Past: Reconstructing German Histories* (Princeton: Princeton University Press, 2003).

peripheral to these national stories or as a topic to be examined within
the separate field of "minority studies" (patterns that to some extent recapitulate the ideological assumptions of the labor recruitment program
itself).[38] At this point, however, it is difficult to maintain such a logic.
As we have seen, the labor recruitment was less a footnote to the economic miracle than one of its sustaining forces. Likewise, the ongoing
national debates on democratization and normative gender relations ultimately dovetailed with questions of ethnic and religious difference that
the guest worker program introduced. What ultimately links the current
strands of postwar historical narrative is the problem of reconstructing
national identity. And on the most fundamental level, the struggle over
what it means to be German is precisely what the guest worker question
was always about. Coming to terms with the labor recruitment, in other
words, was a decidedly national project with far-reaching consequences
that marked the Federal Republic in the Cold War period and continue
to shape German culture and politics today.

German Diversity and the New Europe

At this juncture it is also possible to make some general observations about
how the German guest worker question fits within the larger history of
migration to Europe after World War II. Generally speaking, the guest
worker system entailed a common approach to migrants. Countries that
subscribed to this model, including the Federal Republic, Switzerland,
and Austria, expected the sojourn of foreign laborers to be temporary and
initially targeted single men who were supposed to return home as soon
as their labor was no longer required. Yet none of these nations was able
to prevent long-term residence and family reunion; each one eventually
faced the social, cultural, and political pressures of de facto immigrant
settlement. Within this framework, as Stephen Castles and Mark Miller
have noted, West Germany produced the most developed form of "all the
principles – but also the contradictions" built in to temporary labor
recruitment.[39] The Federal Republic imported the highest number of guest
workers, laying the foundation for the growth of the largest foreign community in Europe; at the same time, West Germans were the most resistant

[38] One might argue, for example, that our tendency to confine scholarship on guest workers
to minority studies serves to reinscribe the older binary distinctions of German/foreign,
center/margin, and so forth.
[39] Stephen Castles and Mark J. Miller, *The Age of Migration: International Population
Movements in the Modern World*, 3rd ed. (New York: Guilford Press, 2003), 71.

to developing new parameters of identity, culture, and citizenship that would incorporate migrants into the nation.

The other dominant model of postwar migration involved the creation of postcolonial societies, as exemplified by Great Britain, France, and the Netherlands. These countries did not typically recruit former colonials to satisfy the demand for surplus manpower. Rather, such migrants came to the metropole on their own initiative in search of employment. What made this seemingly spontaneous immigration possible was the fact that the laborers were already nationals of the former colonial power – and if they did not enjoy the formal status of nationals, they were at least entitled to enter, live, and work there. Such privileges were originally extended to colonized subjects to construct a common sense of belonging as a mechanism for empire building. But one basic premise of colonialism assumed that, except in rare cases, only Europeans traveled between colony and metropole. The imperial powers, in fact, never imagined that large numbers of "native peoples" would claim the rights of entry and citizenship in this new way.

It is important to emphasize that these two different frameworks for postwar migration produced distinct political effects. Because the German system framed the presence of labor recruits as a temporary expedient, guest workers and their families remained outsiders, officially categorized as "foreigners." Until 1992, even those who had been born, raised, and educated in the Federal Republic did not have the right to become citizens and thus were shut out of the conventional channels for political participation. In postcolonial societies such as Britain and France, by contrast, the legacy of empire meant that immigrants did not have to fight in the same way for basic political rights. Many qualified automatically for citizenship, and those who did not were entitled (and even encouraged) to naturalize. From this perspective, the German model seems remarkably retrograde. It took the Federal Republic almost a full half century to begin to offer legal civic inclusion to its postwar migrants.

Yet this stark contrast between migration models only really works to the extent that we bracket out citizenship from ideology and culture. In the case of France, the liberal nationality code was not just a product of empire, but part of a tradition of promoting immigration in order to bolster a declining birthrate.[40] The relative accessibility of citizenship

[40] Several migration scholars have made this point, including Leslie P. Moch, *Moving Europeans: Migration in Western Europe since 1650* (Bloomington: Indiana University Press, 1992); and Saskia Sassen, *Guests and Aliens* (New York: The New Press, 1999), 64–65. For more on French anxieties about the declining birthrate, which began in the nineteenth

went hand in hand with the assumption that immigrants would give up their own customs and adopt the values of French society. As scholar of French literature Alec Hargreaves has observed, the republican tradition "appears universalist and egalitarian" from a political perspective, but "it is particularist and intolerant" in terms of culture.[41] In the well-known Foulard affair, for example, three Muslim girls were suspended in 1989 for wearing headscarves at a state-sponsored school. The headmaster justified his decision by arguing that the girls violated the French law of *laïcité* (secularism), which requires a formal separation of church and state. When Minister of Education Lionel Jospin overturned their expulsion, prominent intellectuals (including Régis Debray and Alain Finkielkraut) decried the reversal as an appeasement of Islamic forces that threatened the core principles of French society.[42] At the level of day-to-day practice, then, the guarantee of citizenship often came with a remarkably strict insistence on cultural conformity.

The situation in postwar Britain was somewhat more complicated. Until the 1962 Commonwealth Immigrants Act, Britain did not make a practical distinction between citizens of the United Kingdom and Colonies (UKC, inhabitants of the British Isles and its colonial possessions), and British subjects (all members of the Commonwealth, including the British Isles, the colonies, and former colonies). Like UKC citizens, all British subjects enjoyed the right to free entry, residence, employment, and suffrage in the United Kingdom.[43] With the influx of former colonials in the post-1945 period, however, the British government sought to maintain universal subjecthood even as it worked to prevent further unwanted immigration. The primary strategy, according to historian Kathleen Paul, was to introduce "competing definitions and communities

century, see E. van de Walle, *The Female Population of France in the Nineteenth Century* (Princeton: Princeton University Press, 1974); Noel Bonneuil, *Transformation of the French Demographic Landscape, 1806–1906* (Oxford: Clarendon, 1997); Joshua Cole, *The Power of Large Numbers: Population, Politics, and Gender in Nineteenth-Century France* (Ithaca, NY: Cornell University Press, 2000).

41 Alec G. Hargreaves, *Immigration, "Race," and Ethnicity in Contemporary France* (London: Routledge, 1995), 162.

42 For more on the headscarf controversy, see David Beriss, "Scarves, Schools, and Segregation: The Foulard Affair," *French Politics and Society* 8.1 (1990): 1–13; Hargreaves, "Immigration," 125–31; and John R. Bowen, "Muslims and Citizens: France's Headscarf Controversy," *Boston Review* February/March (2004): 31–35.

43 In fact, the category of "citizen of the United Kingdom and Colonies" was not created until 1948 in response to the Canadian government's decision to define a distinct category of Canadian national citizenship that would supersede British subjecthood. See Kathleen Paul, *Whitewashing Britain: Race and Citizenship in the Postwar Era* (Ithaca, NY: Cornell University Press, 1997), 14–17.

of Britishness which reflect[ed] separate spheres of nationality: an inclusive formal nationality policy and an exclusive informal national identity."[44] The Commonwealth Immigrants Act, for instance, did not regulate entry into the United Kingdom by revising the definition of British subject, but by singling out unskilled British subjects for yearly quotas.[45] According to Home Secretary Rab Butler, the "great merit" of the new law was that it seemed color-blind even though in practice "its restrictive effect [wa]s intended to, and would in fact, operate on coloured people almost exclusively."[46] In short, after 1962 British policy created racialized spheres of national identity: "the imperial, familial community consisting of white-skinned Britons" remained largely exempt from the letter of immigration law, "while the political community of Britishness consisting of black-skinned Britons" faced tighter restrictions.[47]

More explicitly than France or Germany, then, Britain used the concept of race to mark and enforce social exclusion. Whereas German critics routinely referred to the "foreigner problem," similar debates in Britain were generally described as "race relations." Postwar racial discourse, moreover, was increasingly defined in terms of essentialized cultural differences. As Paul Gilroy has observed, commonsense understandings of race specified who could "legitimately belong to the national community and simultaneously advance[d] reasons for the segregation or banishment" of West Indians and Asians, whose culture and identity "assign[ed] them elsewhere."[48]

At the ground level, both the guest worker and the postcolonial frameworks understood minority populations as perpetually liminal groups, connected to but never quite fully within the boundaries of the nation. In terms of ideology, then, the key differences in migration models had more to do with what kind of liminal position each group was perceived to occupy – and how that liminality was enforced. The pattern in Britain

---

[44] Ibid., 13.
[45] But Paul explains that the new law "created a class of British subjects who were defined as 'belonging' to the United Kingdom and were not subject to immigration control." This group included those who had been born in the United Kingdom or whose passport had been issued on behalf of the United Kigndom. Ibid., 167.
[46] Quoted in Ibid., 166.
[47] Ibid., 173.
[48] Paul Gilroy, *There Ain't No Black in the Union Jack: The Cultural Politics of Race and Nation* (Chicago: University of Chicago Press, 1987), 45–46. This postwar discourse on race was famously described by Martin Barker as the "new racism." See Martin Barker, *The New Racism* (London: Junction Books, 1981).

was to use culture as the very basis for racial formation. This hardening of categories of racial difference supported a system of caste in which nonwhite migrants were understood as the de facto underclass. In France, despite the public rhetoric about equality and universally accessible republican ideals, the intellectual left questioned the willingness and ability of postcolonial migrants to adapt to *laïcité*, while conservatives claimed that anything short of total conformity represented a threat to the nation (as if children wearing headscarves served as agents of fundamentalist contagion).

These arguments about cultural incommensurability echoed the debates in the Federal Republic during the 1980s, when German politicians, journalists, and activists employed criticism of Turkish gender relations to support broader generalizations about the failure of integration. Thus, despite the very different political contexts and historical circumstances, each system produced similar ideological results: migrants were perceived as an ongoing danger to the democratic values of the host country and cultural differences (especially when culture equaled religion) served an essentializing function previously ascribed to biology and/or genealogy. Both postcolonial and guest worker migration models relied upon relatively fixed conceptions of ethnicity, regardless of legal status.

The basic assumptions underlying this logic of incommensurability have emerged somewhat more starkly in the recent debates about a specifically European culture. In 2003, the German philosopher Jürgen Habermas, together with his French counterpart Jacques Derrida, issued an urgent plea for a common European vision grounded in the shared heritage of Western civilization.[49] The Italian author Umberto Eco's contribution to this call included an inventory of the characteristics of a core Europe:

the fundamental principles of the so-called Western world, the Greek and Judeo-Christian heritage, the ideas of freedom and equality born out of the French

---

[49] The Habermas-Derrida intervention was part of a project spearheaded by Habermas in order to provoke public discussion about Europe's place in the world in the wake of the Iraq war. Habermas enlisted a number of leading European intellectuals to write articles on this issue and arranged for these contributions to appear on 31 May 2003 in leading daily newspapers in Germany, France, Italy, Spain, and Switzerland. See Jürgen Habermas and Jacques Derrida, "February 15, Or, What Binds Europeans Together: Plea for a Common Foreign Policy, Beginning in a Core Europe," in Daniel Levy, Max Pensky, and John Torpey, eds., *Old Europe, New Europe, Core Europe: Transatlantic Relations after the Iraq War* (London: Verso, 2005), 3–13.

Revolution, the heritage of modern science that started with Copernicus, Galileo, Kepler, Descartes, and Francis Bacon, the capitalistic form of production, the secularization of the State, Roman or Common Law, the very idea of justice achieved through class struggle.[50]

What was especially striking about this initiative was the unselfconscious way it engaged in boundary-drawing and cultural demarcation. Indeed, the very call for a common European vision presupposed a basic distinction between a "core Europe" and that which lay beyond. And one major effect of the public identification of unique values, traditions, and histories was to mark the line not so much between Europe and the United States (the joint effort's ostensible target), but rather between Europe and its largely Muslim minorities.

This broader set of contexts helps us to clarify the Federal Republic's position within the New Europe. Our tendency has been to think of West Germany as the major exception in the post-1945 period because of its relatively modest colonial empire during the nineteenth century and also its reliance on temporary labor recruitment as the engine driving its multiethnic diversity. I would suggest, however, that a number of arguments push against this portrait. First, most former colonials, came to the metropole for jobs. In both contexts, then, labor migration served as the primary catalyst for transnational movement and social change after 1945. Second, in strictly quantitative terms, West Germany had more foreign residents than any other European country, including France and Britain, between 1955 and 1990.[51] Third, and most significantly, the very idea of the New Europe as a postcolonial product has been dramatically transformed in recent years. As our understanding of empire has shifted from the nineteenth-century model of foreign imperialism and colonization to a late twentieth-century framework that includes the movement of global capital,[52] West Germany's massive labor migration becomes an increasingly crucial case for grasping how this process has operated in the European context. The Federal Republic now looks more and more like the rule rather than the exception: its particular pathways of migration and integration have enormous resonance for how we make sense of the

[50] Umberto Eco, "An Uncertain Europe Between Rebirth and Decline," in Levy et al., *Old Europe*, 15.
[51] Castles and Miller, *Age of Migration*, 80–81.
[52] For more on this new conception of empire see Saskia Sassen, *Globalization and Its Discontents: Essays on the New Mobility of People and Money* (New York: The New Press, 1998); and Michael Hardt and Antonio Negri, *Empire* (Cambridge, MA: Harvard University Press, 2000).

power dynamics and cross-cultural relations that the new model of empire fosters.

West Germany represents the great paradox within the New Europe. On the one hand, its lack of a well-developed colonial framework for difference and citizenship – and especially its prolonged resistance to legal guarantees of civic equality and political participation – often make it seem like the migration model most opposed to meaningful multiethnic democracy. Yet the very fact that West Germany's multiethnic society developed largely outside the nexus of colonialism – and thus required some other framework for multiethnic coexistence – has often produced public debates about pluralism far more ambitious than the rhetorics of one-way assimilation generally championed in postcolonial societies.

Armando Rodrigues Returns

The guest worker question continues to be negotiated in complex ways in Germany today. Consider, for example, the museum exhibition held in 1999 at Berlin's Martin Gropius Bau to commemorate the fiftieth anniversary of the Federal Republic, "Unity and Law and Freedom: Paths of Germans, 1949–1999."[53] One of the most interesting features of the show was the return of the image with which I began the book: Armando Rodrigues's motorcycle. Amid advertising placards for postwar German products such as Pfanni and Aral, a diorama of a set from Bertolt Brecht's *Mother Courage* and movie posters for *Jacob the Liar* and the *Tin Drum* stood the motorbike presented to the one-millionth guest worker thirty-five years before. Locating, retrieving, and including this artifact had not been an easy task. Rodrigues, it turned out, went back to Portugal in the late 1970s and eventually died from a work-related illness. Nevertheless, curators tracked down Rodrigues's family, who agreed to sell the motorcycle for exhibition.[54] Rodrigues's gift thereby completed a kind of grand historical circuit: what had first served as a promotional tool for economic boosterism now returned as a major symbol of national history and collective memory.

This exhibition – a half century removed from the Third Reich – offers some important clues about how the labor migration has reshaped the

---

[53] The exhibit was officially opened by the former Chancellor Helmut Kohl and ran from 23 May 1999 to 3 October 1999. It was organized cooperatively by curators for the Deutsches Historisches Museum in Berlin, the Haus der Geschichte in Bonn, and other art and exhibition halls throughout the country.

[54] It is now part of the permanent collection of the Haus der Geschichte in Bonn.

most fundamental aspects of German self-understanding and national culture. In 1964, Rodrigues was figured in public discourse as fully marginal to West German identity. While officials preached a mantra of mutual benefits, they also insisted that guest workers were just that – temporary labor. The motorcycle underscored his transience: Rodrigues was a man on the move, metaphorically and legally constituted as liminal. In 1999, by contrast, the motorcycle signified a defining event in the nation's history. Within the exhibition, both the motorcycle and the labor migration were represented – and revalued – as historical motors for the creation of multiethnic German democracy.[55] The decision to include this artifact points to the kind of historical revisionism that I have been advocating here, one that understands the labor migration as a foundational event in the constitution of the modern German nation.

This way of understanding postwar German history has not been embraced in universal terms. One need look no further than the regular reports of violence against foreigners on the front pages of leading German newspapers to appreciate just how much the guest worker question remains a flash point of political and social struggle. One could also point to the position on Turkish migrants taken by some of the country's well-known public intellectuals. Consider, for example, Hans-Ulrich Wehler, a decidedly liberal voice in contemporary political debate and one of the nation's most prominent historians. Already in the early 1980s, Wehler sought to differentiate Catholic Italians from Anatolian Muslims, suggesting that certain foreigners simply could not be successfully integrated into West German society.[56] In 2002, he decried the very notion of bringing a Muslim state such as Turkey into the European Union.[57] Invoking rhetoric strikingly similar to that of Helmut Kohl's first election campaign twenty years earlier, Wehler questioned the fundamental capacity of non-Western peoples to participate in liberal democracy. This concern he juxtaposed with the sensational image of Anatolians amassing on the frontier in anticipation of the opening of the EU's labor market. He thus revived one of the

[55] The catalogue for the exhibition shows that the room that contained Rodrigues's motorcycle ("Fremd in Deutschland?") was positioned between two series of rooms, one with the thematic title "Made in Germany" and the other "Muttersprache-Vaterländer." Deutsches Historisches Museum, Haus der Geschichte der Bundesrepublik Deutschland, Kunst- und Ausstellungshalle der Bundesrepublik Deutschland, eds., *50: Einigkeit und Recht und Freiheit, Wege der Deutschen 1949–1999* (Reinbek bei Hamburg: Rowohlt, 1999).
[56] Konrad Adam, "Der Preis der Multikultur. Ausländer und Deutsche – eine kritische Masse?," *Frankfurter Allgemeine Zeitung*, 23 November 1982.
[57] Hans-Ulrich Wehler, "Das Türkenproblem," *Die Zeit*, 12 September 2002.

Enlightenment's oldest tropes of absolute difference, comparing sixty-five million contemporary Turks to Ottoman hordes at the gates of Vienna. More recently, Wehler responded to Habermas's plea for a common European vision by calling for a clear delineation of borders. Turkey and other eastern lands, he maintained, "have never been part of a historic Europe" and did not participate in the defining European experiences (separation of church and state, Reformation, Enlightenment, and construction of the social welfare state).[58] Wehler warned that "cultural divergences are deeply engraved in Europe" and "the Islam of Turkey remains an obvious cultural barrier."[59] For certain leftist critics, then, the integration of guest workers and their descendants was an experiment of the 1980s and an experiment that failed. The only possible recourse, in their view, was to fortify the boundaries between German and foreign, European and Other.

Precisely because such profound skepticism about the possibility of multiethnic coexistence persists, it seems especially crucial now to excavate the ideological history of the guest worker question. In tracking the shifting meanings of Rodrigues's motorcycle, we begin to understand the history of diversity in modern Germany.

---

[58] Hans-Ulrich Wehler, "Let the United States Be Strong! Europe Remains a Mid-Size Power: A Response to Jürgen Habermas," in Levy et al., *Old Europe*, 121.

[59] Ibid.

Index

CPSIA information can be obtained at www.ICGtesting.com
Printed in the USA
LVOW06s1228140815

449973LV00001B/1/P